Family Circle® Quick & Easy Cooking

Editor: Lois White
Contributing Editor: Annie Krumhardt Peterson
Contributing Designer: Mary Pat Crowley
Copy Chief: Doug Kouma
Copy Editor: Kevin Cox
Publishing Operations Manager: Karen Schirm
Edit and Design Production Coordinator: Mary Lee Gavin
Editorial Assistant: Sheri Cord
Book Production Managers: Marjorie J. Schenkelberg, Mark Weaver
Imaging Center Operator: Christopher Sprague
Contributing Copy Editor: Carol DeMasters
Contributing Proofreaders: Jeanette Astor, Stacie Gaylor, Stan West
Contributing Indexer: Elizabeth T. Parson

Meredith® Books

Editorial Director: John Riha
Managing Editor: Kathleen Armentrout
Deputy Editor: Jennifer Darling
Group Editor: Jan Miller

Director, Marketing and Publicity: Amy Nichols
Executive Director, Sales: Ken Zagor
Director, Operations: George A. Susral
Director, Production: Douglas M. Johnston
Business Director: Janice Croat

Vice President and General Manager, SIM: Jeff Myers

Family Circle® Magazine

Editor in Chief: Linda Fears
Editorial Director: Michael Lafavore
Creative Director: Karmen Lizzul
Food Director: Regina Ragone
Senior Food Editor: Julie Miltenberger
Associate Food Editor: Michael Tyrrell
Assistant Food Editor: Cindy Heller
Editorial Assistant: Katie Kemple
Test Kitchen Associate: Althea Needham

Meredith Publishing Group

President: Jack Griffin
Executive Vice President: Doug Olson
Vice President, Corporate Solutions: Michael Brownstein
Vice President, Manufacturing: Bruce Heston
Vice President, Consumer Marketing: David Ball
Consumer Product Marketing Director: Steve Swanson
Consumer Product Marketing Manager: Wendy Merical
Business Manager: Darren Tollefson

Meredith Corporation

Chairman of the Board: William T. Kerr
President and Chief Executive Officer: Stephen M. Lacy

In Memoriam: E.T. Meredith III (1933–2003)

Night after night and bite after bite, families agree that nothing beats fresh home-cooked meals. Busy cooks who pull off the dinnertime challenge with ease admit that some of their best, most requested family meals require only a handful of ingredients and a couple of easy prep steps. They favor no-fuss recipes like these as they continue to look for ways to minimize the stress of family mealtime.

Thumb through the pages of *Quick and Easy Cooking* and discover some of the slickest ways to throw together dinner, even on the days when you have little time or energy to cook a hot meal. This book is bursting with recipes including easy, versatile pastas, quick-grill meats, toss-and-serve salads, and fix-and-forget slow-cooker meals. Recipe ingredient lists specify the familiar basics at any supermarket, including fresh and prepared foods as well as convenience items. Along with that, nearly all of these recipes have the cook out of the kitchen in fewer than 30 minutes.

One of the best ways to experience the convenience of this book is to spend a few minutes on a weekend selecting recipes for the upcoming week. Write each night's menus, do the shopping, and stick the menu list on the fridge. Check it throughout the week to jog your memory for important steps, such as thawing meat or allowing time in the morning to toss ingredients in the slow cooker. The more you do this, the easier it becomes to whip together a weeknight meal, come to the table with a smile, and say, "Dinner is served!"

Because health and timesaving features are paramount these days, look for the following icons throughout the book:

 Healthy: A "healthy" icon means that the recipe meets certain calorie, fat, and sodium guidelines. See page 336 for more information.

One-Pan: A "one-pan" icon means that the recipe uses a single pan in its preparation and that translates to easy cleanup.

Ham and Asparagus Pasta, **page 38**

Grilled Herb Corn On the Cob, **page 225**

Canandian Bacon Pizza, **page 258**

Praline Crunch Bars, **page 319**

Table of Contents:

Pork Medallions with Cranberry
and Fig Chutney, **page 42**

Coriander-Studded Tenderloin, **page 16**

Oven-Baked Cassoulet, **page 46**

Tuscan Lamb Chop Skillet, **page 57**

Meaty Main Dishes

Beef, pork, or lamb assure hearty, satisfying fare. Whether you are planning a special dinner or a quick meal on a busy weeknight, look here for an array of recipes that will become favorites.

Easy Shepherd's Pie ♥ 🔲

To quick-thaw the frozen mixed vegetables, place them in a colander and rinse them under running water for a minute.

Start to Finish: 30 minutes **Makes:** 6 servings

- 1 **pound ground beef or uncooked ground turkey or chicken**
- ½ **cup chopped onion (1 medium)**
- 1 **10-ounce package frozen mixed vegetables, thawed**
- ¼ **cup water**
- 1 **10.75-ounce can condensed tomato soup**
- 1 **teaspoon Worcestershire sauce**
- ¼ **teaspoon dried thyme, crushed**
- 1 **20-ounce package refrigerated mashed potatoes or 3 cups leftover mashed potatoes**
- ½ **cup shredded Cheddar cheese (2 ounces)**

1. In a large skillet, cook ground beef and onion until beef is brown and onion is tender. Drain off fat. Stir vegetables and the water into beef mixture. Bring to boiling; reduce heat. Simmer, covered, about 5 minutes or until vegetables are tender.

2. Stir in tomato soup, Worcestershire sauce, and thyme. Return to boiling; reduce heat. Drop mashed potatoes in six mounds on top of the hot mixture. Sprinkle potatoes with cheese. Simmer, covered, for 10 to 15 minutes or until potatoes are heated through.

Per serving:: 12 g total fat (5 g sat. fat), 58 mg chol., 570 mg sodium, 27 g carbo., 3 g fiber, 20 g pro.

Lemon-Pepper Flank ♥ 🔲 Steak

This recipe relies on fresh oregano, lemon zest, and garlic, instead of bottled lemon-pepper seasoning, for its intense flavor.

Prep: 10 minutes **Broil:** 15 minutes
Makes: 4 servings

- 2 **tablespoons snipped fresh oregano or 2 teaspoons dried oregano, crushed**
- 2 **teaspoons bottled minced garlic (4 cloves)**
- 2 **teaspoons finely shredded lemon peel**
- 2 **teaspoons olive oil or cooking oil**
- ½ **teaspoon coarsely ground black pepper**
- 1½ **pounds beef flank steak**
  Lemon slices (optional)

1. Preheat broiler. In a small bowl, stir together oregano, garlic, lemon peel, oil, and pepper; set aside. Trim fat from steak. Using your fingers, rub oregano mixture onto both sides of steak.

2. Place steak on the unheated rack of a broiler pan. Broil 3 to 4 inches from heat for 15 to 18 minutes or until medium doneness (160°F), turning once halfway through broiling.

3. To serve, thinly slice steak diagonally across the grain. If desired, garnish with lemon slices.

Per serving: 287 cal., 14 g total fat (5 g sat. fat), 68 mg chol., 90 mg sodium, 1 g carbo., 0 g fiber, 39 g pro.

Easy Shepherd's Pie

Lemon-Pepper Flank Steak

Chard-Topped Steaks

Chard-Topped Steaks ♥

Swiss chard sauteed in bacon drippings makes a delicious topping for tender beef tenderloin steaks. Look for chard, a member of the beet family, in yellow, green, and red for lots of color.

Start to Finish: 30 minutes   **Makes:** 4 servings

1   slice bacon, chopped
4   beef tenderloin steaks, cut 1 inch thick (about
       1 pound)
       Salt
       Ground black pepper
3   cups thinly sliced fresh Swiss chard leaves
       (4 ounces)
½   teaspoon dried thyme, crushed
⅛   teaspoon salt
⅛   teaspoon ground black pepper

1. In a large skillet, cook bacon over medium heat until crisp. Remove bacon from skillet, reserving drippings. Crumble bacon; set aside. Remove skillet from heat; set aside.

2. Preheat broiler. Trim fat from steaks. Sprinkle steaks with salt and pepper. Place steaks on the unheated rack of a broiler pan. Broil 3 to 4 inches from the heat for 12 to 14 minutes for medium-rare (145°F) or 15 to 18 minutes for medium (160°F), turning once halfway through broiling.

3. Meanwhile, cook and stir Swiss chard in drippings in skillet over medium heat for 4 to 6 minutes or just until tender. Stir in the crumbled bacon, thyme, the ⅛ teaspoon salt, and the ⅛ teaspoon pepper. To serve, spoon Swiss chard mixture on top of steaks.

Per serving: 208 cal., 11 g total fat (4 g sat. fat), 60 mg chol., 363 mg sodium, 1 g carbo., 1 g fiber, 25 g pro.

Bacon-Cheese Burgers [one]

The cheese and bacon you usually find on top are stuffed inside these double-decker burgers.

Prep: 15 minutes **Broil:** 11 minutes **Makes:** 4 servings

- 1¼ **pounds lean ground beef**
- 8 **thin slices Colby and Monterey Jack cheese or Cheddar cheese (4 ounces)**
- 4 **slices bacon, crisp-cooked and crumbled**
- 4 **hamburger buns, split and toasted**
- ¼ **cup sour cream onion dip**

1. Preheat broiler. Shape ground beef into eight ¼-inch-thick patties. Place one cheese slice on top of each of four of the patties; sprinkle with crumbled bacon. Place remaining four patties on top of the bacon-and-cheese-topped patties. Seal edges well.

2. Place patties on the unheated rack of a broiler pan. Broil 3 to 4 inches from the heat for 10 to 12 minutes or until done (160°F), turning patties once halfway through cooking. Place one of each remaining four cheese slices on top of patties. Broil for 1 minute more.

3. Meanwhile, spread cut sides of toasted buns with the onion dip. Serve burgers on prepared buns.

Per serving: 636 cal., 36 g total fat (17 g sat. fat), 119 mg chol., 778 mg sodium, 23 g carbo., 1 g fiber, 41 g pro.

Beef Steaks with Blue Cheese and Walnuts [one]

Pungent blue cheese, sour cream, and walnuts make a tasty topping for these pan-broiled steaks.

Prep: 10 minutes **Cook:** 10 minutes **Makes:** 4 servings

- 4 **beef tenderloin steaks, cut 1 inch thick**
- ½ **teaspoon garlic salt**
  Nonstick cooking spray
- ⅓ **cup dairy sour cream**
- 3 **tablespoons crumbled blue cheese**
- 3 **tablespoons chopped walnuts, toasted**

1. Sprinkle both sides of steaks with garlic salt. Lightly coat a large skillet with cooking spray. Heat skillet over medium-high heat. Add steaks. Reduce heat to medium and cook for 10 to 13 minutes or until desired doneness (145°F for medium rare or 160°F for medium), turning steaks halfway through cooking. Transfer steaks to a serving platter.

2. Meanwhile, in a small bowl, stir together sour cream and blue cheese; spoon on top of steaks. Sprinkle with walnuts.

Per serving: 264 cal., 17 g total fat (6 g sat. fat), 81 mg chol., 255 mg sodium, 2 g carbo., 0 g fiber, 26 g pro.

Asian-Style Meatballs [one]

Mixing in sweet ginger-sesame grilling sauce or bottled stir-fry sauce and water chestnuts is the key to infusing meatballs with Asian flavor and texture.

Prep: 25 minutes **Cook:** 12 minutes

- 1 **egg, lightly beaten**
- ¾ **cup purchased shredded carrot**
- ½ **cup soft bread crumbs**
- 1 **teaspoon ground ginger**
- ¼ **teaspoon salt**
- ¼ **teaspoon garlic powder**
- 12 **ounces lean ground beef**
- ½ **of a 14-ounce jar sweet ginger-sesame grill sauce (about ¾ cup) or ¾ cup bottled stir-fry sauce**
- ½ **cup water**
- 1 **small onion, cut into thin wedges**
- 1 **8-ounce can sliced water chestnuts, drained**
- 1 **medium red or green sweet pepper, cut into 1-inch pieces**
  Hot cooked rice

1. In a medium bowl, combine egg, ¼ cup of the shredded carrot, the bread crumbs, ginger, salt, and garlic powder. Add beef and mix well. Shape beef mixture into 8 meatballs.

2. In a large skillet, cook meatballs over medium heat until brown, turning to brown evenly (meatballs will not be done). Remove meatballs from skillet. Wipe out skillet with paper towels.

3. Add grill sauce and water to skillet; stir to combine. Add onion, water chestnuts, sweet pepper, and remaining ½ cup shredded carrot to skillet; bring to boiling. Return meatballs to skillet. Reduce heat. Simmer, covered, for 12 to 15 minutes or until meatballs are done (160°F).* Serve meatballs and sauce with hot cooked rice.

Per serving: 537 cal., 10 g total fat (4 g sat. fat), 107 mg chol., 1,367 mg sodium, 83 g carbo., 3 g fiber, 23 g pro.

*Note: To check the doneness of a meatball, insert an instant-read thermometer into the center of meatball.

Mostaccioli with Broccoli Rabe and Pancetta

Mostaccioli with Broccoli Rabe and Pancetta ♥

Also known as rapini, broccoli rabe features small buds that look somewhat like those on broccoli, but its stems are more slender and its jagged leaves are larger.

Start to Finish: 30 minutes **Makes:** 4 to 6 servings

12	**ounces broccoli rabe or 1½ cups broccoli florets**
8	**ounces dried whole wheat or multigrain penne pasta (about 3 cups)**
½	**cup chopped onion (1 medium)**
2	**ounces chopped pancetta or bacon**
2	**cloves garlic, minced**
1⅓	**cups chopped seeded roma tomatoes (4 medium)**
⅓	**cup dry white wine or chicken broth**
¼	**cup finely shredded Asiago cheese (1 ounce)**
1	**tablespoon snipped fresh flat-leaf parsley**
	Salt
	Ground black pepper

1. Thoroughly wash broccoli rabe or broccoli; drain well. If using broccoli rabe, remove large leaves and cut to 4-inch lengths. Set aside.

2. In a large saucepan, cook pasta in a large amount of lightly salted boiling water for 9 minutes. Add broccoli rabe or broccoli. Cook about 3 minutes more or until pasta is tender. Drain well. Return broccoli mixture to hot saucepan; cover and keep warm.

3. Meanwhile, in a medium saucepan, cook onion, pancetta, and garlic over medium heat for 3 to 5 minutes or until pancetta is crisp and onion is tender, stirring occasionally. Reduce heat to low. Add tomatoes and wine; cook for 2 minutes more, stirring frequently.

4. Add tomato mixture to broccoli mixture; toss gently to combine. Transfer to a serving dish. Sprinkle with cheese and parsley. Season to taste with salt and pepper.

Per serving: 348 cal., 8 g total fat (3 g sat. fat), 18 mg chol., 462 mg sodium, 51 g carbo., 8 g fiber, 16 g pro.

Steaks with Creamy Onion Sauce

Onion slices, broiled to perfection, create an irresistible sauce for these juicy ribeye steaks.

Start to Finish: 20 minutes **Makes:** 4 servings

- **1** **medium sweet onion (such as Maui or Walla Walla), thinly sliced**
- **4** **6-ounce beef ribeye steaks, cut 1 inch thick**
- **3** **teaspoons Greek seasoning or lemon-pepper seasoning**
- **1** **8-ounce container sour cream**
- **2** **tablespoons drained capers**

1. Place onion slices on the rack of an unheated broiler pan. Broil 3 to 4 inches from heat for 5 minutes; turn onions. Meanwhile, sprinkle steaks with 1½ teaspoons of the seasoning. Place steaks on the rack with the onion slices.

2. Broil steaks and onions about 5 minutes more or until onions are lightly browned. Transfer onions to a cutting board. Continue to broil steaks until desired doneness. Allow 7 to 9 minutes more for medium rare (145°F) or 10 to 13 minutes more for medium (160°F), turning once.

3. Meanwhile, for the sauce, coarsely chop the cooked onion. In a saucepan, combine the cooked onion, sour cream, capers, and the remaining 1½ teaspoons seasoning. Cook over medium-low heat until heated through (do not boil). Serve steaks with sauce.

Per serving: 398 cal., 22 g total fat (11 g sat. fat), 106 mg chol., 472 mg sodium, 4 g carbo., 0 g fiber, 39 g pro.

Peppered Tenderloins With Asiago Cheese [one]

Buttery, robust Asiago cheese makes a toothsome topping for juicy tenderloin steaks.

Start to Finish: 15 minutes **Makes:** 4 servings

- **4** **beef tenderloin steaks, cut 1 inch thick**
- **1** **teaspoon coarsely ground black pepper**
- **1** **tablespoon butter**
- **1** **ounce Asiago cheese, shaved**
- **¼** **cup beef broth**

1. Rub both sides of steaks with pepper. In a large skillet, melt butter over medium-high heat. Add steaks. Reduce heat to medium and cook for 10 to 13 minutes, turning steaks halfway through cooking (145°F for medium rare or 160°F for medium). Transfer steaks to a serving platter, reserving drippings in skillet. Top steaks with cheese; keep warm.

2. Add beef broth to skillet. Cook and stir until bubbly to loosen any browned bits in bottom of skillet. Pour over steaks.

Per serving: 294 cal., 18 g total fat (8 g sat. fat), 103 mg chol., 225 mg sodium, 1 g carbo., 0 g fiber, 31 g pro.

Salsa Steak ♥

This salsa-smothered steak calls for lots of fresh Mediterranean veggies. For more Mediterranean flavor, try Italian seasoning in place of the chili powder.

Prep: 20 minutes **Bake:** 45 minutes **Oven:** 350°F
Makes: 4 to 6 servings

- **1** **to 1½ pounds boneless beef round steak, cut ½ inch thick**
  Kosher salt
  Freshly ground black pepper
- **1** **tablespoon canola oil**
- **1½** **cups sliced fresh mushrooms**
- **1** **medium green sweet pepper, cut into bite-size strips**
- **1** **medium onion, sliced**
- **1** **8-ounce can tomato sauce**
- **1** **2.25-ounce can sliced pitted ripe olives, drained (optional)**
- **2** **to 3 teaspoons chili powder***

1. Preheat oven to 350°F. Trim fat from steak. Sprinkle both sides of steak with kosher salt and black pepper. Cut steak into 4 to 6 serving-size pieces. In a large skillet, brown steak in hot oil, turning once. Transfer steak to a 2-quart square baking dish.

2. In the same skillet, cook and stir mushrooms, sweet pepper, and onion over medium heat for 5 to 8 minutes or until tender (if necessary, add more oil). Stir in tomato sauce, olives (if desired), and chili powder. Cook and stir until bubbly.

3. Pour mushroom mixture over steak in baking dish. Cover and bake about 45 minutes or until steak is tender.

Per serving: 223 cal., 9 g total fat (2 g sat. fat), 54 mg chol., 454 mg sodium, 8 g carbo., 2 g fiber, 27 g pro.

*Note: Another time, opt for an Italian-flavored dish by substituting 1 to 1½ teaspoons dried Italian seasoning, crushed, for the chili powder.

Peppered Steak with Mushroom Sauce

Peppered Steak with Mushroom Sauce 🄰ne

Sour cream gives the herb-flecked mushroom sauce a smooth, tangy finish.

Start to Finish: 30 minutes **Makes:** 6 servings

- **6** **beef tenderloin steaks or 3 boneless beef top sirloin steaks, cut 1 inch thick (about 1½ pounds total)**
- **½** **teaspoon coarsely ground black pepper**
- **1** **teaspoon dried thyme or oregano, crushed**
- **¼** **teaspoon salt**
  Nonstick cooking spray
- **⅓** **cup water**
- **½** **teaspoon instant beef bouillon granules**
- **¾** **cup sliced fresh shiitake or other mushrooms**
- **¾** **cup milk**
- **2** **tablespoons all-purpose flour**
- **⅔** **cup sour cream**

1. Trim fat from steaks. In a small bowl, stir together pepper, ½ teaspoon of the thyme, and the salt. Sprinkle mixture over both sides of steaks; rub in with your fingers.

2. Lightly coat a large nonstick skillet with cooking spray. Heat over medium-high heat. Add steak; reduce heat to medium. Cook until desired doneness, turning once. Allow 12 to 14 minutes for medium-rare doneness (145°F) or 15 to 18 minutes for medium doneness (160°F). Remove steak from skillet; cover and keep warm.

3. For the sauce, add the water and bouillon granules to skillet. Bring to boiling. Add mushrooms; cook about 2 minutes or until mushrooms are tender. In a small bowl, stir together milk, flour, and the remaining ½ teaspoon dried thyme; add to mushroom mixture. Cook and stir until thickened and bubbly. Stir in sour cream; heat through, but do not boil. Serve steak with sauce.

Per serving: 268 cal., 14 g total fat (6 g sat. fat), 81 mg chol., 252 mg sodium, 8 g carbo., 1 g fiber, 26 g pro.

Hot Italian Beef Salad 🔲

The hot steak and sweet pepper wilt the greens just enough to bring out their flavor.

Start to Finish: 20 minutes **Makes:** 4 servings

- **12** **ounces beef flank steak or beef top round steak, cut 1 inch thick**
- **6** **cups torn mixed salad greens**
- **3** **teaspoons olive oil or salad oil**
- **1** **medium red or green sweet pepper, cut into bite-size strips**
- **½** **cup bottled Italian salad dressing or red wine vinegar and oil salad dressing**
  Coarsely ground black pepper

1. Trim fat from steak. Cut steak into thin, bite-size strips. Arrange salad greens on 4 salad plates; set aside.

2. In a large skillet, heat 2 teaspoons of the oil over medium-high heat; add sweet pepper to skillet. Cook and stir for 1 to 2 minutes or until nearly crisp-tender.

3. Add the remaining 1 teaspoon oil to the skillet; add steak strips. Cook and stir for 2 to 3 minutes or until desired doneness. Add salad dressing to skillet. Cook and stir until heated through.

4. Spoon beef mixture over salad greens. Sprinkle with black pepper.

Per serving: 317 cal., 24 g total fat (5 g sat. fat), 34 mg chol., 284 mg sodium, 7 g carbo., 2 g fiber, 20 g pro.

Upside-Down Pizza Casserole

Refrigerated biscuits top the ground beef mixture in this "pizza."

Prep: 20 minutes **Bake:** 15 minutes **Oven:** 400°F
Makes: 5 servings

- **1½** **pounds lean ground beef**
- **1** **15-ounce can Italian-style tomato sauce**
- **1½** **cups shredded mozzarella cheese (6 ounces)**
- **1** **10-ounce package refrigerated biscuits (10 biscuits)**

1. Preheat oven to 400°F. In a large skillet, cook ground beef over medium heat until brown. Drain off fat. Stir in tomato sauce; heat through. Transfer beef mixture to a 2-quart rectangular baking dish or 10-inch deep-dish pie plate. Sprinkle with cheese. Flatten each biscuit with your hands; arrange the biscuits on top of cheese.

2. Bake, uncovered, about 15 minutes or until biscuits are golden.

Per small serving: 642 cal., 40 g total fat (16 g sat. fat), 116 mg chol., 1,102 mg sodium, 30 g carbo., 2 g fiber, 34 g pro.

Mustard-Crusted Beef Tenderloin

Melt-in-your-mouth beef tenderloin enhanced with the fresh, sharp flavor of mustard makes this a dish you won't soon forget.

Prep: 25 minutes **Roast:** 35 minutes
Stand: 10 minutes **Oven:** 425°F **Makes:** 4 servings

- **¼** **cup coarse-grain mustard**
- **2** **teaspoons honey**
- **¾** **teaspoon dry mustard**
- **¾** **teaspoon freshly ground black pepper**
- **½** **teaspoon finely shredded orange peel**
- **½** **teaspoon finely shredded lemon peel**
- **1** **tablespoon extra-virgin olive oil**
- **1** **1-pound beef tenderloin roast**

1. Preheat oven to 425°F. In a small bowl, combine coarse-grain mustard, honey, dry mustard, the ¾ teaspoon pepper, the orange peel, and lemon peel; set aside.

2. In a large heavy skillet, heat oil over medium-high heat. Quickly brown roast on all sides in hot oil (about 2 minutes total). Transfer roast to a rack set in a shallow roasting pan. Spread mustard mixture over top and sides of roast. Insert an oven-going meat thermometer into center of roast.

3. Roast the beef roast for 35 to 45 minutes or until meat thermometer registers 140°F. Cover roast with foil and let stand for 10 minutes before slicing. The temperature of the roast after standing should be 145°F.

Per serving: 234 cal., 12 g total fat (3 g sat. fat), 70 mg chol., 533 mg sodium, 3 g carbo., 0 g fiber, 24 g pro.

Upside-Down Pizza Casserole

Beef and Noodle Casserole

Mix the ingredients right in the casserole, put them in the oven, and walk away. Thirty minutes of baking does the work.

Prep: 15 minutes **Bake:** 30 minutes **Stand:** 5 minutes
Oven: 350°F **Makes:** 4 servings

- 1 **pound lean ground beef**
- ½ **cup milk**
- ½ **of an 8-ounce tub cream cheese spread with chives and onion (½ cup)**
- ½ **cup shredded carrot (1 medium)**
- 1 **4.6-ounce package vermicelli with garlic and olive oil or one 4.8-ounce package angel hair pasta with herbs**
- 1½ **cups boiling water**

1. Preheat oven to 350°F. Grease a 1½-quart casserole; set aside. In a large skillet, cook ground beef until brown. Drain off fat.

2. Meanwhile, in prepared casserole, gradually whisk milk into cream cheese until smooth. Stir in carrot and seasoning packet from pasta. Stir in browned beef. Break pasta from pasta mix into 1-inch pieces; stir into beef mixture.

3. Slowly pour boiling water over beef mixture. Bake, covered, for 30 to 35 minutes or until pasta is tender, stirring twice. Let stand, covered, for 5 minutes. Stir before serving.

Per serving: 463 cal., 25 g total fat (13 g sat. fat), 101 mg chol., 619 mg sodium, 28 g carbo., 2 g fiber, 28 g pro.

Sweet Potato-Roast Beef Hash

An appealing blend of sweet and regular potatoes makes this hash a cut above the ordinary.

Start to Finish: 30 minutes **Makes:** 4 servings

- 1 **medium sweet potato, peeled and diced**
- 3 **medium potatoes, peeled and diced**
- ½ **cup chopped onion**
- ⅓ **cup chopped red sweet pepper**
- 2 **tablespoons cooking oil**
- 8 **ounces cooked roast beef, cubed**
- 4 **eggs**
- 2 **green onions, chopped**
  Salt
  Ground black pepper

1. In a large covered saucepan, cook diced sweet potato and potatoes in a small amount of boiling water for 3 minutes. Drain; cool slightly.

2. In a large nonstick skillet, cook onion and sweet pepper in hot oil until tender. Stir in potato. Cook and stir about 5 minutes or just until tender. Stir in roast beef.

3. Using the back of a large spoon, make four depressions in the roast beef mixture. Break an egg into each depression. Cook, covered, over medium-low heat about 5 minutes or until the egg whites are completely set and yolks begin to thicken but are not hard. Sprinkle with green onions. Season to taste with salt and black pepper.

Per serving: 420 cal., 19 g total fat (5 g sat. fat), 257 mg chol., 154 mg sodium, 38 g carbo., 4 g fiber, 25 g pro.

Coriander-Studded Tenderloin

Coriander seeds come from the plant commonly called cilantro, but they don't share the same flavor. The seeds taste like a combination of lemon, caraway, and sage. Use a mortar and pestle to crush them. If you don't have a mortar and pestle, crush the seeds with a rolling pin.

Start to Finish: 20 minutes **Makes:** 4 servings

- 4 **3- to 4-ounce beef tenderloin steaks, cut 1 inch thick**
  Salt
- 1 **tablespoon reduced-sodium soy sauce**
- 1 **tablespoon olive oil**
- 1 **tablespoon snipped fresh chives**
- 2 **cloves garlic, minced**
- ½ **teaspoon coriander seeds or cumin seeds, crushed**
- ½ **teaspoon celery seeds**
- ½ **teaspoon coarsely ground black pepper**

1. Trim fat from steaks. Sprinkle lightly with salt. In a small bowl, combine soy sauce, oil, chives, garlic, coriander seeds, celery seeds, and pepper. Brush the mixture onto both sides of each steak.

2. Place steaks on the unheated rack of a broiler pan. Broil 3 to 4 inches from heat until desired doneness, turning once halfway through broiling time. Allow 12 to 14 minutes for medium-rare doneness (145°F) or 15 to 18 minutes for medium doneness (160°F).

Per serving: 164 cal., 9 g total fat (3 g sat. fat), 42 mg chol., 256 mg sodium, 1 g carbo., 0 g fiber, 18 g pro.

Coriander-Studded Tenderloin

Beef and Broccoli with Plum Sauce

Beef and Broccoli with Plum Sauce ♥ [one]

Some supermarkets don't sell plums year-round. When you can't find them, substitute 1 cup frozen unsweetened peach slices, thawed and cut up.

Start to Finish: 30 minutes **Makes:** 4 servings

- 12 **ounces beef top round steak**
- ¾ **cup water**
- ½ **cup bottled plum sauce**
- 2 **tablespoons reduced-sodium soy sauce**
- 1 **tablespoon cornstarch**
- 1 **teaspoon grated fresh ginger**
- 1 **tablespoon cooking oil**
- 1 **cup broccoli florets**
- 1 **small onion, cut into 1-inch pieces**
- 1 **teaspoon bottled minced garlic (2 cloves)**
- 3 **cups lightly packed, coarsely chopped bok choy**
- 2 **medium plums, pitted and cut into thin wedges**
  Hot cooked Chinese egg noodles, fine egg noodles, or rice

1. If desired, partially freeze steak for easier slicing. Trim fat from steak. Thinly slice steak across the grain into bite-size strips. Set aside. For the sauce, in a small bowl, stir together the water, plum sauce, soy sauce, cornstarch, and ginger. Set sauce aside.

2. In a nonstick wok or large skillet, heat oil over medium-high heat. (Add more oil as necessary during cooking.) Add broccoli, onion, and garlic; stir-fry for 3 minutes. Remove broccoli mixture from wok. Add beef to hot wok. Cook and stir for 2 to 3 minutes or until brown. Push beef from center of wok. Stir sauce. Add sauce to center of wok. Cook and stir until thickened and bubbly.

3. Return broccoli mixture to wok. Add bok choy and plums. Stir all ingredients together to coat with sauce. Cover and cook about 2 minutes more or until heated through. Serve over hot cooked noodles.

Per serving: 413 cal., 10 g total fat (3 g sat. fat), 74 mg chol., 533 mg sodium, 54 g carbo., 4 g fiber, 26 g pro.

Top Sirloin with Onions And Mushrooms ♥

Be sure to use a sweet onion for this recipe. Its high sugar content is essential for the sweet and tangy sauce that tops these steaks.

Start to Finish: 30 minutes **Makes:** 4 servings

- 2 **tablespoons dried tomatoes**
  Boiling water
- 8 **ounces fresh button mushrooms (3 cups)**
  Nonstick cooking spray
- 1 **large sweet onion (such as Vidalia, Maui, or Walla Walla), halved crosswise and thinly sliced (2 cups)**
- 1 **tablespoon balsamic vinegar**
- ½ **teaspoon salt**
- ¼ **teaspoon ground black pepper**
- 2 **boneless beef top sirloin steaks, cut 1 inch thick (1 to 1¼ pounds total)**

1. In a small bowl, cover tomatoes with boiling water. Cover and let stand for 5 minutes. Drain and snip tomatoes; set aside. Meanwhile, slice mushrooms.

2. Coat an unheated large nonstick skillet with cooking spray. Heat over medium-low heat. Add onion; cook, covered, for 10 minutes, stirring occasionally. Add mushrooms to onion in skillet. Cook for 8 to 10 minutes more or until onion is golden brown and most of the liquid is evaporated. Stir in snipped tomatoes, balsamic vinegar, ¼ teaspoon of the salt, and ⅛ teaspoon of the pepper; heat through.

3. Meanwhile, preheat broiler. Cut steaks in half. Place steaks on the unheated rack of a broiler pan. Sprinkle with the remaining ¼ teaspoon salt and ⅛ teaspoon pepper. Broil 3 to 4 inches from heat until desired doneness, turning once halfway through cooking time. Allow 15 to 17 minutes for medium-rare (145°F) or 20 to 22 minutes for medium doneness (160°F). Spoon onion mixture over steaks.

Per serving: 197 cal., 6 g total fat (2 g sat. fat), 69 mg chol., 387 mg sodium, 10 g carbo., 2 g fiber, 27 g pro.

Quick Tip For a mushroom medley, use only 3 ounces (1¼ cups) button mushrooms. Add 1 cup chopped shiitake mushrooms and ¾ cup chopped oyster mushrooms (stems removed and discarded from both).

Beef Satay with Peanut Sauce

Staying true to its Indonesian roots, this savory beef satay is skewered and served with a warm peanut sauce, perfect for dipping. For simplified preparation, partially freeze your steak to make slicing easier.

Prep: 25 minutes **Marinate:** 30 minutes
Broil: 4 minutes **Makes:** 5 servings

- 1 **1- to 1¼-pound beef flank steak**
- ⅓ **cup light teriyaki sauce**
- ½ **teaspoon bottled hot pepper sauce**
- ½ **of a medium red onion, cut into thin wedges**
- 4 **green onions, cut into 1-inch pieces**
- 1 **red or green sweet pepper, cut into ¾-inch chunks**
- 3 **tablespoons peanut butter**
- 3 **tablespoons water**
- 2 **tablespoons light teriyaki sauce**

1. If desired, partially freeze steak for easier slicing. Trim fat from steak. Cut steak crosswise into thin slices. For marinade, in a medium bowl, combine the ⅓ cup teriyaki sauce and ¼ teaspoon of the hot pepper sauce. Add steak; toss to coat. Cover and marinate in the refrigerator for 30 minutes. If using wooden skewers, soak them in water for 30 minutes before using.

2. Drain steak, reserving marinade. On wooden or metal skewers, alternately thread steak strips (accordion style), red onion wedges, green onion pieces, and sweet pepper chinks. Brush with reserved marinade. Discard any remaining marinade.

3. Place skewers on the unheated rack of a broiler pan. Broil 4 to 5 inches from the heat about 4 minutes or until steak is slightly pink in center, turning once.

4. For peanut sauce, in a small saucepan, combine peanut butter, the water, the 2 tablespoons teriyaki sauce, and the remaining ¼ teaspoon hot pepper sauce. Cook and stir over medium heat just until smooth and heated through.

5. Serve satay with warm peanut sauce.

Per serving: 230 cal., 10 g total fat (3 g sat. fat), 38 mg chol., 730 mg sodium, 10 g carbo., 2 g fiber, 24 g pro.

Quick Tip Look for flank steak that has a bright red color and even thickness. For the most tender meat, be sure to slice flank steak perpendicular to the grain of the meat.

Stroganoff-Sauced Beef Roast [one]

Dress up a package of ready-to-go beef pot roast with fresh mushrooms and onion-studded sour cream dip and toss it all with hot noodles. Now that's comfort food.

Start to Finish: 30 minutes **Makes:** 3 or 4 servings

- 1 **16-ounce package refrigerated cooked beef pot roast with gravy**
- 2 **cups fresh shiitake, cremini, or button mushrooms**
- ½ **cup sour cream French onion-flavored dip**
- 2 **cups hot cooked noodles**
   Snipped fresh parsley (optional)

1. Transfer beef with gravy to a large skillet (leave beef whole). Remove stems from shiitake mushrooms (if using). Slice, halve, or quarter mushrooms. Add mushrooms to skillet. Cover and cook over medium-low heat about 15 minutes or until cooked through, stirring mushrooms once and turning beef over halfway through cooking time.

2. Using a wooden spoon, break beef into bite-size pieces. Stir onion dip into beef mixture; heat through (do not boil). Stir in hot cooked noodles. If desired, top each serving with snipped fresh parsley.

Per serving: 488 cal., 17 g total fat (9 g sat. fat), 115 mg chol., 771 mg sodium, 48 g carbo., 3 g fiber, 38 g pro.

Quick Tip To make quick work of slicing mushrooms, use an egg slicer.

Chili-Sauced Burgers and Spaghetti [one]

This lively burger version is a twist on Cincinnati chili.

Prep: 20 minutes **Cook:** 15 minutes **Makes:** 6 servings

- ¼ **cup milk**
- ¾ **cup soft bread crumbs (1 slice)**
- ½ **teaspoon salt**
   Dash ground black pepper
- 1 **pound lean ground beef**
- ¼ **cup chopped onion**
- ½ **teaspoon bottled minced garlic (1 clove)**
- 1 **11.25-ounce can condensed chili beef soup**
- ⅔ **cup water**
- 12 **ounces dried spaghetti pasta, cooked according to package directions**
- ⅓ **cup shredded Cheddar cheese**

1. In a medium bowl, combine milk, bread crumbs, salt, and pepper. Add beef; mix well. Shape into six ¾-inch oblong patties. In a large skillet, cook patties over medium heat until brown. Remove from skillet.

2. Cook onion and garlic in drippings in skillet until tender. Stir in soup and the water. Return patties to skillet. Bring soup mixture to boiling; reduce heat. Cover and simmer for 15 minutes.

3. To serve, place patties on top of hot cooked spaghetti. Pour soup mixture over all. Sprinkle with cheese.

Per serving: 461 cal., 13 g total fat (6 g sat. fat), 63 mg chol., 707 mg sodium, 57 g carbo., 3 g fiber, 27 g pro.

Stroganoff-Sauced Beef Roast

Southwestern Pot Roast

Southwestern Pot Roast

Make this pot roast extra special by topping it with sour cream, chopped fresh tomato, and/or sliced avocado.

Start to Finish: 20 minutes **Makes:** 4 servings

- 1 **16- or 17-ounce package refrigerated cooked beef pot roast with juices**
- 1½ **cups sliced fresh mushrooms**
- 1 **cup bottled picante sauce**
- 1 **14-ounce can chicken broth**
- 1 **cup quick-cooking couscous**
- 2 **tablespoons snipped fresh cilantro**

1. Transfer liquid from pot roast package to a large skillet; add mushrooms and picante sauce. Cut pot roast into 1- to 1½-inch pieces; add to skillet. Bring to boiling; reduce heat. Simmer, covered, for 10 minutes.

2. Meanwhile, in a medium saucepan, bring broth to boiling. Stir in couscous; cover and remove from heat. Let stand about 5 minutes or until liquid is absorbed. Fluff couscous with a fork. Stir in cilantro.

3. Place couscous mixture on serving platter. Spoon pot roast mixture over couscous mixture. Serve immediately.

Per serving: 370 cal., 9 g total fat (3 g sat. fat), 61 mg chol., 1,268 mg sodium, 44 g carbo., 3 g fiber, 31 g pro.

Tamale Pie

This pie looks like a party in a pan and tastes just as festive.

Prep: 20 minutes **Bake:** 22 minutes **Oven:** 375°F
Makes: 6 servings

- 1 **8.5-ounce package corn muffin mix**
- 1 **cup shredded cheddar cheese (4 ounces)**
- 1 **4-ounce can diced green chile peppers, drained**
- 1 **pound lean ground beef or bulk pork sausage**
- 1 **15-ounce can kidney beans, rinsed and drained**
- 1 **10-ounce can enchilada sauce**

1. Preheat oven to 375°F. Grease a 2-quart rectangular baking dish; set aside.

2. Prepare muffin mix according to package directions. Stir in ½ cup of the cheese and the drained chile peppers. Spread corn muffin batter into the prepared baking dish.

3. Bake for 12 to 15 minutes or until a wooden toothpick inserted near the center comes out clean.

4. Meanwhile, in a large skillet, cook beef until brown. Drain off fat. Stir drained beans and enchilada sauce into browned beef. Spread beef mixture over baked corn muffin mixture.

5. Bake for 7 minutes more. Sprinkle with remaining ½ cup cheese. Bake about 3 minutes more or until cheese melts and mixture is heated through. To serve, cut into squares. If desired, serve with sour cream.

Per serving: 464 cal., 21 g total fat (8 g sat. fat), 67 mg chol., 778 mg sodium, 44 g carbo., 4 g fiber, 27 g pro.

Quick Honey-Garlic Pot Roast 💙 🔲

Imagine a comforting pot roast dinner in only 30 minutes. Thanks to precooked meat, all you have to do is add a few ingredients to give it a personal touch.

Prep: 10 minutes   **Cook:** 20 minutes   **Makes:** 4 servings

1	**17-ounce package refrigerated cooked beef roast au jus or beef pot roast with juices**
2	**tablespoons honey**
1	**tablespoon Worcestershire sauce**
1	**to 1½ teaspoons bottled roasted minced garlic**
¼	**teaspoon ground black pepper**
2	**cups packaged peeled baby carrots**
12	**ounces small red potatoes, quartered**
1	**medium red onion, cut into thin wedges**
	Snipped fresh parsley (optional)

1. Remove beef from package, reserving juices. In a medium bowl, combine reserved juices, honey, Worcestershire sauce, roasted garlic, and pepper. Place beef in a large nonstick skillet. Arrange carrots, potatoes, and onion wedges around beef. Pour honey mixture over beef and vegetables.

2. Bring beef mixture to boiling; reduce heat. Cover and simmer for 20 to 25 minutes or until vegetables are tender and beef is heated through. Transfer beef and vegetables to a serving platter. Spoon sauce over beef and vegetables. If desired, sprinkle with parsley.

Per serving: 305 cal., 9 g total fat (4 g sat. fat), 64 mg chol., 502 mg sodium, 35 g carbo., 4 g fiber, 26 g pro.

Quick Tip Also called new red potatoes, look for baby red potatoes that are firm and smooth with no dark spots, wrinkles, or sprouts. Store in a cool, dark, well-ventilated place. New potatoes should be used within 3 or 4 days of purchase.

Meatball Lasagna

Jarred pasta sauce and frozen meatballs are the wonderful convenience products that make this lasagna so easy to prepare. Keep them on hand to create easy meals anytime.

Prep: 25 minutes **Bake:** 45 minutes
Stand: 15 minutes **Oven:** 375°F. **Makes:** 8 servings.

- 9 dried lasagna noodles
- ½ of a 15-ounce container ricotta cheese
- 1½ cups shredded mozzarella cheese (6 ounces)
- ¼ cup grated Parmesan cheese
- 1 16-ounce package frozen cooked Italian-style meatballs (½-ounce size), thawed
- 1 26-ounce jar tomato pasta sauce

1. Preheat oven to 375°F. Cook lasagna noodles according to package directions. Drain noodles; rinse with cold water. Drain well; set aside.

2. Meanwhile, for the filling, in a small bowl, stir together ricotta, 1 cup mozzarella cheese, and Parmesan cheese; set aside. In a medium bowl, stir together the meatballs and one-third (about 1 cup) of the pasta sauce; set aside.

3. To assemble, spread a small amount (about 1/2 cup) of the reserved pasta sauce over the bottom of a 2-quart square baking dish. Layer three of the cooked noodles in the dish, trimming or overlapping as necessary to fit. Spoon the meatball mixture over noodles. Layer three more noodles over meatball layer. Spread half of the remaining sauce over noodles. Dollop ricotta mixture over the noodles; spread evenly. Layer remaining noodles over ricotta mixture. Spread remaining sauce over noodles. Cover dish with foil.

4. Bake for 35 minutes. Remove foil and sprinkle remaining mozzarella cheese over lasagna. Bake, uncovered, for 10 minutes more or until heated through. Let stand for 15 to 20 minutes before serving.

Per serving: 410 cal., 21 g total fat (11 g sat. fat), 66 mg chol., 897 mg sodium, 31 g carbo., 4 g fiber, 23 g pro.

Meatball Lasagna

Quick Skillet Lasagna `one`

Talk about quick. The most time-consuming part of this recipe is boiling the water for the pasta.

Start to Finish: 30 minutes **Makes:** 6 servings

- 3 cups (6 ounces) dried mafalda (mini lasagna) noodles
- 12 ounces lean ground beef or bulk pork sausage
- 1 26- to 27.75-ounce jar tomato-base pasta sauce
- 1½ cups shredded mozzarella cheese (6 ounces)
- ¼ cup grated Parmesan cheese (1 ounce)

1. Cook noodles according to package directions; drain.

2. Meanwhile, in a large nonstick skillet, cook beef until brown; drain off fat. Set beef aside. Wipe skillet with paper towel.

3. Spread about half of the cooked noodles in the skillet. Cover with about half of the sauce. Spoon cooked beef over sauce. Sprinkle with 1 cup of the mozzarella cheese. Top with remaining noodles and sauce. Sprinkle remaining mozzarella and the Parmesan cheese over top.

4. Cover and cook over medium heat for 5 to 7 minutes or until heated through and cheese melts. Remove skillet from heat and let stand, covered, for 1 minute.

Per serving: 389 cal., 16 g total fat (6 g sat. fat), 55 mg chol., 1,045 mg sodium, 30 g carbo., 2 g fiber, 25 g pro.

Prosciutto-Wrapped Beef `one`

Prosciutto may seem a little pricey, but because it's so thinly sliced and intensely flavored, a little goes a long way and makes a simple dish special.

Prep: 15 minutes **Broil:** 12 minutes **Makes:** 4 servings

- 1 ounce sliced prosciutto, chopped
- 1 small carrot, shredded
- 1 green onion, sliced
- 4 beef tenderloin steaks, cut 1 inch thick
- 4 thin slices prosciutto

1. Preheat broiler. For the stuffing, combine chopped prosciutto, carrot, and green onion. Cut a horizontal pocket in each steak by cutting from one side almost to, but not through, the other side. Fill pockets with stuffing. Cut the sliced prosciutto into 1-inch strips; wrap prosciutto strips around each steak. Secure with wooden toothpicks.

2. Place steaks on the unheated rack of a broiler pan. Broil 3 to 4 inches from the heat until desired doneness, turning once. Allow 12 to 14 minutes for medium-rare (145°F) and 15 to 18 minutes for medium (160°F).

Per serving: 296 cal., 13 g total fat (5 g sat. fat), 115 mg chol., 516 mg sodium, 1 g carbo., 0 g fiber, 40 g pro.

Basil-Garlic Sirloin ♥ [one] Roast

A regal cut of beef such as this one needs only simple seasonings as enhancements.

Prep: 15 minutes **Roast:** 50 minutes
Stand: 10 minutes **Oven:** 425°F/350°F
Makes: 10 to 12 servings

- **1 3- to 3½-pound boneless beef sirloin roast, cut 1¾ inches thick**
- **¼ teaspoon salt**
- **¼ teaspoon ground black pepper**
- **2 cups lightly packed fresh basil leaves, snipped**
- **8 to 10 cloves garlic, minced, or 2 tablespoons bottled minced garlic**
- **2 teaspoons olive oil**

1. Preheat oven to 425°F. Make five or six 5-inch-long slits along the top of the roast, almost cutting through it; sprinkle with salt and pepper. Combine basil and garlic; stuff into slits in roast. Tie roast with clean heavy-duty string to hold slits closed. Drizzle with olive oil.

2. Place roast on a rack in a shallow roasting pan. Insert a meat thermometer into center of roast. Roast for 15 minutes. Reduce oven temperature to 350°F. Roast for 35 to 45 minutes more or until desired doneness (160°F for medium). Cover and let stand 10 minutes before slicing.

Per serving: 255 cal., 13 g total fat (5 g sat. fat), 91 mg chol., 121 mg sodium, 1 g carbo., 0 g fiber, 31 g pro.

Steak 'n' Bake

This recipe stars a baked potato stuffed with classic steakhouse flavors. Broil the meat or grill it, whichever is more convenient.

Prep: 20 minutes **Broil:** 15 minutes
Stand: 5 minutes **Makes:** 4 servings

- **4 medium baking potatoes**
- **12 to 16 ounces boneless beef sirloin steak, cut 1 inch thick**
- **2 cups fresh baby spinach**
- **¾ cup bottled blue cheese salad dressing**
- **1 small red onion, cut into thin wedges**

1. Wash potatoes; pierce with fork. Arrange potatoes on microwave-safe plate in spoke formation, leaving 1 inch between potatoes. Microwave on high (100% power), uncovered, for 14 to 18 minutes or until tender. Let stand for 5 minutes.

2. Meanwhile, preheat broiler. Trim fat from steak. Place steak on the unheated rack of a broiler pan. Broil 3 to 4 inches from heat for 15 to 17 minutes for medium-rare (145°F) or 20 to 22 minutes for medium (160°F), turning once halfway through broiling. Transfer steak to cutting board; let stand for 5 minutes.

3. To serve, roll each potato gently under your hand. Cut an "X" in top of potato. Press in and up on ends of potato. Cut steak in bite-size strips. Top potatoes with steak strips and spinach; drizzle with dressing. Top with onion wedges.

Per serving: 580 cal., 35 g total fat (9 g sat. fat), 65 mg chol., 577 mg sodium, 35 g carbo., 4 g fiber, 32 g pro.

Peppery Beef with Mushrooms [one]

Steaks, mushrooms, and black pepper combine for unbeatable flavor. Roasted red potatoes make a great side dish.

Start to Finish: 20 minutes **Makes:** 4 servings

- **2 to 3 teaspoons steak seasoning blend or cracked black pepper**
- **4 beef tenderloin steaks or 2 beef top loin steaks, cut 1 inch thick (about 1 pound)**
- **2 tablespoons butter**
- **1 tablespoon olive oil or butter**
- **2 4-ounce packages sliced cremini, shiitaki, or portobello mushrooms or one 8-ounce package sliced button mushrooms (3 cups)**
- **1 large leek, thinly sliced**
- **½ teaspoon dried thyme or oregano, crushed**
- **1 5.5- to 6-ounce can tomato juice**
  Easy Roasted Red Potatoes (optional)

1. Use your fingers to press the steak seasoning onto both sides of the steaks. If using top loin steaks, cut each steak in half crosswise. In a large skillet, cook steaks in hot butter over medium heat to desired doneness, turning once. For tenderloin steaks, allow 10 to 13 minutes for medium-rare (145°F) to medium (160°F). For top loin steaks, allow 12 to 15 minutes for medium-rare to medium. Transfer steaks to a warm serving platter; reserving the drippings in the skillet. Keep warm.

2. Add oil to drippings in skillet. Add mushrooms, leek, and thyme. Cook and stir for 2 minutes. Stir in tomato juice. Bring to boiling; reduce heat. Simmer, uncovered, for 2 to 3 minutes more or until leek is tender. Spoon mushroom mixture over the steak. If desired, serve with Easy Roasted Red Potatoes.

Per serving: 296 cal., 20 g total fat (8 g sat. fat), 86 mg chol., 419 mg sodium, 5 g carbo., 1 g fiber, 26 g pro.

Easy Roasted Red Potatoes: Preheat oven to 400°F. Place one 20-ounce package refrigerated new potato wedges in a 2-quart square baking dish. Sprinkle with ½ teaspoon dried rosemary, crushed; ½ teaspoon seasoned salt; ¼ teaspoon garlic powder; and ¼ teaspoon ground black pepper. Drizzle with 2 tablespoons olive oil; toss gently to coat. Roast for 30 minutes, stirring once. Sprinkle with ⅓ cup finely shredded Parmesan cheese. Roast for 5 to 8 minutes more or until cheese is melted and starts to brown.

Peppery Beef
with Mushrooms

Mediterranean Mostaccioli

Mediterranean Mostaccioli

This tasty beef and veggie pasta dish is sure to be a hit with everyone in your family. Although not required, raisins add a pleasant sweetness to the sauce.

Start to Finish: 25 minutes **Makes:** 4 to 6 servings

4	ounces dried mostaccioli or gemelli pasta
2	cups sliced zucchini
8	ounces ground beef
½	of a medium eggplant, peeled and cubed (about 2½ cups)
1	14.5-ounce can diced tomatoes with basil, oregano, and garlic, undrained
2	tablespoons tomato paste
½	cup shredded carrot
¼	cup snipped fresh basil
2	tablespoons raisins (optional)
¼	teaspoon ground cinnamon
1	tablespoon balsamic vinegar (optional)
½	cup shredded mozzarella cheese (2 ounces)

1. Cook pasta according to package directions, adding zucchini during the last 2 minutes of cooking. Drain; keep warm.

2. Meanwhile, for the sauce, in a large skillet, cook beef and eggplant over medium heat until beef is brown; drain off fat. Stir in undrained tomatoes, tomato paste, carrot, basil, raisins (if desired), and cinnamon. Bring to boiling; reduce heat. Simmer, uncovered, about 2 minutes, or to desired consistency, stirring occasionally. Remove from heat. If desired, stir in vinegar.

3. Transfer pasta mixture to a serving dish. Spoon sauce over pasta mixture. Sprinkle with cheese.

Per serving: 334 cal., 11 g total fat (5 g sat. fat), 47 mg chol., 672 mg sodium, 38 g carbo., 4 g fiber, 21 g pro.

Quick Tip Choose an eggplant that is firm, smooth-skinned, and heavy for its size; avoid those with soft or brown spots. Store eggplants in a cool, dry place and use within 1 to 2 days of purchase. For longer storage (up to 5 days), place them in a plastic bag and store in the vegetable drawer of the refrigerator.

Bail-Out Beef Stroganoff ♥

The horseradish-sour cream topper adds a touch of elegance to this fast-fixing version of the old-world classic.

Start to Finish: 30 minutes **Makes:** 4 servings

3	cups dried wide noodles
3	cups broccoli florets (12 ounces)
½	cup light dairy sour cream
1½	teaspoons prepared horseradish
½	teaspoon fresh dill
1	pound beef ribeye steak
1	small onion, cut into ½-inch slices
½	teaspoon bottled minced garlic (1 clove)
1	tablespoon cooking oil
4	teaspoons all-purpose flour
½	teaspoon ground black pepper
1	14-ounce can beef broth
3	tablespoons tomato paste
1	teaspoon Worcestershire sauce

1. Cook noodles according to package directions, adding broccoli for the last 5 minutes of cooking. Drain well. Return noodle mixture to hot pan; cover to keep warm.

2. Meanwhile, in a small serving bowl, stir together the sour cream, horseradish, and dill; cover and chill until serving time.

3. Trim fat from beef. Cut beef into bite-size strips. In a large skillet, cook and stir half of the beef, the onion, and garlic in hot oil until onion is tender and beef is desired doneness. Remove from skillet. Add remaining beef to skillet; cook and stir until beef is desired doneness. Return all of the beef to the skillet; sprinkle flour and pepper over beef. Stir to coat.

4. Stir in broth, tomato paste, and Worcestershire sauce. Cook and stir until thickened and bubbly. Cook and stir for 1 minute more. Divide noodle-broccoli mixture among 4 bowls. Spoon beef mixture on top of noodle mixture. Top with the horseradish-sour cream mixture.

Per serving: 413 cal., 16 g total fat (6 g sat. fat), 103 mg chol., 504 mg sodium, 33 g carbo., 3 g fiber, 33 g pro.

Bail-Out Beef Stroganoff

Jamaican Pork Kabobs 🖤

A spicy chutney sauce gives these pork tenderloin kabobs sensational flavor. Substitute slices of zucchini or yellow squash for pattypan squash if it's not available.

Prep: 15 minutes **Broil:** 12 minutes **Makes:** 4 servings

2   **ears corn, husked and cleaned, or 2 medium red or yellow sweet peppers, cut into 1-inch pieces**

1   **12- to 14-ounce pork tenderloin**

16 **baby pattypan squash (each about 1 inch in diameter) or 2 small zucchini or yellow summer squash, halved lengthwise and cut into 1-inch slices**

1   **small red onion, cut into ½-inch wedges**

¼   **cup mango chutney, finely chopped**

3   **tablespoons Pickapeppa sauce**

1   **tablespoon cooking oil**

1   **tablespoon water**

1. Cut ears of corn (if using) crosswise into 1-inch pieces. In a medium saucepan, bring a small amount of water to boiling. Add corn pieces to boiling water and cook for 3 minutes; drain and rinse with cold water. Meanwhile, cut pork tenderloin into 1-inch slices.

2. Preheat broiler. For the kabobs, on 8 long metal skewers, alternately thread corn or sweet pepper pieces, pork slices, squash, and onion wedges, leaving a ¼-inch space between pieces. In a small bowl, combine chutney, Pickapeppa sauce, oil, and water; set aside.

3. Place kabobs on the unheated rack of a broiler pan. Broil 3 to 4 inches from the heat for 12 to 14 minutes or until no pink remains in the pork and the vegetables are tender, turning once halfway through broiling and brushing with the chutney mixture for the last 5 minutes of broiling.

Per serving: 254 cal., 6 g total fat (1 g sat. fat), 50 mg chol., 264 mg sodium, 26 g carbo., 3 g fiber, 23 g pro.

Quick Tip If you can't find Pickapeppa sauce, substitute 3 tablespoons Worcestershire sauce mixed with a dash of bottled hot pepper sauce.

Squirt-of-Orange Chops 💜 [one]

It is no secret that oranges impart unbeatable flavor to pork. Here, orange marmalade, fresh orange juice, and rosemary create a tempting glaze on broiled boneless pork chops.

Prep: 10 minutes **Broil:** 9 minutes **Makes:** 4 servings

- **4** boneless pork top loin chops, cut 1 inch thick (about 1¼ pounds)
- **1** large orange
- **½** teaspoon garlic-pepper seasoning
- **¼** teaspoon salt
- **¼** cup orange marmalade
- **2** teaspoons snipped fresh rosemary or ½ teaspoon dried rosemary, crushed

1. Preheat broiler. Trim fat from chops; set chops aside.

2. Cut orange in half. Cut one half of the orange into 4 wedges; set wedges aside. Squeeze juice from remaining orange half. Remove 1 tablespoon of the orange juice and brush on both sides of each chop. Sprinkle chops with garlic-pepper seasoning and salt. In a small bowl, combine remaining orange juice, orange marmalade, and rosemary; set aside.

3. Place chops on the unheated rack of a broiler pan. Broil 3 to 4 inches from the heat for 9 to 11 minutes or until chops are 160°F, turning once and brushing with orange marmalade mixture for the last 2 to 3 minutes of broiling.

4. Serve orange wedges with chops. If desired, squeeze juice from orange wedges over chops.

Per serving: 262 cal., 7 g total fat (3 g sat. fat), 83 mg chol., 343 mg sodium, 17 g carbo., 1 g fiber, 31 g pro.

Tangy Stir-Fried 💜 [one] Pork

When fresh kumquats are in season, use them to add flavor and interest to pork tenderloin. Other times of the year, substitute a thinly sliced orange.

Start to Finish: 25 minutes **Makes:** 4 servings

- **1** teaspoon cooking oil
- **12** ounces pork tenderloin, cut into ½-inch slices
- **¼** cup dry white wine or reduced-sodium chicken broth
- **6** kumquats, thinly sliced, or ¼ of an orange, thinly sliced
- **2** tablespoons bottled hoisin sauce
- **1** green onion, bias-sliced into ¼-inch pieces
- **1** teaspoon sesame seeds, toasted
- **2** cups hot, cooked quick-cooking brown rice

1. In a wok or large nonstick skillet, heat oil over medium-high heat. Add pork; cook for 6 to 8 minutes or until cooked through. Remove from wok or skillet.

2. Add wine, kumquat, and hoisin sauce to wok or skillet. Cook and stir for 1 minute.

3. Return pork to wok or skillet. Heat through. Stir in green onion and sesame seeds. Serve over hot cooked rice.

Per serving: 244 cal., 4 g total fat (1 g sat. fat), 50 mg chol., 126 mg sodium, 26 g carbo., 3 g fiber, 23 g pro.

Quick Tip When selecting kumquats, look for firm, brightly colored fruit without blemishes or shriveled skin. Store kumquats in the refrigerator for up to 2 weeks.

Squirt-of-Orange Chops

Pork Tenderloin with Quinoa and Greens ♥

Enjoy a roasted pork dinner that's ready in minutes, not hours. If you're having a hard time finding curry paste, check the ethnic section of the grocery store or an Indian or Asian market.

Prep: 20 minutes **Roast:** 25 minutes
Stand: 10 minutes + 5 minutes **Oven:** 425°F
Makes: 6 servings

- **2** **tablespoons curry paste**
- **2** **12- to 16-ounce pork tenderloins**
- **2** **14-ounce cans chicken broth**
- **1** **cup quinoa**
- **1** **tablespoon extra-virgin olive oil**
- **2** **cloves garlic, minced (1 teaspoon minced)**
- **12** **ounces fresh kale, stemmed and torn**
- **½** **cup plain lowfat yogurt (optional)**
    Chopped fresh flat-leaf parsley (optional)

1. Preheat oven to 425°F. Using your fingers, rub curry paste on all sides of pork. Place pork on a rack in a shallow roasting pan.

2. Roast pork for 25 to 35 minutes or until an instant-read thermometer inserted in thickest part of tenderloin registers 155°F. Remove pork from oven. Cover with foil and let stand for 10 minutes. The temperature of the pork after standing should be 160°F.

3. Meanwhile, in a medium saucepan, bring 1 can of the broth to boiling over medium-high heat. Add quinoa, olive oil, and garlic; reduce heat. Cover and simmer about 15 minutes or until liquid is absorbed and quinoa is tender. Remove from heat; let stand, covered, for 5 minutes.

4. Meanwhile, in a large saucepan, bring the remaining 1 can broth and the kale to boiling over medium-high heat; reduce heat. Cover and simmer about 20 minutes or until kale is tender, stirring occasionally. Using a slotted spoon, transfer kale to a large serving bowl; stir in quinoa.

5. Thinly slice pork. Serve with quinoa mixture and, if desired, yogurt. If desired, garnish with parsley.

Per serving: 296 cal., 8 g total fat (2 g sat. fat), 74 mg chol., 468 mg sodium, 27 g carbo., 3 g fiber, 30 g pro.

Quick Tip Indian curry paste is available in the ethnic section of many supermarkets. Look for quinoa at a health food store or in the grains section of a large supermarket.

Pork Loin with Vegetables ♥

If you don't usually keep apricot preserves on hand, make this succulent pork dish with peach or pineapple preserves instead.

Prep: 15 minutes **Roast:** 35 minutes **Oven:** 425°F
Stand: 10 minutes **Makes:** 4 servings

- **12** **ounces packaged, peeled baby carrots (2½ cups)**
- **12** **ounces small new potatoes, quartered**
- **1** **12- to 16-ounce pork tenderloin**
- **⅔** **cup apricot preserves**
- **¼** **cup white wine vinegar or white vinegar**

1. Preheat oven to 425°F. In a medium saucepan, cook the carrots and potatoes in a small amount of boiling water for 4 minutes; drain. Meanwhile, place the tenderloin in a 13×9×2-inch baking pan. Arrange carrots and potatoes around meat. Roast, uncovered, for 20 minutes.

2. In a small bowl, stir together the preserves and vinegar; brush some of the mixture over pork. Drizzle remaining preserves mixture over vegetables; toss to coat. Roast, uncovered, about 15 minutes more or until an instant-read thermometer inserted in center of pork registers 155°F. Stir vegetables.

3. Cover pork and vegetables and let stand for 15 minutes. (Temperature will rise 5 to 10°F.) Transfer pork to a platter; slice pork. Using a slotted spoon, transfer vegetables to the platter. Drizzle pan juices over pork and vegetables.

Per serving: 365 cal., 2 g total fat (1 g sat. fat), 50 mg chol., 84 mg sodium, 62 g carbo., 5 g fiber, 23 g pro.

Pork Tenderloin with Quinoa and Greens

Pork Loin with Vegetables

Peppered Pork with Chive Sauce

Peppered Pork with Chive Sauce [one]

There's no complicated sauce to make for these pepper-crusted chops—just cream cheese, chicken broth, and sherry.

Start to Finish: 25 minutes **Makes:** 4 servings

- 4 **boneless pork top loin chops, cut ¾ inch thick**
- 1 **teaspoon coarsely cracked black peppercorns**
- 2 **teaspoons olive oil or cooking oil**
- ¼ **cup chicken broth**
- 3 **tablespoons dry sherry or chicken broth**
- ½ **of an 8-ounce package cream cheese, cut up**
- 1 **tablespoon snipped fresh chives**
     Snipped fresh chives (optional)

1. Sprinkle chops with cracked peppercorns, pressing lightly into pork. In a large skillet, heat oil over medium heat. Add chops; cook for 8 to 12 minutes or until pork juices run clear (160°F), turning once halfway through cooking time. Transfer chops to a serving platter; cover and keep warm.

2. For the sauce, carefully add broth and sherry to skillet. Cook until bubbly, stirring to loosen any browned bits in bottom of skillet. Add cream cheese to skillet. Stir with a wire whisk over medium heat until cream cheese melts. Stir in the 1 tablespoon snipped chives. Spoon sauce over chops. If desired, sprinkle with additional snipped chives.

Per serving: 348 cal., 21 g total fat (10 g sat. fat), 108 mg chol., 204 mg sodium, 2 g carbo., 0 g fiber, 33 g pro.

Citrus and Spice Pork Chops ♥ [one]

For a tangier, less sweet version of these Caribbean-style chops, use grapefruit juice instead of orange juice.

Prep: 10 minutes **Cook:** 9 minutes **Makes:** 4 servings

- 4 **boneless pork loin chops, cut ½-inch thick (about 1½ pounds total)**
- 3 **tablespoons orange juice or grapefruit juice**
- 2 **teaspoons Jamaican jerk or Montreal steak seasoning**
- 1 **tablespoon cooking oil**
- 2 **tablespoons Dijon-style mustard**
- ⅓ **cup orange marmalade**
- ¼ **cup chopped roasted cashews or peanuts (optional)**

1. Brush both sides of pork chops with 1 tablespoon of the orange juice. Sprinkle both sides with seasoning. In a large nonstick skillet, cook chops in hot oil over medium heat for 9 to 11 minutes or until slightly pink in the center, turning once halfway through cooking. Transfer chops to a platter.

2. Remove pan from heat. Stir mustard into pan drippings. Whisk in marmalade and remaining 2 tablespoons orange juice. Return to heat. Cook and stir just until boiling. Pour sauce over chops. If desired, sprinkle with nuts.

Per serving: 342 cal., 11 g total fat (3 g sat. fat), 107 mg chol., 435 mg sodium, 20 g carbo., 0 g fiber, 39 g pro.

Country Chops and ♥ 🔲 Peppers

Any color of sweet pepper looks appetizing and tastes great with pork chops. If you have more than one kind on hand, feel free to mix them.

Start to Finish: 20 minutes **Makes:** 4 servings

- 4 pork loin chops, cut ¾ inch thick
  Seasoned salt
  Ground black pepper
  Nonstick cooking spray
- 1 medium sweet pepper, cut into strips
- 1 tablespoon butter
- ⅓ cup Worcestershire sauce for chicken or
  2 tablespoons Worcestershire sauce and
  ¼ cup water

1. Trim fat from chops. Sprinkle chops on both sides with seasoned salt and black pepper. Lightly coat a large skillet with cooking spray. Heat skillet over medium-high heat. Add chops and cook for 5 minutes. Turn chops; top with sweet pepper strips. Cover and cook for 5 to 7 minutes more or until chops are done (160°F) and sweet pepper strips are crisp-tender. Remove chops and sweet pepper strips from skillet; keep warm.

2. For the sauce, add butter and Worcestershire sauce to hot skillet. Cook over medium heat until sauce thickens slightly, stirring to loosen any brown bits in bottom of skillet. Pour sauce over chops and sweet pepper strips.

Per serving: 282 cal., 11 g total fat (5 g sat. fat), 101 mg chol., 282 mg sodium, 6 g carbo., 1 g fiber, 38 g pro.

Pork and Sweet Potato Stir-Fry ♥

If your supermarket doesn't sell pork strips for stir-frying, cut your own strips from a piece of boneless pork tenderloin.

Start to Finish: 30 minutes **Makes:** 4 servings

- 1½ cups uncooked instant white rice
- ¼ cup thinly sliced green onion (2)
- 1 large sweet potato (about 12 ounces)
- 1 medium tart apple (such as Granny Smith), cored
- 12 ounces packaged pork stir-fry strips
- 2 to 3 teaspoons Jamaican jerk seasoning
- 1 tablespoon cooking oil
- ⅓ cup water

1. Prepare rice according to package directions. Stir half of the green onion into the cooked rice.

2. Meanwhile, peel sweet potato. Cut into quarters lengthwise, then thinly slice crosswise. Place in a microwave-safe pie plate or shallow dish. Cover with vented plastic wrap. Microwave on 100% power (high) for 3 to 4 minutes or until tender, stirring once. Cut apple into 16 wedges. Sprinkle pork with Jamaican jerk seasoning; toss to coat.

3. In a wok or large skillet, heat oil over medium-high heat. Add pork and stir-fry for 2 minutes (add more oil if necessary during cooking). Add apple and remaining green onion. Stir-fry for 1 to 2 minutes more or until no pink remains.

4. Stir in sweet potato and water. Bring to boiling; reduce heat. Simmer, uncovered, for 1 minute. Serve immediately over hot cooked rice mixture.

Per serving: 365 cal., 9 g total fat (2 g sat. fat), 38 mg chol., 131 mg sodium, 54 g carbo., 3 g fiber, 16 g pro.

Jamaican Pork Stir-Fry ♥ 🔲

Take a vacation from the postwork, predinner rush with this Jamaica-inspired dish that features two of this easygoing island's favorite ingredients: lean pork and sweet peppers. For flavor, pick up Jamaican jerk seasoning in the grocery store spice aisle.

Start to Finish: 20 minutes **Makes:** 4 servings

- 1 tablespoon cooking oil
- 1 16-ounce package frozen sweet pepper and onion stir-fry vegetables
- 12 ounces pork strips for stir-frying
- 2 to 3 teaspoons Jamaican jerk seasoning
- ½ cup bottled plum sauce
  Soy sauce (optional)
  Peanuts (optional)
- 2 cups hot cooked rice or pasta

1. In a wok or large skillet, heat oil over medium-high heat. Add frozen vegetables; cook and stir for 5 to 7 minutes or until vegetables are crisp-tender. Remove vegetables from wok.

2. In a medium bowl, toss pork with jerk seasoning; add to wok. Add more oil if necessary. Cook and stir for 2 to 5 minutes or until pork is no longer pink.

3. Add plum sauce to wok; return vegetables to wok. Gently toss to coat; heat through. If desired, season with soy sauce and sprinkle with peanuts. Serve over rice.

Per serving: 357 cal., 9 g total fat (2 g sat. fat), 54 mg chol., 405 mg sodium, 45 g carbo., 2 g fiber, 22 g pro.

Ham and Beans with Spinach `one`

This dish is so good it is reason enough to keep your pantry stocked with beans, olive oil, and garlic. You'll want to make this satisfying supper often.

Start to Finish: 20 minutes **Makes:** 4 servings

- **2   15-ounce cans Great Northern beans**
- **1   tablespoon bottled minced garlic**
- **1   tablespoon olive oil**
- **2   cups cooked ham, cut into bite-size strips**
- **3   cups chopped fresh spinach**

1. Drain beans, reserving liquid. In a large nonstick skillet, cook and stir garlic in hot oil over medium heat for 1 minute. Add beans and ham to skillet. Cook about 5 minutes or until heated through, stirring occasionally.

2. Stir in spinach; cover and cook for 1 to 2 minutes more or until spinach is wilted. If desired, thin mixture with some of the reserved liquid.

Per serving: 324 cal., 8 g total fat (2 g sat. fat), 39 mg chol., 1,443 mg sodium, 33 g carbo., 11 g fiber, 29 g pro.

Scalloped Potatoes and Ham `one`

This stick-to-your-ribs classic comfort dish can be a hearty accompaniment to simple grilled meat, roasted veggies, or a plain salad of mixed greens.

Prep: 15 minutes **Bake:** 45 minutes
Stand: 10 minutes **Oven:** 350°F **Makes:** 6 to 8 servings

- **1   10.75-ounce can condensed cream of onion or cream of celery soup**
- **½   cup milk**
- **⅛   teaspoon ground black pepper**
- **3   cups cubed cooked ham (about 1 pound)**
- **1   20-ounce package refrigerated diced potatoes with onion**
- **¾   cup shredded Swiss or Cheddar cheese (3 ounces)**

1. Preheat oven to 350°F. In a large bowl, stir together soup, milk, and pepper. Stir in ham and potatoes. Transfer to an ungreased 2-quart rectangular baking dish.

2. Bake, covered, for 40 minutes. Stir mixture. Sprinkle with cheese. Bake, uncovered, for 5 to 10 minutes more or until heated through and cheese is melted. Let stand for 10 minutes before serving.

Per serving: 332 cal., 14 g total fat (6 g sat. fat), 64 mg chol., 1,613 mg sodium, 29 g carbo., 2 g fiber, 21 g pro.

Molasses-Glazed Pork Tenderloin

Molasses-Glazed Pork Tenderloin

Consider old-fashioned corn bread as a charming dinner partner for this glazed pork with beans.

Start to Finish: 30 minutes **Makes:** 4 servings

- **¼   cup finely chopped prosciutto or 2 slices bacon, coarsely chopped**
- **2   9-ounce packages frozen cut green beans**
- **½   cup chopped onion**
- **1   tablespoon olive oil**
- **12   ounces pork tenderloin, cut into ½-inch slices (11 to 12 slices)**
- **½   cup orange juice**
- **3   tablespoons molasses**
- **1   teaspoon cornstarch**
- **½   teaspoon salt**
- **¼   teaspoon ground black pepper**
  Steamed spinach (optional)

1. In a large skillet, cook prosciutto over medium heat until crisp; drain and set aside. In the same skillet, cook green beans and onion in ¾ cup water according to bean package directions. Drain bean mixture; set aside.

2. In the same skillet, heat oil over medium-high heat. Add pork; cook for 4 to 5 minutes or just until barely pink in center, turning once halfway through cooking time.

3. Meanwhile, in a small bowl, stir together orange juice, molasses, cornstarch, salt, and pepper. Add to pork in skillet. Cook and stir until thickened and bubbly. Cook and stir for 2 minutes more. Stir bean mixture into mixture in skillet; heat through. If desired, serve with steamed spinach. Top individual servings with prosciutto.

Per serving: 258 cal., 7 g total fat (2 g sat. fat), 61 mg chol., 588 mg sodium, 27 g carbo., 4 g fiber, 23 g pro.

Oven-Fried Pork Chops `one`

Coat the chops with the corn bread stuffing mix to keep them juicy and moist inside and give them a delightful crispy crust.

Prep: 10 minutes **Bake:** 20 minutes **Oven:** 425°F
Makes: 4 servings

- **1 egg**
- **2 tablespoons fat-free milk**
- **1 cup packaged corn bread stuffing mix**
- **4 pork loin chops, cut ½ inch thick (1 to 1½ pounds total)**
- **1 20-ounce package frozen roasted russet potato pieces**

1. Preheat oven to 425°F.

2. In a shallow dish, beat egg with a fork; stir in milk. Place dry stuffing mix in another shallow dish. Trim fat from chops. Dip pork chops into egg mixture. Coat both sides with stuffing mix. Arrange pork chops in a single layer on one side of a 15×10×1-inch baking pan. Add potato pieces to the other side of the same pan, mounding potatoes as needed to fit.

3. Bake, uncovered, about 20 minutes or until pork is done (160°F) and potatoes are lightly browned and crisp, turning pork and stirring potatoes once.

Per serving: 443 cal., 17 g total fat (4 g sat. fat), 88 mg chol., 1,251 mg sodium, 51 g carbo., 2 g fiber, 20 g pro.

Oven-Fried Pork Chops

Pork and Apples

Pork and Apples 🧡 ▣one

For wedges that keep their shape as they cook, make this spicy-sweet medley with Rome Beauty or York Imperial apples.

Start to Finish: 30 minutes   **Makes:** 4 servings

- 1 **12-ounce pork tenderloin**
- ¼ **teaspoon salt**
- ¼ **teaspoon ground black pepper**
- 5 **teaspoons olive oil**
- 1 **large red onion, halved and sliced**
- ¾ **cup apple juice or apple cider**
- 2 **tablespoons red wine vinegar**
- 1 **tablespoon spicy brown mustard**
- 2 **medium cooking apples, cut into wedges**
- 1 **teaspoon snipped fresh rosemary or**
  ½ teaspoon dried rosemary, crushed

1. Cut tenderloin crosswise into ½-inch slices; sprinkle with salt and pepper.

2. In a 12-inch skillet, heat 3 teaspoons of the oil over medium heat. Add pork; cook for 6 to 8 minutes or until done (160°F), turning once. Remove pork from skillet.

3. Add the remaining 2 teaspoons oil and the onion to skillet. Cook and stir for 2 minutes. Carefully stir in apple juice, vinegar, and mustard. Bring to boiling; reduce heat.

4. Add apple wedges and rosemary to skillet. Cook about 4 minutes or just until apples are tender and most of the liquid has evaporated. Add the pork slices; heat through.

Per serving: 225 cal., 9 g total fat (2 g sat. fat), 55 mg chol., 240 mg sodium, 18 g carbo., 2 g fiber, 19 g pro.

Pork Skillet with ▣one Sauerkraut and Apples

The sweet-tart taste of sauerkraut and apples goes well with the pork. Use red apples for color.

Start to Finish: 25 minutes   **Makes:** 4 servings

- 1 **12- to 16-ounce pork tenderloin**
- 1 **tablespoon olive oil**
- 1 **14.5-ounce can sauerkraut, rinsed and well drained**
- 1 **large apple, cored and thinly sliced**
- ¼ **cup apple juice**

1. Trim fat from pork. Cut pork crosswise into 12 slices. Place one slice, cut side down, between 2 pieces of plastic wrap. Using the flat side of a meat mallet, pound pork from center to edges to ½-inch thickness. Repeat with remaining pork slices.

2. In a 12-inch nonstick skillet, heat oil over medium-high heat. Add pork; cook for 6 to 8 minutes or until slightly pink in the center (160°F), turning once halfway through cooking. Reduce heat to medium if oil starts to spatter. Transfer pork to a serving platter; cover to keep warm.

3. Add sauerkraut, apple slices, and apple juice to hot skillet. Cover and cook over medium heat for 4 to 6 minutes or just until apples are tender, stirring occasionally. Serve apple mixture with pork.

Per serving: 200 cal., 8 g total fat (2 g sat. fat), 47 mg chol., 695 mg sodium, 12 g carbo., 4 g fiber, 21 g pro.

Greek-Stuffed Roasted Pork Loin ♥ [one]

Greek seasoning is actually a blend of 10 or more spices, so you're guaranteed that this dish is well-seasoned.

Prep: 25 minutes **Roast:** 1 hour **Stand:** 10 minutes
Oven: 325°F **Makes:** 8 servings

- 1   **2- to 2½-pound boneless pork top loin roast (single loin)**
- 1   **tablespoon chopped fresh mint or dill**
- 1   **tablespoon chopped fresh flat-leaf parsley**
      Salt
      Freshly ground black pepper
- 1   **12-ounce jar roasted red sweet peppers, drained**
- ½   **cup crumbled feta cheese (2 ounces)**
- 2   **cloves garlic, minced (1 teaspoon minced)**

1. Preheat oven to 325°F. To butterfly the pork roast, make a lengthwise cut down the center of the roast, cutting to within ½ inch of the opposite side, to form a "V". Spread roast open. Make a parallel slit on each side of the original cut. Open pork roast to lay flat. Place between 2 pieces of plastic wrap. Working from center to edges, pound with the flat side of a meat mallet to ½-inch thickness. Remove plastic wrap.

2. Sprinkle mint and parsley on pounded side of pork loin. Sprinkle with kosher salt and pepper. If necessary, split drained roasted sweet peppers to lay flat. Arrange peppers in an even layer on top of the pork roast. In a small bowl, combine feta cheese and garlic. Sprinkle over sweet peppers on pork roast. Roll up, starting from a short side; tie with 100-percent-cotton string at 1½-inch intervals. Season with salt and black pepper.

3. Place roast on a rack in a shallow roasting pan. Insert an oven-going meat thermometer into center of roast. Roast for 1 to 1½ hours or until the thermometer registers 155°F. Cover with foil and let stand for 10 minutes before slicing. The temperature of the roast after standing should be 160°F.

Per serving: 196 cal., 8 g total fat (3 g sat. fat), 68 mg chol., 181 mg sodium, 2 g carbo., 1 g dietary fiber, 26 g protein.

Soy and Sesame Pork ♥ [one]

Toast sesame seeds over medium-low heat in a dry skillet, stirring often, until they are light brown and fragrant.

Prep: 5 minutes **Roast:** 20 minutes
Marinate: 4 to 24 hours **Oven:** 425°F **Makes:** 4 servings

- 1   **1-pound pork tenderloin**
- ¼   **cup reduced-sodium soy sauce**
- 1   **tablespoon ketchup**
- ¼   **teaspoon garlic powder**
- 2   **to 3 tablespoons sesame seeds, toasted**

1. Trim fat from pork. Place pork in a large resealable plastic bag set in a shallow dish. For the marinade, in a small bowl, combine soy sauce, ketchup, and garlic powder. Pour marinade over pork. Seal bag; turn to coat pork. Marinate in the refrigerator for 4 to 24 hours, turning bag occasionally.

2. Preheat oven to 425°F. Drain pork, discarding marinade. Place pork on a rack in a shallow roasting pan. Roast for 20 to 30 minutes or until done (160°F). Sprinkle sesame seeds on a piece of foil; roll pork in sesame seeds.

Per serving: 162 cal., 5 g total fat (1 g sat. fat), 73 mg chol., 357 mg sodium, 2 g carbo., 1 g fiber, 25 g pro.

Greek-Stuffed
Roasted Pork Loin

Pork Medallions with
Fennel and Pancetta

3. In the same skillet, cook pancetta over medium-high heat until crisp. Add fennel, onion, and garlic and cook for 3 to 5 minutes or until crisp-tender. Add lemon juice; stir in whipping cream. Bring to boiling; return pork to pan. Cook until pork is heated through and sauce is slightly thickened.

4. Transfer the meat to a serving platter. Spoon the sauce over the meat.

Per serving: 341 cal., 23 g total fat (10 g sat. fat), 105 mg chol., 175 mg sodium, 12 g carbo., 12 g fiber, 22 g pro.

Ham and Asparagus Pasta [one]

Cream cheese spread thinned with a little milk makes a super easy creamy pasta sauce for this delectable weeknight meal. So rich and delicious, no one will guess it took only 20 minutes to prepare.

Start to Finish: 20 minutes **Makes:** 4 servings

- **4 cups dried bow tie pasta, rotini, or other medium-size pasta**
- **1 10-ounce package frozen cut asparagus or broccoli**
- **8 ounces sliced cooked ham, cut into thin strips**
- **1 8-ounce tub cream cheese spread with chives and onion**
- **⅓ cup milk**

1. Cook pasta according to package directions, adding the frozen asparagus for the last 5 minutes and the ham for the last 1 minute of the cooking time. Drain and return to the pan.

2. In a medium bowl, whisk together cream cheese and milk; add to the pasta mixture in the pan. Stir gently over medium heat until heated through. If necessary, add additional milk, to reach desired consistency. Serve immediately.

Per serving: 459 cal., 24 g total fat (15 g sat. fat), 89 mg chol., 1,001 mg sodium, 38 g carbo., 3 g fiber, 19 g pro.

Pork Medallions with Fennel and Pancetta [one]

The ingredients with wow-power are fennel, which adds licoricelike tones, and pancetta, a flavorful Italian bacon. Of course, a touch of cream doesn't hurt matters either. It all adds up to a bistro-style dish ready in just 30 minutes.

Start to Finish: 30 minutes **Makes:** 4 servings

- **1 12-ounce pork tenderloin**
- **¼ cup all-purpose flour**
  Dash salt
  Dash ground black pepper
- **2 tablespoons olive oil**
- **2 ounces pancetta (Italian bacon) or bacon, finely chopped**
- **2 fennel bulbs, trimmed and cut crosswise into ¼-inch slices**
- **1 small onion, thinly sliced**
- **2 cloves garlic, minced**
- **2 tablespoons lemon juice**
- **½ cup whipping cream**

1. Trim fat from pork. Cut pork crosswise into 1-inch slices. Place each slice between 2 pieces of plastic wrap. Pound pork lightly with the flat side of a meat mallet to a ¼-inch thickness. Remove plastic wrap. In a shallow dish, combine flour, salt, and pepper. Dip pork slices in flour mixture to coat.

2. In a large heavy skillet, heat oil over high heat. Add pork, half at a time, and cook for 2 to 3 minutes or until pork is slightly pink in center, turning once. (If necessary, add more oil.) Remove meat from skillet; set aside.

Ham and Asparagus Pasta

Thyme Pork Chops with
Roasted Cauliflower

Thyme Pork Chops with Roasted Cauliflower ♥ [one]

Thyme and pork are a match made in heaven. Try the combo alongside savory pan-roasted cauliflower and onions.

Start to Finish: 30 minutes   **Makes:** 4 servings

- **4** **pork rib chops, cut ¾ inch thick**
- **4** **teaspoons snipped fresh thyme or 1 teaspoon dried thyme or Italian seasoning, crushed**
- **¼** **teaspoon salt**
- **¼** **teaspoon ground black pepper**
   Nonstick cooking spray
- **6** **cups packaged cauliflower florets**
- **2** **small onions, cut into wedges**
- **2** **tablespoons olive oil**

1. Trim fat from chops. In a small bowl, stir together thyme, salt, and pepper; sprinkle evenly on both sides of chops. Set chops aside.

2. Coat an unheated very large nonstick skillet with nonstick cooking spray. Preheat over medium-high heat. Add cauliflower and onion; cook and stir about 5 minutes or until almost tender. Remove skillet from heat.

3. Push cauliflower and onion to the edge of the skillet. Add oil to the skillet. Arrange the seasoned chops in a single layer in skillet. Return skillet to heat and cook over medium heat for 10 to 15 minutes or until pork chops are 160°F and vegetables are tender, turning chops to brown evenly and stirring the vegetable mixture often.

Per serving: 296 cal., 14 g total fat (3 g sat. fat), 70 mg chol., 389 mg sodium, 11 g carbo., 4 g fiber, 32 g pro.

Pork with Berry-Dressed Greens

Pork with Berry-Dressed Greens [one]

Think of this salad when raspberry season rolls around. Reduced-fat raspberry vinaigrette and lean pork loin help keep this fresh-tasting salad low in calories and fat.

Start to Finish: 20 minutes   **Makes:** 4 servings

- **2** **boneless pork loin chops, cut ¾ inch thick (about 12 ounces total)**
- **¼** **teaspoon salt**
- **¼** **teaspoon ground ginger**
- **⅛** **teaspoon ground black pepper**
- **1** **teaspoon cooking oil**
- **1** **teaspoon bottled minced garlic (2 cloves)**
- **½** **cup fresh sugar snap peas**
- **⅓** **cup sliced fresh mushrooms**
- **⅔** **cup bottled reduced-fat raspberry vinaigrette salad dressing**
- **½** **cup fresh raspberries**
- **8** **cups torn fresh spinach and/or romaine or purchased torn mixed salad greens**

1. Trim fat from chops. Sprinkle both sides of each chop with salt, ginger, and pepper. In a large nonstick skillet, heat oil over medium heat. Add chops; cook for 8 to 10 minutes or until pork juices run clear (160°F), turning once. Remove chops from skillet, reserving drippings. Cover chops; keep warm.

2. In the same skillet, cook and stir garlic in reserved drippings for 30 seconds. Add peas and mushrooms to skillet. Pour dressing over all. Cover and cook for 2 to 3 minutes or until heated through. Remove from heat. Gently stir in the raspberries; set aside and keep warm.

3. Divide spinach evenly among 4 dinner plates. Thinly slice pork. Arrange pork on spinach. Pour warm raspberry mixture over all.

Per serving: 248 cal., 12 g total fat (2 g sat. fat), 46 mg chol., 617 mg sodium, 12 g carbo., 7 g fiber, 21 g pro.

Quick Tip Choose brightly colored , fresh-smelling, plump berries without hulls. Attached hulls indicate that the berries were picked too early and will undoubtedly be tart. Avoid soft, shriveled, or moldy berries. If fresh raspberries are not available, you may substitute blackberries, strawberries, or blueberries.

Cranberry- and Citrus-Glazed Pork Roast 🖤

The leftover pork roast is delicious when made into sandwiches with any remaining chilled sauce.

Prep: 15 minutes **Roast:** 1½ hours **Stand:** 15 minutes
Oven: 325°F **Makes:** 8 to 10 servings

- ¼ **teaspoon salt**
- ¼ **teaspoon ground black pepper**
- ½ **teaspoon ground sage**
- 1 **2½- to 3-pound boneless pork top loin roast**
- 1 **16-ounce can whole or jellied cranberry sauce**
- ½ **teaspoon finely shredded orange peel**
- ⅓ **cup orange juice**

1. Preheat oven to 325°F. For the rub, in a small bowl, stir together salt, pepper, and ¼ teaspoon of the sage. Sprinkle rub evenly all over sides of pork roast; rub in mixture with your fingers. Place roast on rack in a shallow roasting pan. Roast, uncovered, for 1 hour.

2. For the sauce, in a medium saucepan, stir together cranberry sauce, orange peel, orange juice, and the remaining ¼ teaspoon sage. Bring to boiling; reduce heat. Simmer, uncovered, about 10 minutes or until sauce has thickened slightly.

3. Spoon about ¼ cup of the sauce over pork. Roast, uncovered, for 30 to 45 minutes more or until done (155°F). Remove from oven. Cover pork loosely with foil; let stand for 15 minutes before slicing. (The temperature of the pork will rise 5°F during standing.) Reheat remaining sauce. Serve warm sauce with pork.

Per serving: 290 cal., 7 g total fat (2 g sat. fat), 77 mg chol., 132 mg sodium, 23 g carbo., 1 g fiber, 31 g pro.

Orecchiette with Pancetta And Broccoli Rabe 🖤

To prepare broccoli rabe (also called rapini), trim away any leaves and the woody stem ends.

Prep: 20 minutes **Cook:** 15 minutes **Makes:** 6 servings

- 4 **ounces pancetta, coarsely chopped**
- 6 **ounces dried orecchiette or gemelli pasta**
- 2 **teaspoons olive oil**
- 2 **teaspoons bottled minced garlic (4 cloves)**
- ¼ **teaspoon crushed red pepper**
- 3 **cups cut-up broccoli rabe or broccoli**
- ⅓ **cup reduced-sodium chicken broth**
- ¼ **cup pitted Greek black olives or pitted ripe olives or 2 tablespoons drained capers**
- ¼ **cup finely shredded Parmesan cheese**

1. In a large skillet, cook pancetta over medium heat about 10 minutes or until crisp. Drain on paper towels, reserving 1 tablespoon drippings in skillet. Set pancetta aside.

2. In a large saucepan, cook pasta according to package directions. Drain; return pasta to pan. Toss with oil; keep warm.

3. In the same skillet, heat reserved drippings over medium heat. Add garlic and crushed red pepper; cook and stir for 30 seconds. Add broccoli rabe and broth. Bring to boiling; reduce heat. Cover and simmer for 3 minutes or until broccoli rabe is tender. Stir in pancetta and olives; heat through. Add broccoli rabe mixture to pasta mixture in saucepan. Add half of the Parmesan cheese and toss to combine. Transfer pasta mixture to a serving dish and sprinkle with remaining Parmesan cheese.

Per serving: 211 cal., 9 g total fat (3 g sat. fat), 11 mg chol., 244 mg sodium, 25 g carbo., 2 g fiber, 8 g pro.

Pork Medallions with 🖤 Cranberry and Fig Chutney

This is a great dish to make when fresh cranberries come into season, about mid fall.

Start to Finish: 20 minutes **Makes:** 4 servings

- 1 **cup fresh cranberries or ½ cup canned whole cranberry sauce**
- ½ **cup apple juice**
- ¼ **cup snipped dried figs**
- 2 **tablespoons packed brown sugar or granulated sugar**
- 1 **teaspoon snipped fresh rosemary or ½ teaspoon dried rosemary, crushed**
   Salt
   Ground black pepper
- 12 **ounces pork tenderloin**
- 4 **teaspoons cooking oil**

1. For the chutney, in a small heavy saucepan, stir together cranberries, apple juice, figs, brown sugar, and rosemary. Bring to boiling; reduce heat. Simmer, uncovered, for 5 to 8 minutes or until chutney is of desired consistency, stirring occasionally. Season to taste with salt and pepper. Set aside.

2. Meanwhile, trim fat from pork. Cut pork crosswise into 12 pieces. Press each piece with palm of hand to make an even thickness. In a large nonstick skillet, heat oil over medium-high heat. Add pork; cook the pork for 2 to 3 minutes or until juices run clear, turning once.

3. To serve, spoon some of the warm chutney over pork and pass remaining chutney.

Per serving: 227 cal., 7 g total fat (1 g sat. fat), 55 mg chol., 185 mg sodium, 23 g carbo., 3 g fiber, 18 g pro.

Pork Medallions with Cranberry
and Fig Chutney

Pork Chops with Raspberries

Pork Chops with Raspberries ♥ 🍽 one

Pan drippings mix with vinegar, brown sugar, and spices to create a thick and bubbly sauce dotted with fresh berries.

Start to Finish: 25 minutes **Makes:** 4 servings

¾	cup reduced-sodium chicken broth
1	tablespoon white balsamic vinegar
1	tablespoon packed brown sugar
1½	teaspoons cornstarch
	Dash ground allspice
4	pork rib chops, cut ¾ inch thick (about 1½ pounds total)
½	teaspoon salt
¼	teaspoon ground black pepper
¼	teaspoon dried basil, crushed
1	tablespoon cooking oil
1	cup fresh raspberries

1. In a small bowl, stir together broth, balsamic vinegar, brown sugar, cornstarch, and allspice; set aside.

2. Trim fat from chops. Sprinkle both sides of each chop with salt, pepper, and basil. In a 12-inch skillet, heat oil over medium heat. Add chops; cook for 8 to 12 minutes or until pork juices run clear (160°F). Transfer chops to a serving platter. Cover and keep warm. Drain fat from skillet.

3. Stir vinegar mixture. Add to skillet. Cook and stir over medium heat until slightly thickened and bubbly. Cook and stir for 2 minutes more. Gently stir in raspberries; heat through. To serve, spoon raspberry mixture over chops.

Per serving: 207 cal., 9 g total fat (2 g sat. fat), 53 mg chol., 444 mg sodium, 8 g carbo., 2 g fiber, 22 g pro.

Baked Penne Cordon Bleu

The classic cheese-and-ham-stuffed chicken breast is recast into a mouthwatering casserole.

Prep: 20 minutes **Bake:** 40 minutes **Chill:** 6 hours
Oven: 350°F **Makes:** 6 servings

- **8** ounces dried penne pasta (2½ cups)
- **1** 10.75-ounce can condensed cream of chicken soup
- **½** cup dry white wine or chicken broth
- **2** tablespoons Dijon-style mustard
- **1½** cups chopped cooked chicken
- **¾** cup chopped cooked ham
- **1** cup shredded Swiss cheese
- **⅓** cup seasoned fine dry bread crumbs
- **1** tablespoon butter, melted

1. Preheat oven to 350°F. Prepare pasta according to package directions; drain. Rinse pasta with cold water; drain again.

2. In a large bowl, combine soup, wine, and mustard. Stir in cooked pasta, chicken, ham, and cheese. Spoon into a 2-quart baking dish.

3. In a small bowl, combine bread crumbs and melted butter. Sprinkle over the top of the pasta mixture. Bake, uncovered, 40 minutes or until heated through and topping is golden brown.

Per serving: 427 cal., 16 g total fat (7 g sat. fat), 71 mg chol., 1,011 mg sodium, 40 g carbo., 2 g fiber, 28 g pro.

Ham and Potato Scramble [one]

This all-in-one skillet breakfast needs nothing more than orange juice and some fresh fruit to round out the menu.

Start to Finish: 25 minutes **Makes:** 4 servings

- **8** eggs
- **¼** cup milk
- **¼** teaspoon garlic salt
- **¼** teaspoon ground black pepper
- **¼** cup thinly sliced green onion
- **1** tablespoon butter or margarine
- **1** cup refrigerated shredded hash brown potatoes
- **½** cup diced cooked ham (about 2 ounces)
- **⅓** cup shredded Cheddar cheese

1. In a medium bowl, combine eggs, milk, garlic salt, and pepper; beat with a rotary beater or whisk until well mixed. Stir in green onion. Set aside.

2. In a large nonstick skillet, melt butter over medium heat. Add potatoes and ham to skillet; cook for 6 to 8 minutes or until light brown, stirring occasionally. Add egg mixture. Cook over medium heat, without stirring, until mixture begins to set on the bottom and around edge.

3. Using a large spatula, lift and fold the partially cooked egg mixture so the uncooked portion flows underneath. Continue cooking and folding for 2 to 3 minutes more or until egg mixture is cooked through but is still glossy and moist. Remove from heat immediately. Sprinkle with cheese. Serve warm.

Per serving: 289 cal., 18 g total fat (8 g sat. fat), 453 mg chol., 540 mg sodium, 11 g carbo., 1 g fiber, 20 g pro.

Ham and Potato Scramble

Dijon Pork Salad [one]

Brush the pork using the same bottled salad dressing you toss with the greens.

Prep: 10 minutes **Roast:** 20 minutes **Oven:** 425°F
Makes: 4 servings

1	**1-pound pork tenderloin**
	Salt and ground black pepper
²/₃	**cup bottled Dijon lime salad dressing or oil and vinegar salad dressing**
8	**cups torn mixed salad greens**
2	**ounces Gouda or white Cheddar cheese, cut into bite-size strips**
12	**cherry tomatoes, quartered**

1. Preheat oven to 425°F. Trim fat from pork. Place pork on a rack in a shallow roasting pan. Sprinkle with salt and pepper. Brush pork with 2 tablespoons of the salad dressing. Roast, uncovered, for 20 to 30 minutes or until done (160°F).

2. Meanwhile, arrange salad greens on 4 salad plates. Top with cheese and tomatoes. Thinly slice pork; arrange pork slices on salads. Serve with remaining salad dressing.

Per serving: 336 cal., 24 g total fat (5 g sat. fat), 71 mg chol., 535 mg sodium, 5 g carbo., 2 g fiber, 23 g pro.

Oregano and Pork Chop Skillet ♥ [one]

If you love winter squash, but don't happen to have an hour or so to roast it, you'll appreciate this quick-cooking chop-and-simmer method.

Start to Finish: 30 minutes **Makes:** 4 servings

1	**pound boneless pork sirloin chops, cut ½ inch thick**
2	**tablespoons all-purpose flour**
½	**teaspoon salt**
½	**teaspoon ground black pepper**
2	**tablespoons olive oil**
1	**1-pound whole winter squash (such as butternut or banana), peeled, seeded, and cut into 1-inch cubes (2 cups)**
1	**medium onion, cut into thin wedges**
1	**tablespoon snipped fresh oregano or 1 teaspoon dried oregano, crushed**
¼	**cup chicken broth**
¼	**cup orange juice**
2	**medium zucchini, quartered lengthwise and cut into 1-inch pieces (about 2½ cups)**

1. Trim fat from pork; if necessary, cut meat into four serving-size portions. Sprinkle both sides of each chop with some of the flour, salt, and pepper.

2. In a large skillet, heat oil over medium-high heat. Add chops and brown for 4 minutes, turning once. Add winter squash and onion; sprinkle with dried oregano, if using. Pour broth and orange juice over vegetables and pork. Bring to boiling; reduce heat. Cover and simmer for 10 minutes.

3. Add zucchini. Cover and cook about 5 minutes more or until chops are tender and no longer pink. Transfer chops to a serving platter.

4. Stir fresh oregano, if using, into vegetables. Serve with chops.

Per serving: 276 cal., 11 g total fat (3 g sat. fat), 71 mg chol., 417 mg sodium, 17 g carbo., 2 g fiber, 26 g pro.

Oven-Baked Cassoulet ♥ [one]

A French cassoulet traditionally simmers for hours. This version bakes in the oven, slashing the cooking time to 40 minutes. For a touch of freshness, top with snipped fresh herb before serving.

Prep: 20 minute **Bake:** 40 minutes
Oven: 325°F **Makes:** 5 servings

	Nonstick cooking spray
12	**ounces lean boneless pork, cut into ½-inch cubes**
1	**teaspoon cooking oil**
1	**cup chopped onion (1 large)**
1	**cup chopped carrot (2 medium)**
3	**cloves garlic, minced**
2	**15-ounce cans cannellini beans (white kidney beans), rinsed and drained**
4	**roma tomatoes, chopped**
²/₃	**cup reduced-sodium chicken broth**
²/₃	**cup water**
2	**ounces smoked turkey sausage, halved lengthwise and cut into ¼-inch slices**
1	**teaspoon dried thyme, crushed**
¼	**teaspoon dried rosemary, crushed**
¼	**teaspoon ground black pepper**
2	**tablespoons snipped fresh thyme or flat-leaf parsley**

1. Lightly coat an unheated Dutch oven with nonstick cooking spray. Preheat over medium-high heat. Add pork to Dutch oven; cook and stir until pork is browned. Remove pork from Dutch oven. Reduce heat. Carefully add oil to hot Dutch oven. Add onion, carrot, and garlic; cook until onion is tender. Stir pork, beans, tomatoes, broth, the water, turkey sausage, thyme, rosemary, and pepper into Dutch oven.

2. Bake, covered, in a 325° oven for 40 to 45 minutes or until pork and carrots are tender. To serve, spoon into individual casseroles or bowls; sprinkle each serving with thyme.

Per serving: 263 cal., 6 g total fat (2 g sat. fat), 48 mg chol., 500 mg sodium, 33 g carbo., 10 g fiber, 28 g pro.

Oven-Baked Cassoulet

White Beans and Spinach Ragout

White Beans and Spinach Ragout one

Tomatoes, beans, and spinach make this tri-colored combination as eye-catching as it is tasty.

Start to Finish: 20 minutes **Makes:** 3 servings

- 1   **14.5-ounce can diced tomatoes**
- 2   **slices bacon, cut into 1-inch pieces**
- 1   **medium onion, halved and thinly sliced**
- 1   **15-ounce can cannellini beans (white kidney beans) or navy beans, rinsed and drained**
- 4   **cups torn fresh spinach**
- 4   **teaspoons bottled balsamic or red wine vinaigrette salad dressing**

1. Drain tomatoes, reserving ⅓ cup of the liquid; set aside. In a large skillet, cook bacon pieces over medium heat until crisp. Remove with slotted spoon, reserving 1 tablespoon of the drippings in skillet. Drain bacon on paper towels.

2. Add onion to bacon drippings in skillet; cook about 3 minutes or just until tender. Stir in drained beans, tomatoes, and reserved tomato liquid. Cook and stir over medium heat about 2 minutes or until heated through. Stir in 3 cups of the spinach; cover and cook about 30 seconds or just until wilted. Stir in cooked bacon and the remaining 1 cup spinach. Drizzle individual servings with vinaigrette salad dressing.

Per serving: 221 cal., 9 g total fat (3 g sat. fat), 10 mg chol., 678 mg sodium, 31 g carbo., 8 g fiber, 12 g pro.

Apricot-Glazed Pork Roast

Apricot-Glazed Pork Roast ♥

A five-spice roast rub imparts a symphony of flavor to roast pork, which is finished with several brushings of shiny apricot glaze.

Prep: 20 minutes **Roast:** 1¼ hours **Stand:** 15 minutes
Chill: 1 to 2 hours **Oven:** 325°F **Makes:** 8 servings

- 1½ **teaspoons ground cumin**
- ½   **teaspoon garlic salt**
- ½   **teaspoon ground cinnamon**
- ½   **teaspoon ground ginger**
- ¼   **teaspoon ground cloves**
- 1   **2½- to 3-pound boneless pork top loin roast (single loin)**
- 1   **cup apricot preserves**
- 2   **to 3 tablespoons white wine vinegar**

1. For the rub, in a small bowl, stir together cumin, garlic salt, cinnamon, ginger, and cloves. Sprinkle rub mixture evenly over roast; rub into roast. Wrap roast in plastic wrap and refrigerate for 1 to 2 hours.

2. Preheat oven to 325°F. Unwrap roast and discard plastic wrap. Place roast on a rack in a shallow roasting pan. Insert an oven-going meat thermometer into center of roast. Roast for 1 to 1½ hours or until meat thermometer registers 135°F.

3. Meanwhile, for the glaze, in a small saucepan, cook and stir apricot preserves and vinegar over medium heat until preserves are melted. Remove from heat. Brush roast generously with the glaze. Roast about 15 minutes more or until meat thermometer registers 155°F, brushing 2 or 3 times with the glaze.

4. Remove roast from oven; cover with foil. Let stand for 15 minutes. The temperature of the roast after standing should be 160°F. Reheat remaining glaze and pass with roast.

Per serving: 326 cal., 9 g total fat (3 g sat. fat), 77 mg chol., 125 mg sodium, 28 g carbo., 1 g fiber, 31 g pro.

Quick Tip Ground spices, such as cumin, coriander, ginger, and cloves, lose their aroma and flavor quickly, so it's wise to purchase them in small quantities. Store spices in a cool, dark place for up to 6 months. Avoid storing spices over the stovetop or any other hot location.

Pasta with Prosciutto

Pasta with Prosciutto

Prosciutto may seem expensive when you first spot the price, but a little prosciutto goes a long way to add flavor to a dish. If you have any extra, wrap pieces around pear slices or steamed, chilled asparagus for elegant appetizers.

Start to Finish: 20 minutes   **Makes:** 4 servings

- 6   **ounces dried angel hair pasta**
- 2   **tablespoons olive oil**
- 1   **tablespoon butter**
- 4   **cloves garlic, minced**
- 8   **ounces fresh mushrooms, sliced (3 cups)**
- 1   **medium red onion, thinly sliced**
- 3   **ounces thinly sliced prosciutto, cut into ¾-inch strips**
- 4   **ounces fresh spinach, torn (3 cups loosely packed)**
- ⅓   **cup finely shredded Parmesan cheese**
- ¼   **teaspoon salt**
- ¼   **teaspoon freshly ground black pepper**
      Parmesan cheese curls or finely shredded Parmesan cheese (optional)

1. Cook pasta according to package directions; drain. Cover and keep warm.

2. Meanwhile, in a 12-inch skillet, heat oil and butter over medium heat. Add garlic and cook for 30 seconds. Add mushrooms, onion, and prosciutto. Cook over medium-high heat for 4 to 5 minutes or until mushrooms and onion are tender, stirring occasionally. Add spinach to skillet; remove from heat. Add cooked pasta, the ⅓ cup Parmesan cheese, salt, and pepper. Toss well.

3. Transfer pasta mixture to serving bowls or plates. If desired, sprinkle with additional Parmesan cheese.

Per serving: 382 cal., 19 g total fat (5 g sat. fat), 17 mg chol., 676 mg sodium, 37 g carbo., 2 g fiber, 17 g pro.

Cavatappi with Tomatoes And Ham ♥

Check out the flavored olive oils at your supermarket or specialty foods store. You'll find garlic-, basil-, rosemary-, and lemon-flavor oils, among others.

Start to Finish: 30 minutes   **Makes:** 4 servings

- 1   **medium onion, cut into ¼-inch slices**
- 12   **red and/or yellow cherry and/or pear tomatoes, halved**
- 8   **ounces dried cavatappi or gemelli pasta**
- ¼   **teaspoon crushed red pepper (optional)**
- 2   **ounces thinly sliced cooked ham, cut into strips**
- 3   **tablespoons thinly sliced basil**
- 2   **tablespoons garlic-flavor olive oil or olive oil**
      Arugula leaves (optional)

1. Place onion slices on the foil-lined rack of a broiler pan. Broil onions 4 inches from heat for 5 minutes. Add tomato halves to pan; broil about 5 minutes more or until edges are brown.

2. Meanwhile, cook pasta according to package directions, adding crushed red pepper to water, if desired. Drain and return pasta to pan.

3. Cut up onion slices. Toss onion pieces and tomato halves with pasta, ham, basil, and olive oil. If desired, garnish with arugula leaves.

Per serving: 341 cal., 11 g total fat (2 g sat. fat), 16 mg chol., 381 mg sodium, 47 g carbo., 2 g fiber, 13 g pro.

Cavatappi with Tomatoes and Ham

Quick Pepperoni Pasta

Quick Pepperoni Pasta

Whip up pizza-like flavors in less time than it takes to order takeout. Because pepperoni is already cooked, it's a quick choice for adding hearty, robust flavor without a long simmering time.

Start to Finish: 30 minutes **Makes:** 4 servings

- 6 ounces dried spaghetti pasta, broken in half
- 3 cups sliced fresh mushrooms (8 ounces)
- ⅔ cup cubed pepperoni (3 ounces)
- 1 tablespoon butter
- 8 ounces fresh spinach, torn (6 cups)
- ¼ cup grated Parmesan cheese
- 2 tablespoons snipped fresh basil
- 1 teaspoon lemon juice
   Breadsticks (optional)

1. Cook pasta according to package directions; drain.

2. Meanwhile, in a very large skillet, cook mushrooms and pepperoni in butter over medium heat for 5 minutes or until mushrooms are just tender. Drain fat. Stir in spinach. Cook and stir for 1 minute or until spinach begins to wilt. Remove from heat.

3. In a large mixing bowl, toss together pasta, pepperoni mixture, 3 tablespoons of the Parmesan cheese, the basil, and lemon juice. Sprinkle with remaining Parmesan cheese. If desired, serve with breadsticks.

Per serving: 344 cal., 14 g total fat (5 g sat. fat), 32 mg chol., 604 mg sodium, 39 g carbo., 2 g fiber, 15 g pro.

Sausage-Cavatelli Skillet

Bullet-shaped cavatelli joins meat, pasta sauce, and mozzarella cheese for a quick, hearty meal. Together with a green salad and a glass of wine, a weeknight meal couldn't be better.

Start to Finish: 30 minutes **Makes:** 4 servings

- 8 ounces dried cavatelli pasta (1¾ cups)
- 1 pound bulk Italian sausage or ground beef
- ¾ cup chopped green sweet pepper (1 medium) (optional)
- 1 20-ounce jar pasta sauce with mushrooms
- 1 cup shredded mozzarella cheese (4 ounces)

1. Cook cavatelli according to package directions. Drain well.

2. Meanwhile, in a large skillet, cook sausage and, if desired, sweet pepper over medium heat until sausage is brown. Drain off fat. Stir in pasta sauce; cook about 2 minutes or until heated through. Stir in the drained cavatelli. Sprinkle with cheese. Cover and cook about 2 minutes more or until cheese melts.

Per serving: 700 cal., 31 g total fat (15 g sat. fat), 96 mg chol., 1,513 mg sodium, 60 g carbo., 4 g fiber, 33 g pro.

Rotini-Sausage Skillet

For this colorful dish, rotini—the corkscrew-shaped pasta—adds a pleasing, fun texture. Or you can use rotelle pasta with its wagon-wheel shape. Both will add kid-pleasing whimsy to this flavorful skillet meal.

Start to Finish: 35 minutes **Makes:** 6 servings

- 2 cups dried rotini or rotelle pasta (about 6 ounces)
- 1 tablespoon olive oil
- 1 medium onion, cut into wedges
- 2 cloves garlic, minced
- 1 pound cooked smoked sausage or kielbasa, halved lengthwise and sliced diagonally
- 1 small zucchini, cut into matchstick-size strips
- 1 yellow or orange sweet pepper, cut into small strips
- 1 teaspoon dried Italian seasoning, crushed
- ⅛ teaspoon ground red pepper
- 8 roma tomatoes, cored and chopped (about 1 pound)

1. Cook pasta according to package directions; drain. Meanwhile, in a very large skillet, heat oil over medium-high heat. Add onion and garlic and cook for 1 minute. Add sausage; cook until onion is tender, stirring frequently.

2. Add zucchini, sweet pepper, Italian seasoning, and ground red pepper; cook and stir for 5 minutes. Stir in tomatoes and cooked pasta. Heat through, stirring occasionally. If desired, garnish with fresh herbs.

Per serving: 410 cal., 26 g total fat (0 g sat. fat), 0 mg chol., 714 mg sodium, 31 g carbo., 2 g fiber, 14 g pro.

Rotini-Sausage Skillet

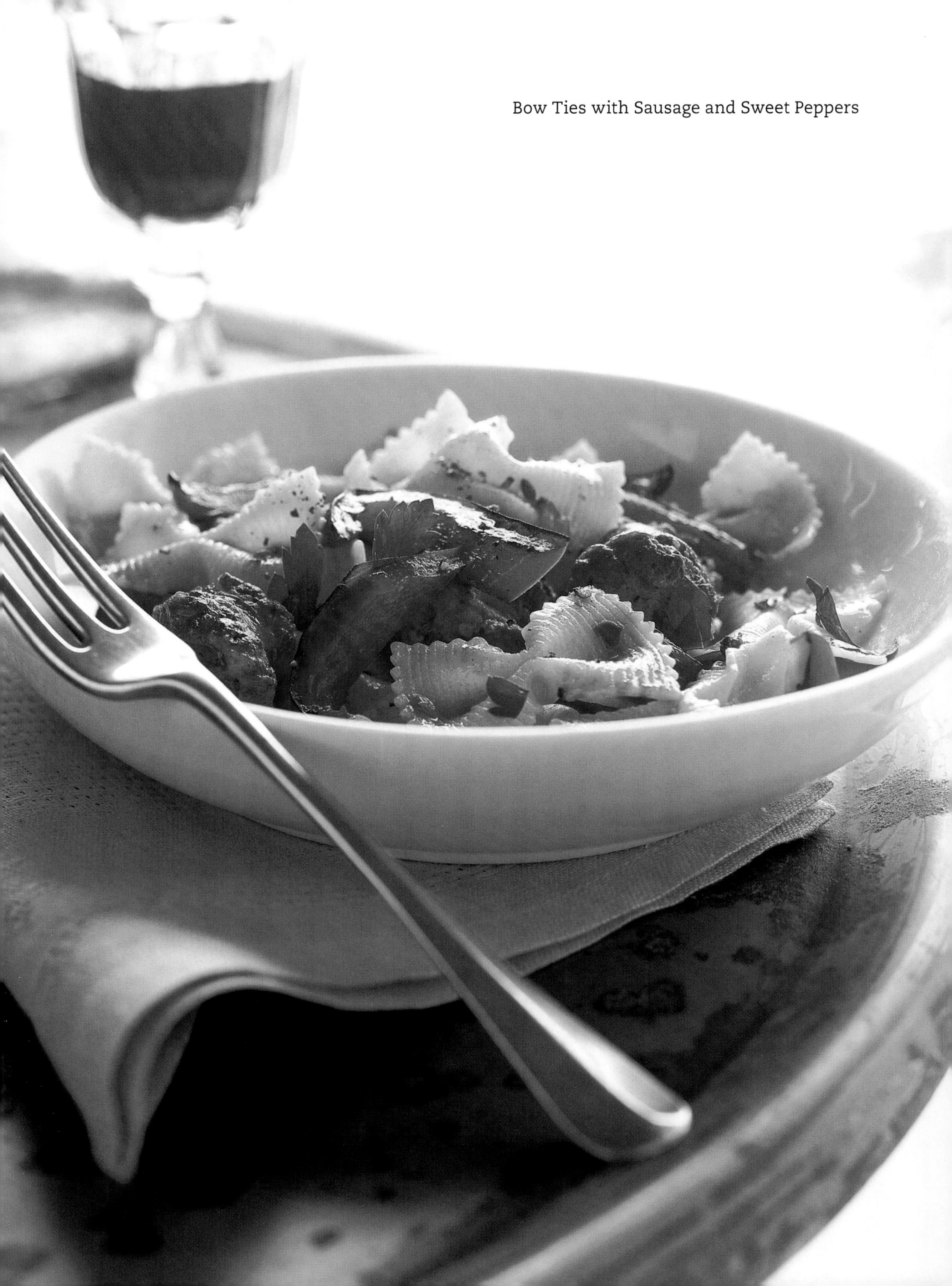

Bow Ties with Sausage and Sweet Peppers

Bow Ties with Sausage And Sweet Peppers

Italian sausages—often spiced with fennel and red pepper flakes—make it easy to create a boldly flavored, highly satisfying meal. Here's a delicious example.

Start to Finish: 30 minutes **Makes:** 4 servings

- **8 ounces dried large bow tie pasta**
- **12 ounces spicy Italian sausage links**
- **2 medium red sweet peppers, cut into ¾-inch pieces**
- **½ cup vegetable broth or beef broth**
- **¼ teaspoon coarsely ground black pepper**
- **¼ cup snipped fresh flat-leaf parsley**

1. Cook pasta according to package directions; drain. Return pasta to saucepan.

2. Meanwhile, cut the sausage into 1-inch pieces. In a large skillet, cook sausage and sweet peppers over medium-high heat until sausage is brown. Drain off fat.

3. Stir the broth and pepper into skillet. Bring to boiling. Reduce heat and simmer, uncovered, for 5 minutes. Remove from heat. Pour over pasta; add parsley. Toss gently to coat. Transfer to a warm serving dish.

Per serving: 397 cal., 18 g total fat (6 g sat. fat), 94 mg chol., 713 mg sodium, 38 g carbo., 3 g fiber, 24 g pro.

Italian Sausage Manicotti

Mild and slightly sweet, zucchini adds texture and bright flecks of green to the marinara sauce that tops this baked pasta dish.

Prep: 25 minutes **Bake:** 40 minutes
Stand: 10 minutes **Oven:** 350°F **Makes:** 4 servings

- **8 dried manicotti pasta shells**
- **12 ounces bulk sweet or hot Italian sausage**
- **1 egg, lightly beaten**
- **1 cup ricotta cheese**
- **1 teaspoon Italian seasoning, crushed**
- **1 15-ounce container refrigerated marinara sauce**
- **½ cup shredded zucchini**
- **1 cup shredded Italian blend cheeses**

1. Preheat oven to 350°F. Cook manicotti according to package directions. Drain. Cool manicotti in a single layer on a piece of greased foil.

2. Meanwhile, in a large skillet, cook sausage until browned; drain off fat.

3. In a medium bowl, stir together egg, ricotta cheese, sausage, and Italian seasoning. Use a small spoon to fill manicotti shells with filling. Arrange 2 filled shells in each of 4 individual baking dishes. In a medium bowl, stir together marinara sauce and zucchini. Spoon sauce over manicotti. Top with shredded cheese.

4. Bake, covered, for 40 to 45 minutes or until heated through. Let stand, uncovered, for 10 minutes before serving.

Per serving: 683 cal., 46 g total fat (19 g sat. fat), 169 mg chol., 1,222 mg sodium, 33 g carbo., 1 g fiber, 34 g pro.

Sausage and Polenta with Balsamic Vinaigrette

Ever wonder what to do with those tubes of refrigerated polenta you've spotted in the produce section? Here's a delicious answer: Slice and bake the polenta, then serve it plus savory sausage over mixed greens.

Start to Finish: 27 minutes **Bake:** 10 minutes
Oven: 400°F **Makes:** 4 servings

- **3 sweet Italian sausage links, each cut into four pieces (about 12 ounces)**
- **½ of a 16-ounce tube refrigerated polenta, plain or flavored**
- **1 tablespoon olive oil**
- **6 cups Mediterranean- or Italian-blend purchased torn mixed greens**
- **½ cup apple juice**
- **¼ cup balsamic vinegar**
- **2 tablespoons snipped dried tomato**
- **¼ cup toasted pine nuts or slivered almonds (optional)**

1. Preheat oven to 400° F.

2. In a 10-inch skillet, cook sausage over medium heat for 5 minutes, turning to brown evenly. Meanwhile, slice polenta ¼ inch thick; cut each slice crosswise in half. Brush top of each polenta slice with oil. Arrange in a single layer on a baking sheet. Bake for 10 to 12 minutes or until golden, turning once.

3. Divide greens among 4 dinner plates; set aside.

4. Remove sausage from skillet; drain fat and wipe out skillet. Return sausage to skillet and add apple juice, vinegar, and dried tomato. Bring to boiling; reduce heat. Cover and simmer for 8 to 10 minutes or until sausage is cooked through (165°F).

5. Arrange polenta slices over greens on plates. Add sausage pieces to plates; drizzle with balsamic mixture. If desired, sprinkle with nuts.

Per serving: 380 cal., 22 g total fat (8 g sat. fat), 57 mg chol., 741 mg sodium, 23 g carbo., 4 g fiber, 15 g pro.

Rosemary-Rubbed
Lamb Chops

Rosemary-Rubbed Lamb Chops 🖤

Rosemary and lamb are a natural pairing. Apricot preserves and Dijon-style mustard make for an irresistible glaze atop these chops.

Start to Finish: 25 minutes **Makes:** 4 servings

8	lamb rib chops, cut 1 inch thick (about 1½ pounds total)
2	tablespoons olive oil
½	teaspoon dried rosemary, crushed
½	teaspoon ground black pepper
1	teaspoon bottled minced garlic
½	cup apricot or peach preserves
1	tablespoon Dijon-style mustard
1	teaspoon chicken bouillon granules

1. Trim fat from chops. In a small bowl, combine 1 tablespoon of the oil, ¼ teaspoon of the rosemary, ¼ teaspoon of the pepper, and the garlic. Use your fingers or a pastry brush to rub or brush the garlic mixture over all sides of the chops.

2. For the glaze, in a small saucepan, combine apricot preserves, ¼ cup water, mustard, bouillon granules, remaining ¼ teaspoon rosemary, and remaining ¼ teaspoon pepper; heat and stir until bubbly. Remove from heat; set aside.

3. In a large skillet, heat remaining 1 tablespoon oil over medium heat. Add chops; cook for 9 to 11 minutes or until medium doneness (160°F), turning once halfway through cooking time. Serve chops with glaze.

Per serving: 289 cal., 12 g total fat (3 g sat. fat), 48 mg chol., 361 mg sodium, 29 g carbo., 1 g fiber, 15 g pro.

Tuscan Lamb Chop Skillet ♥ 🄰

White kidney beans, also called cannellini beans, have a mild flavor and smooth, creamy texture. They taste wonderful when paired with balsamic vinegar and fresh rosemary.

Start to Finish: 18 minutes **Makes:** 4 servings

- **8 lamb rib chops, cut 1 inch thick (1½ pounds)**
- **2 teaspoons olive oil**
- **3 cloves garlic, minced**
- **1 19-ounce can cannellini beans (white kidney beans), rinsed and drained**
- **1 8-ounce can Italian-style stewed tomatoes, undrained**
- **1 tablespoon balsamic vinegar**
- **2 teaspoons snipped fresh rosemary**
  Fresh rosemary sprigs (optional)

1. Trim fat from chops. In a large skillet, heat oil over medium heat. Cook chops about 8 minutes for medium doneness, turning once. Transfer chops to a plate; keep warm.

2. Stir garlic into drippings in skillet. Cook and stir for 1 minute. Stir in beans, undrained tomatoes, vinegar, and snipped rosemary. Bring to boiling; reduce heat. Simmer, uncovered, for 3 minutes.

3. Spoon bean mixture onto 4 dinner plates; arrange two chops on each serving of beans. If desired, garnish with rosemary sprigs.

Per serving: 272 cal., 9 g total fat (3 g sat. fat), 67 mg chol., 466 mg sodium, 24 g carbo., 6 g fiber, 30 g pro.

Tuscan Lamb Chop Skillet

Lamb with Herbed Mushrooms

Lamb with Herbed Mushrooms ♥ 🄰

Featuring fresh tarragon and mushrooms, the low-calorie topper makes an ideal accent to the distinctive flavor of the lamb. Try it with other broiled or grilled meats such as pork, chicken, or beef.

Start to Finish: 25 minutes **Makes:** 4 servings

- **8 lamb loin chops, cut 1 inch thick (about 1½ pounds total)**
- **2 teaspoons olive oil**
- **1 small onion, thinly sliced**
- **2 cups sliced fresh mushrooms**
- **1 tablespoon balsamic vinegar**
- **1 teaspoon bottled minced garlic (2 cloves)**
- **¼ teaspoon salt**
- **¼ teaspoon ground black pepper**
- **1 teaspoon snipped fresh tarragon or basil or ¼ teaspoon dried tarragon or basil, crushed**

1. Trim fat from chops. In a large nonstick skillet, heat oil over medium heat. Add chops; cook for 9 to 11 minutes or until medium doneness (160°F), turning once. Transfer chops to a serving platter; keep warm.

2. Stir onion into drippings in skillet. Cook and stir for 2 minutes. Stir in mushrooms, vinegar, garlic, salt, and pepper. Cook and stir for 3 to 4 minutes or until mushrooms are tender. Stir in tarragon. Spoon mushroom mixture over chops on platter.

Per serving: 165 cal., 9 g total fat (3 g sat. fat), 48 mg chol., 280 mg sodium, 4 g carbo., 1 g fiber, 16 g pro.

Chicken, Goat Cheese, and Greens, **page 65**

Balsamic Chicken and Vegetables, **page 79**

Lemon-Dill Butter Chicken and Cucumbers **page 70**

Honey-Orange Chicken, **page 95**

Quick Poultry

Busy cooks rely on chicken because it is quick-cooking, inexpensive, and incredibly versatile. Team it with other fast-cooking ingredients, and chicken is a sure winner at any table.

20-Minute Chicken Fettuccine

20-Minute Chicken Fettuccine

For great weeknight meals in a flash, stock your kitchen with refrigerated pasta. It comes in several flavors and is the quickest-cooking pasta around! If red sweet pepper fettuccine isn't available, you can substitute refrigerated linguine or plain, spinach, or herb fettuccine.

Start to Finish: 20 minutes **Makes:** 4 servings

- 1 **9-ounce package refrigerated red sweet pepper fettuccine or linguine**
- ¼ **of a 7-ounce jar oil-packed, dried tomato strips or pieces (¼ cup)**
- 1 **large zucchini or yellow summer squash, halved lengthwise and sliced (about 2 cups)**
- ½ **pound skinless, boneless chicken breast strips for stir-frying**
- ½ **cup finely shredded Parmesan, Romano, or Asiago cheese (2 ounces)**
    Freshly ground black pepper
    Arugula (optional)

1. Use kitchen scissors to cut pasta in half. Cook according to package directions; drain. Return pasta to hot pan.

2. Meanwhile, drain tomato strips, reserving 2 tablespoons oil from jar; set aside. In a large skillet, heat 1 tablespoon reserved oil over medium-high heat. Add zucchini; cook and stir 2 to 3 minutes or until crisp-tender. Remove from skillet. Add remaining reserved oil to skillet. Add chicken; cook and stir 2 to 3 minutes or until no longer pink. Add zucchini, chicken, tomato strips, and cheese to cooked pasta; toss gently to combine. Season with pepper to taste. If desired, garnish with arugula.

Per serving: 381 cal., 14 g total fat (1 g sat. fat), 40 mg chol., 334 mg sodium, 40 g carbo., 3 g fiber, 24 g pro.

Dijon Chicken and Mushrooms `one`

Dijon-style mustard contains seasonings and white wine—we use it here to add sharp flavor to an earthy, quickly cooked chicken-mushroom dinner.

Start to Finish: 30 minutes **Makes:** 4 servings

- 3 **tablespoons butter or margarine**
- 2 **cups sliced fresh mushrooms**
- 4 **skinless, boneless chicken breast halves (about 1¼ pounds)**
- 1 **10.75-ounce can condensed cream of chicken soup**
- ¼ **cup dry white wine**
- ¼ **cup water**
- 2 **tablespoons Dijon-style mustard**
- ½ **teaspoon dried thyme or tarragon, crushed Hot cooked pasta**

1. In a large skillet, melt 1 tablespoon of the butter over medium-high heat. Add mushrooms; cook for 3 to 4 minutes or until tender. Remove mushrooms from skillet. In the same skillet, cook chicken in remaining 2 tablespoons butter for 8 to 10 minutes or until tender and no longer pink (170°F), turning to brown evenly.

2. Meanwhile, in a small bowl, stir together soup, wine, the water, mustard, and thyme.

3. Return mushrooms to skillet; add soup mixture. Bring to boiling; reduce heat. Simmer, uncovered, for 2 minutes. Serve chicken and soup mixture over hot cooked pasta.

Per serving: 498 cal., 18 g total fat (8 g sat. fat), 112 mg chol., 947 mg sodium, 37 g carbo., 2 g fiber, 41 g pro.

Quick Tip Because other white wines can impart a sweet flavor to food, be sure to choose a dry white wine, such as Sauvignon Blanc, Pinot Grigio, or Chardonnay, for use in this dish.

Chicken with Basil Cream Sauce ♥

Use fresh basil for this recipe if you have it. It will give the sauce a brighter, more intense flavor than dried basil.

Start to Finish: 30 minutes **Oven:** 400°F
Makes: 4 servings

¼	**cup fine dry bread crumbs**
3	**teaspoons snipped fresh basil or ¾ teaspoon dried basil, crushed**
⅛	**teaspoon ground black pepper**
⅛	**teaspoon paprika**
1	**tablespoon butter, melted**
4	**skinless, boneless chicken breast halves (about 1¼ pounds)**
⅔	**cup milk**
2	**teaspoons all-purpose flour**
¾	**teaspoon instant chicken bouillon granules**

1. Preheat oven to 400°F. In a small bowl, stir together bread crumbs, 2 teaspoons of the fresh basil or ½ teaspoon of the dried basil, the pepper, and paprika. Add melted butter; toss to coat.

2. Arrange chicken in a 2-quart rectangular baking dish. Sprinkle chicken with the crumb mixture, pressing onto the chicken to coat. Bake for 20 to 25 minutes or until chicken is no longer pink (170°F).

3. Meanwhile, in a small saucepan, stir together milk, flour, bouillon granules, and remaining ¼ teaspoon dried basil (if using) until combined. Cook and stir until thickened and bubbly. Cook and stir for 1 minute more. Stir in remaining 1 teaspoon fresh basil (if using). Serve over chicken.

Per serving: 238 cal., 6 g total fat (3 g sat. fat), 93 mg chol., 460 mg sodium, 8 g carbo., 0 g fiber, 35 g pro.

Chicken-Tortilla Bake ♥ one

Just toss together five ingredients, and let the oven do the rest of the work for this Mexican-style casserole.

Prep: 15 minutes **Bake:** 45 minutes **Oven:** 350°F
Makes: 8 servings

- 2 **10.75-ounce cans reduced-sodium condensed cream of chicken soup**
- 1 **10-ounce can diced tomatoes with green chiles, undrained**
- 12 **6- or 7-inch corn tortillas, cut into thin bite-size strips**
- 3 **cups cubed cooked chicken (1 pound)**
- 1 **cup shredded taco cheese (4 ounces)**

1. Preheat oven to 350°F. In a medium bowl, combine soup and undrained tomatoes; set aside.

2. Sprinkle one-third of the tortilla strips over the bottom of an ungreased 3-quart rectangular baking dish. Layer half of the chicken over tortilla strips; spoon half of the soup mixture on top. Repeat layers. Sprinkle with remaining tortilla strips.

3. Bake, covered, about 40 minutes or until bubbly around edges and center is hot. Uncover and sprinkle with cheese. Bake about 5 minutes more or until cheese is melted.

Per serving: 291 cal., 10 g total fat (4 g sat. fat), 64 mg chol., 658 mg sodium, 28 g carbo., 2 g fiber, 22 g pro.

Mediterranean Cheese-Stuffed Chicken one

Take your choice of two Mediterranean cheeses to fill these chicken rolls. Creamy mascarpone and tangy feta both taste terrific.

Prep: 20 minutes **Cook:** 25 minutes **Makes:** 4 servings

- 4 **skinless, boneless chicken breast halves**
  Salt
  Ground black pepper
- 4 **oil-packed dried tomatoes, drained and cut into thin strips**
- 2 **ounces mascarpone cheese or crumbled feta cheese**
- 4 **teaspoons snipped fresh oregano, basil, tarragon, or parsley, or ½ teaspoon dried oregano, basil, or parsley, crushed**
- 2 **tablespoons olive oil**

1. Place each chicken breast half between 2 pieces of plastic wrap. Pound lightly with the flat side of a meat mallet to ¼-inch thickness. Remove plastic wrap. Sprinkle chicken with salt and pepper.

2. On each chicken breast half, layer tomato strips, cheese, and oregano. Fold narrow ends over filling; fold in sides. Roll up each chicken breast half from a short side. Secure with wooden toothpicks.

3. In a medium skillet, heat oil over medium-low heat. Add chicken; cook about 25 minutes or until chicken is no longer pink (170°F), turning to brown evenly.

Per serving: 257 cal., 17 g total fat (6 g sat. fat), 77 mg chol., 114 mg sodium, 2 g carbo., 0 g fiber, 25 g pro.

Tarragon Chicken Linguine ♥

Cooking broccoli with the linguine lets you use less pasta overall and save on cleanup time. To save even more time, purchase chicken that has already been cut up for stir-frying from the meat counter at your supermarket.

Start to Finish: 25 minutes
Makes: 4 servings

- 6 **ounces dried linguine or fettuccine pasta**
- 2 **cups broccoli florets**
- ½ **cup reduced-sodium chicken broth**
- 2 **teaspoons cornstarch**
- ¼ **teaspoon lemon-pepper seasoning or ground black pepper**
- 3 **skinless, boneless chicken breast halves (12 ounces total), cut into bite-size strips**
- 2 **teaspoons olive oil or cooking oil**
- 1 **tablespoon snipped fresh tarragon or dill or ½ teaspoon dried tarragon or dill, crushed**

1. Cook pasta according to directions, adding broccoli the last 4 minutes. Drain; keep warm.

2. Combine broth, cornstarch, and seasoning; set aside.

3. In a large nonstick skillet, cook chicken in hot oil 4 minutes or until no longer pink, stirring often.

4. Stir cornstarch mixture; add to skillet. Cook and stir until thickened. Stir in tarragon; cook for 2 minutes. Serve over pasta.

Per serving: 293 cal., 4 g total fat (1 g sat. fat), 49 mg chol., 153 mg sodium, 36 g carbo., 2 g fiber, 27 g pro.

Quick Tip If you don't have cornstarch on hand, you may substitute 4 teaspoons of all-purpose flour for the 2 teaspoons of cornstarch in this recipe.

Tarragon Chicken Linguine

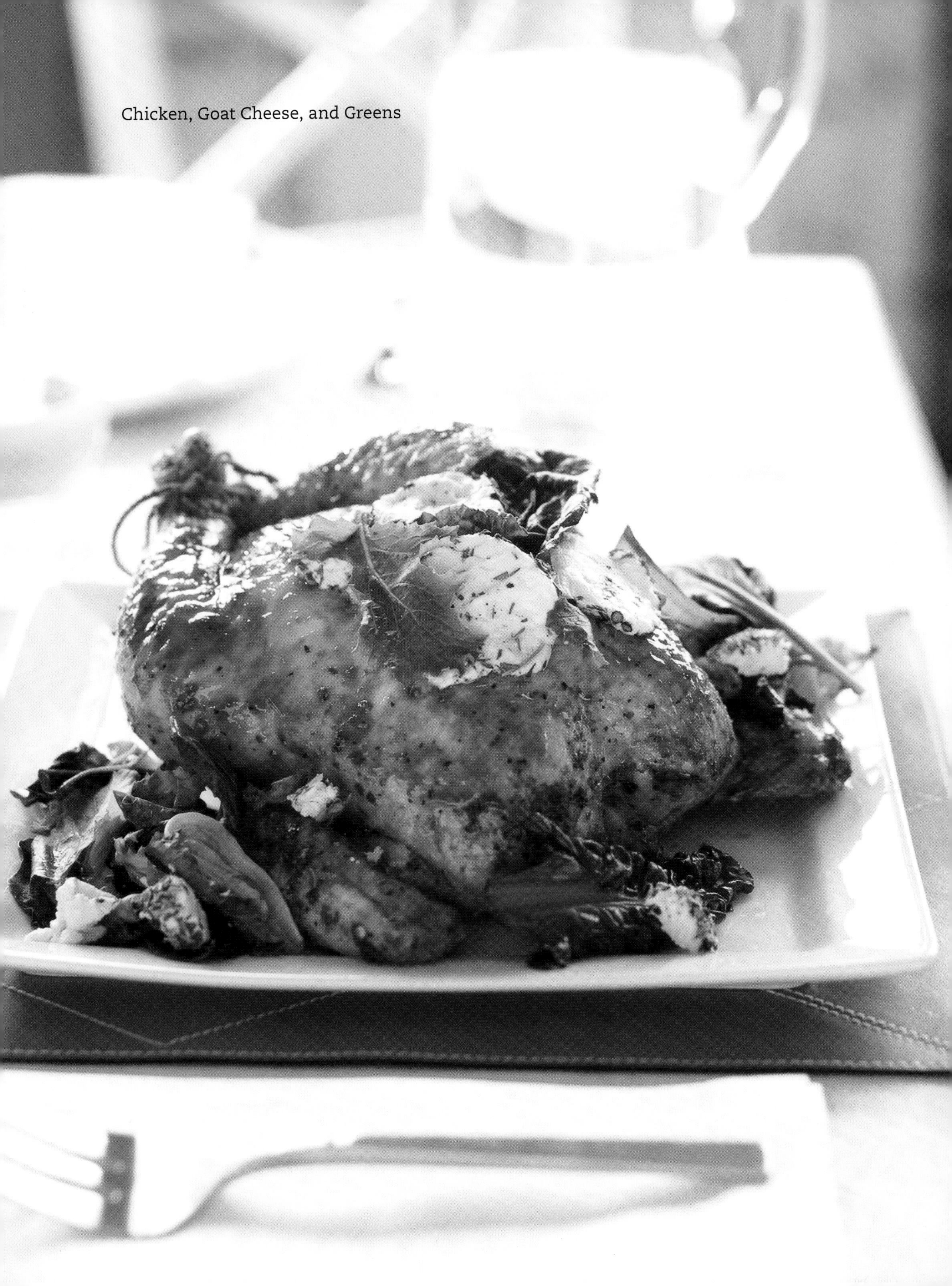
Chicken, Goat Cheese, and Greens

Asian Chicken Salad ♥

When you need something quick for lunch or dinner, this salad is it. The dressing and oranges add a distinctly Asian flavor to ready-to-use torn salad greens.

Start to Finish: 15 minutes **Makes:** 4 servings

- 1   **10-ounce package torn mixed salad greens**
- 8   **ounces cooked chicken, cut into bite-size pieces**
- ⅓   **cup bottled Asian vinaigrette salad dressing**
- 1   **11-ounce can mandarin orange sections, drained**
- 3   **tablespoons sliced almonds, toasted**

1. In a large bowl, combine greens and chicken. Add salad dressing; toss to coat. Divide greens mixture among 4 salad plates. Top with mandarin orange sections and almonds. Serve immediately.

Per serving: 218 cal., 9 g total fat (1 g sat. fat), 50 mg chol., 502 mg sodium, 15 g carbo., 2 g fiber, 19 g pro.

Chicken, Goat Cheese, And Greens [one]

Go ahead, invite guests over at the last minute. Dinner can be a cinch. Just stop at the supermarket to pick up a ready-to-eat deli-roasted chicken and a few other ingredients.

Prep: 15 minutes **Bake:** 15 minutes **Oven:** 350°F
Makes: 4 servings

- 1½   **pounds Swiss chard, beet greens, and/or mustard greens, trimmed and washed**
- 1   **2- to 2½-pound purchased deli-roasted chicken**
- 3   **tablespoons olive oil**
- 2   **tablespoons lemon juice**
- 2   **tablespoons snipped fresh dill, oregano, and/or sage**
- ¼   **teaspoon sea salt, kosher salt, or salt**
- ⅛   **teaspoon cracked black pepper**
- 1   **3- to 4-ounce log goat cheese (chèvre), sliced into rounds or coarsely crumbled**
- ⅛   **teaspoon cracked black pepper**

1. Preheat oven to 350°F. Reserve one or two small leaves of the Swiss chard. Tear remaining chard and place in a 3-quart rectangular baking dish. Remove string from chicken; use the string to tie the chicken legs together. Place chicken on chard in baking dish.

2. In a small bowl, combine oil and lemon juice. Drizzle oil mixture over chicken and chard in baking dish. Sprinkle 1 tablespoon of the dill, oregano, and/or sage over the chicken and chard. Sprinkle the salt and ⅛ teaspoon pepper only over the torn chard.

3. Loosely cover baking dish with foil. Bake for 15 to 20 minutes or until torn chard is tender. Meanwhile, sprinkle cheese with remaining 1 tablespoon snipped dill and ⅛ teaspoon pepper.

4. Transfer chicken to a serving platter. Place some of the goat cheese on top of chicken. Add reserved chard leaves. Toss cooked chard in dish to evenly coat with cooking liquid. Serve cooked chard and remaining cheese with chicken.

Per serving: 542 cal., 36 g total fat (10 g sat. fat), 143 mg chol., 620 mg sodium, 7 g carbo., 3 g fiber, 48 g pro.

Quick Tip This recipe doubles easily to serve 8. Double the ingredients and prepare as directed, except place all the greens and both chickens in a large shallow roasting pan.

Spicy Chinese Chicken With Eggplant ♥ [one]

Light and healthy, this Asian dish gets its kick from fresh jalapeño chiles, garlic, and ginger.

Start to Finish: 30 minutes
Makes: 6 servings

- 4   **cups eggplant cut into thin bite-size strips**
    Boiling water
- 2   **tablespoons soy sauce**
- 1   **tablespoon cornstarch**
- 1   **tablespoon dry sherry or water**
- ½   **pound cooked chicken, cut into bite-size strips**
- 2   **tablespoons cooking oil**
- 4   **or 5 fresh jalapeño chile peppers, seeded and thinly sliced***
- ½   **cup chicken broth**
- 1   **clove garlic, minced**
- 1   **tablespoon very finely chopped fresh ginger**
- 3   **cups hot cooked rice or cellophane noodles**

1. In a large bowl, cover eggplant strips with boiling water; let stand for 5 minutes. Drain and set aside. (Eggplant may darken.)

2. Meanwhile, in a large bowl, combine soy sauce, cornstarch, and sherry. Add chicken, stirring to coat; set aside.

3. In a large saucepan, heat oil; add peppers. Cook and stir for 4 minutes or until tender. Remove peppers from pan. Add chicken mixture to pan; cook and stir for 3 to 4 minutes or until chicken is heated through and sauce has thickened. Stir in eggplant, peppers, broth, garlic, and ginger. Heat through. Serve with rice.

Per serving: 340 cal., 8 g total fat (2 g sat. fat), 50 mg chol., 655 mg sodium, 42 g carbo., 4 g fiber, 22 g pro.

*Note: Because chile peppers contain volatile oils that can burn your skin and eyes, avoid direct contact with them as much as possible. When working with chile peppers, wear plastic or rubber gloves. If your bare hands do touch the peppers, wash your hands and nails well with soap and warm water.

Chicken and Rigatoni With Roasted Red Peppers 🖤

Meet the new Chicken Parmesan. Reminiscent of that Italian restaurant favorite, this irresistible recipe with less cheese plus flavorful tomatoes, basil, and roasted sweet peppers, brings a lighter, fresher take on the classic.

Start to Finish: 30 minutes **Makes:** 6 servings

- 1 **pound skinless, boneless chicken breast halves**
- ½ **cup seasoned fine dry bread crumbs**
- 2 **tablespoons grated Parmesan or Romano cheese**
- 1 **egg**
- 1 **tablespoon water**
- 1 **7-ounce jar roasted red sweet peppers**
  Chicken broth
- 2 **teaspoons cornstarch**
- 3 **cups dried rigatoni pasta**
- 2 **tablespoons olive oil**
- 2 **cloves garlic, minced**
- 3 **plum tomatoes, seeded and chopped (1 cup)**
- 2 **tablespoons dry white wine**
- 2 **tablespoons snipped fresh basil**
- 2 **tablespoons grated Parmesan or Romano cheese**

1. Halve each chicken piece lengthwise. In a shallow bowl, combine crumbs and 2 tablespoons Parmesan cheese. In another shallow bowl, beat together egg and water. Dip each chicken piece in egg mixture and then in crumb mixture, turning to coat all sides. Set chicken aside.

2. Drain peppers, reserving liquid. Add chicken broth to reserved liquid to equal ⅔ cup; stir in cornstarch and set aside. Cut peppers into thin strips; set aside.

3. Cook pasta according to package directions; drain. Return to warm pan.

4. Meanwhile, in a 12-inch skillet, cook chicken, uncovered, in hot oil over medium-high heat for 10 to 12 minutes or until chicken is tender and no longer pink, turning once. Remove from skillet; cover and keep warm.

5. Add garlic to skillet; cook and stir 1 minute. Carefully add the broth mixture; cook and stir until thickened and bubbly. Stir in tomatoes, pepper strips, wine, and basil; cook 1 minute more. Toss mixture with drained rigatoni and 2 tablespoons Parmesan cheese; arrange chicken over top.

Per serving: 379 cal., 10 g total fat (2 g sat. fat), 79 mg chol., 442 mg sodium, 41 g carbo., 1 g fiber, 24 g pro.

Chicken Quesadillas

Chicken Quesadillas

Easy to fix and neat to eat, quesadillas are a sure family favorite. Serve with the dip your family likes best.

Start to Finish: 25 minutes **Makes:** 4 servings

- **Nonstick cooking spray**
- 1 **cup sliced fresh mushrooms**
- 1 **2- to 2¼-pound deli-roasted chicken**
- 4 **8- to 10-inch flour tortillas**
  Fresh spinach leaves
- 2 **cups shredded Monterey Jack cheese (8 ounces)**
  Salsa, guacamole, and sour cream (optional)

1. Coat a small nonstick skillet with cooking spray. Add mushrooms to skillet; cook over medium-high heat until tender. Remove skillet from heat; set aside.

2. Remove meat from chicken (discard skin and bones). Chop meat; reserve 2 cups. Cover and chill or freeze remaining chicken for another use.

3. Spoon reserved chicken evenly on one half of each tortilla. Top with spinach and mushrooms. Sprinkle cheese evenly over mushrooms. Fold tortillas in half.

4. Preheat a griddle over medium heat. Cook quesadillas on hot griddle until browned on both sides and cheese is melted. If desired, serve with salsa, guacamole, and sour cream.

Per serving: 472 cal., 28 g total fat (15 g sat. fat), 120 mg chol., 513 mg sodium, 18 g carbo., 2 g fiber, 37 g pro.

White Beans, Pasta, and Chicken

Canned beans are one of the all-time great staples of the cook's pantry. They're always ready when you are. Here, they add heartiness to a satisfying dish that comes together in just 30 minutes.

Start to Finish: 30 minutes **Makes:** 4 servings

- 8 ounces dried cavatappi, fusilli, rotini, ditalini, or other short pasta tubes
- 1 15- to 19-ounce can cannellini (white kidney) beans, rinsed and drained
- ½ cup chicken broth
- 3 cloves garlic, thinly sliced
- 1 tablespoon olive oil
- 6 plum tomatoes, coarsely chopped (about 2 cups)
- 12 ounces cooked chicken, shredded
- ¼ cup snipped fresh Italian flat-leaf parsley
- ½ to 1 teaspoon cracked black pepper
- ½ teaspoon salt
  Fresh Italian flat-leaf parsley sprigs (optional)
  Olive oil (optional)

1. In a large saucepan, cook pasta according to package directions; drain well and set aside.

2. In a blender or food processor, combine ¾ cup of the drained beans and the chicken broth. Cover and blend or process until smooth. Place bean puree in pan used for cooking the pasta; bring to boiling. Return pasta to pan.

3. Meanwhile, in a large skillet, cook garlic in 1 tablespoon hot oil for 1 minute. Add tomatoes; cook for 1 minute. Add the remaining beans, shredded chicken, snipped parsley, pepper, and salt. Heat through.

4. Add the tomato mixture to hot pasta; toss to coat. Top with parsley sprigs and, if desired, additional olive oil. Serve immediately.

Per serving: 602 cal., 9 g total fat (1 g sat. fat), 102 mg chol., 1,051 mg sodium, 87 g carbo., 10 g fiber, 49 g pro.

White Beans, Pasta, and Chicken

Chipotle Chicken Enchiladas [one]

Simple, sassy, and satisfying, this enchilada dish comes together quickly and bakes in less than an hour. Take the bake time to unwind, walk the dog, or play a game of catch.

Prep: 25 minutes **Bake:** 40 minutes **Oven:** 350°F
Makes: 4 servings

- 2½ cups chopped cooked chicken (12 ounces)
- 1 to 2 teaspoons ground dried chipotle chile pepper
- 1 10.75-ounce can condensed cream of chicken soup
- 1 8-ounce carton dairy sour cream
- 1 4-ounce can diced green chile peppers
- 8 7- to 8-inch flour tortillas
- 2 cups shredded Cheddar cheese (8 ounces)
- ¼ cup sliced green onion (1)

1. Preheat oven to 350°F. Grease a 3-quart rectangular baking dish; set aside. In a medium bowl, combine chicken and chipotle chile pepper; set aside.

2. For the sauce, in a large bowl, combine soup, sour cream, and undrained green chile peppers. Stir ½ cup of the sauce into the chicken mixture.

3. Divide chicken mixture among tortillas. Sprinkle 1½ cups of the cheese and the green onion over chicken mixture on tortillas. Roll up tortillas; place, seam sides down, in prepared baking dish. Pour remaining sauce over all. Cover with foil.

4. Bake for 35 minutes or until edges are bubbly. Uncover; sprinkle with the remaining ½ cup cheese. Bake, uncovered, about 5 minutes more or until cheese is melted.

Per serving: 786 cal., 47 g total fat (24 g sat. fat), 169 mg chol., 1,376 mg sodium, 42 g carbo., 2 g fiber, 47 g pro..

Quick Tip To save time during the dinnertime rush, make this chicken dish ahead of time. Prepare the recipe through Step 3 and chill for up to 8 hours. Bake as directed.

Feta-Stuffed Chicken Breasts

Buffalo-Style Chicken [one] Strips with Blue Cheese

Work-saving chicken breast tenders make this homemade adaptation of restaurant-style Buffalo wings easy on the cook.

Start to Finish: 25 minutes **Makes:** 4 servings

- ⅓ **cup all-purpose flour**
- ¾ **teaspoon salt**
- ½ **teaspoon ground black pepper**
- ¼ **cup milk**
- 1 **pound chicken breast tenderloins**
- ½ **cup olive oil or cooking oil**
- 4 **teaspoons butter or margarine, melted**
- 2 **teaspoons bottled hot pepper sauce**
- ⅓ **cup bottled blue cheese salad dressing**

1. In a shallow dish, combine flour, salt, and pepper. Pour milk into another shallow dish. Dip chicken in milk; coat with flour mixture.

2. In a large skillet, heat oil over medium heat. Add half of the chicken; cook about 4 minutes or until no longer pink (170°F), turning once. Repeat with remaining chicken.

3. Meanwhile, in a small bowl, stir together melted butter and hot pepper sauce. Drizzle butter mixture over chicken strips. Serve chicken strips with blue cheese salad dressing for dipping.

Per serving: 369 cal., 24 g total fat (6 g sat. fat), 81 mg chol., 784 mg sodium, 10 g carbo., 0 g fiber, 29 g pro.

Herb-Rubbed Roaster [one]

Get this bird ready for the oven the night before you plan to serve it. The next day all you have to do is pile potatoes around the chicken and bake it.

Prep: 20 minutes **Roast:** 1¼ hours
Stand: 10 minutes **Marinate:** 2 to 24 hours
Oven: 375°F **Makes:** 6 servings

- 1 **3½- to 4-pound whole broiler-fryer chicken**
- ¼ **cup olive oil**
- 2 **tablespoons herbes de Provence**
- 1 **teaspoon salt or smoked salt**
- 1 **teaspoon crushed red pepper**
- ¾ **teaspoon coarsely ground black pepper**
- 1½ **pounds tiny yellow and purple potatoes and/or fingerling potatoes, halved**

1. Remove the neck and giblets from chicken. Rinse chicken; pat dry with paper towels. Skewer neck skin to back; tie legs to tail with 100-percent-cotton string. Twist wings under back. Brush chicken with 2 tablespoons of the olive oil.

2. In a small bowl, stir together herbes de Provence, salt, crushed red pepper, and black pepper. Rub 2 tablespoons of the herb mixture onto the chicken.

Cover the remaining herb mixture; set aside. Place chicken in a large resealable plastic bag. Seal bag and place in the refrigerator for 2 to 24 hours.

3. Preheat oven to 375°F. Remove chicken from bag. Place chicken, breast side up, on a rack in a shallow roasting pan. Insert an oven-proof meat thermometer into center of an inside thigh muscle. Do not allow thermometer bulb to touch bone.

4. In a large bowl, combine the remaining 2 tablespoons oil and remaining herb mixture. Add the potatoes and toss to combine. Arrange potatoes around the chicken. Roast, uncovered, for 1¼ to 1¾ hours or until drumsticks move easily in their sockets and meat thermometer registers 180°F. Remove chicken from oven. Cover and let stand for 10 minutes before carving.

5. To serve, place the chicken on a large serving platter. Arrange the potatoes around the chicken.

Per serving: 543 cal., 35 g total fat (9 g sat. fat), 134 mg chol., 492 mg sodium, 18 g carbo., 3 g fiber, 37 g pro.

Feta-Stuffed Chicken Breasts ♥

A filling made of feta cheese, dried tomatoes, and basil embellishes these succulent chicken breasts.

Start to Finish: 30 minutes **Makes:** 4 servings

- 1 **tablespoon snipped dried tomatoes (not oil-packed)**
  Boiling water
- 4 **skinless, boneless chicken breast halves (about 1¼ pounds)**
- ¼ **cup crumbled feta cheese (1 ounce)**
- 2 **tablespoons softened cream cheese (1 ounce)**
- ½ **teaspoon dried basil, crushed**
- ½ **teaspoon ground black pepper**
- 1 **teaspoon olive oil or cooking oil**

1. Place tomatoes in a small bowl. Cover with boiling water. Let stand for 10 minutes. Drain and pat dry; set aside. Meanwhile, using a sharp knife, cut a pocket in each chicken breast by cutting horizontally through the thickest portion to, but not through, the opposite side; set aside.

2. In a small bowl, combine feta, cream cheese, basil, and tomatoes. Spoon about 1 rounded tablespoon into each chicken pocket. If necessary, secure openings with wooden toothpicks. Sprinkle chicken with black pepper.

3. In a large nonstick skillet, heat oil over medium-high heat. Add chicken; cook for 12 to 14 minutes or until chicken is no longer pink (170°F), turning once (reduce heat to medium if chicken browns too quickly).

Per serving: 186 cal., 7 g total fat (4 g sat. fat), 82 mg chol., 203 mg sodium, 1 g carbo., 0 g fiber, 28 g pro.

Mediterranean Chicken And Pasta ♥ [one]

The zesty flavors of the Mediterranean dominate this dish. Artichokes, oregano, kalamata olives, and feta cheese mingle with chicken pieces, garlic, and a splash of white wine.

Start to Finish: 20 minutes **Makes:** 4 servings

- 1 **6-ounce jar marinated artichoke hearts**
- 1 **tablespoon olive oil**
- 12 **ounces skinless, boneless chicken breasts, cut into bite-size pieces**
- 3 **cloves garlic, thinly sliced**
- ¼ **cup chicken broth**
- ¼ **cup dry white wine**
- 1 **teaspoon dried oregano, crushed**
- 1 **cup roasted red sweet peppers, drained and cut into strips**
- ¼ **cup pitted kalamata olives**
- 3 **cups hot cooked campanelle or penne pasta**
- ¼ **cup crumbled feta cheese (optional)**

1. Drain artichokes, reserving marinade. Cut up any large pieces. Set aside. In a large skillet, heat oil over medium-high heat. Add chicken and garlic. Cook and stir until chicken is brown. Add the reserved artichoke marinade, broth, wine, and, oregano.

2. Bring to boiling; reduce heat. Simmer, covered, for 10 minutes. Stir in artichokes, peppers, and olives. Heat through.

3. To serve, spoon the chicken mixture over pasta. If desired, sprinkle with feta cheese.

Per serving: 347 cal., 9 g total fat (1 g sat. fat), 49 mg chol., 323 mg sodium, 38 g carbo., 3 g fiber, 26 g pro.

Zesty Chicken with Black Beans and Rice [one]

This recipe is a great example of how to turn a packaged mix into a satisfying dinner for the whole family. Additions such as sour cream, sliced green onions, and wedges of lime make this dish extra special.

Start to Finish: 30 minutes **Makes:** 4 servings

- 2 **tablespoons cooking oil**
- 1 **pound skinless, boneless chicken breast halves, cut into 2-inch pieces**
- 1 **6- to 7.4-ounce package Spanish rice mix**
- 1¾ **cups water**
- 1 **15-ounce can black beans, rinsed and drained**
- 1 **14.5-ounce can diced tomatoes, undrained**
  Sour cream, sliced green onion, and lime wedges (optional)

1. In a 12-inch skillet, heat 1 tablespoon of the oil over medium-high heat. Add chicken pieces; cook in hot oil until chicken is lightly browned. Remove chicken from skillet and keep warm.

2. Add rice mix (reserve seasoning packet) and remaining 1 tablespoon oil to skillet; cook and stir for 2 minutes over medium heat. Stir in seasoning packet from rice mix, the water, drained beans, and undrained tomatoes; add chicken. Bring to boiling; reduce heat. Cover and simmer for 15 to 20 minutes, or until rice is tender and chicken is no longer pink. Remove from heat and let stand, covered, for 5 minutes.

3. If desired, serve with sour cream, green onion, and lime wedges.

Per serving: 424 cal., 9 g total fat (2 g sat. fat), 66 mg chol., 1,080 mg sodium, 52 g carbo., 6 g fiber, 37 g pro.

Lemon-Dill Butter ♥ Chicken and Cucumbers

Cook the cucumber until it just begins to soften but still retains a bit of crispness. If you like, seed the cucumber before chopping it. Or, purchase an English cucumber (also called hothouse cucumbers) which is naturally seedless.

Prep: 10 minutes **Broil:** 12 minutes **Makes:** 4 servings

- 4 **skinless, boneless chicken breast halves (about 1¼ pounds)**
- 1 **medium lemon**
- 3 **tablespoons butter**
- ½ **teaspoon dried dill**
- ¼ **teaspoon salt**
- ¼ **teaspoon ground black pepper**
- 1½ **cups coarsely chopped cucumber or zucchini**

1. Preheat broiler. Place chicken on the unheated rack of a broiler pan. Broil 4 to 5 inches from heat for 12 to 15 minutes or until no longer pink (170°F), turning once halfway through broiling.

2. Meanwhile, finely shred ½ teaspoon peel from the lemon. Cut lemon in half; squeeze lemon to get 2 tablespoons juice.

3. In a small skillet, melt butter over medium heat. Stir in lemon peel, lemon juice, dill, salt, and pepper. Stir in cucumber. Cook and stir over medium heat for 3 to 4 minutes or until cucumber is just tender. Spoon sauce over chicken.

Per serving: 244 cal., 11 g total fat (6 g sat. fat), 107 mg chol., 477 mg sodium, 2 g carbo., 0 g fiber, 33 g pro.

Quick Tip Choose lemons with smooth, brightly colored skin with no tinge of green. They should be firm, plump, and heavy for their size. Store lemons in a plastic bag in the refrigerator for 2 to 3 weeks.

Lemon-Dill Butter Chicken and Cucumbers

Couscous Chicken Salad

Couscous Chicken Salad one

Couscous is a tiny grain-shape pasta made from semolina flour. Once cooked and fluffed up, it's a good substitute for rice or polenta. Look for it near the rice and pasta at your supermarket.

Start to Finish: 15 minutes **Makes:** 4 servings

1	**14-ounce can chicken broth**
1¼	**cups quick-cooking couscous**
½	**cup mango chutney, large pieces cut up**
¼	**cup bottled olive oil and vinegar salad dressing, white wine vinaigrette salad dressing, or roasted garlic vinaigrette salad dressing**
1	**6-ounce package cooked, refrigerated lemon-pepper chicken breast strips, cut into bite-size pieces (about 1½ cups)**
½	**cup golden raisins or raisins (optional)**
1	**cup coarsely chopped radishes or seeded cucumber**
	Salt
	Freshly ground black pepper
1	**small cucumber, cut into spears**

1. In a medium saucepan, bring chicken broth to boiling. Stir in couscous. Cover and remove from heat. Let stand for 5 minutes. Fluff couscous lightly with a fork.

2. In a medium bowl, combine chutney and salad dressing. Add chicken, raisins (if using), chopped radishes, and cooked couscous. Toss to coat. Season to taste with salt and pepper. Serve with cucumber spears.

Per serving: 411 cal., 10 g total fat (2 g sat. fat), 22 mg chol., 848 mg sodium, 63 g carbo., 4 g fiber, 16 g pro.

Quick Tip Choose radishes that feel firm when gently squeezed. If a radish gives to pressure when pressed, the inside will likely be pithy instead of crisp. Any attached leaves should be green and unwilted. Store radishes in a plastic bag in the refrigerator for up to 1 week.

Plum Wonderful Chicken ♥

A quick skillet browning, then a bake in the oven with a plum sauce spiked with ginger, dry mustard, and frozen lemonade concentrate, produces a chicken dish with a tantalizing sweet-sour flavor.

Prep: 40 minutes **Bake:** 35 minutes **Oven:** 350°F
Makes: 6 servings

- 2 tablespoons olive oil or cooking oil
- 2½ to 3 pounds meaty chicken pieces (breast halves, thighs, and/or drumsticks), skinned
- ¼ cup chopped onion
- 1 teaspoon grated fresh ginger
- ½ teaspoon bottled minced garlic (1 clove)
- ⅓ cup bottled plum sauce
- ¼ cup frozen lemonade concentrate
- ¼ cup bottled chili sauce
- 2 tablespoons reduced-sodium soy sauce
- 1 tablespoon lemon juice
- 1 teaspoon dry mustard
- 3 cups hot cooked rice
   Thinly sliced green onions (optional)
   Sesame seeds, toasted (optional)

1. Preheat oven to 350°F. In a large skillet, heat oil over medium heat. Add half of the chicken; cook about 10 minutes or until brown, turning often to brown evenly on all sides. Transfer browned chicken pieces to a 3-quart rectangular baking dish. Repeat with remaining chicken. Drain fat from skillet, reserving 1 tablespoon in the skillet. Add onion, ginger, and garlic to skillet. Cook and stir about 5 minutes or until onion is tender.

2. Meanwhile, for the sauce, in a small bowl, stir together plum sauce, lemonade concentrate, chili sauce, soy sauce, lemon juice, and dry mustard. Carefully stir into onion mixture in skillet. Bring to boiling; reduce heat. Cover and simmer for 5 minutes; spoon sauce over chicken in dish.

3. Bake, uncovered, for 35 to 40 minutes or until chicken is tender and no longer pink (170°F for breast pieces; 180°F for thighs and drumsticks), spooning sauce over chicken twice during baking. Serve chicken and sauce over rice. If desired, sprinkle with green onions and sesame seeds.

Per serving: 366 cal., 12 g total fat (2 g sat. fat), 77 mg chol., 405 mg sodium, 37 g carbo., 1 g fiber, 28 g pro.

Plum Wonderful Chicken

Italian-Style Chicken Cutlets ♥ 🔲one

This recipe for pan-fried cutlets is quick and easy. The blend of bread crumbs, parsley, rosemary, and Parmesan creates an Italian-flavored crust around the chicken.

Prep: 15 minutes **Cook:** 10 minutes **Makes:** 4 servings

- 4 skinless, boneless chicken breast halves (about 1¼ pounds)
- ¼ teaspoon kosher salt
- ¼ teaspoon freshly ground black pepper
- ¾ cup fine dry whole wheat bread crumbs
- 2 tablespoons freshly grated Parmesan cheese
- 1 tablespoon chopped fresh flat-leaf parsley
- 1 teaspoon chopped fresh rosemary
- 1 egg
- 1 egg white
- 2 tablespoons extra-virgin olive oil
   Lemon wedges (optional)

1. Place each chicken piece between 2 pieces of plastic wrap. Using the flat side of a meat mallet, pound chicken lightly until ½-inch thickness. Remove plastic wrap. Season chicken with kosher salt and black pepper.

2. In a shallow dish, combine bread crumbs, Parmesan cheese, parsley, and rosemary. Place whole egg and egg white in another shallow dish; beat slightly. Dip chicken in egg mixture, then coat with crumb mixture.

3. In a large skillet, heat oil over medium-high heat. Add chicken and cook for 10 to 12 minutes or until chicken is no longer pink, turning once. If desired, serve chicken with lemon wedges.

Per serving: 264 cal., 11 g total fat (2 g sat. fat), 121 mg chol., 349 mg sodium, 9 g carbo., 1 g fiber, 31 g pro.

Fresh Garlic and Pecan Chicken 🔳

Garlic-infused roast chicken gets a crunchy twist with a butter and pecan coating.

Prep: 30 minutes **Roast:** 1¼ hours **Stand:** 10 minutes
Oven: 375°F **Makes:** 4 servings

1	**3- to 3½-pound whole broiler-fryer chicken**
6	**cloves garlic, thinly sliced**
⅔	**cup finely chopped pecans**
¼	**cup butter or margarine, melted**
1	**tablespoon snipped fresh thyme or 1 teaspoon dried thyme, crushed**
½	**teaspoon ground black pepper**
¼	**teaspoon salt**

1. Preheat oven to 375°F. Rinse inside of chicken; pat dry with paper towels. Skewer neck skin of chicken to back; tie legs to tail with 100-percent-cotton string. Twist wing tips under back. Using a small, sharp knife, make numerous slits about 1 inch wide and ½ inch deep in the breast portions of the chicken. Stuff garlic in slits.

2. In a small bowl, combine pecans, melted butter, thyme, pepper, and salt. Pat mixture onto top of chicken.

3. Place chicken, breast side up, on a rack in a shallow roasting pan. Insert an oven-proof meat thermometer into center of an inside thigh muscle, not touching bone.

4. Roast, uncovered, for 1¼ to 1½ hours or until drumsticks move easily in their sockets and thermometer registers 180°F. (If necessary, cover chicken loosely with foil for the last 10 to 15 minutes of roasting to prevent pecans from overbrowning.) Remove chicken from oven. Cover and let stand for 10 minutes before carving. If desired, spoon any pecans from roasting pan over each serving.

Per serving: 725 cal., 59 g total fat (18 g sat. fat), 205 mg chol., 400 mg sodium, 4 g carbo., 2 g fiber, 45 g pro.

Honey-Glazed Chicken 🖤

Get double the kick from the honey-mustard mixture by using it as a marinade for the chicken and as the dressing for the greens or hot pasta.

Prep: 15 minutes **Bake:** 20 minutes
Marinate: 2 to 4 hours **Oven:** 400°F **Makes:** 4 servings

1½	**pounds skinless, boneless chicken breast halves**
½	**cup honey**
3	**tablespoons lemon juice**
1	**tablespoon reduced-sodium soy sauce**
1	**tablespoon spicy brown mustard**
	Torn mixed salad greens or hot cooked pasta (optional)

1. Place chicken breast halves in a resealable plastic bag set in a shallow bowl. For marinade, in a small bowl, whisk together honey, lemon juice, soy sauce, and mustard. Set aside ¼ cup of the marinade. Pour remaining marinade over chicken in the bag. Seal bag; turn to coat chicken. Marinate in the refrigerator for 2 to 4 hours.

2. Preheat the oven to 400°F. Remove chicken from marinade, reserving remaining marinade. Place the chicken in a shallow baking pan.

3. Bake chicken, uncovered, about 20 minutes or until no longer pink (170°F), turning once and basting with some of the remaining marinade halfway through roasting time. Discard any leftover marinade. Thinly slice chicken. If desired, serve chicken on greens or pasta. Drizzle the ¼ cup reserved marinade over chicken.

Per serving: 325 cal., 2 g total fat (1 g sat. fat), 99 mg chol., 299 mg sodium, 36 g carbo., 0 g fiber, 40 g pro.

Orange Chicken and Fried Rice

Orange juice concentrate is just one of the secrets to this quick-cooking skillet meal. Infused with ginger and garlic, and served with flavored fried rice and chopped cashews, the dish has plenty of texture, too.

Start to Finish: 25 minutes **Makes:** 4 servings

1	**6-ounce package Oriental-flavor fried rice mix**
2	**tablespoons butter or margarine**
1	**pound packaged skinless, boneless chicken breast strips (stir-fry strips)**
8	**green onions, bias-sliced into 1-inch pieces**
1	**teaspoon bottled minced garlic (2 cloves) or ¼ teaspoon garlic powder**
1	**teaspoon ground ginger**
1	**tablespoon frozen orange juice concentrate, thawed**
¼	**cup chopped cashews**

1. Cook rice according to package directions.

2. Meanwhile, in a large skillet, melt butter over medium-high heat. Add chicken strips, green onion, garlic, and ginger; cook and stir for 3 to 5 minutes or until chicken is no longer pink (170°F).

3. Stir orange juice concentrate into cooked rice. Stir rice mixture into chicken mixture in skillet. Cook and stir until heated through. Sprinkle each serving with cashews.

Per serving: 396 cal., 13 g total fat (5 g sat. fat), 82 mg chol., 985 mg sodium, 38 g carbo., 2 g fiber, 32 g pro.

Asian Chicken and Vegetables ♥ [one]

Pop this easy chicken dish in the oven and relax; the one-pan meal means simple cleanup too.

Prep: 10 minutes **Bake:** 40 minutes **Oven:** 400°F
Makes: 4 servings

- **8**   **chicken drumsticks and/or thighs, skinned (about 2 pounds total)**
- **1**   **tablespoon cooking oil**
- **1½**   **teaspoons five-spice powder**
- **⅓**   **cup bottled plum sauce or sweet-and-sour sauce**
- **1**   **14-ounce package frozen baby whole potatoes, broccoli, carrots, baby corn, and red pepper mix or one 16-ounce package frozen stir-fry vegetables (any combination)**

1. Preheat oven to 400°F. Arrange the chicken pieces in a 13×9×2-inch baking pan, making sure pieces do not touch. Brush chicken pieces with cooking oil; sprinkle with 1 teaspoon of the five-spice powder. Bake, uncovered, for 25 minutes.

2. Meanwhile, in a large bowl, combine plum sauce and the remaining ½ teaspoon five-spice powder. Add frozen vegetables; toss to coat.

3. Move chicken pieces to one side of the baking pan. Add vegetable mixture to the other side of the baking pan. Bake for 15 to 20 minutes more or until chicken is no longer pink (180°F), stirring vegetables once during baking. Using a slotted spoon, transfer chicken and vegetables to a serving platter.

Per serving: 277 cal., 9 g total fat (2 g sat. fat), 98 mg chol., 124 mg sodium, 21 g carbo., 2 g fiber, 30 g pro.

Pepper and Peach Fajita Chicken ♥ 🎬

Seasoning blends, such as fajita seasoning, contain several spices and herbs, simplifying both shopping and cooking. Here the fajita seasoning gives a spicy kick to juicy peaches, sweet peppers, and moist chicken breasts.

Start to Finish: 20 minutes **Makes:** 4 servings

- **4**   **skinless, boneless chicken breast halves**
- **1½** **teaspoons fajita seasoning**
- **2**   **tablespoons olive oil or butter**
- **1½** **cups sweet pepper strips**
- **1**   **medium fresh peach or nectarine, cut into thin slices, or 1 cup frozen peach slices, thawed**

1. Sprinkle both sides of chicken breast halves with fajita seasoning. In a large skillet, heat 1 tablespoon of the oil over medium-high heat. Add chicken to skillet; cook for 8 to 10 minutes or until chicken is no longer pink (170°F), turning once. Transfer chicken to a serving platter; keep warm.

2. Add remaining oil to skillet; add sweet pepper strips. Cook and stir about 3 minutes or until crisp-tender. Gently stir in peach slices. Cook and stir for 1 to 2 minutes more or until heated through. Spoon over chicken.

Per serving: 243 cal., 9 g total fat (1 g sat. fat), 82 mg chol., 150 mg sodium, 7 g carbo., 2 g fiber, 33 g pro.

Saucy Cranberry Chicken 🎬

For a fresh take on easy baked chicken, stir French onion soup mix into whole cranberry sauce and some French dressing, pour it over a pan of chicken and bake.

Prep: 15 minutes **Bake:** 1½ hours **Oven:** 325°F
Makes: 4 to 6 servings

- **1**   **16-ounce can whole cranberry sauce**
- **1**   **cup bottled French salad dressing**
- **1**   **envelope (½ of a 2.2-ounce package) onion soup mix**
- **2½** **to 3 pounds meaty chicken pieces (breast halves, thighs, and drumsticks)**
  Hot cooked rice (optional)

1. Preheat oven to 325°F. In a medium bowl, stir together cranberry sauce, salad dressing, and dry soup mix. If desired, skin chicken. Arrange chicken pieces, meaty sides down, in a 3-quart rectangular baking dish. Pour cranberry mixture over chicken pieces.

2. Bake, uncovered, for about 1½ hours or until the chicken is tender and no longer pink (170°F for breast pieces; 180°F for thighs and drumsticks), stirring glaze and spooning over chicken. If desired, serve over cooked rice.

Per serving: 810 cal., 47 g total fat (7 g sat. fat), 141 mg chol., 901 mg sodium, 54 g carbo., 2 g fiber, 43 g pro.

Pepper and Peach Fajita Chicken

Cool-as-a-Cucumber
Chicken Salad

Cool-as-a-Cucumber Chicken Salad

Purchase cut-up cantaloupe, found in most supermarket produce sections, for this quick-fix salad. Take advantage of cut-up fruits—they are a great way to save time in the kitchen.

Start to Finish: 25 minutes **Makes:** 4 to 6 servings

2   cups shredded cooked chicken (10 ounces)
2   cups purchased cut-up cantaloupe and/or
       halved seedless red grapes
1   cup chopped cucumber
⅓   cup orange juice
3   tablespoons salad oil
1   tablespoon snipped fresh mint or cilantro
       Salt
       Ground black pepper
4   cups shredded romaine or leaf lettuce

1. In a large bowl, toss together chicken, cantaloupe and/or grapes, and cucumber.

2. For the dressing, in a screw-top jar, combine orange juice, oil, and cilantro. Cover and shake well. Season to taste with salt and pepper. Drizzle over chicken mixture; toss lightly to coat.

3. Arrange lettuce on 4 salad plates. Top with chicken and fruit mixture.

Per serving: 269 cal., 16 g total fat (3 g sat. fat), 62 mg chol., 114 mg sodium, 11 g carbo., 1 g fiber, 22 g pro.

Quick Tip Choose cucumbers with smooth, brightly colored skins. Be sure they have no shriveled or soft spots. Smaller cucumbers are generally not as bitter and have thinner skin and fewer seeds than larger ones. Store whole cucumbers , unwashed, in a plastic bag in the refrigerator for up to 10 days. Cut cucumbers can be wrapped in plastic wrap and refrigerated for up to 5 days.

Balsamic Chicken and Vegetables

Balsamic Chicken and Vegetables ♥ [one]

Balsamic vinegar, with its hallmark dark color, syrupy body, and slight sweetness, brings a wonderful touch to any recipe.

Start to Finish: 30 minutes **Makes:** 4 servings

- ¼ **cup bottled Italian salad dressing**
- 2 **tablespoons balsamic vinegar**
- 1 **tablespoon honey**
- ⅛ **to ¼ teaspoon crushed red pepper**
- 2 **tablespoons olive oil**
- 1 **pound chicken breast tenderloins**
- 10 **ounces fresh asparagus, trimmed and cut into 2-inch pieces, or one 10-ounce package frozen cut asparagus, thawed and well drained**
- 1 **cup purchased shredded carrot**
- 1 **small tomato, seeded and chopped**

1. In a small bowl, stir together salad dressing, vinegar, honey, and crushed red pepper. Set aside.

2. In a large skillet, heat oil over medium-high heat. Add chicken; cook for 5 to 6 minutes or until chicken is tender and no longer pink, turning once. Add half of the dressing mixture to skillet; turn chicken to coat. Transfer chicken to a serving platter; cover and keep warm.

3. Add asparagus and carrot to skillet. Cook and stir for 3 to 4 minutes or until asparagus is crisp-tender; transfer to serving platter.

4. Stir remaining dressing mixture; add to skillet. Cook and stir for 1 minute, scraping up browned bits from bottom of skillet. Drizzle the dressing mixture over chicken and vegetables. Sprinkle with tomato.

Per serving: 269 cal., 12 g total fat (2 g sat. fat), 66 mg chol., 323 mg sodium, 12 g carbo., 2 g fiber, 27 g pro.

Cheesy Corn and Chicken Turnovers [one]

Cutting refrigerated piecrust into quarters is an easy way to form triangle-shape packets.

Prep: 25 minutes **Bake:** 15 minutes **Oven:** 400°F
Makes: 4 servings

- 2 **cups chopped cooked chicken**
- 1 **11-ounce can whole kernel corn with sweet peppers, drained**
- 1 **10.5-ounce can condensed cream of chicken and herbs or cream of mushroom soup**
- 1 **cup shredded Cheddar cheese (4 ounces)**
- 1 **15-ounce package rolled refrigerated unbaked piecrust (2 crusts)**

1. Preheat oven to 400°F. Grease a large baking sheet; set aside. In a medium bowl, combine chicken, corn, soup, and cheese. Unfold piecrusts according to package directions.

2. On a lightly floured surface or pastry cloth, roll each piecrust into a 13-inch circle. Cut each piecrust into quarters. Spoon about ½ cup chicken mixture along one straight side of each triangle, about ¾ inch from edge. Brush edges of triangle with a little water. Fold other straight side of triangle over the filling. Seal edges with a fork. Prick the top of the triangle several times with a fork. Repeat with remaining pastry triangles and filling. Place wedges on prepared baking sheet.

3. Bake about 15 minutes or until wedges are golden brown. Serve hot.

Per serving: 862 cal., 47 g total fat (21 g sat. fat), 118 mg chol., 1,625 mg sodium, 73 g carbo., 3 g fiber, 33 g pro.

Chicken with Cranberry And Olive Couscous [one]

Just five ingredients add up to a delicious dinner when three of them are as flavorful as dried cranberries, kalamata olives, and fresh mint.

Start to Finish: 15 minutes **Makes:** 4 servings

- 1 **cup uncooked quick-cooking couscous**
- ¼ **cup dried cranberries**
- 3 **tablespoons sliced pitted kalamata olives**
- 2 **6-ounce packages refrigerated grilled chicken breast strips**
- 1 **tablespoon snipped fresh mint**
  Salt
  Ground black pepper

1. Prepare the couscous according to package directions, adding cranberries and olives with the couscous. Fluff with a fork. Stir in chicken breast strips. Sprinkle each serving with fresh mint. Season to taste with salt and pepper.

Per serving: 337 cal., 4 g total fat (1 g sat. fat), 60 mg chol., 1,011 mg sodium, 43 g carbo., 3 g fiber, 28 g pro.

Quick Tip When you have extra time, try grilling the chicken yourself to use in this recipe. For a charcoal grill, grill 2 chicken breast halves (8 ounces total) on the rack of an uncovered grill directly over medium coals for 12 to 15 minutes or until chicken is no longer pink (170°F), turning once halfway through grilling and brushing with sauce during the last 5 minutes of grilling. (For a gas grill, preheat grill. Reduce heat to medium. Place chicken on grill rack over heat. Cover and grill as above.)

Spicy Chicken Breasts with Fruit

Spicy Chicken Breasts With Fruit  ♥ one

This Caribbean-style dish exhibits sweet and spicy flavors in magnificent harmony.

Start to Finish: 25 minutes **Makes:** 4 servings

- 1 **tablespoon Jamaican jerk seasoning**
- 4 **skinless, boneless chicken breast halves (about 1¼ pounds)**
- 1 **tablespoon cooking oil**
- 3 **green onions, cut into 1-inch pieces**
- ½ **cup peach nectar**
- 1 **teaspoon cornstarch**
- 2 **cups frozen peach slices**
- ½ **cup frozen unsweetened pitted dark sweet cherries**
- 1 **tablespoon packed brown sugar**
- ⅛ **teaspoon salt**
- 1 **cup sliced plums**
  Hot cooked instant rice (optional)

1. Sprinkle jerk seasoning evenly over both sides of chicken; rub in with your fingers. Add oil to a large skillet; heat over medium heat. Add chicken. Cook for 10 to 12 minutes or until chicken is tender and no longer pink (170°F), turning once and adding the green onions the last 2 to 3 minutes of cooking. Transfer chicken to serving platter; cover and keep warm.

2. Meanwhile, in a medium bowl, combine nectar and cornstarch. Add peaches, cherries, brown sugar, and salt.

Add to skillet. Cook and stir 3 minutes or until slightly thickened and bubbly. Stir in plums; cook and stir 1 minute more.

3. To serve, spoon fruit mixture over chicken. If desired, serve with hot cooked rice.

Per serving: 294 cal., 6 g total fat (1 g sat. fat), 82 mg chol., 380 mg sodium, 26 g carbo., 3 g fiber, 34 g pro.

Thai Chicken Pasta

If your supermarket doesn't stock unsweetened coconut milk, look for it at an Asian market. To add some extra kick to this pasta dish, add a dash of crushed red pepper.

Start to Finish: 20 minutes **Makes:** 4 servings

- 8 **ounces dried angel hair or vermicelli pasta**
- 3 **cups cooked chicken, cut into strips**
- 1 **14-ounce can unsweetened coconut milk**
- 1 **teaspoon Thai seasoning**
- ¼ **cup roasted peanuts**
- 2 **tablespoons snipped fresh cilantro**

1. Cook pasta according to package directions. Drain and return pasta to warm pan.

2. Meanwhile, in a large skillet, combine chicken, coconut milk, and Thai seasoning. Cook and gently stir over medium heat until mixture is heated through. Pour hot chicken mixture over cooked pasta in pan. Add peanuts and cilantro. Toss gently to coat.

Per serving: 644 cal., 31 g total fat (19 g sat. fat), 93 mg chol., 236 mg sodium, 47 g carbo., 2 g fiber, 42 g pro.

Thai Chicken Pasta

Lemon Chicken with Garlic and Rosemary [one]

This easy baked chicken features the classic Mediterranean flavors of rosemary, lemon, and garlic.

Prep: 15 minutes **Bake:** 35 minutes **Oven:** 425°F
Makes: 6 servings

- 1 tablespoon snipped fresh rosemary or 1 teaspoon dried rosemary, crushed
- 1 teaspoon salt
- 1 teaspoon ground black pepper
- 2½ to 3 pounds meaty chicken pieces (breast halves, thighs, and drumsticks)
- 1 medium lemon
- 2 tablespoons olive oil
- 2 cloves garlic, minced, or 1 teaspoon bottled minced garlic

1. Preheat oven to 425°F. In a small bowl, combine rosemary, salt, and pepper. Using your fingers, rub rosemary mixture onto both sides of chicken pieces. Place chicken pieces, bone sides up, in a lightly greased 13×9×2-inch baking pan.

2. Finely shred 1 teaspoon peel from the lemon. Cut lemon in half; squeeze lemon to get 1 tablespoon juice. In a small bowl, combine lemon peel, lemon juice, oil, and garlic; drizzle over chicken pieces.

3. Bake chicken for 20 minutes. Turn chicken pieces bone sides down; spoon pan juices over chicken. Bake for 15 to 20 minutes more or until chicken is no longer pink (170°F for breasts; 180°F for thighs and drumsticks).

Per serving: 257 cal., 15 g total fat (4 g sat. fat), 86 mg chol., 464 mg sodium, 1 g carbo., 0 g fiber, 28 g pro.

Poached Chicken and [heart] [one] Pasta with Pesto Dressing

The chicken cooks in the same pot with the pasta, and a sprightly veggie-studded pesto sauce stirs together in a hurry to create a creamy and colorful version of chicken salad.

Start to Finish: 30 minutes **Makes:** 4 servings

- 6 ounces dried rotelle macaroni or rotini (about 2 cups)
- 12 ounces skinless, boneless chicken breast halves, cut into 1-inch pieces
- ¼ cup refrigerated pesto sauce
- ½ cup fat-free dairy sour cream
- 1 cup chopped fresh vegetables, such as red, yellow, or green sweet pepper; broccoli florets; zucchini; or cucumber
- 1 small tomato, chopped
- ¼ cup pine nuts or chopped walnuts, toasted (optional)

1. Cook pasta according to package directions, adding chicken the last 5 to 6 minutes of cooking. Cook until pasta is tender but firm and chicken is no longer pink. Drain pasta and chicken. Rinse with cold water and drain again.

2. In a large mixing bowl, combine pesto and sour cream. Add pasta mixture, chopped vegetables, and tomato. Toss lightly to coat. If desired, sprinkle with nuts.

Per serving: 404 cal., 13 g total fat (1 g sat. fat), 47 mg chol., 183 mg sodium, 43 g carbo., 1 g fiber, 26 g pro.

Pappardelle with Chicken And Peas [heart]

Pappardelle, which means "gulp down" in Italian, are long, wide, flat strands of pasta that perfectly pair with this chunky sauce.

Prep: 10 minutes **Cook:** 10 minutes **Makes:** 4 servings

- 6 ounces dried pappardelle or other wide egg noodles
- 1½ cups shelled sweet peas
- ½ of a 14.5-ounce can Italian-style stewed tomatoes, undrained
- 2 teaspoons olive oil
- 8 ounces skinless, boneless chicken breast, cut into large bite-size pieces
- 1 small onion, cut into thin wedges
- ¼ teaspoon coarsely ground black pepper
- ¼ cup chicken broth
- ¼ cup heavy whipping cream
- 2 tablespoons freshly grated Parmesan cheese (optional)

1. Cook pasta according to package directions, adding peas the last 3 minutes of cooking time. Meanwhile, place undrained tomatoes in a blender or food processor. Cover and blend or process until smooth; set aside.

2. In a large skillet, heat oil over medium-high heat. Add chicken, onion, and pepper; cook for 2 to 4 minutes or until chicken is just cooked through and no longer pink.

3. Carefully stir in broth and the blended tomato mixture. Return to boiling. Reduce heat and boil gently, uncovered, for 2 minutes. Stir in cream; boil gently for 3 minutes more or until sauce thickens slightly.

4. Drain pasta and peas; transfer to a warm serving dish. Spoon sauce over pasta and peas; toss gently. If desired, top with grated Parmesan cheese.

Per serving: 378 cal., 11 g total fat (4 g sat. fat), 94 mg chol., 214 mg sodium, 46 g carbo., 5 g fiber, 23 g pro.

Pappardelle with Chicken and Peas

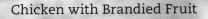

Chicken with Brandied Fruit

Chicken with Brandied Fruit ♥ [one]

Orange juice or apple juice makes a delicious substitute for the brandy in this recipe.

Start to Finish: 30 minutes **Makes:** 4 servings

- 4 **skinless, boneless chicken breast halves (about 1¼ pounds)**
- ¼ **cup all-purpose flour**
- ¼ **teaspoon salt**
- ¼ **teaspoon ground black pepper**
- 2 **tablespoons olive oil**
- 3 **cups thinly sliced nectarines or peaches**
- 3 **tablespoons brandy, orange juice, or apple juice**
- 2 **tablespoons water**
- 1 **tablespoon lemon juice**
- 2 **tablespoons sliced almonds, toasted**

1. Place each chicken breast half between 2 pieces of plastic wrap. Using the flat side of a meat mallet, pound chicken lightly to about ¼ inch thick.*

2. In a shallow dish, combine flour, salt, and pepper. Lightly coat chicken pieces on both sides with flour mixture; shake off excess.

3. In a large skillet, heat oil over medium-high heat. Add chicken; reduce heat to medium. Cook for 6 to 8 minutes or until chicken is no longer pink, turning occasionally to brown evenly. Remove skillet from heat. Remove chicken from skillet; cover to keep warm.

4. Add nectarines, brandy, water, and lemon juice to the skillet. Return skillet to heat and cook for 1 minute, stirring gently. Spoon fruit mixture over chicken. Sprinkle with almonds.

Per serving: 346 cal., 12 g total fat (2 g sat. fat), 82 mg chol., 242 mg sodium, 18 g carbo., 3 g fiber, 36 g pro.

*Note: If you like, skip pounding the chicken in Step 1. Prepare as above, except cook the chicken in the hot oil over medium heat for 10 to 12 minutes or until no longer pink (170°F), turning occasionally to brown evenly.

Chicken in a Phyllo Nest ♥

Leftover grilled steak or chunks of cooked salmon are appetizing substitutes for the chicken in this attractive main dish.

Start to Finish: 25 minutes **Makes:** 6 servings

	Nonstick cooking spray
10	sheets frozen phyllo dough (14×9-inch rectangles), thawed
2	tablespoons olive oil
1	cup 2-inch-long pieces green onions (1 bunch)
12	ounces refrigerated grilled chicken breast strips (3 cups)
1	6-ounce package fresh baby spinach
¾	cup cherry tomatoes, halved or quartered
1	tablespoon snipped fresh tarragon
¼	teaspoon freshly ground black pepper
½	cup bottled balsamic vinaigrette salad dressing

1. Preheat oven to 425°F. Lightly coat a 15×10×1-inch baking pan with cooking spray; set aside. Roll stack of phyllo sheets into a cylinder shape. Using a sharp knife, cut phyllo roll crosswise into ¼- to ½-inch slices. Gently separate phyllo into strips; spread strips evenly in the prepared baking pan. Coat phyllo generously with cooking spray. Bake for 8 to 10 minutes or until phyllo strips are golden brown.

2. Meanwhile, in a 12-inch skillet, heat oil over medium-high heat. Add green onions; cook about 1 minute or just until tender. Add chicken; cook and stir until heated through. Remove skillet from heat. Add spinach, cherry tomatoes, tarragon, and pepper. Toss to combine.

3. Divide phyllo among 6 bowls. Spoon chicken mixture over phyllo. Drizzle with salad dressing. Serve immediately.

Per serving: 197 cal., 10 g total fat (2 g sat. fat), 40 mg chol., 760 mg sodium, 14 g carbo., 1 g fiber, 14 g pro.

Chicken in a Phyllo Nest

Lemon Chicken

Lemon Chicken 🔲one

You'll love how the zingy flavors of lemon and garlic combine with the smoky-flavored adobo seasoning in this quick-to-make chicken dish. Bread crumbs from the coating on the chicken help thicken the sauce.

Prep: 20 minutes **Cook:** 15 minutes **Makes:** 4 servings

- 4 **skinless, boneless chicken breast halves (about 1¼ pounds)**
- ¼ **cup fat-free milk**
- ⅔ **cup fine dry bread crumbs**
- 2 **teaspoons adobo seasoning***
- 2 **tablespoons cooking oil**
- 1¾ **cups water**
- 1 **clove garlic, minced**
- 1 **lemon, halved crosswise**
- 1 **tablespoon snipped fresh parsley**
  Shredded lemon peel (optional)
  Lemon slices (optional)

1. Split chicken breast halves in half horizontally. Place milk in a shallow bowl. In a shallow dish, combine bread crumbs and adobo seasoning. Dip chicken pieces into milk, allowing excess to drip off. Dip chicken pieces into crumb mixture, turning to coat evenly.

2. In a very large nonstick skillet, heat cooking oil over medium heat. Add chicken; cook about 5 minutes or until browned, turning occasionally.

3. Add the water and garlic to skillet. Squeeze juice from one of the lemon halves over chicken. Bring to boiling; reduce heat. Simmer, uncovered, about 15 minutes or until sauce is thickened, stirring occasionally. Cut the remaining lemon half in half and then into slices.

4. Sprinkle chicken with parsley and, if desired, lemon peel. If desired, serve with the lemon slices.

Per serving: 254 cal., 8 g total fat (2 g sat. fat), 66 mg chol., 999 mg sodium, 15 g carbo., 1 g fiber, 29 g pro.

***Note:** Look for this seasoning blend at a market that specializes in Hispanic foods.

Quick Tip Before you halve the lemon for this recipe, finely shred the peel to sprinkle onto the finished dish for additional flavor. When shredding peel, be sure to remove only the yellow-colored part of the rind; the white pith could impart a bitter flavor.

Stuffed Chicken Breasts ♥ 🔲one

For extra zip, make the stuffing with a flavored feta cheese.

Prep: 25 minutes **Cook:** 12 minutes **Makes:** 4 servings

- 4 **skinless, boneless chicken breast halves (about 1¼ pounds)**
- 4 **ounces crumbled feta cheese with peppercorn, feta cheese with garlic and herb, or plain feta cheese**
- ½ **of a 7-ounce jar roasted red sweet peppers, drained and cut into strips (½ cup)**
- 1 **tablespoon olive oil**
- ¼ **cup chicken broth**

1. Place each chicken breast half between 2 pieces of plastic wrap. Pound lightly with the flat side of a meat mallet to ¼-inch thickness. Remove plastic wrap.

2. Sprinkle each chicken breast half with cheese. Place sweet pepper strips in center of each breast half. Fold narrow ends over filling; fold in sides. Roll up each breast half from a short side. Secure with wooden toothpicks.

3. In a medium nonstick skillet, heat oil over medium-high heat. Add chicken to skillet; cook about 5 minutes, turning to brown evenly. Add broth. Bring to boiling; reduce heat. Simmer, covered, for 7 to 8 minutes or until chicken is no longer pink (170°F). To serve, spoon juices over chicken.

Per serving: 265 cal., 11 g total fat (5 g sat. fat), 107 mg chol., 449 mg sodium, 2 g carbo., 0 g fiber, 37 g pro.

Tuscan Chicken 🔲one

If you can't find pesto seasoning, substitute dried Italian seasoning, which contains some of the same herbs.

Prep: 5 minutes **Cook:** 45 minutes **Makes:** 4 servings

- 2 **tablespoons olive oil**
- 2 **to 2½ pounds meaty chicken pieces (breast halves, thighs, and drumsticks)**
- 1¼ **teaspoons pesto seasoning or dried Italian seasoning, crushed**
- ½ **cup whole pitted kalamata olives**
- ½ **cup white wine or chicken broth**

1. In a 12-inch skillet, heat oil over medium heat. Add chicken to skillet; cook for 15 minutes, turning to brown evenly. Reduce heat. Drain off excess oil in skillet. Sprinkle pesto seasoning evenly over chicken. Add olives to skillet. Pour wine over all.

2. Cook, covered, for 25 minutes. Uncover; cook for 5 to 10 minutes more or until chicken is no longer pink (170°F for breasts; 180°F for thighs and drumsticks).

Per serving: 334 cal., 18 g total fat (4 g sat. fat), 104 mg chol., 280 mg sodium, 2 g carbo., 1 g fiber, 34 g pro.

Spring Chicken Scallopini

Spring Chicken Scallopini ♥ one

A buttery white wine sauce and fresh herbs dress up this chicken dish and add incredible fresh flavor. Best of all, the cutlets are fast and flashy.

Start to Finish: 25 minutes   **Makes:** 4 servings

- **4   skinless, boneless chicken breast halves (about 1¼ pounds)**
- ¼   **cup all-purpose flour**
- ¼   **teaspoon salt**
- **4   tablespoons butter**
- ½   **cup dry white wine (such as Sauvignon Blanc) and/or chicken broth**
- ¼   **cup sliced green onion**
- ½   **cup snipped mixed fresh herbs (such as oregano, thyme, lemon thyme, and/or mint)**
- ¼   **teaspoon coarsely ground black pepper**
- ⅛   **teaspoon salt***
       Steamed fresh asparagus (optional)

1. Place each chicken piece between 2 pieces of plastic wrap. Working from the center to the edges, pound lightly with the flat side of a meat mallet until chicken pieces are an even ¼-inch thickness. Remove plastic wrap. In a shallow dish, combine flour and the ¼ teaspoon salt. Coat chicken pieces with flour mixture.

2. In a 12-inch skillet, heat 2 tablespoons of the butter over medium heat. Add chicken; cook for 6 to 8 minutes or until chicken is tender and no longer pink (170°F), turning once. Transfer chicken to a serving platter; cover and keep warm.

3. Add white wine and/or broth and green onion to the skillet. Cook and stir for 1 minute, scraping up any browned bits from bottom of skillet. Cook about 1 minute more or until wine mixture is reduced to ⅓ cup. Remove from heat. Whisk in the remaining 2 tablespoons butter until melted. Stir in half of the snipped fresh herbs, the pepper, and the ⅛ teaspoon salt.

4. Drizzle wine sauce over individual servings; sprinkle with remaining fresh herbs. If desired, serve with steamed asparagus.

Per serving: 317 cal., 14 g total fat (8 g sat. fat), 113 mg chol., 380 mg sodium, 7 g carbo., 0 g fiber, 34 g pro.

***Note:** If using chicken broth rather than wine, omit the ⅛ teaspoon salt.

Quick Tip To steam asparagus, snap off and discard woody bases from fresh asparagus. Bias-slice asparagus into 1-inch-long pieces. Steam asparagus for 3 to 5 minutes or until tender.

Szechwan-Fried Chicken Breasts ♥ [one]

Szechwan Chinese cuisine is known for its hot, spicy dishes. In this dish, while chile oil spikes up the heat, the sweetness from the apricot preserves tempers it.

Start to Finish: 30 minutes **Makes:** 4 servings

- 1 **tablespoon soy sauce**
- 1 **teaspoon grated fresh ginger**
- 1 **teaspoon chile oil**
- ½ **teaspoon sugar**
- ½ **cup all-purpose flour**
- 4 **skinless, boneless chicken breast halves (about 1¼ pounds)**
- 1 **tablespoon cooking oil**
- ¼ **cup apricot preserves**
- ¼ **cup chicken broth**
  Shredded orange peel (optional)
  Snipped fresh chives (optional)
  Hot cooked rice (optional)

1. In a small bowl, stir together soy sauce, ginger, ½ teaspoon of the chile oil, and the sugar; set aside.

2. Place flour in a shallow bowl. Brush both sides of each chicken breast half with soy sauce mixture; dip in flour to coat. In a large nonstick skillet, heat cooking oil over medium-high heat. Add chicken; cook for 8 to 10 minutes or until tender and no longer pink (170°F), turning once. Remove chicken from skillet; cover and keep warm.

3. For the sauce, add apricot preserves, chicken broth, and the remaining ½ teaspoon chile oil to skillet. Cook and stir over medium heat until preserves melt and mixture is heated through. Spoon sauce over chicken. If desired, sprinkle with orange peel. If desired, stir chives into hot cooked rice; serve with chicken.

Per serving: 315 cal., 7 g total fat (1 g sat. fat), 82 mg chol., 374 mg sodium, 25 g carbo., 1 g fiber, 35 g pro.

Quick Tip If you don't have chicken broth on hand, stir together ¼ cup hot water and ¼ teaspoon instant bouillon granules until dissolved.

Szechwan-Fried Chicken Breasts

BBQ Chicken Burgers and Waffle Fries

Mini burgers bake in just 12 minutes, so let the waffle fries get a head start in the oven before popping in the burgers.

Start to Finish: 30 minutes **Oven:** 425°F
Makes: 4 servings

⅓ **cup bottled barbecue sauce**
⅓ **cup grape jelly or seedless raspberry jam**
3 **cups frozen waffle-cut or thick-cut french-fried potatoes**
4 **slices packaged ready-to-serve cooked bacon, chopped**
2 **tablespoons fine dry bread crumbs**
2 **tablespoons finely chopped honey-roasted walnuts or almonds**
1 **tablespoon bottled barbecue sauce**
½ **teaspoon poultry seasoning**
¼ **teaspoon salt**
⅛ **teaspoon ground black pepper**
8 **ounces uncooked ground chicken or turkey**
½ **cup shredded Italian-blend cheeses or Monterey Jack cheese with jalapeño peppers**
Snipped fresh chives
8 **dinner rolls or cocktail-size hamburger buns, split**
Tomato slices and/or lettuce leaves

1. Preheat oven to 425°F. In a small bowl, combine the ⅓ cup barbecue sauce and the jelly. Mix with a wire whisk until smooth. Set aside.

2. Arrange waffle-cut potatoes in a single layer on an ungreased baking sheet. Sprinkle with chopped bacon. Bake for 8 minutes.

3. Meanwhile, in a medium bowl, combine bread crumbs, nuts, the 1 tablespoon barbecue sauce, poultry seasoning, salt, and pepper. Add ground chicken; mix well. Shape into 8 balls; place 2 inches apart on greased shallow baking pan. Moisten the bottom of a glass and press each ball to about ¼-inch thickness.

4. Place pan of burgers in oven. Bake fries and burgers for 5 minutes. Stir fries; turn burgers. Continue baking burgers and potatoes for 5 minutes more.

5. Sprinkle cheese over fries. Brush barbecue-jelly mixture on burgers. Bake burgers and potatoes 2 minutes more or until burgers are no longer pink in center and cheese is melted on fries.

6. To serve, sprinkle fries with snipped chives. Place burgers in dinner rolls with additional barbecue-jelly mixture spooned over. Top with tomato slices and/or lettuce leaves.

Per serving: 537 cal., 21 g total fat (7 g sat. fat), 20 mg chol., 902 mg sodium, 66 g carbo., 4 g fiber, 22 g pro.

Tomato Pesto Chicken Rolls ♥

If tomato pesto isn't available at your grocery store, use traditional basil pesto instead.

Prep: 30 minutes **Bake:** 10 minutes + 15 minutes
Oven: 400°F **Makes:** 6 servings

Nonstick cooking spray
6 **skinless, boneless chicken breast halves (about 1¾ pounds)**
⅛ **teaspoon ground black pepper**
½ **of an 8-ounce tub fat-free cream cheese**
2 **tablespoons purchased dried tomato pesto**
2 **tablespoons olive oil**
⅓ **cup seasoned fine dry bread crumbs**
1 **pound fresh asparagus spears**

1. Preheat oven to 400°F. Lightly coat a 9×9×2-inch baking pan and a shallow roasting pan with nonstick cooking spray; set aside.

2. Place a chicken breast half between 2 pieces of plastic wrap. Using the flat side of a meat mallet, pound chicken until ¼ inch thick. Remove plastic wrap. Repeat with remaining chicken breast halves. Sprinkle chicken with pepper.

3. In a small bowl, stir together cream cheese and tomato pesto. Place 2 tablespoons of the cream cheese mixture in the center of each chicken breast. Fold in sides and roll up. Secure with wooden toothpicks. Brush chicken rolls with 1 tablespoon of the oil; roll in bread crumbs. Place, seam sides down, in prepared baking pan.

4. Bake, uncovered, for 10 minutes. Meanwhile, snap off and discard woody bases from asparagus. If desired, scrape off scales. Toss asparagus with remaining 1 tablespoon oil; arrange in prepared roasting pan. Place in oven alongside chicken.

5. Bake, uncovered, for 15 to 20 minutes more or until asparagus is crisp-tender and chicken is no longer pink (170°F).

Per serving: 254 cal., 8 g total fat (2 g sat. fat), 79 mg chol., 326 mg sodium, 8 g carbo., 1 g fiber, 36 g pro.

Tomato Pesto Chicken Rolls

Chicken Thighs and Orzo  one

Pancetta—Italy's famous unsmoked bacon—is flavored with white wine and black pepper. It adds superb flavor to this Mediterranean-inspired main dish.

Prep: 20 minutes **Cook:** 25 minutes **Makes:** 6 servings

- 1 **4-ounce package pancetta, chopped, or 4 slices bacon, chopped**
   Olive oil
- 6 **chicken thighs (about 2¼ pounds), skinned**
- 2 **14.5-ounce cans diced tomatoes with garlic and onion**
- 1 **cup dried orzo**
- 2 **cloves garlic, minced**
- ⅓ **cup pitted kalamata olives**
- ¼ **cup snipped fresh basil**
- 1 **6-ounce bag prewashed baby spinach leaves**
- 3 **ounces goat cheese with basil and roasted garlic (about ⅓ cup)**

1. In a 5- to 6-quart Dutch oven, oven cook pancetta over medium heat until browned. Remove pancetta, reserving 2 tablespoons of drippings in pan (if necessary, add olive oil to equal 2 tablespoons). Drain pancetta on paper towels; set aside. Cook chicken in drippings about 10 minutes or until light brown, turning to brown evenly; drain off fat. Add undrained tomatoes, orzo, garlic, and 1 cup water. Bring to boiling; reduce heat.

2. Simmer, covered, 25 to 30 minutes or until chicken is no longer pink (180°F) and orzo is tender. If necessary, cook, uncovered, 2 to 3 minutes or until sauce is desired consistency. Stir in pancetta, olives, and basil; heat through. Divide spinach among 6 plates. Top each with a thigh, some of the orzo mixture, and some of the cheese.

Per serving: 395 cal., 18 g total fat (5 g sat. fat), 77 mg chol., 1,229 mg sodium, 32 g carbo., 2 g fiber, 26 g pro.

Quick Tip If you like, use baby arugula in place of the spinach. It adds an aromatic, peppery flavor to the dish.

Chicken Thighs and Orzo

Chicken and Pasta

Bottled minced garlic is a hurried cook's friend. You'll find it in your supermarket's produce section.

Start to Finish: 30 minutes   **Makes:** 4 servings

- 1½   **teaspoons coarsely ground pepper blend**
- ¾   **teaspoon salt**
- ½   **teaspoon bottled minced garlic (1 clove)**
- 4   **skinless, boneless chicken breasts (about 1¼ pounds total)**
- 2   **tablespoons olive oil**
- 2   **large onions, sliced**
- 3   **medium tomatoes, chopped**
- 1   **tablespoon tomato paste**
- 2   **to 3 teaspoons grated fresh ginger**
- 8   **ounces dried spaghetti pasta**
- ¼   **cup purchased pesto**
  Parmesan cheese shavings (optional)

1. In a small bowl, combine 1 teaspoon of the pepper blend, ½ teaspoon of the salt, and the garlic. Sprinkle evenly over chicken. In a large skillet, heat oil over medium heat. Add chicken and onions; cook about 15 minutes or until chicken is tender and no longer pink (170°F) and onions are tender, turning chicken once and stirring onions occasionally.

2. Remove chicken from skillet; slice crosswise into strips. Return chicken to skillet; add tomatoes, tomato paste, ginger, the remaining ½ teaspoon pepper blend, and the remaining ¼ teaspoon salt. Cook and stir just until heated through.

3. Meanwhile, cook spaghetti according to package directions. Drain. Return spaghetti to the hot pan and stir in pesto.

4. Serve the chicken and tomato mixture on top of pesto-coated spaghetti. If desired, top with shavings of Parmesan cheese.

Per serving: 597 cal., 20 g total fat (2 g sat. fat), 84 mg chol., 641 mg sodium, 59 g carbo., 4 g fiber, 44 g pro.

Peruvian-Style Chicken Tacos ♥ 🄾🄽🄴

Potatoes, plums, and green olives create a South American accent in these chicken tacos.

Start to Finish: 30 minutes   **Oven:** 350°F
Makes: 12 tacos (4 servings)

- 1   **pound uncooked ground chicken**
- ½   **cup chopped onion**
- 2   **teaspoons ground coriander**
- 2   **teaspoons ground cumin**
- 1   **14.5-ounce can diced tomatoes**
- 1   **potato, peeled and finely chopped**
- ¼   **cup snipped pitted dried plums**
- ¼   **cup chopped pimiento-stuffed green olives**
- 12   **6- to 7-inch corn or flour tortillas**
- 4   **to 6 ounce Cotija or Monterey Jack cheese, shredded**

1. Preheat oven to 350°F. In a large skillet, cook chicken and onion until chicken is no longer pink; stir to break up pieces. If necessary, drain off fat. Add coriander, cumin, and 1 teaspoon salt; cook and stir for 1 to 2 minutes.

2. Add undrained tomatoes, potato, plums, and olives. Bring to boiling; reduce heat. Simmer, covered, 12 to 15 minutes or until potatoes are tender. Uncover; cook 5 minutes more or until most of the liquid has evaporated. Wrap tortillas in foil; bake for 15 minutes or until heated.

3. To assemble, place ⅓ cup chicken mixture in center of each tortilla; top with cheese. Fold tortillas in half.

Per taco: 194 cal., 10 g total fat (0 g sat. fat), 9 mg chol., 328 mg sodium, 18 g carbo., 3 g fiber, 11 g pro.

Chicken and Pasta

Chicken with Cherry Tomatoes

Chicken with Cherry Tomatoes ♥ one

The simple topping of delightfully tangy red and yellow cherry tomatoes makes this meal perfect for busy weeknights.

Prep: 15 minutes **Cook:** 10 minutes **Makes:** 4 servings

- 4 **skinless, boneless chicken breast halves (about 1¼ pounds)**
- ½ **teaspoon salt**
- ¼ **teaspoon ground black pepper**
- 2 **teaspoons extra-virgin olive oil**
- 2 **cups red and/or yellow cherry tomatoes, halved**
- 2 **tablespoons water**
- ½ **teaspoon dried parsley, basil, or tarragon, crushed**
- 1 **tablespoon white wine vinegar**

1. Sprinkle chicken with ¼ teaspoon of the salt and ⅛ teaspoon of the pepper. In a large nonstick skillet, heat oil over medium-high heat. Add chicken; cook for 10 to 12 minutes or until chicken is no longer pink (170°F), turning once. Transfer chicken to a serving platter; cover and keep warm.

2. Drain fat from skillet. Add tomatoes, the water, parsley, vinegar, the remaining ¼ teaspoon salt, and the remaining ⅛ teaspoon pepper to skillet.

3. Bring to boiling; reduce heat. Simmer, uncovered, for 3 to 4 minutes or until tomatoes begin to soften, stirring occasionally. Serve tomato mixture over chicken.

Per serving: 163 cal., 4 g total fat (1 g sat. fat), 66 mg chol., 320 mg sodium, 4 g carbo., 1 g fiber, 27 g pro.

Chicken Fingers

Chicken Fingers ♥ 🔲

A mixture of egg, honey, and mustard serves as the glue to hold crunchy cornflake crumbs onto chicken strips. They are baked instead of fried for a healthier entrée.

Prep: 15 minutes **Bake:** 12 minutes **Oven:** 450°F
Makes: 4 servings

- **12   ounces skinless, boneless chicken breast halves**
- **1   egg, lightly beaten**
- **1   tablespoon honey**
- **1   teaspoon prepared mustard**
- **1   cup packaged cornflake crumbs or 2 cups cornflakes, finely crushed**
-    **Dash ground black pepper**
-    **Purchased dipping sauce (optional)**

1. Preheat oven to 450°F. Cut chicken into 3×¾-inch strips. In a shallow dish, combine egg, honey, and mustard. In another shallow dish, stir together cornflake crumbs and pepper. Dip chicken strips into the egg mixture; roll in crumb mixture to coat. Arrange chicken strips on an ungreased baking sheet.

2. Bake about 12 minutes or until golden and chicken is no longer pink. If desired, serve with your favorite dipping sauce.

Per serving: 212 cal., 3 g total fat (1 g sat. fat), 102 mg chol., 236 mg sodium, 23 g carbo., 0 g fiber, 23 g pro.

Quick Tip Store poultry in the coldest part of the refrigerator (40°F or below) as soon as you get it home from the supermarket. Raw poultry can be refrigerated for up to 2 days and frozen for up to 6 months.

Honey-Orange Chicken ♥

Removing skin from chicken reduces the fat while the marinade enhances the flavor and keeps the chicken moist during baking.

Prep: 20 minutes **Bake:** 45 minutes **Oven:** 375°F
Marinate: 2 to 4 hours **Makes:** 4 servings

- 2 **pounds meaty chicken pieces (breast halves, thighs, and drumsticks)**
- ½ **cup orange juice**
- 1 **tablespoon olive oil**
- 1 **tablespoon grated fresh ginger**
- 1 **teaspoon paprika**
- 1 **teaspoon ground cumin**
- ½ **teaspoon ground coriander**
- ¼ **teaspoon crushed red pepper**
- ⅛ **teaspoon salt**
- 2 **teaspoons finely shredded orange peel**
- 2 **tablespoons honey**
- 2 **teaspoons orange juice**

1. Remove skin from chicken. Place chicken in large resealable plastic bag and set in shallow dish. For the marinade, in a small bowl, combine ½ cup orange juice, oil, ginger, paprika, cumin, coriander, crushed red pepper, and salt. Pour over chicken; seal bag. Marinate in refrigerator for 2 to 4 hours, turning bag occasionally.

2. Meanwhile, in small bowl, combine orange peel, honey, and 2 teaspoons orange juice; set aside. Drain chicken, discarding marinade.

3. Preheat oven to 375°F. Place chicken, skinned sides up, in a shallow baking dish. Bake for 45 to 55 minutes or until chicken is done (170°F for breast halves; 180°F for thighs and drumsticks); brush occasionally with honey mixture during the last 10 minutes of baking.

Per serving: 217 cal., 5 g total fat (1 g sat. fat), 94 mg chol., 141 mg sodium, 11 g carbo., 0 g fiber, 30 g pro.

Honey-Orange Chicken

Southern Chicken Salad

Layer Texas toast with greens, fresh herbs, and a lively tasting dressing, then top with peaches and chicken for a tasty Southern treat. Serve this salad next time you plan to take dinner outdoors—it makes great picnic fare.

Start to Finish: 20 minutes **Makes:** 4 servings

- ½ **cup purchased crème fraîche or dairy sour cream**
- ¼ **cup white wine vinegar**
- 3 **to 4 tablespoons Dijon mustard**
- 2 **cloves garlic, minced**
- ½ **teaspoon salt**
- ¼ **teaspoon ground black pepper**
- 6 **cups torn mixed salad greens, such as romaine, spinach, baby mustard greens, or tatsoi**
- ½ **cup lightly packed small fresh mint leaves**
- 2 **tablespoon shredded fresh basil or marjoram leaves**
- 4 **slices Texas toast or large slices sourdough bread, toasted**
- 2 **to 4 tablespoons honey butter**
- 1 **2- to 2½-pound purchased roasted chicken, quartered***
- 4 **medium peaches or nectarines, pitted and sliced**

1. For the dressing, in a small bowl, whisk together crème fraîche, white wine vinegar, mustard, garlic, salt, and pepper; set aside.

2. In a large bowl, toss together the greens, mint, and basil or marjoram. Spread each toast slice with honey butter and place one slice on each of 4 serving plates. Top each with some of the greens. Arrange chicken and peaches on top of greens. Drizzle with dressing.

Per serving: 677 cal., 36 g total fat (13 g sat. fat), 218 mg chol., 965 mg sodium, 37 g carbo., 3 g fiber, 52 g pro.

*Note: Chicken can be warm or chilled in this salad.

Quick Tip If you don't have honey butter on hand, you can make it yourself: In a small bowl, stir together ¼ cup unsalted butter (softened), ¼ cup honey, and 1 teaspoon lemon juice. Cover and store in the refrigerator for up to one week.

Basil-Tomato Chicken Skillet

Basil-Tomato Chicken Skillet ♥ [one]

To cut the fat, cook in a skillet coated with cooking spray instead of oil. Always spray the pan before heating.

Start to Finish: 20 minutes **Makes:** 4 servings

- 1 to 1¼ pounds chicken breast tenderloins
  Nonstick cooking spray
- ⅛ teaspoon salt
- ⅛ teaspoon ground black pepper
- 1 14.5-ounce can no-salt-added diced tomatoes, drained
- ¼ cup snipped fresh basil
- 1 9- to 10-ounce package prewashed spinach
- 2 tablespoons finely shredded Parmesan cheese

1. Cut any large chicken tenderloins in half lengthwise. Coat an unheated 12-inch skillet with cooking spray.

2. Heat skillet over medium heat. Add chicken; cook and stir about 5 minutes or until no longer pink. Sprinkle with salt and pepper.

3. Add tomatoes and basil; heat through. Remove from heat. Add spinach; toss until wilted. Divide among 4 plates. Sprinkle with Parmesan cheese.

Per serving: 170 cal., 2 g total fat (1 g sat. fat), 68 mg chol., 265 mg sodium, 7 g carbo., 3 g fiber, 30 g pro.

Pan-Roasted Chicken With Shallots ♥ [one]

So simple but so delicious, this bistro-style dish is great for a special-occasion dinner.

Start to Finish: 20 minutes **Makes:** 4 servings

- 8 shallots or 1 large onion
- 4 skinless, boneless chicken breast halves (about 1¼ pounds)
  Salt and ground black pepper
- 1 tablespoon olive oil
- 1 medium zucchini, halved lengthwise and cut into ¼-inch slices
- ¼ cup snipped fresh parsley

1. Peel shallots; halve small shallots and quarter large shallots. If using onion, cut into thin wedges (you should have about 1 cup); set aside. Sprinkle chicken with salt and pepper. In a large skillet, heat oil over medium heat. Add chicken; cook for 2 minutes.

2. Turn chicken. Add shallots to skillet. Sprinkle shallots lightly with additional salt and pepper. Cook for 8 to 10 minutes more or until chicken is no longer pink (170°F), stirring shallots frequently and turning chicken, if necessary, to brown evenly. If necessary, add additional oil to prevent sticking. Reduce heat to medium low if chicken or shallots brown too quickly.

3. Transfer chicken and shallots to a serving platter. Cover to keep warm. Add zucchini to skillet. Cook and stir for 3 to 5 minutes or until crisp-tender. Add to platter with chicken. Sprinkle with parsley.

Per serving: 193 cal., 5 g total fat (1 g sat. fat), 66 mg chol., 231 mg sodium, 9 g carbo., 1 g fiber, 28 g pro.

Mexican Chicken Casserole

A deli-roasted chicken tops the list of convenient chicken products. Here we jazz it up with Mexican seasonings.

Prep: 15 minutes **Bake:** 15 minutes **Oven:** 350°F
Makes: 4 servings

- 1 15-ounce can black beans, rinsed and drained
- ½ cup chunky salsa
- ½ teaspoon ground cumin
- 1 2- to 2¼-pound deli-roasted chicken
- ¼ cup shredded Monterey Jack cheese with jalapeño peppers (1 ounce)
  Dairy sour cream (optional)

1. Preheat oven to 350°F. In a small bowl, stir together drained beans, ¼ cup of the salsa, and the cumin. Divide bean mixture among 4 individual au gratin dishes or casseroles; set aside.

2. Cut chicken into quarters. Place one piece on bean mixture in each dish. Spoon remaining ¼ cup salsa evenly over chicken pieces. Sprinkle evenly with cheese.

3. Bake for 15 to 20 minutes or until heated through. If desired, serve with sour cream.

Per serving: 468 cal., 23 g total fat (7 g sat. fat), 140 mg chol., 596 mg sodium, 16 g carbo., 5 g fiber, 50 g pro.

Mexican Chicken Casserole

Turkey and Soba Noodle Stir-Fry

Turkey and Soba Noodle Stir-Fry 🖤

Japanese buckwheat noodles, also called soba noodles, give this stir-fry a nutty flavor and pleasant chewy texture.

Start to Finish: 25 minutes **Makes:** 4 servings

- **6 ounces dried soba (buckwheat) noodles or whole wheat spaghetti pasta**
- **2 teaspoons extra-virgin olive oil**
- **2 cups fresh sugar snap peas**
- **1 medium red sweet pepper, cut into thin strips**
- **2 teaspoons minced fresh ginger**
- **4 cloves garlic, minced (2 teaspoons minced)**
- **4 green onions, bias-sliced into 1-inch pieces**
- **12 ounces turkey breast tenderloin, cut into bite-size strips**
- **1 teaspoon toasted sesame oil**
- **½ cup bottled plum sauce**
- **¼ teaspoon crushed red pepper**

1. Cook soba noodles according to package directions; drain. Return to hot pan; cover and keep warm.

2. Meanwhile, pour oil into a wok or large skillet. (Add more olive oil as necessary during cooking.) Heat over medium-high heat. Stir-fry peas, sweet pepper, ginger, and garlic in hot oil for 2 minutes. Add green onion. Stir-fry for 1 to 2 minutes more or until vegetables are crisp-tender. Remove vegetables from wok.

3. Add turkey and sesame oil to the hot wok. Stir-fry for 3 to 4 minutes or until turkey is tender and no longer pink. Add plum sauce and crushed red pepper. Return cooked vegetables to wok; stir to coat all ingredients with sauce. Heat through. Serve immediately over noodles.

Per serving: 368 cal., 5 g total fat (1 g sat. fat), 53 mg chol., 409 mg sodium, 55 g carbo., 4 g fiber, 29 g pro.

Quick Tip If your supermarket doesn't carry soba noodles, look for them at Asian food stores. Or opt for whole wheat spaghetti for a similar nutty flavor.

Turkey Supper Salad

Look for prewashed and presliced white button mushrooms in your supermarket's produce section. That way, you save time cleaning and slicing the mushrooms. Serve this satisfying salad with breadsticks or thick slices of crusty bread.

Start to Finish: 15 minutes **Makes:** 4 servings

- **4   cups packaged torn mixed greens**
- **2   cups sliced mushrooms**
- **8   ounces smoked turkey, cut into bite-size strips**
- **¾   cup mild Cheddar cheese cubes**
- **¼   cup bottled light Caesar or Italian salad dressing**

1. In a very large salad bowl, combine greens, mushrooms, turkey, and cheese. Drizzle with salad dressing and toss to coat. Serve immediately.

Per serving: 212 cal., 13 g total fat (6 g sat. fat), 57 mg chol., 1,017 mg sodium, 5 g carbo., 1 g fiber, 20 g pro.

Turkey-Pesto Pot Pie

These breadstick-topped mini pot pies excel in eye appeal as well as flavor. Additional breadsticks bake alongside the individual casseroles, so you'll have extra for sopping up every last bit of the turkey gravy.

Prep: 15 minutes **Bake:** 15 minutes **Oven:** 375°F
Makes: 6 servings

- **1   12-ounce jar turkey gravy**
- **⅓   cup purchased basil or dried tomato pesto**
- **3   cups cubed cooked turkey (about 1 pound)**
- **1   16-ounce package frozen peas and carrots**
- **1   11-ounce package refrigerated breadsticks (12)**
       Grated Parmesan cheese (optional)
       Dried basil (optional)

1. Preheat oven to 375°F. In a large saucepan, combine turkey gravy and pesto; stir in turkey and vegetables. Bring to boiling, stirring frequently. Divide turkey mixture evenly among six 8-ounce casseroles.

2. Cut 6 of the breadsticks into 6 pieces. Place remaining breadsticks onto a baking sheet. Divide breadstick pieces among the dishes.

3. Bake casseroles about 15 minutes or until breadsticks are golden. Bake remaining breadsticks according to package directions.

Per serving: 365 cal., 16 g total fat (5 g sat. fat), 52 mg chol., 964 mg sodium, 36 g carbo., 4 g fiber, 20 g pro.

Five-Spice Turkey Stir-Fry

Use a wok if you have one, or a skillet, to get this easy sizzling stir-fry to the table in a flash. Five-spice powder—a seasoning blend of ground cinnamon, cloves, star anise, fennel seed, and Szechwan peppercorns—will lend a familiar Chinese flavor.

Start to Finish: 25 minutes **Makes:** 4 servings

- **1   4.4-ounce package beef lo mein noodle mix**
- **12   ounces turkey breast tenderloin, cut into bite-size strips**
- **¼   teaspoon five-spice powder**
- **¼   teaspoon salt**
- **¼   teaspoon ground black pepper**
- **2   tablespoons cooking oil**
- **½   of a 16-ounce package (2 cups) frozen stir-fry vegetables (yellow, green, and red peppers and onion)**
- **2   tablespoons chopped honey-roasted peanuts or peanuts**

1. Prepare noodle mix according to package directions. Set aside. In a small bowl, toss together turkey strips, five-spice powder, salt, and pepper; set aside.

2. Pour 1 tablespoon of the oil into a wok or large skillet. Heat over medium-high heat. Carefully add frozen vegetables to wok; cook and stir for 3 minutes. Remove vegetables from wok. Add remaining 1 tablespoon oil to hot wok. Add turkey mixture to wok; cook and stir for 2 to 3 minutes or until turkey is no longer pink. Return cooked vegetables to wok. Cook and stir about 1 minute more or until heated through.

3. To serve, divide noodle mixture among 4 dinner plates. Top with turkey mixture. Sprinkle with peanuts.

Per serving: 314 cal., 11 g total fat (2 g sat. fat), 76 mg chol., 670 mg sodium, 26 g carbo., 3 g fiber, 27 g pro.

Turkey-Pesto Pot Pie

Turkey-Potato Bake

If you grew up loving those saucy, delicious poultry-and-cheese casseroles—but find them too rich and heavy now—this is a light, modern version every bit as comforting. Quick and simple to make, too, with just 5 ingredients to blend then bake.

Prep: 15 minutes **Bake:** 30 minutes
Stand: 10 minutes **Oven:** 400°F **Makes:** 4 servings

2¼ **cups water**
1 **4.5- to 5-ounce package dry julienne potato mix**
2 **cups chopped cooked turkey or chicken breast (10 ounces)**
1 **cup shredded Cheddar cheese (4 ounces)**
1 **teaspoon dried parsley flakes**
⅔ **cup milk**

1. Preheat oven to 400°F. In a medium saucepan, bring the water to boiling. Meanwhile, in a 2-quart square baking dish, combine dry potatoes and sauce mix from potato mix. Stir in turkey, ½ cup of the Cheddar cheese, and the parsley flakes. Stir in the boiling water and the milk.

2. Bake, uncovered, for 30 to 35 minutes or until potatoes are tender. Sprinkle with the remaining ½ cup cheese. Let stand for 10 minutes before serving (mixture will thicken on standing).

Per serving: 370 cal., 15 g total fat (8 g sat. fat), 87 mg chol., 1,050 mg sodium, 27 g carbo., 1 g fiber, 32 g pro.

Parmesan-Sesame-Crusted Turkey one

Parmesan cheese and crunchy sesame seeds create a flavorful, crispy coating for lean turkey tenders.

Start to Finish: 20 minutes **Makes:** 4 servings

½ **cup finely shredded Parmesan cheese**
¼ **cup sesame seeds**
1 **egg, lightly beaten**
4 **turkey breast tenders, ½ inch thick**
¼ **teaspoon salt**
¼ **teaspoon ground black pepper**
1 **tablespoon olive oil or cooking oil**

1. In a shallow dish, combine Parmesan cheese and sesame seeds. Place egg in another shallow dish. Dip turkey slices into egg; coat with Parmesan cheese mixture. Sprinkle turkey slices with salt and pepper.

2. In a large skillet, heat oil over medium-high heat. Add turkey; cook turkey in hot oil for 8 to 10 minutes or until turkey is no longer pink (170°F), turning once.

Per serving: 498 cal., 28 g total fat (13 g sat. fat), 171 mg chol., 1,336 mg sodium, 3 g carbo., 1 g fiber, 57 g pro.

Turkey and Peppers

How can something so low in calories taste so good? The contrast of sweet and hot peppers does the trick. Serve the turkey slices over rice to soak up the flavorful juices.

Start to Finish: 25 minutes **Makes:** 4 servings

4 **¼- to ⅜-inch turkey breast slices (about 12 ounces)**
Salt
Ground black pepper
1 **tablespoon olive oil**
2 **medium red, yellow, and/or green sweet peppers, cut into thin strips**
1 **medium onion, halved lengthwise and sliced**
1 **fresh jalapeño pepper, seeded and thinly sliced***
¾ **cup chicken broth**
1 **tablespoon all-purpose flour**
1 **teaspoon paprika**
Hot cooked rice (optional)

1. Sprinkle turkey lightly with salt and black pepper. In a large nonstick skillet, cook turkey in hot oil over medium-high heat for 4 to 5 minutes or until turkey is tender and no longer pink (170°F), turning once. (If necessary, reduce heat to medium to prevent overbrowning.) Transfer turkey to a serving platter; cover and keep warm.

2. Add sweet pepper, onion, and jalapeño pepper to skillet. Cook, covered, for 4 to 5 minutes or until vegetables are crisp-tender, stirring occasionally.

3. In a screw-top jar combine broth, flour, and paprika; shake well. Add to sweet pepper mixture. Cook and stir over medium heat until thickened and bubbly. Cook and stir for 1 minute more. If desired, serve turkey on hot cooked rice. Spoon the sweet pepper mixture over turkey and rice.

Nutrition Facts per serving: 167 cal., 5 g total fat (1 g sat. fat), 51 mg chol., 260 mg sodium, 8 g carbo., 2 g fiber, 22 g pro.

*****Note:** Because chile peppers can contain volatile oils that can burn your skin and eyes, avoid direct contact with them as much as possible. When working, with chile peppers, wear plastic or rubber gloves. If your bare hands do touch the chile peppers, wash your hands and nails well with soap and warm water.

Turkey and Peppers

Sausage and Vegetables With Polenta one

Refrigerated cooked polenta is a wonderful time saver. Look for it in the produce section of the supermarket.

Start to Finish: 30 minutes **Makes:** 4 servings

1	tablespoon olive oil
1	1-pound tube refrigerated cooked polenta, cut into 12 slices and quartered
8	ounces light smoked turkey sausage, halved lengthwise and cut into ½-inch slices
2	medium red, green, and/or yellow sweet peppers, cut into bite-size pieces
1	medium onion, cut into bite-size pieces
1	cup sliced fresh mushrooms
½	cup bottled pasta sauce

1. In a 12-inch nonstick skillet, heat the oil over medium heat. Add polenta in a single layer; cook for 10 to 12 minutes or until light brown, stirring occasionally. Remove polenta from skillet; keep warm.

2. Add sausage, sweet pepper, onion, and mushrooms to skillet. Cook and stir until sausage is brown and vegetables are crisp-tender. Stir in pasta sauce. Add polenta; gently toss to combine all ingredients. Heat through.

Per serving: 260 cal., 9 g total fat (2 g sat. fat), 38 mg chol., 1,088 mg sodium, 32 g carbo., 5 g fiber, 14 g pro.

Quick Tip Purchase mushrooms that are firm and evenly colored with tightly closed caps. Avoid those that are broken, damaged, or have soft spots. Store fresh mushrooms, unwashed, in a paper bag in the refrigerator for up to 3 days. Clean mushrooms with a damp paper towel just before using.

Apricot Turkey Steaks 🔲

These moist, tender turkey steaks receive a double dose of fruit flavor from apricot nectar and apricot preserves. Packaged rice mix—a great starting point for fast dishes—gives this entrée lots of flavor and makes it easy to prepare.

Start to Finish: 25 minutes **Makes:** 4 servings

- **1 6-ounce package chicken-flavored rice and vermicelli mix**
- **2 turkey breast tenderloins (about 1¼ pounds)**
- **1 5.5-ounce can apricot nectar**
- **½ teaspoon salt**
- **⅛ teaspoon ground cinnamon**
   Dash ground black pepper
- **3 tablespoons apricot preserves**
- **1½ teaspoons cornstarch**

1. Prepare rice mix according to package directions. Set aside.

2. Meanwhile, split each turkey breast tenderloin in half horizontally to make a total of four turkey steaks. In a large skillet, combine apricot nectar, salt, cinnamon, and pepper. Add turkey steaks. Bring to boiling; reduce heat. Cover and simmer about 10 minutes or until turkey is no longer pink (170°F).

3. Transfer turkey steaks to a serving platter, reserving cooking liquid in the skillet. Cover turkey; keep warm.

4. For the sauce, in a small bowl, stir together apricot preserves and cornstarch; stir into reserved cooking liquid in the skillet. Cook and stir until thickened and bubbly. Cook and stir for 2 minutes more. Spoon rice mixture onto the serving platter. Pour some of the sauce over turkey; pass remaining sauce.

Per serving: 374 cal., 2 g total fat (1 g sat. fat), 88 mg chol., 1,054 mg sodium, 48 g carbo., 1 g fiber, 39 g pro.

Quick Tip To split the turkey breast tenderloins in half horizontally, lay the tenderloin flat on a plastic cutting board. Place one hand on top of the tenderloin. Hold the tenderloin down while you carefully glide a sharp knife horizontally through the center of the tenderloin. Note: If your cutting board tends to slip, place a damp paper towel underneath the board to hold it in place while cutting.

Turkey Marsala with Mushrooms 🔲

To cut up parsley or any fresh herb quickly, place the leaves in a glass measuring cup and use kitchen scissors to finely snip the herb. Look for sliced baby portobello mushrooms, also called cremini mushrooms, for the most robust flavor in this dish.

Start to Finish: 30 minutes **Makes:** 4 servings

- **1 turkey breast tenderloin (about 8 ounces)**
- **2 tablespoons all-purpose flour**
- **¾ teaspoon salt**
- **¼ teaspoon ground black pepper**
- **4 teaspoons olive oil or cooking oil**
- **12 ounces packaged sliced fresh mushrooms (4½ cups)**
- **½ cup chopped onion**
- **¼ teaspoon dried thyme, crushed**
- **½ cup chicken broth**
- **⅓ cup dry Marsala wine or dry sherry**
- **1 teaspoon cornstarch**

1. Cut turkey tenderloin crosswise into ¼-inch slices. In a shallow dish, combine flour, ½ teaspoon of the salt, and the pepper. Dip turkey slices into flour mixture to coat.

2. In a large skillet, cook turkey slices, half at a time, in hot oil for 2 to 4 minutes or until golden brown and no longer pink, turning once halfway through cooking time. (Add more oil as necessary during cooking.) Remove turkey from skillet.

3. Add mushrooms, onion, thyme, and the remaining ¼ teaspoon salt to the skillet. Cook and stir for 4 to 5 minutes or until mushrooms and onion are tender. In a small bowl, stir together broth, wine, and cornstarch; carefully stir into mixture in skillet. Cook and stir until thickened and bubbly. Cook and stir for 2 minutes more.

4. Return turkey slices to skillet; heat through.

Per serving: 235 cal., 8 g total fat (1 g sat. fat), 68 mg chol., 621 mg sodium, 8 g carbo., 1 g fiber, 30 g pro.

Turkey Marsala with Mushrooms

Turkey and Pasta with Peanut Sauce

Turkey and Pasta with Peanut Sauce 🖤

Sweet pineapple, lime juice, and peanut butter create an intriguing sauce in this Thai-syle dish.

Start to Finish: 30 minutes **Makes:** 4 servings

- **6** **ounces dried fettuccine or linguine pasta**
- **2** **cups fresh pea pods, tips trimmed, or one 6-ounce package frozen pea pods**
- **1** **cup cooked turkey or chicken strips**
- **1** **cup coarsely chopped fresh pineapple or one 8-ounce can pineapple chunks, drained**
- **¼** **cup reduced-sodium chicken broth**
- **2** **tablespoons creamy peanut butter**
- **1** **tablespoon reduced-sodium soy sauce**
- **1** **tablespoon lime juice or lemon juice**
- **¼** **teaspoon crushed red pepper**
- **1** **clove garlic, minced**

1. Cook pasta according to package directions. Meanwhile, halve the fresh pea pods diagonally. Place the pea pods and turkey in a large colander. Pour hot cooking liquid from pasta over pea pods and turkey in colander; drain well. Return pasta, pea pods, and turkey to the hot pan. Add the pineapple.

2. Meanwhile, for the sauce, in a small saucepan, stir chicken broth into peanut butter. Heat and stir with a whisk until peanut butter melts. Stir in soy sauce, lime juice, red pepper, and garlic; heat through.

3. Add sauce to the pasta mixture. Gently stir to coat pasta with sauce.

Per serving: 317 cal., 7 g total fat (2 g sat. fat), 30 mg chol., 254 mg sodium, 44 g carbo., 3 g fiber, 21 g pro.

Turkey Burgers with Cranberry Sauce

Turkey Burgers with Cranberry Sauce 🖤 one

All the goodness of Thanksgiving dinner comes together in this healthful entrée that features cranberry sauce, turkey, stuffing, and sage.

Prep: 12 minutes **Broil:** 11 minutes **Makes:** 4 servings

- **⅓** **cup herb-seasoned stuffing mix, crushed (¼ cup)**
- **2** **tablespoons milk**
- **1** **tablespoon snipped fresh sage or ½ teaspoon dried sage, crushed**
- **¼** **teaspoon salt**
- **1** **pound uncooked ground turkey or ground chicken**
- **1** **cup torn mixed salad greens, watercress leaves, or shredded fresh spinach**
- **4** **whole wheat hamburger buns, split and toasted**
- **½** **cup whole cranberry sauce**

1. Preheat broiler. In a large bowl, combine stuffing mix, milk, sage, and salt. Add ground turkey; mix well. Shape into four ½-inch patties. Place patties on the unheated rack of a broiler pan. Broil 4 to 5 inches from the heat for 11 to 13 minutes or until done (165°F),* turning once halfway through broiling.

2. Divide greens among bottoms of buns; top with patties and cranberry sauce. Top with bun tops.

Per serving: 350 cal., 11 g total fat (3 g sat. fat), 71 mg chol., 503 mg sodium, 37 g carbo., 3 g fiber, 28 g pro.

*Note: The internal color of a burger is not a reliable doneness indicator. A turkey or chicken patty cooked to 165°F is safe, regardless of color. To measure the doneness of a patty, insert an instant-read thermometer through the side of the patty to a depth of 2 to 3 inches.

Smoked Turkey and Tortellini Salad

Smoked Turkey and Tortellini Salad 🅾️one

To speed up prep for this main-dish salad, use refrigerated cheese tortellini, which cooks in less time than dried tortellini.

Start to Finish: 25 minutes **Makes:** 4 servings

- 1 **7- to 8-ounce package dried cheese-filled tortellini**
- 1 **cup chopped cooked, smoked turkey, ham, or chicken (5 ounces)**
- 8 **cherry tomatoes, quartered**
- ½ **cup coarsely chopped green sweet pepper**
- ¼ **cup sliced pitted ripe olives (optional)**
- ¼ **cup bottled Italian vinaigrette or balsamic vinaigrette salad dressing**
   Ground black pepper

1. Cook tortellini according to package directions; drain. Rinse with cold water; drain again.

2. In a large bowl, combine tortellini, turkey, tomatoes, sweet pepper, and, if desired, olives. Drizzle salad dressing over mixture; toss to coat. Season to taste with black pepper.

Per serving: 330 cal., 15 g total fat (2 g sat. fat), 20 mg chol., 897 mg sodium, 32 g carbo., 1 g fiber, 17 g pro.

Quick Tip For a vegetarian salad, replace the turkey with 1 cup chopped fresh broccoli or cauliflower.

Turkey Tetrazzini ♥

Prepared the original way, this dish has the potential to be astoundingly high in calories and fat. This version is much healthier but tastes just as terrific. Serve it with a side salad tossed with reduced-calorie Italian dressing.

Prep: 30 minutes **Bake:** 10 minutes **Oven:** 400°F
Makes: 6 servings

- 4 **ounces dried whole wheat spaghetti pasta**
- 2 **cups sliced fresh cremini, stemmed shiitake, or button mushrooms**
- ¾ **cup chopped red and/or green sweet pepper**
- ½ **cup cold water**
- 3 **tablespoons all-purpose flour**
- 1 **12-ounce can evaporated fat-free milk**
- ½ **teaspoon instant chicken bouillon granules**
- ⅛ **teaspoon salt**
- ⅛ **teaspoon ground black pepper**
   Dash ground nutmeg
- 1 **cup chopped cooked turkey breast or chicken breast (5 ounces)**
- ¼ **cup finely shredded Parmesan cheese (1 ounce)**
- 2 **tablespoons snipped fresh parsley**
   Nonstick cooking spray

1. Preheat oven to 400°F. Cook the spaghetti according to package directions. Drain well and return to warm pan.

2. Meanwhile, in a covered large saucepan, cook the mushrooms and sweet pepper in a small amount of boiling water for 3 to 6 minutes or until the vegetables are tender. Drain well; return to saucepan.

3. In a screw-top jar, combine the ½ cup cold water and the flour; cover and shake until well mixed. Stir flour mixture into the vegetable mixture in saucepan. Stir in evaporated milk, bouillon granules, salt, black pepper, and nutmeg. Cook and stir until thickened and bubbly. Stir in the cooked spaghetti, turkey, Parmesan cheese, and parsley.

4. Lightly coat a 2-quart square baking dish with nonstick cooking spray. Spoon spaghetti mixture into dish. Bake, covered, for 10 to 15 minutes or until heated through.

Per serving: 202 cal., 2 g total fat (1 g sat. fat), 24 mg chol., 253 mg sodium, 32 g carbo., 2 g fiber, 17 g pro.

Quick Tip If you don't have cooked turkey or chicken, poach raw chicken breasts to use in this recipe. In a medium skillet, place 6 ounces skinless, boneless chicken breasts and 1 cup water. Bring to boiling; reduce heat. Simmer, covered, for 12 to 14 minutes, or until chicken is no longer pink (170°F). Drain well; cool. Chop chicken.

Turkey Tetrazzini

Balsamic Turkey with Zucchini ♥ [one]

In this recipe, a small amount of honey and crushed red pepper combine with the delightful flavor of balsamic vinegar, resulting in a tantalizing spicy-sweet blend.

Start to Finish: 25 minutes **Makes:** 4 servings

- 2 **tablespoons balsamic vinegar**
- 2 **tablespoons cooking oil**
- 1 **tablespoon honey**
- ⅛ **to ¼ teaspoon crushed red pepper**
- 2 **turkey breast tenderloins (about 1 pound total)**
  Salt
  Ground black pepper
- 2 **medium zucchini, halved lengthwise and cut into ¼-inch slices**
- 2 **cups hot cooked pasta or rice**
- ½ **cup chopped tomato**
  Shredded fresh basil

1. For the dressing, in a small bowl, stir together balsamic vinegar, 1 tablespoon of the oil, the honey, and crushed red pepper; set aside. Split each turkey breast tenderloin in half horizontally to make a total of four ½-inch portions. Lightly sprinkle turkey with salt and pepper.

2. In a large nonstick skillet, heat the remaining 1 tablespoon of oil over medium-high heat. Add turkey; cook for 8 to 10 minutes or until tender and no longer pink (170°F), turning once. Remove from skillet; cover and keep warm.

3. Add zucchini to skillet; cook and stir about 3 minutes or until crisp-tender. Cut turkey into bite-size pieces. In a large bowl, combine turkey, zucchini, and dressing. Spoon over hot cooked pasta. Sprinkle with chopped tomato and basil.

Per serving: 328 cal., 9 g total fat (2 g sat. fat), 68 mg chol., 96 mg sodium, 30 g carbo., 2 g fiber, 31 g pro.

Quick Tip Choose zucchini with brightly colored skin free of spots or bruises. In general, the smaller the zucchini, the more tender it will be. Store zucchini in a plastic bag in the refrigerator for up to 5 days.

Bacon-Wrapped Turkey Mignons ♥

Cook the bacon until brown but not crisp, so it is pliable enough to wrap around the turkey mignons.

Prep: 25 minutes **Bake:** 30 minutes **Oven:** 400°F
Makes: 6 servings

- 6 **slices bacon**
- 2 **turkey breast steaks**
  Salt and ground black pepper
- ¼ **cup bottled honey-mustard dipping sauce**

1. In a large skillet, cook bacon slices over medium heat until lightly browned but still limp, turning once. Drain the bacon on paper towels and cool until easy to handle.

2. Preheat oven to 400°F. Season turkey steaks with salt and pepper. Cut both steaks crosswise into four pieces. Press the two end pieces of each steak together to form one piece (you should have six "mignons"). Wrap one slice of partially cooked bacon around each mignon; secure with wooden toothpicks. Place mignons in a 13×9×2-inch baking pan.

3. Bake for 30 to 40 minutes or until turkey is no longer pink (170°F), brushing with dipping sauce the last 15 minutes of baking.

Per serving: 239 cal., 7 g total fat (2 g sat. fat), 109 mg chol., 401 mg sodium, 2 g carbo., 0 g fiber, 39 g pro.

Turkey Steaks with Cranberry-Orange Sauce

Purchased relish, plus a splash of orange juice or liqueur, joins wild rice mix as a fitting pairing with sautéed turkey tenderloin.

Start to Finish: 30 minutes **Makes:** 4 servings

- 1 **6-ounce package long grain and wild rice mix**
- 1 **pound turkey breast tenderloin**
  Salt
  Ground black pepper
- 2 **tablespoons butter or margarine**
- 1 **10-ounce package frozen cranberry-orange relish, thawed**
- 2 **tablespoons orange liqueur or orange juice**

1. Cook rice mix according to package directions.

2. Meanwhile, split turkey breast tenderloin in half horizontally. Cut each piece in half, making 4 portions. Sprinkle turkey with salt and pepper. In a large skillet, melt butter over medium heat. Add turkey; cook for 10 to 12 minutes or until tender and no longer pink (170°F), turning once.

3. Transfer turkey to a serving platter. Keep warm. Remove skillet from heat; let cool for 2 minutes. Carefully add cranberry-orange relish to drippings in skillet; stir in liqueur. Return to heat; cook and stir over low heat until heated through. Spoon sauce over turkey. Serve with rice.

Per serving: 481 cal., 8 g total fat (4 g sat. fat), 84 mg chol., 941 mg sodium, 68 g carbo., 0 g fiber, 31 g pro.

Turkey Piccata with Fettuccine ♥

The tasty juices and crusty flavor bits left in the pan after cooking the turkey jump start the snappy pan sauce. To complete the meal, serve this dish with steamed broccoli or asparagus.

Start to Finish: 30 minutes **Makes:** 4 servings

- **6** ounces dried fettuccine or linguine pasta
- **¼** cup all-purpose flour
- **½** teaspoon lemon-pepper seasoning or ground black pepper
- **2** turkey breast tenderloins (about 1 pound total)
- **2** tablespoons olive oil or cooking oil
- **⅓** cup dry white wine
- **2** tablespoons lemon juice
- **2** tablespoons water
- **½** teaspoon instant chicken bouillon granules
- **1** tablespoon capers, rinsed and drained (optional)
- **2** tablespoons snipped fresh parsley
  Lemon wedges (optional)
  Fresh parsley sprigs (optional)

1. Cook pasta according to package directions. Drain well. Return pasta to hot pan; cover to keep warm. Meanwhile, in a small bowl, stir together flour and lemon-pepper seasoning; set aside.

2. Cut each turkey tenderloin crosswise into ½-inch slices. Dip turkey slices in flour mixture to coat.

3. In a large skillet, heat oil over medium-high heat. Add turkey; cook for 6 to 10 minutes or until light golden brown and no longer pink (170°F), turning once halfway through cooking time. Remove turkey from skillet; cover and keep warm.

4. For the sauce, add wine, lemon juice, the water, and bouillon granules to skillet, scraping up crusty bits from bottom of skillet. If desired, stir in capers. Bring to boiling; reduce heat. Simmer, uncovered, for 2 minutes. Remove from heat; stir in snipped parsley.

5. To serve, divide pasta among 4 dinner plates. Top pasta with turkey slices. Spoon sauce over all. If desired, serve with lemon wedges and garnish with fresh parsley sprigs.

Per serving: 377 cal., 9 g total fat (2 g sat. fat), 68 mg chol., 301 mg sodium, 36 g carbo., 1 g fiber, 33 g pro.

Turkey Piccata with Fettuccine

Scallops with Tropical Salsa, **page 140**

Flounder with
Roma Tomatoes, **page 114**

Red Snapper Veracruz, **page 127**

Roasted Salmon
and Tomatoes, **page 129**

Seafood Favorites

Because they are best
cooked quickly, fish
and seafood are smart
choices for fast, easy
meals. Their mild,
fresh-from-the-sea
taste pairs deliciously
with both simple and
intense flavors.

Basil-Buttered Salmon

Basil-Buttered Salmon [one]

Use the leftover basil-and-butter mixture to season your favorite cooked vegetables.

Prep: 15 minutes **Broil:** 8 minutes **Makes:** 4 servings

- **4 fresh or frozen skinless salmon, halibut, or sea bass fillets (about 1¼ pounds)**
- **½ teaspoon salt-free lemon-pepper seasoning**
- **2 tablespoons butter, softened**
- **1 teaspoon snipped fresh lemon basil or regular basil, or ¼ teaspoon dried basil**
- **1 teaspoon snipped fresh parsley or cilantro**
- **¼ teaspoon finely shredded lemon peel**

1. Thaw fish, if frozen. Rinse fish; pat dry with paper towels. Sprinkle with lemon-pepper seasoning.

2. Place fish on the greased unheated rack of a broiler pan. Turn any thin portions under to make uniform thickness. Broil 4 inches from the heat for 5 minutes. Carefully turn fish over. Broil for 3 to 7 minutes more or until fish flakes easily when tested with a fork.

3. Meanwhile, in a small bowl, stir together butter, basil, parsley, and lemon peel. To serve, spoon 1 teaspoon of the butter mixture on top of each fish piece. Cover and refrigerate remaining butter mixture for another use.

Grilling Directions: Place fish on the greased rack of an uncovered grill directly over medium coals. Grill for 8 to 12 minutes or until fish flakes easily when tested with a fork, carefully turning once halfway through grilling.

Per serving: 294 cal., 19 g total fat (5 g sat. fat), 94 mg chol., 113 mg sodium, 0 g carbo., 0 g fiber, 28 g pro.

Broiled Snapper with Fennel ♥

Fennel has a mild, sweet flavor that may remind you of licorice. Save some of the delicate, fernlike tops to use as a garnish.

Prep: 15 minutes
Broil: 4 to 6 minutes per ½-inch thickness
Makes: 4 servings

- **4 6- to 8-ounce fresh or frozen red snapper fillets
  Salt and ground black pepper**
- **1 medium lemon**
- **1 tablespoon butter**
- **1 fennel bulb, trimmed and cut crosswise into thin slices (about 1¼ cups)**
- **1 teaspoon snipped fresh dill or thyme**

1. Thaw fish, if frozen. Rinse fish; pat dry with paper towels. Preheat broiler. Measure thickness of fish. Place fish on the greased unheated rack of a broiler pan. Sprinkle fish with salt and pepper. Broil 4 inches from heat until fish flakes easily when tested with a fork (allow 4 to 6 minutes per ½-inch thickness of fish).

2. Meanwhile, finely shred 1 teaspoon peel from lemon. Cut lemon in half; squeeze to get 4 teaspoons juice. Cut remaining lemon half into wedges; set wedges aside.

3. In a small saucepan, melt butter over medium-high heat. Add fennel and cook in hot butter for 5 to 8 minutes or just until tender. Stir in lemon peel, lemon juice, and dill. Season to taste with salt and pepper. Spoon fennel over fish. Serve with lemon wedges.

Per serving: 237 cal., 6 g total fat (2 g sat. fat), 81 mg chol., 318 mg sodium, 4 g carbo., 2 g fiber, 41 g pro.

Fish Fillets with Yogurt Dressing ♥ [one]

Choose a favorite fish fillet, then bake it in a poppy seed dressing that you'll also combine with yogurt for a refreshing sauce.

Prep: 15 minutes   **Marinate:** 20 minutes
Bake: 4 to 6 minutes per ½-inch thickness
Oven: 450°F   **Makes:** 4 servings

- **1 pound fresh or frozen skinless cod, orange roughy, or other fish fillets, ½ to 1 inch thick**
- **⅔ cup bottled poppy seed salad dressing**
- **3 tablespoons thinly sliced green onion**
- **1 teaspoon snipped fresh thyme or ¼ teaspoon dried thyme, crushed**
- **½ cup plain yogurt**

1. Thaw fish, if frozen. Rinse fish; pat dry with paper towels. Cut into 4 serving-size pieces. For the marinade, in a large bowl, combine ½ cup of the salad dressing, 2 tablespoons of the green onion, and ½ teaspoon of the fresh thyme (or ¼ teaspoon dried thyme). Add fish fillets. Turn to coat. Cover and marinate in the refrigerator for 20 to 30 minutes.

2. Preheat oven to 450°F. Drain fillets; discard the marinade. Measure the thickness of the fish. Place fish in a greased 2-quart rectangular baking dish, tucking under any thin edges before baking.

3. Bake fish, uncovered, until fish flakes easily when tested with a fork (allow 4 to 6 minutes per ½-inch thickness of fish). Transfer fish to a serving platter.

4. Meanwhile, for the sauce, in a small serving bowl, stir together yogurt, remaining salad dressing, remaining 1 tablespoon green onion, and remaining ½ teaspoon fresh thyme. Serve sauce with fish.

Per serving: 182 cal., 9 g total fat (2 g sat. fat), 55 mg chol., 201 mg sodium, 3 g carbo., 0 g fiber, 22 g pro.

Salmon-Sour Cream Turnovers one

This is a lovely way to enjoy salmon! Flaked and folded into sour cream dip with fresh chopped celery and sweet pepper then baked in a piecrust envelope.

Prep: 15 minutes **Bake:** 25 minutes
Stand: 20 minutes **Oven:** 375°F **Makes:** 4 servings

- 1 **15-ounce package folded refrigerated unbaked piecrusts (2 crusts)**
- ⅓ **cup dairy sour cream chive-flavor dip**
- 1 **tablespoon all-purpose flour**
- 2 **6-ounce cans skinless, boneless salmon, drained and flaked**
- ½ **cup chopped celery (1 stalk)**
- ¼ **cup finely chopped red or green sweet pepper**
  Milk
- 1 **teaspoon sesame seeds**

1. Preheat oven to 375°F. Let piecrusts stand at room temperature for 15 minutes as directed on package.

2. Meanwhile, in a medium bowl, stir together sour cream dip and flour. Fold in salmon, celery, and sweet pepper.

3. Unfold piecrusts. Spread half of the salmon mixture onto one half of each piecrust, spreading to within 1 inch of the edges. Moisten edges with water. Carefully lift and fold piecrusts in half over filling; turn edges under. Seal edges with the tines of a fork. Cut slits in tops of turnovers to allow steam to escape. Brush tops of turnovers with milk; sprinkle with sesame seeds. Transfer turnovers to a large baking sheet.

4. Bake for 25 to 30 minutes or until pastry is golden. Let stand for 5 minutes before removing from baking sheet.

Per serving: 658 cal., 36 g total fat (15 g sat. fat), 80 mg chol., 996 mg sodium, 57 g carbo., 1 g fiber, 20 g pro.

Beer-Battered Cod one

When you're buying frozen fish fillets, look for a package of individually wrapped fillets. You can remove just the number you need and save the rest for another meal.

Start to Finish: 35 minutes **Oven:** 300°F
Makes: 4 servings

- 6 **4- to 6-ounce fresh or frozen cod fillets**
  Cooking oil for deep-fat frying
- 2 **cups self-rising flour**
- ½ **teaspoon salt**
- ½ **teaspoon ground black pepper**
- 1 **12-ounce can beer**

1. Thaw fish, if frozen. Rinse fish; pat dry with paper towels. In a heavy 3-quart saucepan or deep-fat fryer, heat 2 inches of oil to 365°F.

2. Meanwhile, in a large bowl, stir together flour, salt, and pepper. Sprinkle both sides of fish with 2 tablespoons of the flour mixture. Add beer to remaining flour mixture and stir until combined. (Batter will be thick.) Dip fish pieces, one at a time, into the batter, coating well.

3. Fry fish, one or two pieces at a time, for 4 to 6 minutes or until golden and fish flakes easily when tested with a fork. Drain on paper towels; keep warm in a 300°F oven while frying remaining fish.

Per serving: 635 cal., 29 g total fat (4 g sat. fat), 72 mg chol., 1,181 mg sodium, 50 g carbo., 2 g fiber, 37 g pro.

Flounder with Roma Tomatoes ♥ one

Mild flavored flounder fillets take on a Mediterranean flavor with capers and black olives. Other white fish fillets, such as cod, tilapia, or sole, also work well in this recipe.

Start to Finish: 25 minutes **Makes:** 4 servings

- 1 **pound fresh or frozen flounder fillets or other thin, mild fish fillets**
- 1 **tablespoon olive oil**
- 1 **cup finely chopped onion (2 medium)**
- 1 **medium fresh mild green chile pepper, such as Anaheim, seeded and chopped (½ cup)**
- 2 **cups chopped roma tomato (4 medium)**
- 2 **tablespoons capers, drained**
- ¼ **cup sliced, pitted imported black olives, such as kalamata or niçoise**
- ¼ **teaspoon salt**
- ⅛ **teaspoon ground black pepper**

1. Thaw fish, if frozen. Rinse fish; pat dry with paper towels. Cut fish into 4 serving-size pieces, if necessary. Set fish aside.

2. In a large skillet, heat oil over medium heat. Add onion and chile pepper; cook about 4 minutes or until tender. Stir in tomato, capers, olives, and ⅛ teaspoon of the salt. Arrange fish on top of the vegetable mixture. Sprinkle fish with the remaining ⅛ teaspoon salt and the black pepper. Cook, covered, over medium heat for 4 to 5 minutes or until fish begins to flake when tested with a fork.

Per serving: 188 cal., 6 g total fat (1 g sat. fat), 54 mg chol., 500 mg sodium, 10 g carbo., 2 g fiber, 23 g pro.

Flounder with Roma Tomatoes

Fish with Tangerine Relish

Fish with Tangerine Relish 🖤

To prepare the tangerines, peel and separate them into segments. Then cut off the thick membrane of each segment next to the seed, slip out the seed, and coarsely chop the fruit.

Prep: 25 minutes
Broil: 4 to 6 minutes per ½-inch thickness
Makes: 6 servings

6	**4-ounce fresh or frozen skinless halibut, cod, sole, or other white fish fillets**
¼	**teaspoon salt**
¼	**teaspoon ground black pepper**
⅓	**cup orange juice**
¼	**cup finely chopped red onion or shallots**
2	**teaspoons white balsamic vinegar**
1	**teaspoon snipped fresh tarragon or ½ teaspoon dried tarragon, crushed**
1	**teaspoon olive oil**
1	**clove garlic, minced**
	Dash bottled hot pepper sauce
	Nonstick cooking spray
4	**medium tangerines**
2	**tablespoons snipped fresh parsley**
6	**cups torn mixed salad greens (optional)**

1. Thaw fish fillets, if frozen. Rinse fish; pat dry with paper towels. Sprinkle with salt and black pepper. Measure thickness of fish; set aside.

2. Preheat broiler. In a small saucepan, combine orange juice, red onion, balsamic vinegar, tarragon, olive oil, garlic, and hot pepper sauce. Bring to boiling; reduce heat. Simmer, uncovered, for 5 to 6 minutes or until reduced to about ⅓ cup. Remove from heat. Remove 2 tablespoons of the liquid; set both mixtures aside.

3. Coat the unheated rack of a broiler pan with cooking spray. Place fish fillets on rack. Brush both sides of each fish fillet with the reserved 2 tablespoons liquid. Turn under any thin portions of fish to make uniform thickness. Broil 4 inches from the heat for 4 to 6 minutes per ½-inch thickness or until fish flakes easily when tested with a fork.

4. Meanwhile, for the tangerine relish, peel tangerines and separate into segments. Remove seeds and cut up tangerine segments. In a small bowl, combine chopped tangerines, the remaining orange juice mixture, and the parsley. To serve, divide greens, if using, among serving plates. Top with fish; spoon tangerine relish over fish.

Per serving: 175 cal., 4 g total fat (1 g sat. fat), 36 mg chol., 161 mg sodium, 11 g carbo., 1 g fiber, 24 g pro.

Lime-Steamed Salmon ♥

Use a rice steamer if you have one. If not, follow the directions for steaming using a steamer basket and skillet.

Start to Finish: 30 minutes **Makes:** 3 servings

1	pound fresh or frozen salmon fillet, skinned
2	limes
2	tablespoons toasted sesame oil
1	tablespoon grated fresh ginger
⅛	teaspoon salt
⅛	teaspoon ground black pepper
2	cups trimmed baby (small) green beans (about 8 ounces) or one 9-ounce package frozen French-cut green beans
	Lime wedges (optional)

1. Thaw fish, if frozen. Rinse fish; pat dry with paper towels. Cut fish into three pieces about 1 inch thick; set aside.

2. Finely shred 2 teaspoons of peel from the limes; set limes aside. In a small bowl, stir together lime peel, sesame oil, ginger, salt, and pepper. Set oil mixture aside.

3. In a small covered saucepan, cook green beans in a small amount of boiling salted water about 15 minutes (5 to 6 minutes for frozen beans) or until crisp-tender.

4. Meanwhile, place 4 cups water in a very large skillet. Bring to boiling; reduce heat. Thinly slice limes. Place lime slices and fish in a steamer basket. Generously brush fish with oil mixture. Carefully place steamer basket in the skillet. Cover and steam over gently boiling water about 10 minutes or until fish flakes when tested with a fork.

5. To serve, arrange green beans in a serving dish; remove fish from lime slices and arrange fish on top of beans. If desired, serve with lime wedges.

Per serving: 293 cal., 14 g total fat (2 g sat. fat), 78 mg chol., 204 mg sodium, 11 g carbo., 4 g fiber, 32 g pro.

Halibut with Tomatoes And Olives ♥ [one]

Fished from cold northern waters, halibut is white and firm with a mild flavor. Steaks are more commonly available than fillets.

Start to Finish: 20 minutes **Makes:** 4 servings

4	6-ounce fresh or frozen halibut steaks, 1 inch thick
2	tablespoons olive oil
	Salt and ground black pepper
⅓	cup coarsely chopped tomato
⅓	cup Greek black olives, pitted and coarsely chopped
2	tablespoons snipped fresh flat-leaf parsley or 1 tablespoon snipped fresh oregano
	Mixed salad greens (optional)

1. Thaw fish, if frozen. Rinse fish; pat dry with paper towels. Brush fish with 1 tablespoon of the oil; sprinkle with salt and pepper.

2. Preheat broiler. Place fish on the greased unheated rack of a broiler pan. Broil fish 4 inches from heat for 8 to 12 minutes or until fish flakes easily when tested with a fork, turning once halfway through broiling.

3. Meanwhile, in a small bowl, stir together the remaining 1 tablespoon oil, the tomato, olives, and parsley. Spoon tomato mixture over fish. If desired, serve with salad greens.

Per serving: 262 cal., 12 g total fat (2 g sat. fat), 54 mg chol., 264 mg sodium, 2 g carbo., 1 g fiber, 36 g pro.

Lime-Poached Mahi Mahi ♥ [one]

Basmati rice from India is an aromatic rice that's prized for its nutty flavor and sweet aroma. In this recipe, it is extraordinary with the margarita-accented fish.

Start to Finish: 20 minutes **Makes:** 4 servings

4	6-ounce fresh or frozen mahi mahi or catfish fillets, ½ to ¾ inch thick
2	teaspoons seasoned pepper
1	tablespoon olive oil or cooking oil
⅓	cup frozen margarita mix concentrate, thawed Hot cooked basmati or long grain rice

1. Thaw fish, if frozen. Skin fish, if necessary. Rinse fish; pat dry with paper towels. Sprinkle both sides of each fish fillet with seasoned pepper.

2. In a large nonstick skillet, heat oil over medium-high heat. Add fish fillets; cook for 2 to 4 minutes or until lightly browned, turning to brown evenly. Reduce heat to medium low. Carefully add margarita mix concentrate to skillet. Cook, covered, for 6 to 8 minutes or until fish flakes easily when tested with a fork. Serve fish and cooking liquid with rice.

Per serving: 336 cal., 5 g total fat (1 g sat. fat), 124 mg chol., 150 mg sodium, 41 g carbo., 0 g fiber, 34 g pro.

Fish Fillets with Orange-Ginger Sauce [one]

If you sometimes opt for a fast-food fish sandwich for a quick lunch, consider this healthier alternative. It's just as fast as eating out (it only takes 15 minutes) and twice as tasty.

Start to Finish: 15 minutes **Oven:** 450°F
Makes: 4 servings

- **4** **fresh or frozen fish fillets (such as cod, orange roughy, or pike), about ½ inch thick (about 1 pound total)**
  Nonstick cooking spray
- ¼ **cup fine dry bread crumbs**
- ¼ **teaspoon ground ginger**
- ⅛ **teaspoon salt**
- ⅛ **teaspoon cayenne pepper**
- **2** **tablespoons butter or margarine, melted**
  Orange-Ginger Sauce
- **4** **lettuce leaves (optional)**
- **4** **baguette-style rolls or kaiser rolls, split and toasted (optional)**

1. Preheat oven to 450°F. Thaw fish, if frozen. Rinse fish; pat dry with paper towels.

2. Lightly coat a shallow baking pan with cooking spray; set aside. In a small bowl, combine bread crumbs, ginger, salt, and cayenne pepper; set aside. Place fish fillets on waxed paper. Brush tops and sides of the fish with melted butter; coat tops and sides with crumb mixture.

3. Arrange the fish fillets in a single layer, crumb sides up, in prepared baking pan. Bake for 4 to 6 minutes or until fish flakes easily when tested with a fork.

4. Top fish with Orange-Ginger Sauce. If desired, place fish onto a lettuce-lined roll to make a sandwich.

Orange-Ginger Sauce: In a small bowl, stir together ¼ cup low-fat mayonnaise dressing, 1 teaspoon orange marmalade, and ¼ teaspoon ground ginger.

Per serving: 319 cal., 10 g total fat (5 g sat. fat), 68 mg chol., 711 mg sodium, 31 g carbo., 2 g fiber, 25 g pro.

Buttery Sole with ♥ [one] Almonds and Cilantro

Cilantro adds a bit of zing and almonds add a pleasant crunch to these baked fish fillets. You'll love how the butter lightly browns under the broiler, giving it a nutty flavor that pairs deliciously with the slivered almonds.

Start to Finish: 15 minutes **Makes:** 4 to 6 servings

- 1½ **pounds sole fillets**
  Salt
  Ground black pepper
- **2** **tablespoons butter, softened**
- **2** **tablespoons slivered almonds, toasted**
- **2** **teaspoons snipped fresh cilantro**
  Lemon wedges

1. Preheat the broiler. Season fish with salt and pepper. Rub 1 tablespoon of the butter on the inside of a 13×9×2-inch baking pan or a shallow broiler-proof baking dish.

2. Place the fillets in the pan in a single layer and spread with remaining butter. Broil about 4 inches from the heat for 4 to 6 minutes or until fish flakes easily when tested with a fork. Sprinkle with almonds and cilantro just before serving. Serve with lemon wedges.

Per serving: 228 cal., 9 g total fat (4 g sat. fat), 97 mg chol., 325 mg sodium, 4 g carbo., 2 g fiber, 33 g pro.

Quick Tip Toasting almonds heightens their flavor. To toast the slivered almonds, spread them in a single layer in a shallow roasting pan. Bake them in a 350°F oven for 5 to 10 minutes or until light golden brown, watching carefully and stirring once or twice so the almonds don't burn.

Fish Fillets with Orange-Ginger Sauce

Maple-Hoisin Glazed Halibut

Maple-Hoisin Glazed Halibut ♥ one

Maple syrup adds a sweet accent to these Asian-style halibut steaks. Ginger and crushed red pepper add just the right amount of spice.

Prep: 10 minutes **Broil:** 8 minutes **Makes:** 4 servings

- **4 5- to 6-ounce fresh or frozen halibut steaks, 1 inch thick**
- **3 tablespoons hoisin sauce**
- **2 tablespoons seasoned rice vinegar**
- **2 tablespoons maple syrup**
- **1 teaspoon grated fresh ginger**
- **½ teaspoon bottled minced garlic (1 clove)**
- **¼ teaspoon crushed red pepper**
- **¼ teaspoon ground black pepper**
   Shredded leaf lettuce or napa cabbage (optional)

1. Thaw fish, if frozen. Preheat broiler. Rinse fish; pat dry with paper towels. In a small bowl, stir together hoisin sauce, vinegar, syrup, ginger, garlic, and crushed red pepper. Set aside.

2. Sprinkle fish with black pepper. Place fish on the greased unheated rack of a broiler pan. Broil 4 inches from the heat for 5 minutes. Brush with glaze; turn fish. Brush with remaining glaze. Broil for 3 to 7 minutes more or until fish begins to flake when tested with a fork. If desired, serve on a bed of lettuce.

Per serving: 210 cal., 4 g total fat (1 g sat. fat), 45 mg chol., 285 mg sodium, 13 g carbo., 0 g fiber, 30 g pro.

Quick Tip After you purchase fresh fish, be sure to cook it as soon as possible. When you have to wait a couple of days to use it, wrap the fish loosely in plastic wrap. Store it in the coldest part of your refrigerator for up to 2 days. Cover and refrigerate any leftover cooked fish and use within 2 days.

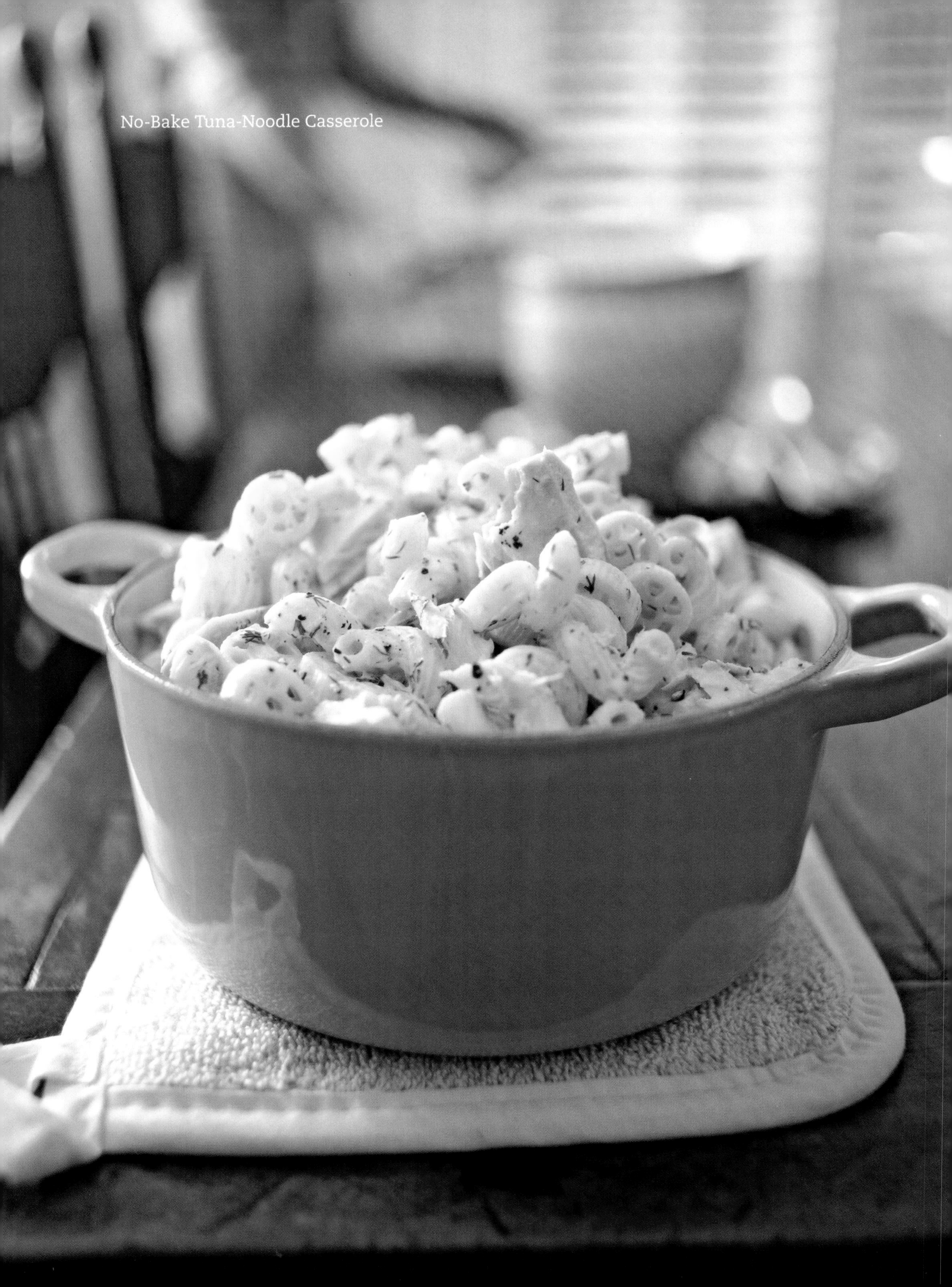

No-Bake Tuna-Noodle Casserole

No-Bake Tuna-Noodle Casserole ♥ [one]

Cavatappi is a short spiral tube pasta with ridges, which are good for capturing the velvety sauce.

Start to Finish: 20 minutes   **Makes:** 4 servings

- **8   ounces dried cavatappi, rotelle, or medium shell macaroni pasta**
- **1½ cups desired frozen vegetables (optional)**
- **¼   to ½ cup milk**
- **1   6.5-ounce container or two 4-ounce containers light semisoft cheese with garlic and herb**
- **1   12.25-ounce can solid white tuna (water pack), drained and broken into chunks**
  Salt and ground black pepper

1. Cook pasta in lightly salted water according to package directions. If desired, add frozen vegetables during the last 4 minutes of cooking. Drain and return to warm pan.

2. Add ¼ cup milk and the cheese to pasta in pan. Cook and stir over medium heat until cheese is melted and pasta is coated, adding additional milk as necessary to make desired consistency. Gently fold in tuna; heat through. Season to taste with salt and pepper.

Per serving: 417 cal., 10 g total fat (7 g sat. fat), 66 mg chol., 552 mg sodium, 45 g carbo., 2 g fiber, 33 g pro.

Ginger Fish ♥ [one]

Sea bass pairs well for the strong flavors of ginger, garlic, and jalapeño chiles. Mahi mahi, halibut, or swordfish also works well.

Start to Finish: 20 minutes   **Makes:** 4 servings

- **4   4-ounce fresh or frozen skinless sea bass or other firm-fleshed white fish fillets, ¾ to 1 inch thick**
- **⅔   cup thinly sliced green onion**
- **4   teaspoons lemon juice or dry sherry**
- **2   teaspoons grated fresh ginger**
- **1   teaspoon bottled minced garlic (2 cloves)**
- **2   teaspoons bottled fish sauce or reduced-sodium soy sauce**
- **1   small fresh jalapeño chile pepper, seeded and finely chopped***

1. Thaw fish, if frozen. Rinse fish; pat dry with paper towels. In a small bowl, stir together green onion, 2 teaspoons of the lemon juice, the ginger, and garlic.

2. Arrange fish fillets in a single layer in a microwave-safe shallow baking dish, tucking under any thin edges. Spoon scallion mixture over fish. Cover dish with vented plastic wrap. Microwave on 100% (high) power for 3 to 5 minutes or until fish flakes easily when tested with a fork, giving the dish a half-turn halfway through cooking.

3. Using a slotted spatula, transfer fish to 4 dinner plates. In a small bowl, stir together fish sauce, jalapeño pepper, and remaining 2 teaspoons lemon juice; drizzle over fish.

Per serving: 121 cal., 2 g total fat (1 g sat. fat), 46 mg chol., 312 mg sodium, 3 g carbo., 1 g fiber, 22 g pro.

*Note: Because chile peppers contain volatile oils that can burn your skin and eyes, avoid direct contact with them as much as possible. When working with chile peppers, wear plastic or rubber gloves. If your bare hands do touch the peppers, wash your hands and nails well with soap and warm water.

Orange Roughy with Puttanesca Sauce ♥ [one]

Orzo, an almond-shape pasta, resembles rice, but you can bring it to the table in much less time.

Start to Finish: 30 minutes   **Makes:** 4 servings

- **1   pound skinless orange roughy or cod fillets**
- **1   teaspoon dried oregano, crushed**
- **½   teaspoon coarsely ground black pepper**
- **1   tablespoon olive oil**
- **4   medium plum tomatoes, chopped (about 1⅓ cups)**
- **1   small onion, cut into thin wedges**
- **½   of a 2.25-ounce can sliced ripe olives, drained (¼ cup)**
- **1   tablespoon capers, drained**
- **2   cloves garlic, minced**
- **¼   cup dry white wine or chicken broth**
  Hot cooked orzo (optional)

1. Measure thickness of fish. Cut fish into four portions. Sprinkle with half of the oregano and half of the pepper.

2. In a large skillet, heat oil over medium heat. Add fish, seasoned side down, and cook for 2 minutes, turning once. Add tomatoes, onion, drained olives, capers, garlic, wine or broth, and the remaining oregano and pepper. Bring to boiling; reduce heat. Simmer, covered, for 4 to 6 minutes per ½-inch thickness of fish or until fish flakes easily when tested with a fork.

3. Transfer fish to serving platter with a slotted spatula. Boil sauce, uncovered, until slightly thickened, about 1½ to 2 minutes. Spoon sauce over fish. If desired, serve with hot cooked orzo.

Per serving: 152 cal., 6 g total fat (1 g sat. fat), 23 mg chol., 211 mg sodium, 5 g carbo., 2 g fiber, 18 g pro.

Oven-Fried Fish

Oven-Fried Fish 💙 🔲

No need to haul out the skillet to enjoy fried fish. This version bakes in as little as four minutes. What's more, there are no messy cooking oil splatters to clean up.

Prep: 15 minutes
Bake: 4 to 6 minutes per ½-inch thickness
Oven: 450°F **Makes:** 4 servings

- **1 pound fresh or frozen skinless cod, orange roughy, or catfish fillets**
- **¼ cup milk**
- **⅓ cup all-purpose flour**
- **½ cup fine dry bread crumbs**
- **2 tablespoons grated Parmesan cheese**
- **¼ teaspoon lemon-pepper seasoning**
- **2 tablespoons butter or margarine, melted**
  Lemon wedges (optional)

1. Preheat oven to 450°F. Thaw fish, if frozen. Rinse fish; pat dry with paper towels. If necessary, cut into four serving-size pieces. Measure the thickness of each piece. Place milk in a shallow dish. Place flour in another shallow dish. In a third shallow dish, combine bread crumbs, Parmesan cheese, and lemon-pepper seasoning. Add melted butter to bread crumb mixture; stir until well mixed.

2. Grease a shallow baking pan; set aside. Dip fish in the milk; coat with flour. Dip again in the milk; dip in the crumb mixture, turning to coat all sides. Place fish in a single layer in prepared baking pan. Bake, uncovered, for 4 to 6 minutes per ½-inch thickness or until fish flakes easily when tested with a fork. If desired, serve with lemon wedges.

Per serving: 254 cal., 9 g total fat (5 g sat. fat), 75 mg chol., 565 mg sodium, 15 g carbo., 1 g fiber, 26 g pro.

South-of-the-Border Snapper ♥ [one]

Can you say super-cinchy? It's easy to meet your fish and seafood quotient with this dish. Just bake snapper, orange roughy, sole, or cod with your favorite chunky salsa and a dressing of shredded cheese.

Prep: 10 minutes   **Bake:** 15 minutes   **Oven:** 425°F
Makes: 4 servings

- 4   **4-ounce fresh or frozen red snapper, sole, or cod fillets, about ½ inch thick**
- ½   **cup bottled chunky salsa**
- ¾   **cup shredded reduced-fat Monterey Jack and/or Cheddar cheese**

1. Thaw fish, if frozen. Rinse fish; pat dry with paper towels. Preheat oven to 425°F.

2. Place fish in a 2-quart rectangular baking dish, tucking under any thin edges. Spoon salsa over fish and sprinkle with cheese.

3. Bake about 15 minutes or until fish flakes easily when tested with a fork.

Per serving: 177 cal., 5 g total fat (3 g sat. fat), 56 mg chol., 277 mg sodium, 1 g carbo., 0 g fiber, 29 g pro.

Pizza Fish Fillets ♥

Orange roughy, cod, or haddock fillets are excellent choices for this recipe because they have firm texture and delicate flavor.

Start to Finish: 20 minutes   **Oven:** 450°F
Makes: 6 servings

- 1½   **pounds fresh or frozen fish fillets, ½ to ¾ inch thick**
- ½   **teaspoon lemon-pepper seasoning**
     Nonstick cooking spray
- 12   **ounces dried spinach fettuccine pasta**
- 2   **cups sliced fresh mushrooms**
- 1   **medium green sweet pepper, chopped (¾ cup)**
- 1   **medium onion, chopped (½ cup)**
- ¼   **cup water**
- 1   **8-ounce can pizza sauce**
- ½   **cup shredded mozzarella cheese (2 ounces)**

1. Preheat oven to 450°F.

2. Thaw fish, if frozen. Cut the fish into six portions. Measure thickness of fish. Sprinkle fish with lemon-pepper seasoning. Coat a 2-quart rectangular baking dish with cooking spray. Place fish in the prepared baking dish, tucking under any thin edges so fish cooks evenly.

3. Bake, uncovered, until fish flakes easily with a fork (allow 6 to 9 minutes per ½-inch thickness of fish). Drain off any liquid.

4. Meanwhile, cook fettuccine according to package directions. Combine mushrooms, sweet pepper, onion, and the water in a medium saucepan; cover and cook for 5 minutes or until just tender. Drain; add pizza sauce. Heat through.

5. Serve fish on fettuccine; spoon sauce over fish. Sprinkle with cheese.

Per serving: 147 cal., 3 g total fat (1 g sat. fat), 50 mg chol., 419 mg sodium, 7 g carbo., 1 g fiber, 22 g pro.

Sea Bass with Lemon-Caper Butter [one]

If it's more convenient, make the lemon-caper butter ahead, cover it, and store in the refrigerator. Let it stand at room temperature before serving.

Start to Finish: 20 minutes   **Makes:** 4 servings

- 4   **6-ounce fresh or frozen sea bass steaks, 1 inch thick**
     Salt
     Ground black pepper
- 1   **medium lemon**
- ¼   **cup butter, softened**
- 1   **tablespoon capers, drained**
- 1   **clove garlic, minced, or ½ teaspoon bottled minced garlic**

1. Thaw fish, if frozen. Rinse fish; pat dry with paper towels. Preheat broiler. Sprinkle fish with salt and pepper. Place fish on the greased unheated rack of a broiler pan. Broil 4 inches from heat for 8 to 12 minutes or until fish flakes easily when tested with a fork, turning once halfway through broiling.

2. Meanwhile, finely shred 1 teaspoon peel from lemon. Cut lemon in half; squeeze to get 2 teaspoons juice. Cut remaining lemon half into wedges; set wedges aside.

3. For the lemon-caper butter, in a small bowl, stir together lemon peel, lemon juice, butter, drained capers, and garlic. Top fish with lemon-caper butter. Serve with lemon wedges.

Per serving: 277 cal., 16 g total fat (8 g sat. fat), 102 mg chol., 449 mg sodium, 2 g carbo., 1 g fiber, 32 g pro.

Pan-Seared Tilapia with Almond Browned Butter

Pan-Seared Tilapia With Almond Browned Butter ♥ 🔲

Pan-searing gives the fish a golden crust and locks in flavor and natural juices. If you try to turn the fish fillets and there's some resistance, cook them a little longer, then try again.

Start to Finish: 25 minutes   **Makes:** 4 servings

- **4   4- to 5-ounce fresh or frozen skinless tilapia or other white fish fillets**
- **3   cups fresh pea pods, trimmed**
  Salt
  Ground black pepper
- **1   teaspoon all-purpose flour**
- **1   tablespoon olive oil**
- **2   tablespoons butter**
- **¼   cup coarsely chopped almonds**
  Snipped fresh parsley (optional)

1. Thaw fish, if frozen. Rinse fish; pat dry with paper towels. Set aside. In a large saucepan, bring a large amount of lightly salted water to boiling. Add pea pods; cook for 2 minutes. Drain and set aside.

2. Meanwhile, sprinkle one side of each fish fillet with salt, pepper, and flour. Heat a large skillet over medium-high heat. Add oil, tilting skillet to coat. Add fish, floured side up (if necessary, cook half the fish at a time). Cook fish for 4 to 5 minutes or until it is easy to remove with spatula. Gently turn fish and cook for 2 to 3 minutes more or until fish begins to flake when tested with a fork. Arrange pea pods on a platter; place fish on top of pea pods.

3. Reduce heat to medium. In same skillet, melt butter; stir in almonds. Cook for 30 to 60 seconds or until nuts are lightly toasted (do not let butter burn). Spoon over fish fillets. If desired, sprinkle with snipped fresh parsley.

Per serving: 266 cal., 15 g total fat (5 g sat. fat), 71 mg chol., 210 mg sodium, 7 g carbo., 3 g fiber, 24 g pro.

Seasoned Cod ♥ [one]

Sprinkle with seasonings, broil a few minutes, and the succulent fish is ready to serve.

Prep: 10 minutes
Broil: 4 to 6 minutes per ½-inch thickness
Makes: 8 servings

- **2 pounds fresh or frozen skinless cod fillets, ¾ to 1 inch thick**
- **1 teaspoon paprika**
- **½ teaspoon ground black pepper**
- **½ teaspoon seasoned salt**
- **Lemon wedges and/or fresh parsley sprigs (optional)**

1. Preheat broiler. Thaw fish, if frozen. Rinse fish; pat dry with paper towels. In a small bowl, combine paprika, pepper, and seasoned salt. Sprinkle paprika mixture over both sides of each fish fillet. Measure thickness of fish.

2. Place fish on the greased unheated rack of a broiler pan. Broil 4 inches from the heat for 4 to 6 minutes per ½-inch thickness of fish or until fish flakes easily when tested with a fork. If desired, garnish with lemon wedges and/or parsley sprigs.

Per serving: 93 cal., 1 g total fat (0 g sat. fat), 48 mg chol., 156 mg sodium, 0 g carbo., 0 g fiber, 20 g pro.

Microwave directions: Prepare as directed through Step 1. In a microwave-safe 2-quart square baking dish, arrange fish in a single layer (fish may be tight in the dish but do not overlap). Cover with vented plastic wrap. Microwave on 100% power (high) for 5 to 7 minutes or until fish flakes easily when tested with a fork, turning dish once halfway through cooking, if necessary. If desired, garnish with lemon wedges and/or parsley sprigs.

Tuna with Tuscan Beans

Navy beans add an unbeatable creamy richness to tuna.

Start to Finish: 20 minutes **Makes:** 4 servings

- **1 pound fresh or frozen tuna or swordfish steaks, cut 1 inch thick**
- **¼ teaspoon salt**
- **¼ teaspoon ground black pepper**
- **1 tablespoon olive oil**
- **2 cloves garlic, minced**
- **2 teaspoons olive oil**
- **1 14.5-ounce can Italian-style stewed tomatoes, undrained and cut up**
- **2 teaspoons snipped fresh sage or ¼ teaspoon ground sage**
- **1 15-ounce can navy beans, rinsed and drained**
- **Lemon wedges**
- **Fresh sage sprigs (optional)**

1. Thaw fish, if frozen. Cut fish into four portions; sprinkle with salt and pepper. Heat the 1 tablespoon oil in a large skillet over medium heat. Add the fish. Cook for 10 to 12 minutes or until fish flakes easily with a fork, turning once. (If using tuna, fish may still be pink in the center.)

2. Meanwhile, in a medium skillet, cook garlic in 2 teaspoons hot oil for 15 seconds. Stir in the undrained tomatoes and the sage. Bring to boiling; reduce heat. Simmer, uncovered, for 5 minutes. Stir in beans; heat through.

3. To serve, remove the skin from fish, if present. Spoon some of the bean mixture onto 4 dinner plates. Place a fish portion on top of bean mixture on each plate. Serve with lemon wedges. If desired, garnish with sage sprigs.

Per serving: 339 cal., 8 g total fat (1 g sat. fat), 51 mg chol., 883 mg sodium, 30 g carbo., 6 g fiber, 36 g pro.

Red Snapper with Carrots and Fennel ♥

Red snapper is a natural for low-calorie meals not only because it's low in fat, but because of how good it tastes with veggies.

Prep: 25 minutes **Bake:** 4 minutes **Oven:** 450°F
Makes: 4 servings

- **1 pound fresh or frozen skinless red snapper fillets, about ½ inch thick**
- **1 cup sliced fennel bulb**
- **½ cup chopped onion (1 medium)**
- **½ cup chopped carrot (1 medium)**
- **2 cloves garlic, minced**
- **1 tablespoon olive oil**
- **1 tablespoon snipped fresh dill**
- **¼ teaspoon salt**
- **¼ teaspoon ground black pepper**
- **¼ cup dry white wine or reduced-sodium chicken broth**
- **Fresh dill sprigs (optional)**

1. Thaw fish, if frozen. Rinse fish; pat dry. Preheat oven to 450°F. In a large skillet, cook fennel, onion, carrot, and garlic in oil over medium heat for 5 to 7 minutes or until vegetables are tender and lightly browned. Remove from heat. Stir in dill, salt, and pepper. Stir in wine.

2. Spoon about 1 cup of the vegetable mixture into a 2-quart square baking dish. Place fish on top of vegetables, tucking under any thin edges. Spoon remaining vegetable mixture on top of fish.

3. Bake, uncovered, for 4 to 6 minutes or until fish flakes easily when tested with a fork. Transfer fish and vegetables to dinner plates. If desired, garnish with dill sprigs.

Per serving: 182 cal., 6 g total fat (1 g sat. fat), 41 mg chol., 260 mg sodium, 6 g carbo., 7 g fiber, 24 g pro.

Saucy Shrimp over Polenta ♥ [one]

A tube of prepared polenta is your leg up on getting a simple but brilliant spicy shrimp sauté to the table fast.

Start to Finish: 25 minutes **Makes:** 6 servings

- **18** fresh or frozen peeled and deveined, cooked shrimp, tails removed (about 8 ounces)
- **1** 16-ounce tube refrigerated cooked polenta, cut crosswise into 12 slices
- **1** tablespoon cooking oil
- **2** cups frozen whole kernel corn
- **1⅓** cups chopped roma tomatoes (4 medium)
- **3** tablespoons balsamic vinegar
- **1** teaspoon dried thyme, crushed
- **½** teaspoon ground cumin
- **¼** teaspoon salt

1. Thaw shrimp, if frozen. Rinse shrimp; pat dry with paper towels. Set aside. In a large skillet, cook polenta slices in hot oil for 5 to 8 minutes or until golden brown, turning once. Transfer to a serving platter; keep warm.

2. In the same large skillet, combine corn, tomatoes, balsamic vinegar, thyme, cumin, and salt. Cook and stir about 5 minutes or until heated through. Stir in shrimp. Cook and stir until heated through.

3. Using a slotted spoon, spoon shrimp mixture over polenta slices.

Per serving: 196 cal., 3 g total fat (1 g sat. fat), 74 mg chol., 483 mg sodium, 30 g carbo., 4 g fiber, 12 g pro.

Citrus-Glazed Salmon ♥ [one]

Orange marmalade adds a hint of sweetness and five-spice powder a hint of intrigue to this fork-tender baked salmon.

Prep: 15 minutes
Bake: 4 to 6 minutes per ½-inch thickness
Oven: 450°F **Makes:** 8 servings

- **1** 2-pound fresh or frozen salmon fillet, skin removed
  Salt
  Ground black pepper
- **¾** cup orange marmalade
- **2** green onions, sliced
- **2** teaspoons dry white wine
- **1** teaspoon grated fresh ginger
- **1** teaspoon Dijon-style mustard
- **½** teaspoon bottled minced garlic (1 clove)
- **¼** teaspoon cayenne pepper
- **⅛** teaspoon five-spice powder
- **3** tablespoons sliced almonds, toasted
  Steamed fresh asparagus spears (optional)

1. Preheat oven to 450°F. Thaw fish, if frozen. Rinse fish; pat dry with paper towels. Measure the thickest portion of the fish fillet. Sprinkle fish with salt and black pepper. Place in a shallow baking pan; set aside.

2. In a small bowl, stir together marmalade, green onion, wine, ginger, mustard, garlic, cayenne pepper, and five-spice powder. Spoon mixture over fish.

3. Bake for 4 to 6 minutes per ½-inch thickness or until fish flakes easily when tested with a fork. Sprinkle individual servings with almonds. If desired, serve fish with asparagus.

Per serving: 227 cal., 6 g total fat (1 g sat. fat), 59 mg chol., 170 mg sodium, 21 g carbo., 1 g fiber, 24 g pro.

Quick Tip To steam asparagus spears, snap off and discard woody bases from fresh asparagus. Steam spears for 4 to 6 minutes or until tender.

Salmon, Rice, and Pesto Salad [one]

If you're in a crunch, use frozen cut green beans in place of the sugar snap peas or fresh asparagus.

Start to Finish: 25 minutes **Makes:** 4 servings

- **1½** cups sugar snap peas or 1-inch pieces fresh asparagus
- **1** 8.8-ounce pouch cooked long grain and wild rice
- **¼** cup purchased basil or dried tomato pesto
- **¼** cup light mayonnaise or salad dressing
- **1** 8-ounce piece smoked salmon, flaked, with skin and bones removed
- **1** cup cherry tomatoes, halved
- **⅓** cup thinly sliced radishes
  Lettuce leaves

1. In a medium saucepan, cook sugar snap peas in a small amount of boiling, lightly salted water for 2 minutes; drain. Place in a bowl of ice water to chill; drain.

2. In a large bowl, combine rice, pesto, and mayonnaise. Gently stir in peas, salmon, tomatoes, and radishes.

3. Spoon salad onto lettuce-lined plates.

Per serving: 312 cal., 14 g total fat (3 g sat. fat), 23 mg chol., 892 mg sodium, 28 g carbo., 3 g fiber, 16 g pro.

Quick Tip Sugar snap peas are a cross between the snow pea and the English pea (common green pea). Choose sugar snap peas that are plump, crisp, and bright green. Store unwashed peas in a plastic bag in the refrigerator for up to 3 days. Before using, snap off the stem ends, using them to pull on and remove the string, if present.

Red Snapper Veracruz

Red Snapper Veracruz 🖤

Couscous is granular semolina that steams in just minutes. It is a perfect alternative to pasta when cooking time is short.

Start to Finish: 20 minutes **Makes:** 4 servings

- **4   4- to 5-ounce fresh or frozen skinless red snapper or orange roughy fillets, ½ to 1 inch thick**
- **1   14-ounce can vegetable broth**
- **1   cup quick-cooking couscous**
- **¼   cup thinly sliced green onion (2) or coarsely chopped fresh cilantro**
- **Salt**
- **Ground black pepper**
- **⅓   cup bottled salsa**
- **Lemon wedges (optional)**

1. Thaw fish, if frozen. Preheat broiler. In a medium saucepan, bring broth to boiling. Stir in couscous. Cover saucepan and remove from heat. Let stand about 5 minutes or until liquid is absorbed. Stir in green onion.

2. Meanwhile, rinse fish; pat dry. Sprinkle fish with salt and pepper. Place fish on the greased unheated rack of a broiler pan, tucking under any thin edges to make pieces of uniform thickness. Measure thickness of the fish. Broil 4 to 5 inches from the heat until fish flakes when tested with a fork. (Allow 4 to 6 minutes per ½-inch thickness of fish; if fillets are 1 inch thick, turn once halfway through broiling.) Spoon the salsa over fish; broil 1 minute more or until salsa is heated through.

3. To serve, arrange fish on couscous mixture. If desired, serve with lemon wedges.

Per serving: 298 cal., 2 g total fat (0 g sat. fat), 42 mg chol., 603 mg sodium, 38 g carbo., 3 g fiber, 29 g pro.

Creamy Sea Bass ♥ [one]

This is definitely not your typical casserole! The generous Parmesan-bread crumb topping and decadent Dijon sauce are luscious on top of tender fish.

Prep: 20 minutes **Bake:** 20 minutes **Oven:** 450°F
Makes: 6 servings

1½	**pounds fresh or frozen sea bass or other white fish fillets, ½ inch thick**
½	**cup cream cheese with chive and onion**
2	**tablespoons mayonnaise or salad dressing**
1	**tablespoon milk**
1	**teaspoon lemon juice**
1	**teaspoon Dijon-style mustard**
¾	**cup soft bread crumbs**
¼	**cup grated Parmesan cheese**
4	**teaspoons dried parsley flakes, crushed**
½	**teaspoon paprika**

1. Thaw fish, if frozen. Rinse fish; pat dry. Cut fillets into 6 serving-size portions if necessary. Arrange fillets in a single layer in an ungreased 2-quart square baking dish. Set aside. Preheat oven to 450°F.

2. In a small bowl, combine cream cheese, mayonnaise, milk, lemon juice, and mustard. Spread cream cheese mixture over fillets. Bake for 10 minutes.

3. Meanwhile, combine bread crumbs, cheese, parsley, and paprika; sprinkle over fillets. Bake, uncovered, about 10 minutes more or until crumbs are golden and fish flakes easily when tested with a fork.

Per serving: 243 cal., 13 g total fat (6 g sat. fat), 71 mg chol., 300 mg sodium, 5 g carbo., 0 g fiber, 24 g pro.

Make-Ahead Directions: Prepare cream cheese mixture; cover and chill up to 4 hours. Prepare bread crumb mixture; cover and let stand at room temperature for up to 4 hours.

Quick Tip Use a blender or food processor to make fluffy soft bread crumbs. One slice yields ¾ cup crumbs.

Sesame-Crusted Salmon

Sesame-Crusted Salmon [one]

A quick turn in the skillet keeps the fish firm and juicy while enhancing the toasty crunch of the sesame.

Start to Finish: 30 minutes **Makes:** 4 servings

1	**pound fresh or frozen skinless salmon or halibut fillet**
½	**cup mayonnaise**
⅓	**cup chopped roasted red sweet pepper**
2	**teaspoons lemon juice**
1	**teaspoon snipped fresh chives**
	Salt
	Ground black pepper
⅓	**cup all-purpose flour**
1	**tablespoon white sesame seeds**
1	**tablespoon black sesame seeds**
¼	**teaspoon salt**
¼	**cup milk**
2	**tablespoons cooking oil**
	Lemon or lime wedges (optional)
	Fresh watercress (optional)

1. Thaw fish, if frozen. Rinse fish; pat dry with paper towels. Cut into 4 serving-size pieces. Set aside.

2. In a small bowl, combine mayonnaise, sweet pepper, lemon juice, and chives. Season to taste with salt and black pepper. Cover and chill until serving time.

3. In another small bowl, combine flour, white sesame seeds, black sesame seeds, and the ¼ teaspoon salt. Place milk in a shallow dish. Dip salmon in milk. Firmly press both sides of fish in sesame seed mixture.

4. In a large skillet, heat oil over medium-high heat; cook coated fish fillets in hot oil for 8 to 10 minutes or until fish flakes when tested with a fork, turning once. To serve, spoon sweet pepper sauce on dinner plates; top with fish. If desired, garnish with lemon or lime wedges and fresh watercress.

Per serving: 539 cal., 44 g total fat (8 g sat. fat), 78 mg chol., 404 mg sodium, 10 g carbo., 1 g fiber, 25 g pro.

Make-Ahead Directions: Prepare sweet pepper sauce; cover and chill up to 24 hours. Stir before serving; if necessary, stir in a little extra water.

Quick Tip If you can't find black sesame seeds, just use all white sesame seeds. Mix all of the sesame seeds with all of the flour and salt in one bowl, and dredge both sides of fish in mixture.

Roasted Salmon and Tomatoes ♥ one

Tomatoes sweeten as they roast alongside salmon fillets. A quick toss with fresh marjoram and Dijon-style mustard dresses them up in satisfying style.

Prep: 15 minutes **Bake:** 12 minutes **Oven:** 450°F
Makes: 4 servings

1	1¼-pound fresh salmon fillet, about 1 inch thick
	Nonstick cooking spray
¼	teaspoon salt
6	roma tomatoes, seeded and chopped (about 1 pound)
1	tablespoon Worcestershire sauce for chicken
¼	teaspoon ground black pepper
1	tablespoon Dijon-style mustard
1	tablespoon snipped fresh marjoram or oregano

1. Thaw fish, if frozen. Preheat oven to 450°F. Coat a 13×9×2-inch baking pan with nonstick cooking spray. Rinse fish; pat dry with paper towels. Cut fish into 4 serving-size pieces. Sprinkle with ⅛ teaspoon of the salt. Place fillet in pan, skin side up, tucking under any thin edges to make fish of uniform thickness. Arrange tomatoes around salmon. Sprinkle tomatoes with Worcestershire sauce, pepper, and the remaining ⅛ teaspoon salt.

2. Bake, uncovered, for 12 to 16 minutes or until fish begins to flake when tested with a fork. Remove skin from fish; discard skin. Transfer fish to 4 dinner plates. Stir mustard and marjoram into tomatoes. Serve tomato mixture with fish.

Per serving: 231 cal., 10 g total fat (2 g sat. fat), 75 mg chol., 370 mg sodium, 6 g carbo., 1 g fiber, 30 g pro.

Salmon Caesar Salad

Salmon Caesar Salad ♥

Smoked salmon is especially flavorful, but any form of salmon works well in this main-dish salad.

Start to Finish: 15 minutes **Makes:** 3 servings

- 1 **10-ounce package Caesar salad (includes lettuce, dressing, croutons, and cheese)**
- 1 **small yellow, red, or green sweet pepper, cut into thin strips**
- 1 **small cucumber, quartered lengthwise and sliced**
- 6 **ounces smoked, poached, or canned salmon, skinned, boned, and broken into chunks (1 cup)**
- ½ **of a lemon, cut into 3 wedges**

1. In a large bowl, combine the lettuce and dressing from the packaged salad, sweet pepper, and cucumber; toss gently to coat.

2. Add salmon and the croutons and cheese from the packaged salad; toss gently to mix. Divide among 3 dinner plates. Before serving, squeeze juice from a lemon wedge over each salad.

Per serving: 199 cal., 11 g total fat (1 g sat. fat), 16 mg chol., 564 mg sodium, 10 g carbo., 2 g fiber, 14 g pro.

Salmon Potato Cakes ♥

Seafood seasoning, sometimes called Old Bay seasoning, originated in Maryland crab houses and typically is a mix of celery salt or seeds, bay leaves, and spices. It varies by brand and makes a delicious addition to fish dishes such as this one. Look for it in the herb and spice aisle of your supermarket.

Start to Finish: 30 minutes **Makes:** 6 servings

- 1 **pound fresh or frozen salmon fillets**
- 3 **cups frozen shredded hash brown potatoes, thawed**
- 2 **eggs, lightly beaten**
- 1 **tablespoon seafood seasoning**
- 2 **tablespoons butter or margarine**

1. Thaw fish, if frozen. Rinse fish; pat dry with paper towels. In a covered large skillet, cook fish in a small amount of boiling water for 6 to 9 minutes or until fish flakes easily when tested with a fork. Remove skin, if present. Place fish in a large bowl and flake with a fork; cool slightly.

2. Add potatoes, eggs, and seafood seasoning to the fish; stir gently to combine. Shape fish mixture into 6 patties. In a 12-inch skillet, melt butter over medium heat. Add fish patties; cook about 8 minutes or until browned and heated through, turning once halfway through cooking time.

Per serving: 235 cal., 9 g total fat (4 g sat. fat), 121 mg chol., 466 mg sodium, 19 g carbo., 1 g fiber, 19 g pro.

Sole with Caponata ♥ [one]

Zesty caponata (the Italian cousin of France's ratatouille) turns ordinary fish into a fresh and lively dinner. Another time, try the caponata on your favorite sandwich or use it to top off broiled chicken.

Start to Finish: 20 minutes **Makes:** 4 servings

- 4 **4-ounce fresh or frozen skinless sole fillets**
- 1 **14.5-ounce can Italian-style stewed tomatoes, undrained**
- 2 **tablespoons olive oil**
- 2 **cups chopped, peeled eggplant**
- 1 **small yellow, green, or red sweet pepper, coarsely chopped**
- ¼ **cup bottled picante sauce**
- ½ **teaspoon bottled minced garlic (1 clove)**
- 1 **tablespoon balsamic vinegar**
- ⅛ **teaspoon salt**
- ⅛ **teaspoon ground black pepper**
  Lemon wedges (optional)

1. Thaw fish, if frozen. Rinse fish; pat dry with paper towels.

2. For the caponata, cut up any large tomato pieces; set aside. In a large nonstick skillet, heat 1 tablespoon of the oil over medium-high heat. Add eggplant; cook about 3 minutes or until golden brown, stirring occasionally. Stir in undrained tomatoes, sweet pepper, picante sauce, and garlic. Bring to boiling; reduce heat. Simmer, uncovered, for 4 to 5 minutes or until slightly thickened. Stir in balsamic vinegar. Remove from skillet; set aside.

3. Wipe out skillet with paper towels. Sprinkle fish with the salt and pepper. In the same skillet, heat the remaining 1 tablespoon oil over medium heat. Add fish; cook for 4 to 6 minutes or until fish flakes easily when tested with a fork. Serve caponata with fish. If desired, garnish with lemon wedges.

Per serving: 225 cal., 9 g total fat (1 g sat. fat), 49 mg chol., 481 mg sodium, 13 g carbo., 3 g fiber, 22 g pro.

Pineapple-Glazed
Orange Roughy

Tuna Salad Niçoise [one]

This classic French salad originated in the city of Nice in Provence. Anchovies are a traditional addition, but may be omitted if preferred.

Prep: 30 minutes **Marinate:** 4 hours
Makes: 4 servings

- **8   ounces tiny new potatoes (5 or 6)**
- **1½   cups cut green beans**
       Caper Vinaigrette
- **1   9.25-ounce can chunk white tuna (water pack), drained and broken into chunks,**
- **1   medium green sweet pepper, cut into strips**
- **1   cup cherry tomatoes, halved**
- **4   cups torn romaine and/or Boston or Bibb lettuce**
- **¾   cup pitted ripe olives**
- **½   of a 2-ounce can anchovy fillets, drained and halved (optional)**

1. In a covered medium saucepan, cook potatoes and beans in boiling, lightly salted water about 15 minutes or until vegetables are tender; drain. Rinse with cold water; drain again.

2. Prepare Caper Vinaigrette. Place tuna in small bowl; add ⅔ cup of the vinaigrette. Quarter potatoes. In a medium bowl, combine potatoes, sweet pepper, tomatoes, olives, and ⅔ cup of the vinaigrette. Cover each bowl and marinate in refrigerator for 4 hours.

3. To serve, line dinner plates with lettuce. Using slotted spoon, place tuna and potato mixture on top of lettuce. If desired, top with anchovies. Pass remaining vinaigrette.

Caper Vinaigrette: In a screw-top jar, combine ½ cup olive oil or salad oil, ½ cup white wine vinegar or white vinegar, 1 tablespoon dry mustard, 1 tablespoon drained capers, 1 teaspoon bottled minced garlic, 1 tablespoon snipped fresh basil or 1 teaspoon crushed dried basil, and 1 tablespoon snipped fresh oregano or 1 teaspoon crushed dried oregano. Cover and shake well.

Per serving: 404 cal., 23 g total fat (3 g sat. fat), 55 mg chol., 551 mg sodium, 19 g carbo., 5 g fiber, 31 g pro.

Pineapple-Glazed Orange Roughy ♥ [one]

A glaze may seem elegant but in most cases it's just a few tablespoons of preserves mixed with seasonings and vinegar. Be sure to try this one on chicken or pork as well.

Start to Finish: 20 minutes **Makes:** 4 servings

- **1   pound fresh or frozen orange roughy fillets, about ¾ inch thick**
- **3   tablespoons pineapple preserves**
- **2   tablespoons rice vinegar**
- **2   teaspoons snipped fresh thyme**
- **⅛   teaspoon crushed red pepper**
- **1   clove garlic, minced**
- **¼   teaspoon ground black pepper**
- **⅛   teaspoon salt**
       Fresh thyme sprigs (optional)
       Fresh pineapple wedges (optional)

1. Thaw fish, if frozen. Preheat broiler. In a small bowl, stir together preserves, vinegar, thyme, red pepper, and garlic; set aside.

2. Rinse fish; pat dry. Cut into 4 serving-size portions. Sprinkle fish with black pepper and salt. Place fish on the greased unheated rack of a broiler pan. Broil about 4 inches from the heat for 6 to 9 minutes or until the fish flakes easily when tested with a fork, brushing occasionally with the preserves mixture. If desired, garnish with thyme sprigs and pineapple wedges.

Per serving: 125 cal., 1 g total fat (0 g sat. fat), 22 mg chol., 150 mg sodium, 11 g carbo., 0 g fiber, 17 g pro.

Easy Baked Fish ♥ [one]

Easy says it all. Frozen fish portions plus stuffing mix brightened with a splash of lemon juice—dinner is ready in just 18 minutes.

Prep: 10 minutes **Bake:** 18 minutes **Oven:** 425°F
Makes: 4 servings

- **½   cup packaged herb-seasoned stuffing mix, finely crushed**
- **2   tablespoons butter, melted**
- **2   7.6-ounce packages frozen grill-flavored fish portions (4 portions total)**
- **2   teaspoons lemon juice**

1. Preheat oven to 425°F. In a small bowl, combine dry stuffing mix and melted butter; toss until well mixed.

2. Place frozen fish portions in a greased 2-quart rectangular baking dish. Sprinkle with lemon juice. Sprinkle stuffing mixture over fish.

3. Bake for 18 to 20 minutes or until fish flakes easily when tested with a fork.

Per serving: 183 cal., 9 g total fat (4 g sat. fat), 76 mg chol., 401 mg sodium, 6 g carbo., 1 g fiber, 18 g pro.

Linguine with Garlic Shrimp

Linguine with Garlic Shrimp ♥

Pick up the phone and invite some friends over tonight. This stylish recipe comes together quickly, making it perfect for a spontaneous get-together.

Start to Finish: 25 minutes **Makes:** 4 servings

8	**ounces refrigerated linguine or fettuccine pasta**
½	**cup chicken broth**
2	**teaspoons cornstarch**
1	**tablespoon snipped fresh basil or ½ teaspoon dried basil, crushed**
1	**tablespoon olive oil**
2	**cups sliced fresh mushrooms**
1	**medium yellow or green sweet pepper, chopped (1 cup)**
2	**tablespoons bottled minced garlic**
1	**14.5 ounce can Italian-style stewed tomatoes, undrained**
8	**ounces fresh or frozen shrimp, thawed, peeled, and deveined**
¼	**cup finely shredded Parmesan cheese (1 ounce)**
	Fresh basil leaves (optional)

1. Cook pasta according to package directions; drain and return to pan to keep warm.

2. In a small mixing bowl, combine broth, cornstarch, and snipped basil; set aside.

3. Meanwhile, in a large skillet, heat oil. Add mushrooms, sweet pepper, and garlic; cook until sweet pepper is just tender, about 3 minutes. Add broth mixture and undrained tomatoes; cook and stir until boiling. Add the shrimp; cover and simmer about 2 minutes or until shrimp turn opaque.

4. To serve, spoon shrimp mixture over pasta. Top with Parmesan cheese. If desired, garnish with fresh basil leaves.

Per serving: 420 cal., 9 g total fat (2 g sat. fat), 92 mg chol., 482 mg sodium, 59 g carbo., 3 g fiber, 25 g pro.

Quick Tip When purchasing shrimp, look for firm meat, translucent and moist shells without black spots, and a fresh scent (ammonia indicates spoilage). To store, refrigerate shrimp for up to 2 days. Keep frozen shrimp in the freezer for up to 6 months.

Cajun Shrimp with
Mango-Edamame Salsa

Cajun Shrimp with ♥ [one] Mango-Edamame Salsa

Stir up our homemade Cajun seasoning if you can't find salt-free seasoning mix for the shrimp.

Start to Finish: 30 minutes **Makes:** 4 servings

- **1 pound fresh or frozen large shrimp with tails**
- **2 teaspoons purchased salt-free Cajun seasoning or Homemade Cajun Seasoning**
- **1 tablespoon soybean cooking oil**
  Mango-Edamame Salsa
  Belgian endive leaves (optional)

1. Thaw shrimp, if frozen. Peel and devein shrimp, leaving tails intact if desired. Rinse shrimp; pat dry with paper towels. Set aside.

2. In a large bowl, toss shrimp with Cajun seasoning. In a large heavy skillet, heat oil over medium-high heat. Add shrimp; cook and stir about 5 minutes or until shrimp are opaque.

3. Serve shrimp warm with Mango-Edamame Salsa and, if desired, Belgian endive leaves.

Per serving: 317 cal., 12 g total fat (2 g sat. fat), 129 mg chol., 287 mg sodium, 29 g carbo., 6 g fiber, 27 g pro.

Homemade Cajun Seasoning: In a small bowl, stir together ½ teaspoon onion powder, ½ teaspoon paprika, ¼ teaspoon ground white pepper, ¼ teaspoon garlic powder, ¼ teaspoon cayenne pepper, and ¼ teaspoon ground black pepper.

Mango-Edamame Salsa: In a medium bowl, combine 2 seeded, peeled, and chopped mangoes; 1 cup fresh or frozen shelled sweet soybeans (edamame), cooked and cooled; 1 red sweet pepper, chopped; ½ cup finely chopped green onion; ¼ cup snipped fresh cilantro; 2 teaspoons soybean cooking oil; and ¼ teaspoon salt. Toss gently to mix. Cover and chill until serving time or up to 2 hours. Makes 3 cups.

Buttery Garlic Shrimp With Red Pepper

For extra color and flavor, add broccoli florets to this dish. Add the florets to the boiling pasta for the last 4 minutes of cooking time, or cook and stir with the shrimp.

Start to Finish: 10 minutes **Makes:** 4 servings

- **1½ pounds fresh or frozen medium shrimp, peeled and deveined**
- **8 ounces dried angel hair pasta**
- **2 tablespoons butter**
- **2 cloves garlic, minced, or 1 teaspoon bottled minced garlic**
  Salt
- **¼ teaspoon crushed red pepper**

1. Thaw shrimp, if frozen. Rinse shrimp; pat dry with paper towels. Cook pasta according to package directions. Drain pasta; keep warm.

2. Meanwhile, in a large skillet, melt butter over medium heat. Add garlic; cook for 30 seconds. Add the shrimp; sprinkle with salt. Cook and stir the shrimp for 2 to 4 minutes or until shrimp are opaque. Sprinkle with crushed red pepper. Serve shrimp over hot cooked pasta.

Per serving: 444 cal., 10 g total fat (4 g sat. fat), 274 mg chol., 438 mg sodium, 44 g carbo., 1 g fiber, 42 g pro.

Quick Tip To thaw frozen shrimp, place in a bowl of cold water for 30 to 60 minutes or until thawed.

Brown Rice Salad with Shrimp ♥ [one]

Brown rice comes in a quick-cooking variety that's ready in just 10 minutes. Its nutty flavor combines well with shrimp and asparagus, tempered with sweet-hot mustard and vivid bits of dried tomatoes.

Start to Finish: 20 minutes **Makes:** 4 servings

- **8 ounces fresh asparagus, trimmed and cut into 1½-inch pieces**
- **½ pound peeled and deveined uncooked shrimp**
- **3 cups cooked brown rice***
- **3 tablespoons chopped oil-packed dried tomatoes, drained**
- **2 tablespoons sweet-hot mustard or honey Dijon-style mustard**
- **2 tablespoons sliced almonds, toasted**

1. In a large saucepan, cook asparagus and shrimp, covered, in lightly salted boiling water for 3 minutes or until asparagus is crisp-tender and shrimp turn opaque. Drain; rinse under cold water.

2. In a large bowl, toss together asparagus and shrimp, rice, and drained tomatoes. Add mustard; toss lightly to coat. Sprinkle with almonds.

Per serving: 286 cal., 5 g total fat (1 g sat. fat), 86 mg chol., 158 mg sodium, 40 g carbo., 4 g fiber, 17 g pro.

*Note: For 3 cups cooked brown rice, use two 8.8-ounce pouches cooked whole grain brown rice, cook 1¾ cups uncooked instant brown rice according to the package directions, or cook 1 cup uncooked regular brown rice and 2 cups water, covered, in a medium saucepan over medium-low heat for 40 minutes or until rice is tender. To cool the rice quickly, spread in a shallow baking pan and freeze for 20 minutes.

Citrus Scallops ♥ [one]

Sea scallops are the larger of the two varieties of scallops. Even though they're quite thick, they cook in just 2 to 3 minutes.

Start to Finish: 15 minutes **Makes:** 4 servings

- 1 **pound fresh or frozen sea scallops**
- 1 **medium orange**
- 1 **tablespoon olive oil**
- 2 **cloves garlic, minced, or 1 teaspoon bottled minced garlic**
- ½ **teaspoon snipped fresh thyme**
  Salt and ground black pepper

1. Thaw scallops, if frozen. Rinse scallops; pat dry with paper towels. Set scallops aside. Finely shred 1 teaspoon peel from the orange. Cut orange in half; squeeze to get ⅓ cup juice.

2. In a large skillet, heat oil over medium-high heat. Add scallops. Cook, stirring frequently, for 2 to 3 minutes or until scallops turn opaque. Transfer scallops to a serving platter; keep warm.

3. For the sauce, add garlic to skillet; cook and stir for 30 seconds (add more oil to skillet if necessary). Add orange peel, orange juice, and thyme to skillet. Bring to boiling; reduce heat. Simmer, uncovered, for 1 to 2 minutes or until desired consistency. Season to taste with salt and pepper. Pour over scallops.

Per serving: 142 cal., 4 g total fat (1 g sat. fat), 37 mg chol., 218 mg sodium, 5 g carbo., 0 g fiber, 19 g pro.

Chipotle-Topped Crab Cakes [one]

The smoky flavor of chipotle chile peppers gives the stir-together sauce gusto that complements the subtly seasoned crab cakes. To tame the spiciness of the sauce, remove the seeds from the pepper before you add it.

Start to Finish: 30 minutes **Makes:** 4 servings

- 1 **egg, lightly beaten**
- ¾ **cup soft bread crumbs (1 slice)**
- 2 **tablespoons sliced green onion**
- 2 **tablespoons mayonnaise or salad dressing**
- 1 **tablespoon milk**
- ½ **teaspoon lemon-pepper seasoning**
- 2 **6.5-ounce cans crabmeat, drained, flaked, and cartilage removed**
  Nonstick cooking spray
- 4 **cups torn mixed salad greens**
  Chipotle Sauce
  Lime wedges (optional)

1. In a large bowl, stir together egg, bread crumbs, green onion, mayonnaise, milk, and lemon-pepper seasoning. Add crabmeat; mix well. Shape into eight 2½-inch crabmeat patties.

2. Lightly coat an unheated large nonstick skillet with cooking spray. Preheat over medium heat. Add patties. Cook for 6 to 8 minutes or until browned, turning once. Serve crab patties on greens with Chipotle Sauce. If desired, garnish with lime wedges.

Chipotle Sauce: In a small bowl, combine ⅓ cup mayonnaise or salad dressing; ¼ cup dairy sour cream; 2 tablespoons milk; 2 teaspoons snipped fresh cilantro; 1 canned chipotle chile pepper in adobo sauce, drained and finely chopped;* and a dash of salt.

Per serving: 359 cal., 26 g total fat (6 g sat. fat), 150 mg chol., 712 mg sodium, 8 g carbo., 1 g fiber, 23 g pro.

Spicy Jalapeño Shrimp Pasta ♥

Serve this robust pasta toss with slices of toasted baguette drizzled with extra-virgin olive oil.

Start to Finish: 30 minutes **Makes:** 4 servings

- 12 **ounces fresh or frozen large shrimp in shells**
- 8 **ounces dried linguine pasta**
- 2 **tablespoons extra-virgin olive oil**
- 1 **or 2 fresh jalapeño chile peppers, finely chopped***
- 1 **teaspoon bottled minced garlic (2 cloves)**
- ½ **teaspoon salt**
- ⅛ **teaspoon ground black pepper**
- 2 **cups chopped tomato and/or cherry tomatoes, halved or quartered**
  Finely shredded Parmesan cheese (optional)

1. Thaw shrimp, if frozen. Peel and devein shrimp. Rinse shrimp; pat dry with paper towels. Cook linguine according to package directions; drain well. Return to pan. Cover and keep warm.

2. In a large skillet, heat oil over medium-high heat. Add chile pepper, garlic, salt, and black pepper; cook and stir for 1 minute. Add shrimp; cook about 3 minutes more or until shrimp are opaque. Stir in tomato; heat through.

3. Toss cooked linguine with shrimp mixture. If desired, sprinkle with Parmesan cheese.

Per serving: 363 cal., 9 g total fat (1 g sat. fat), 97 mg chol., 396 mg sodium, 48 g carbo., 3 g fiber, 21 g pro.

***Note:** Because chile peppers contain volatile oils that can burn your skin and eyes, avoid direct contact with them as much as possible. When working with chile peppers, wear plastic or rubber gloves. If your bare hands do touch the chile peppers, wash your hands and nails well with soap and warm water.

Spicy Jalapeño Shrimp Pasta

Spinach-Pasta Salad with Shrimp

Spinach-Pasta Salad with Shrimp ♥ [one]

Frozen cooked shrimp are an easy way to add protein to a meal without lots of work. Simply thaw and use in recipes like this one.

Start to Finish: 20 minutes **Makes:** 6 servings

- **4 ounces shell pasta or elbow macaroni**
- **1 pound frozen cooked shrimp, thawed, or 1 pound cooked deli shrimp**
- **1 cup chopped red sweet pepper**
- **⅓ cup bottled creamy onion or Caesar salad dressing**
- **2 tablespoons snipped fresh dill (optional)**
- **1 6-ounce package baby spinach**
  Salt
  Ground black pepper
- **4 ounces goat cheese, sliced, or feta cheese, crumbled**
  Bottled creamy onion or Caesar dressing (optional)

1. Cook pasta according to package directions. Drain and rinse with cold water.

2. In an extra large bowl, combine cooked pasta, shrimp, and sweet pepper. Drizzle with ⅓ cup salad dressing; sprinkle with dill, if desired. Toss to coat. Season to taste with salt and pepper. Divide spinach between salad plates or bowls. Top with shrimp mixture and cheese. Drizzle with additional dressing, if desired.

Per serving: 247 cal., 10 g total fat (4 g sat. fat), 156 mg chol., 435 mg sodium, 17 g carbo., 2 g fiber, 23 g pro.

Pesto Pasta with Shrimp [one]

For convenience, turn to refrigerated pesto, adding some lemon peel for a fresh taste.

Start to Finish: 20 minutes **Makes:** 4 servings

- **12 ounces fresh or frozen, peeled and deveined medium shrimp (leave tails intact, if desired)**
- **1 9-ounce package refrigerated linguine pasta**
- **1 7-ounce container refrigerated basil pesto**
- **2 teaspoons finely shredded lemon peel**
- **2 tablespoons snipped fresh chives**
- **1 teaspoon finely shredded lemon peel (optional)**

1. Thaw shrimp, if frozen. Rinse shrimp; pat dry with paper towels. In a large saucepan, cook linguine in a large amount of boiling water for 1 minute. Add shrimp; cook about 2 minutes more or until shrimp turn opaque. Drain well.

2. Meanwhile, in a small bowl, stir together pesto and the 2 teaspoons lemon peel.

3. To serve, divide pasta mixture among 4 shallow bowls or dinner plates. Spoon pesto mixture over pasta mixture. Sprinkle with chives and, if desired, the 1 teaspoon lemon peel.

Per serving: 497 cal., 23 g total fat (6 g sat. fat), 186 mg chol., 562 mg sodium, 42 g carbo., 3 g fiber, 30 g pro.

Spanish-Style Rice with Seafood ♥ [one]

A package of Spanish-flavored rice is the base for this quick, one-skillet meal.

Start to Finish: 25 minutes **Makes:** 4 servings

- **1 5.6- to 6.2-ounce package Spanish-style rice mix**
- **1¾ cups water**
- **1 tablespoon butter or margarine**
  Several dashes bottled hot pepper sauce
- **1 12-ounce package frozen peeled, deveined shrimp**
- **1 cup frozen peas**
- **½ cup chopped tomato (1 medium)**

1. In a large skillet, stir together rice mix, the water, butter, and hot pepper sauce. Bring to boiling; reduce heat. Cover and simmer for 5 minutes.

2. Stir shrimp into rice mixture. Return to boiling; reduce heat. Cover and simmer for 2 to 3 minutes more or until shrimp turn opaque. Remove from heat. Stir in peas. Cover and let stand for 10 minutes. Sprinkle with chopped tomato before serving.

Per serving: 197 cal., 6 g total fat (2 g sat. fat), 137 mg chol., 414 mg sodium, 15 g carbo., 2 g fiber, 21 g pro.

Roasted Curried Shrimp ♥ [one]

Thirty minutes is exactly the right time for marinating the shrimp. Less than that and they won't absorb enough flavor; more than that and they may toughen.

Prep: 10 minutes **Bake:** 8 minutes
Marinate: 30 minutes **Oven:** 350°F
Makes: 4 to 6 servings

- 1½ **pounds fresh or frozen medium shrimp, peeled and deveined**
- ¼ **cup reduced-sodium soy sauce**
- 1 **tablespoon lemon juice**
- 2 **teaspoons curry powder**
- 2 **cloves garlic, minced, or 1 teaspoon bottled minced garlic**
  Hot cooked rice (optional)

1. Thaw shrimp, if frozen. Rinse shrimp; pat dry with paper towels. In a shallow baking dish, whisk together soy sauce, lemon juice, curry powder, and garlic. Add the shrimp and stir to coat well. Cover and refrigerate for 30 minutes.

2. Preheat the oven to 350°F. Line a baking sheet with foil. Using a slotted spoon, remove the shrimp from marinade and spread in a single layer on the prepared baking sheet. Discard remaining marinade.

3. Bake for 8 to 9 minutes or until the shrimp turn opaque. If desired, serve with hot cooked rice.

Per serving: 186 cal., 3 g total fat (1 g sat. fat), 259 mg chol., 378 mg sodium, 2 g carbo., 0 g fiber, 35 g pro.

Shrimp Capellini with Pesto Sauce ♥

Who has time to fix a romantic dinner? You do! With ready-made pesto, you can make a quick, elegant shrimp dish that's worthy of candlesticks and a tablecloth.

Start to Finish: 20 minutes **Makes:** 4 servings

- 12 **ounces fresh or frozen peeled and deveined shrimp**
- 8 **ounces dried tomato-flavored angel hair pasta (capellini), fettuccine, or linguine**
  Nonstick cooking spray
- 2 **medium yellow summer squash and/or zucchini, cut into ½-inch chunks (about 2 cups)**
- ⅓ **cup purchased pesto**
- 1 **medium plum tomato, chopped**

1. Thaw shrimp, if frozen. Cook pasta according to package directions; drain and keep warm.

2. Meanwhile, spray an unheated large nonstick skillet with cooking spray (or, brush it with a little oil drained from the pesto). Heat skillet over medium-high heat. Add shrimp; cook and stir for 2 minutes. Add squash; cook and stir about 2 minutes more or until shrimp turn opaque and squash is crisp-tender. Remove skillet from heat. Add pesto; toss gently to coat.

3. Serve shrimp mixture over pasta; sprinkle with tomato.

Per serving: 428 cal., 16 g total fat (0 g sat. fat), 134 mg chol., 316 mg sodium, 47 g carbo., 3 g fiber, 25 g pro.

Scallops with Tropical Salsa ♥ [one]

Sweet-tart bursts of papaya enliven this dish of succulent scallops. Scallops are quite delicate, so be cautious not to overcook them or they will toughen and lose their subtle texture.

Start to Finish: 25 minutes **Makes:** 4 servings

- 1 **cup finely chopped papaya or mango**
- ½ **cup seeded and chopped red sweet pepper**
- ½ **cup finely chopped, seeded cucumber**
- 2 **tablespoons chopped fresh cilantro**
- 1 **fresh jalapeño chile pepper, seeded and finely chopped***
- 4 **teaspoons lime juice**
- 1 **teaspoon extra-virgin olive oil**
- 12 **ounces fresh or frozen scallops**
  Kosher salt
  Freshly ground black pepper
- 2 **teaspoons extra-virgin olive oil**
- 1 **clove garlic, minced (½ teaspoon minced)**
  Lime wedges (optional)

1. For salsa, in a small bowl, stir together papaya, sweet pepper, cucumber, cilantro, chile pepper, lime juice, and oil. Let stand at room temperature for at least 15 minutes to allow flavors to blend.

2. Meanwhile, thaw scallops, if frozen. Rinse scallops; pat dry with paper towels. Halve any large scallops. Season lightly with kosher salt and black pepper.

3. In a large nonstick skillet, heat olive oil over medium heat. Add garlic; cook for 30 seconds. Add scallops. Cook and stir for 2 to 3 minutes or until scallops are opaque. Use a slotted spoon to remove scallops; drain on paper towels. Serve the scallops with the salsa. If desired, serve with lime wedges.

Per serving: 134 cal., 4 g total fat (1 g sat. fat), 28 mg chol., 262 mg sodium, 9 g carbo., 1 g fiber, 15 g pro.

***Note:** Because chile peppers contain volatile oils that can burn your skin and eyes, avoid contact with them as much as possible. When working with chile peppers, wear plastic or rubber gloves. If your bare hands do touch the chile peppers, wash your hands and nails well with soap and warm water.

Scallops with Tropical Salsa

Shrimply Divine Pasta

Shrimply Divine Pasta 🖤

Mafalda pasta, which looks like skinny lasagna noodles, is a great pasta pairing for this shrimp-Parmesan-spinach combo. Bow ties or fettuccine work well too.

Start to Finish: 25 minutes **Makes:** 4 servings

12	**ounces fresh or frozen peeled and deveined medium shrimp**
6	**ounces dried mafalda (or other pasta)**
1½	**teaspoons bottled minced garlic (3 cloves)**
1	**tablespoon olive oil or cooking oil**
2	**tablespoons butter**
2	**tablespoons all-purpose flour**
1	**teaspoon dried basil, crushed**
¼	**teaspoon salt**
⅛	**teaspoon ground black pepper**
2	**cups half-and-half or light cream**
4	**cups packaged prewashed baby spinach or torn spinach**
½	**cup finely shredded Parmesan cheese**
	Freshly ground black pepper or crushed red pepper (optional)

1. Thaw shrimp, if frozen. Rinse shrimp; pat dry with paper towels. Cook pasta according to the package directions. Drain well; keep warm.

2. Meanwhile, for the sauce, in a large skillet, cook garlic in hot oil over medium-high heat for 15 seconds. Add shrimp. Cook and stir for 2 to 3 minutes or until shrimp turn opaque. Remove shrimp.

3. In the same skillet, melt butter. Stir in flour, basil, salt, and pepper. Stir in half-and-half. Cook and stir over medium heat until thickened and bubbly. Cook and stir for 1 minute more. Return shrimp to skillet and add spinach and Parmesan cheese. Cook for 1 to 2 minutes more or until shrimp is heated through and spinach is wilted.

4. Toss shrimp mixture and pasta together. If desired, sprinkle with ground black pepper.

Per serving: 333 cal., 7 g total fat (1 g sat. fat), 136 mg chol., 422 mg sodium, 39 g carbo., 3 g fiber, 25 g pro.

Quick Tip To devein shrimp, use a sharp knife to make a shallow slit along the back from the head to the tail. If the vein is visible, hold the shrimp under cold running water to rinse it away.

Tossed Shrimp Salad

This refreshing salad gets you in and out of the kitchen fast, allowing plenty of time for after-dinner activities.

Start to Finish: 10 minutes **Makes:** 4 servings

- 2 **8-ounce packages frozen peeled, cooked shrimp, thawed**
- 1 **10-ounce package torn mixed salad greens**
- ¼ **cup thinly sliced green onion (2)**
- ⅓ **cup bottled Italian salad dressing**
  Salt (optional)
  Ground black pepper (optional)
- ¼ **cup sliced almonds, toasted**

1. Drain shrimp; pat dry with paper towels.

2. In a large salad bowl, combine shrimp, salad greens, and green onions. Pour dressing over salad; toss to coat. If desired, season to taste with salt and pepper. Sprinkle with almonds.

Per serving: 301 cal., 20 g total fat (2 g sat. fat), 185 mg chol., 483 mg sodium, 6 g carbo., 2 g fiber, 26 g pro.

White Clam Sauce with Spaghetti ♥

Here's a great recipe for nights when you forget about dinner. The dish can be made almost entirely from ingredients that have long shelf lives in the cupboard, fridge, and freezer.

Start to Finish: 22 minutes **Makes:** 4 servings

- 8 **ounces dried spaghetti, linguine, or twisted spaghetti pasta**
- 2 **6.5-ounce cans minced clams, undrained**
- 2 **teaspoons olive oil**
- 1 **medium onion, chopped (½ cup)**
- 2 **cloves garlic, minced**
- ¾ **cup milk**
- ⅓ **cup all-purpose flour**
- ¼ **teaspoon salt**
- ¼ **teaspoon lemon-pepper seasoning**
- ½ **cup frozen peas**
- ¼ **cup snipped fresh parsley**
- ¼ **cup dry white wine or chicken broth**
- 1 **tablespoon snipped fresh basil or ½ teaspoon dried basil, crushed**
  Grated Parmesan cheese (optional)

1. Cook pasta according to package directions; drain and keep warm.

2. Meanwhile, drain clams, reserving the liquid. Set clams aside. Add water, if necessary, to the reserved liquid to equal 1 cup. Set aside.

3. For the sauce, in a medium saucepan, heat oil. Add onion and garlic and cook until onion is tender. Place milk and flour in a screw-top jar; cover and shake until smooth. Add milk mixture to saucepan along with salt, lemon-pepper seasoning, and the clam liquid. Cook and stir over medium heat until thickened and bubbly. Cook and stir for 1 minute more. Stir in the clams, peas, parsley, wine, and basil. Heat through.

4. Serve sauce over hot pasta. If desired, sprinkle each serving with Parmesan cheese.

Per serving: 384 cal., 6 g total fat (1 g sat. fat), 24 mg chol., 364 mg sodium, 59 g carbo., 3 g fiber, 19 g pro.

Scallops and Spinach with Parmesan Sauce

The pairing of a hot mixture with cool greens sets this dish apart. You'll love the way the greens wilt pleasantly as they meld with the luscious, creamy scallop mixture.

Start to Finish: 25 minutes **Makes:** 4 servings

- 1 **pound fresh or frozen large sea scallops**
- 6 **cups purchased torn Italian-blend salad greens or prewashed baby spinach**
- 4 **small red and/or yellow tomatoes, cut into chunks or wedges**
- 3 **tablespoons butter or margarine**
- 1 **teaspoon bottled minced garlic (2 cloves)**
- ¼ **teaspoon cayenne pepper**
- 1 **tablespoon all-purpose flour**
- ¾ **cup half-and-half or light cream**
- ⅓ **cup grated Parmesan cheese**

1. Thaw scallops, if frozen. Rinse scallops; pat dry with paper towels.

2. Preheat broiler. Divide greens among 4 dinner plates. Arrange tomato chunks on top of greens; set aside.

3. Arrange scallops on the unheated rack of a broiler pan; set aside. In a small saucepan, melt butter over medium heat; stir in garlic and cayenne pepper. Remove from heat. Brush half of the butter mixture on scallops. Broil scallops 4 inches from heat about 8 minutes or until opaque, turning once halfway through broiling time. (If desired, for easier turning, thread scallops on metal skewers before broiling.)

4. Meanwhile, return saucepan to heat; stir flour into remaining butter mixture in saucepan. Add half-and-half and Parmesan cheese; cook and stir until thickened and bubbly. Cook and stir for 1 minute more.

5. Arrange broiled scallops on top of tomato chunks on dinner plates; drizzle with Parmesan cheese mixture.

Per serving: 310 cal., 18 g total fat (11 g sat. fat), 85 mg chol., 464 mg sodium, 12 g carbo., 2 g fiber, 26 g pro.

Couscous-Stuffed Peppers, **page 165**

Pasta Rosa-Verde, **page 149**

Spring Peas Risotto, **page 153**

Trattoria-Style Spinach
Fettuccine, **page 162**

Meatless Main Dishes

These scrumptious,
savory dishes feature
vegetables, cheese,
grains, and pasta
that allow health
conscious eaters to cut
back on meat without
sacrificing flavor.

Mediterranean Frittata

This open-face omelet calls on a windfall of convenience products to make a colorful, simple dish that's perfect for brunch, lunch, or supper.

Start to Finish: 30 minutes **Makes:** 6 servings

- 3 **tablespoons olive oil**
- 1 **cup chopped onion**
- 1 **teaspoon bottled minced garlic**
- 8 **eggs**
- ¼ **cup half-and-half, light cream, or milk**
- ½ **cup crumbled feta cheese (2 ounces)**
- ½ **of a 7-ounce jar (½ cup) roasted red sweet peppers, drained and chopped**
- ½ **cup sliced kalamata or pitted ripe olives**
- ¼ **cup slivered fresh basil**
- ⅛ **teaspoon ground black pepper**
- ½ **cup onion-and-garlic croutons, coarsely crushed**
- 2 **tablespoons finely shredded Parmesan cheese**
  Fresh basil leaves (optional)

1. Preheat broiler. In a 10-inch broilerproof skillet, heat 2 tablespoons of the oil over medium heat. Add onion and garlic; cook until onion is just tender.

2. Meanwhile, in a large mixing bowl, beat together eggs and half-and-half. Stir in feta cheese, roasted sweet peppers, olives, basil, and black pepper. Pour over onion mixture in skillet. Cook over medium heat. As mixture sets, run a spatula around the edge of the skillet, lifting egg mixture to allow the uncooked portion to flow underneath. Continue cooking and lifting edges until egg mixture is almost set (surface will be moist). Reduce heat as necessary to prevent overcooking.

3. Combine crushed croutons, Parmesan cheese, and the remaining 1 tablespoon of oil; sprinkle mixture over frittata.

4. Broil 4 to 5 inches from heat for 1 to 2 minutes or until top is set. Cut frittata in wedges to serve. If desired, garnish with fresh basil leaves.

Per serving: 242 cal., 19 g total fat (6 g sat. fat), 297 mg chol., 339 mg sodium, 7 g carbo., 1 g fiber, 12 g pro.

Mediterranean Frittata

Polenta with Fresh Tomato Sauce

Polenta with Fresh Tomato Sauce 🤍

Making polenta the traditional way takes a strong stirring hand and time for cooking, chilling, and slicing. This expeditious version serves up medallions of polenta that are crisp on the outside and creamy on the inside, placed on top of a savory rosemary-olive tomato sauce.

Start to Finish: 20 minutes **Makes:** 4 servings

4	**teaspoons olive oil**
½	**teaspoon bottled minced garlic**
6	**plum tomatoes, coarsely chopped (about 2 cups)**
¼	**cup pitted halved kalamata olives or sliced pitted ripe olives**
2	**teaspoons snipped fresh rosemary or 2 tablespoons snipped fresh thyme**
1	**16-ounce package prepared polenta**
½	**cup shredded smoked Gouda or Swiss cheese (2 ounces)**

1. For the sauce, in a medium saucepan, heat 2 teaspoons of the oil and the garlic over medium heat. Add tomatoes; cook for 2 minutes. Stir in olives and rosemary. Bring to boiling; reduce heat. Simmer, uncovered, for 8 minutes, stirring occasionally. Season to taste with salt and pepper.

2. Meanwhile, cut polenta into 8 slices. In a large nonstick skillet or on a griddle, heat the remaining 2 teaspoons oil over medium heat. Add polenta; cook about 6 minutes or until golden brown, turning once. Sprinkle with cheese. Serve on top of tomato sauce.

Per serving: 226 cal., 10 g total fat (3 g sat. fat), 16 mg chol., 608 mg sodium, 27 g carbo., 5 g fiber, 8 g pro.

Quick Tip Purchase fresh tomatoes that are firm, richly colored, and noticeably fragrant. They should be free of any blemishes, heavy for their size, and give slightly when lightly pressed. Store ripe tomatoes at room temperature away from direct sunlight and use within a few days. Never refrigerate fresh tomatoes; it will damage the texture and the flavor.

Pasta Rosa-Verde

Pasta Rosa-Verde ♥

Sometimes, all it takes to bring an irresistible out-of-the-ordinary flourish to an Italian dish is simply to call on a couple of knockout ingredients. Here, the starring touches are toasted pine nuts and sharp Gorgonzola cheese.

Start to Finish: 30 minutes
Makes: 4 main-dish servings

- 8 ounces dried penne or ziti pasta
- 1 tablespoon olive oil
- 1 medium onion, thinly sliced
- 2 cloves garlic, minced
- 4 to 6 medium tomatoes, seeded and coarsely chopped (3 cups)
- 1 teaspoon salt
- ½ teaspoon ground black pepper
- ¼ teaspoon crushed red pepper (optional)
- 3 cups arugula, watercress, and/or spinach, coarsely chopped
- ¼ cup pine nuts or slivered almonds, toasted
- 2 tablespoons crumbled Gorgonzola or other blue cheese

1. Cook pasta according to package directions; drain. Cover and keep warm.

2. Meanwhile, in a large skillet, heat oil over medium heat. Add onion and garlic and cook until onion is tender. Add tomatoes, salt, black pepper, and, if desired, crushed red pepper. Cook and stir over medium-high heat about 2 minutes or until the tomatoes are warm and release some of their juices. Stir in arugula, watercress, and/or spinach and heat just until greens are wilted.

3. To serve, divide pasta among individual serving bowls. Top with tomato mixture. Sprinkle with toasted pine nuts and cheese.

Per serving: 352 cal., 11 g total fat (2 g sat. fat), 3 mg chol., 610 mg sodium, 54 g carbo., 2 g fiber, 12 g pro.

Quick Tip To get the best flavor from your pasta, cook it only until it is al dente, or firm and somewhat chewy. In Italian, al dente means "to the tooth" and describes the doneness of pasta and other foods such as vegetables. For the best results, follow cooking directions on the package of dried or fresh pasta carefully.

Cashew Vegetable ♥ [one] Stir-Fry

Buttery roasted cashews provide protein in this quick, vegetarian stir-fry. Frozen vegetables and bottled stir-fry sauce make it quick to prepare.

Prep: 5 minutes **Cook:** 6 minutes **Makes:** 4 servings

- 1 tablespoon cooking oil
- 1 16-ounce package frozen stir-fry vegetables
- ⅓ cup bottled stir-fry sauce
- 3 cups hot cooked rice
- ¾ cup dry roasted cashews

1. In a large skillet, heat oil over medium-high heat. Add vegetables; cook and stir about 3 minutes or until crisp-tender. Add the sauce; stir-fry for 1 to 2 minutes more or until heated through.

2. Serve vegetable mixture over rice. Sprinkle with cashews.

Per serving: 393 cal., 16 g total fat (3 g sat. fat), 0 mg chol., 720 mg sodium, 54 g carbo., 4 g fiber, 9 g pro.

Gardener's Pie [one]

Smoky Cheddar and dried thyme give this simple mashed-potato-topped dish an earthy taste. Personalize the dish by adding your favorite frozen mixed vegetables..

Prep: 15 minutes **Bake:** 45 minutes **Oven:** 350°F
Makes: 4 servings

- 1 16-ounce package frozen mixed vegetables (any combination), thawed
- 1 11-ounce can condensed Cheddar cheese soup
- ½ teaspoon dried thyme, crushed
- 1 20-ounce package refrigerated mashed potatoes
- 1 cup shredded smoked Cheddar cheese (4 ounces)

1. Preheat oven to 350°F. In a 1½-quart casserole, combine thawed vegetables, soup, and thyme. Stir mashed potatoes to soften. Spread mashed potatoes carefully over vegetable mixture to cover surface.

2. Bake, covered, for 30 minutes. Uncover and bake about 15 minutes more or until heated through, topping with cheese for the last 5 minutes of baking. Serve in shallow bowls.

Per serving: 349 cal., 17 g total fat (8 g sat. fat), 39 mg chol., 1,031 mg sodium, 40 g carbo., 4 g fiber, 15 g pro.

Ramen Noodles with Vegetables

Use clean kitchen scissors to snip through the long noodles a few times to make shorter, easier-to-eat lengths.

Start to Finish: 15 minutes **Makes:** 2 to 3 servings

- 1   **3-ounce package ramen noodles (any flavor)**
- 1   **tablespoon cooking oil**
- 6   **ounces fresh asparagus, trimmed and cut into 1-inch pieces (1 cup)**
- 1   **medium carrot, shredded, or ½ cup purchased shredded carrot**
- ¼   **cup light teriyaki sauce**

1. Cook noodles according to package directions (discard seasoning packet or save for another use). Drain noodles and keep warm.

2. Meanwhile, in a large skillet, heat oil over medium-high heat. Add asparagus and carrot. Cook and stir for 3 to 5 minutes or until asparagus is crisp-tender. Stir in teriyaki sauce and noodles; toss to coat.

Per serving: 291 cal., 14 g total fat (4 g sat. fat), 0 mg chol., 1,396 mg sodium, 36 g carbo., 3 g fiber, 7 g pro.

Quick Tip Purchase firm, bright green asparagus stalks with tight tips. Choose stalks that are all approximately the same size and thickness—they'll cook more evenly. Generally, the thinner the spear, the more tender it will be.

Ramen Noodles with Vegetables

Roasted Vegetable Couscous

Roasted Vegetable Couscous ♥

Line a salad bowl with butterhead lettuce for a sensational presentation for palatable couscous.

Prep: 20 minutes   **Roast:** 45 minutes
Stand: 20 minutes   **Oven:** 375°F
Makes: 6 servings

	Nonstick cooking spray
1	**Japanese eggplant or 1 small eggplant, halved lengthwise**
1	**small sweet onion (such as Walla Walla or Vidalia), halved**
1	**carrot, halved lengthwise, or 4 ounces packaged peeled baby carrots**
1	**yellow or red sweet pepper, halved lengthwise and seeded**
1	**or 2 yellow banana peppers, halved lengthwise and seeded**
1	**cup water**
¾	**cup quick-cooking couscous**
	Balsamic-Mustard Dressing
	Butterhead lettuce leaves (optional)

1. Preheat oven to 375°F. Lightly coat a shallow baking pan with cooking spray. Place all vegetables, cut sides down, in prepared baking pan. Roast for 45 to 60 minutes or until tender.

2. Wrap eggplant and peppers in foil; let stand for 20 minutes. Set remaining vegetables aside. Peel eggplant and peppers. Cut all vegetables into bite-size pieces.

3. In a medium saucepan, bring the water to boiling. Stir in couscous. Remove from heat; let stand, covered, for 5 minutes.

4. In a large bowl, combine vegetables, couscous, and Balsamic-Mustard Dressing. Toss gently to coat. If desired, line a shallow serving bowl with lettuce leaves. Spoon in couscous mixture. Serve chilled or at room temperature.

Balsamic-Mustard Dressing: In a screw-top jar, combine ¼ cup white or regular balsamic vinegar, 1 tablespoon canola oil, 1½ teaspoons Dijon-style mustard, ¼ teaspoon ground black pepper, and ¼ teaspoon garlic powder. Cover; shake.

Per serving: 141 cal., 3 g total fat (0 g sat. fat), 0 mg chol., 105 mg sodium, 25 g carbo., 3 g fiber, 4 g pro.

Quick Tip If you like, use half of a yellow sweet pepper and half of a red sweet pepper.

Spring Peas Risotto

Spring Peas Risotto

Serve the classic Venetian dish with a simple fresh tomato salad and some Italian bread, and you're set for a lovely Northern Italian dinner.

Start to Finish: 30 minutes   **Makes:** 4 servings

- 2   **tablespoons olive oil**
- 1   **medium onion, chopped (½ cup)**
- 2   **cloves garlic, minced**
- 1   **cup arborio rice**
- 2   **14-ounce cans vegetable broth (3½ cups)**
- 1   **cup frozen tiny or regular-size shelled peas**
- ¼   **cup coarsely shredded carrot**
- 2   **cups fresh spinach, shredded**
- ¼   **cup grated Parmesan cheese**
- 1   **tablespoon snipped fresh thyme**

1. In a large saucepan, heat oil over medium heat. Cook onion and garlic until onion is tender. Add the rice. Cook and stir about 5 minutes or until rice is golden.

2. Meanwhile, in a medium saucepan, bring broth to boiling; reduce heat and simmer. Carefully add 1 cup of the broth to the rice mixture, stirring constantly. Continue to cook and stir over medium heat until liquid is absorbed.

3. Add another 1 cup of the broth to the rice mixture, stirring constantly. Continue to cook and stir until liquid is absorbed. Add another 1 cup broth, ½ cup at a time, stirring constantly until the broth has been absorbed. (This should take about 18 to 20 minutes.)

4. Stir in remaining ½ cup broth, the peas, and carrot. Cook and stir until the rice is slightly creamy and just tender.

5. Stir in the spinach, Parmesan cheese, and thyme; heat through. Serve immediately.

Per serving: 263 cal., 10 g total fat (2 g sat. fat), 5 mg chol., 1,047 mg sodium, 388 g carbo., 3 g fiber, 9 g pro.

Chili Corn Pie one

Refrigerated corn bread twists make a tasty, and easy, topping on this Texas-style casserole.

Prep: 20 minutes   **Bake:** 20 minutes   **Stand:** 5 minutes
Oven: 375°F   **Makes:** 4 servings

- 2   **11-ounce packages frozen bean chili**
- 1   **11.5-ounce package refrigerated corn bread twists**
- ⅓   **cup shredded Cheddar cheese**
- 1   **tablespoon snipped fresh cilantro**
- ¼   **cup dairy sour cream**

1. Preheat oven to 375°F. Heat the chili according to microwave package directions.

2. Meanwhile, on a lightly floured surface, unroll sheet of corn bread twist dough (do not separate into strips). Press at perforations to seal. Roll to an 11×7-inch rectangle.

3. Spoon hot chili into a 2-quart rectangular baking dish. Immediately place corn bread dough on top of chili in baking dish. Using a sharp knife, cut slits in corn bread dough to allow steam to escape.

4. Bake about 20 minutes or until corn bread is lightly browned. Sprinkle with cheese and cilantro. Let stand for 5 minutes before serving. Top individual servings with sour cream.

Per serving: 512 cal., 24 g total fat (9 g sat. fat), 44 mg chol., 1,429 mg sodium, 50 g carbo., 3 g fiber, 22 g pro.

Chipotle Bean Enchiladas one

Here's a pantry casserole that fits the bill for Sunday supper—a little festive, a lot easy, and destined to be a family favorite.

Prep: 25 minutes   **Bake:** 40 minutes   **Oven:** 350°F
Makes: 5 servings

- 10   **6-inch corn tortillas**
- 1   **15-ounce can pinto beans or black beans, rinsed and drained**
- 1   **tablespoon chopped chipotle pepper in adobo sauce***
- 1   **8-ounce package shredded Mexican cheese blend (2 cups)**
- 2   **10-ounce cans enchilada sauce**

1. Preheat oven to 350°F. Grease a 2-quart rectangular baking dish; set aside. Stack the tortillas and wrap tightly in foil. Warm tortillas in the preheated oven for 10 minutes.

2. Meanwhile, for the filling, in a medium bowl, combine drained beans, chipotle pepper, 1 cup of the cheese, and ½ cup of the enchilada sauce. Spoon about ¼ cup of the filling onto one edge of each tortilla. Starting at the edge with the filling, roll up each tortilla.

3. Arrange tortillas, seam sides down, in the prepared baking dish. Top with remaining enchilada sauce. Cover with foil.

4. Bake about 25 minutes or until heated through. Remove foil. Sprinkle with remaining 1 cup cheese. Bake, uncovered, about 5 minutes more or until cheese melts.

Per serving: 487 cal., 19 g total fat (8 g sat. fat), 40 mg chol., 1,091 mg sodium, 63 g carbo., 14 g fiber, 23 g pro.

***Note:** Because chile peppers can contain volatile oils that can burn your skin and eyes, avoid direct contact with them as much as possible. When working, with chile peppers, wear plastic or rubber gloves. If your bare hands do touch the chile peppers, wash your hands and nails well with soap and warm water.

Broccoli Rabe and Penne ♥

Broccoli rabe has a pleasant, slightly bitter flavor.

Start to Finish: 25 minutes **Makes:** 6 servings

- **1** pound broccoli rabe
- **8** ounces dried multigrain penne pasta
- **2** tablespoons extra-virgin olive oil
- **6** cloves garlic, minced (1 tablespoon minced)
- **¼** to ½ teaspoon crushed red pepper
- **¼** cup grated Parmesan cheese
- **1** tablespoon lemon juice
  Salt and ground black pepper
- **⅓** cup shredded Parmesan cheese

1. Trim tough stems from broccoli rabe; discard stems. Coarsely chop the broccoli rabe leaves. In a Dutch oven, cook broccoli rabe in a large amount of boiling salted water for 5 to 7 minutes or until tender. Drain; submerse broccoli rabe into a large bowl of ice water to cool quickly. When cool, drain well.

2. Meanwhile, cook pasta according to package directions. Drain pasta, reserving ¾ cup of the cooking water.

3. In a large skillet, heat olive oil over medium heat. Add garlic and red pepper; cook for 1 minute. Add broccoli rabe; toss to coat with oil. Add the drained pasta, reserved pasta cooking water, grated Parmesan cheese, and lemon juice. Cook and stir until heated through. Season to taste with salt and black pepper. Sprinkle each serving with shredded Parmesan cheese.

Per serving: 238 cal., 7 g total fat (2 g sat. fat), 6 mg chol., 263 mg sodium, 30 g carbo., 5 g fiber, 12 g pro.

Skillet Eggplant Parmigiana

This range-top version satisfies diners just as much as the classic long-baking casserole. A bonus topping of heady basil and crunchy walnuts gives the dish a fresh, up-to-date touch.

Start to Finish: 30 minutes **Makes:** 4 servings

- **1** medium eggplant (1 pound)
- **¼** cup seasoned fine dry bread crumbs
- **½** cup grated Parmesan cheese
- **1** egg
- **1** tablespoon water
- **2** tablespoons olive oil or cooking oil
- **1¼** cup meatless spaghetti sauce
- **1** cup shredded mozzarella cheese (4 ounces)
- **¼** cup snipped fresh basil
- **2** tablespoons finely chopped walnuts

1. Peel eggplant, if desired. Cut eggplant into ¾-inch slices. In a shallow dish, combine bread crumbs and ¼ cup of the Parmesan cheese. In another shallow dish, combine egg and the water. Dip eggplant slices into the egg mixture and then into the crumb mixture to coat.

2. In a 12-inch skillet, heat oil over medium heat. Cook eggplant for 6 to 8 minutes or until golden, turning once. Add spaghetti sauce; sprinkle with mozzarella cheese and remaining ¼ cup Parmesan cheese. Reduce heat to medium-low. Cook, covered, for 5 minutes.

3. Sprinkle fresh basil and walnuts over eggplant just before serving.

Per serving: 295 cal., 20 g total fat (7 g sat. fat), 48 mg chol., 850 mg sodium, 18 g carbo., 5 g fiber, 15 g pro.

Broccoli Rabe and Penne

Vegetable Medley au Gratin

Vegetable Medley au Gratin

No peeling or chopping the vegetables! An easy-to-use bag of frozen vegetables goes gourmet with a buttery walnut topping.

Prep: 20 minutes **Bake:** 65 minutes
Oven: 300°F/375°F **Makes:** 5 servings

- 1 **10.75-ounce can condensed cream of chicken and mushroom soup**
- ½ **cup dairy sour cream**
- ½ **teaspoon dried dill, crushed**
- 2 **16-ounce packages loose-pack frozen broccoli, cauliflower, and carrots, thawed**
- ⅔ **cup crushed stone-ground wheat crackers (about 15 crackers)**
- ⅓ **cup finely chopped walnuts**
- ¼ **cup shredded Parmesan cheese**
- 2 **tablespoons butter, melted**

1. Preheat oven to 300°F. In a large bowl, combine soup, sour cream, and dill; stir in thawed vegetables. Transfer mixture to an ungreased 2-quart rectangular baking dish.

2. In a small bowl, combine crackers, walnuts, cheese, and melted butter. Cover and chill until needed.

3. Bake, covered, for 50 minutes. Increase oven temperature to 375°F. Sprinkle crumb mixture over vegetable mixture. Bake, uncovered, about 15 minutes more or until topping is golden brown.

Per serving: 314 cal., 20 g total fat (8 g sat. fat), 32 mg chol., 904 mg sodium, 22 g carbo., 6 g fiber, 10 g pro.

Harvest Vegetable Hash ♥ ⬛

This vibrant mix of veggies taste great on a chilly fall day.

Prep: 30 minutes **Roast:** 30 minutes **Oven:** 425°F
Makes: 4 to 6 servings

- ⅓ **teaspoon ancho chili powder**
- ⅓ **teaspoon coarse sea salt or kosher salt**
- ⅓ **teaspoon cracked black pepper**
- ¼ **teaspoon ground turmeric**
- 5 **to 6 cups coarsely chopped vegetables, such as peeled sweet potatoes, carrots, tiny new potatoes, and/or onions, cut into wedges**
- 3 **cloves garlic, peeled and cut in half**
- 2 **tablespoons olive oil or cooking oil**
- 1 **cup packed spinach leaves**

1. Preheat oven to 425°F. In a small bowl, combine chili powder, salt, pepper, and turmeric.

2. In a large roasting pan, toss vegetables and garlic with the oil. Sprinkle with the chili powder mixture; toss again to distribute seasonings.

3. Roast vegetables, uncovered, for 30 to 35 minutes or until lightly browned and tender, stirring once or twice. Remove from oven. Add spinach and toss until wilted.

Per serving: 193 cal., 7 g total fat (1 g sat. fat), 0 mg chol., 231 mg sodium, 31 g carbo., 5 g fiber, 3 g pro.

Barley and Bean Skillet ⬛

If you have a few extra minutes, you can shred your own carrot.

Start to Finish: 30 minutes **Makes:** 4 servings

- 1 **14-ounce can vegetable broth**
- ⅓ **cup water**
- 1¼ **cups quick-cooking barley**
- 2 **cups loose-pack frozen cut green beans**
- 1 **10.75-ounce can condensed cream of onion soup**
- ½ **cup purchased shredded carrot**
- ½ **cup milk**
- ½ **teaspoon dried thyme, crushed**
- 1 **cup shredded cheddar cheese (4 ounces)**

1. In a large skillet, combine vegetable broth and the water; bring to boiling. Stir in barley. Return to boiling; reduce heat. Cover and simmer for 5 minutes.

2. Stir in green beans, soup, carrot, milk, and thyme. Bring to boiling; reduce heat. Cover and simmer for 12 to 15 minutes more or until barley is tender and most of the liquid is absorbed, stirring occasionally. Stir in half of the cheese. Sprinkle with remaining cheese. Let stand for 2 to 3 minutes or until cheese is melted.

Per serving: 394 cal., 15 g total fat (8 g sat. fat), 45 mg chol., 1,193 mg sodium, 52 g carbo., 8 g fiber, 16 g pro.

Ziti with Eggplant and Dried Tomato Pesto

Ziti with Eggplant and Dried Tomato Pesto

Treat your family to this full-flavor pasta sauce made richer and sweeter with roasted vegetables. Refrigerate or freeze the remaining Dried Tomato Pesto to toss with pasta for other meals.

Start to Finish: 35 minutes   **Oven:** 425°F
Makes: 4 servings

- **1**   **medium onion, cut into 8 wedges**
- **2**   **tablespoons olive oil**
- **1**   **medium eggplant (about 1 pound), halved lengthwise**
- **6**   **ounces dried ziti, rigatoni, or penne pasta**
- **⅓**   **cup Dried Tomato Pesto or ⅓ cup purchased dried tomato pesto**
- **¼**   **teaspoon coarsely ground black pepper**
    Salt
- **2**   **tablespoons crumbled goat cheese (chèvre) or feta cheese (optional)**
    Snipped fresh basil (optional)

1. Preheat oven to 425°F. Place onion in a large shallow baking pan; brush with 1 tablespoon of the olive oil. Roast for 10 minutes; stir. Brush eggplant with remaining olive oil. Place eggplant in pan, cut sides down. Roast 15 minutes more or until onion is golden brown and eggplant is tender.

2. Meanwhile, cook pasta according to package directions; drain. Add Dried Tomato Pesto and black pepper to pasta; toss gently to coat. Transfer pasta to a warm serving dish; keep warm.

3. Cut eggplant into ½-inch slices. Toss eggplant and onion with pasta. Season to taste with salt. Top with cheese and basil, if desired.

Dried Tomato Pesto: Drain ¾ cup oil-pack dried tomatoes, reserving oil. Add enough olive oil to the reserved oil to make ½ cup; set aside. Place tomatoes, ¼ cup pine nuts or slivered almonds, ¼ cup snipped fresh basil, ½ teaspoon salt, and 4 teaspoons bottled minced garlic in a food processor. Cover; process until finely chopped. With machine running, gradually add the oil, processing until almost smooth. Divide pesto into thirds. Refrigerate or freeze unused portions. Makes three ⅓-cup portions.

Per serving: 370 cal., 19 g total fat (3 g sat. fat), 0 mg chol., 112 mg sodium, 43 g carbo., 4 g fiber, 8 g pro.

Spinach-Feta Shells with Minted Tomato Sauce ♥

Garlic and mint add subtle flavor to plump, cheese-and-spinach-filled shells. They contain no meat, but you'll never miss it.

Prep: 25 minutes **Bake:** 30 minutes **Oven:** 350°F
Makes: 4 servings

- **12   jumbo pasta shells**
- **1   10-ounce package frozen chopped spinach, thawed and well-drained**
- **½   cup crumbled feta cheese (2 ounces)**
- **½   cup ricotta cheese**
- **¼   cup chopped walnuts, toasted**
- **1   egg**
- **¼   teaspoon salt**
- **⅛   teaspoon ground black pepper**
- **1   14.5-ounce can diced tomatoes, undrained**
- **½   of a 6-ounce can tomato paste (⅓ cup)**
- **1½   teaspoons dried mint, crushed**
- **¼   teaspoon garlic powder**
- **½   cup shredded mozzarella cheese (2 ounces)**

1. Preheat oven to 350°F. Cook pasta shells according to package directions. Drain and set aside.

2. Meanwhile, in a medium mixing bowl, combine spinach, feta cheese, ricotta cheese, walnuts, egg, salt, and pepper. Stir to mix. Set aside.

3. For the sauce, in a medium saucepan, combine undrained tomatoes, tomato paste, mint, and garlic powder. Bring to boiling; reduce heat. Simmer, uncovered, for 5 minutes.

4. Fill each shell with about 2 tablespoons of the spinach mixture. Arrange in an ungreased 2-quart square baking dish. Spoon sauce over shells. Bake, covered, for 30 to 35 minutes or until heated through. Sprinkle with mozzarella cheese. Bake, uncovered, for 2 to 3 minutes more or until cheese melts.

Per serving: 339 cal., 16 g total fat (7 g sat. fat), 92 mg chol., 677 mg sodium, 30 g carbo., 4 g fiber, 17 g pro.

Spinach-Feta Shells with
Minted Tomato Sauce

Orzo Pasta with Mushrooms
and Leeks

Orzo Pasta with ♥ Mushrooms and Leeks

Even devout meat eaters will enjoy this simple, earthy dish.

Start to Finish: 25 minutes **Makes:** 4 servings

- **¾   cup dried orzo pasta**
- **1   tablespoon margarine or butter**
- **4   ounces assorted fresh mushrooms (such as porcini, cremini, chanterelle, shiitake, or button), sliced or quartered (1½ cups)**
- **1   leek or 2 large green onions, chopped (about ⅓ cup)**
- **¼   teaspoon ground black pepper**
- **⅛   teaspoon salt**
- **1   clove garlic, minced**
- **¼   cup water**
- **½   to 1 teaspoon snipped fresh marjoram or ¼ teaspoon dried marjoram, crushed**
- **½   teaspoon instant beef or chicken bouillon granules**
- **Grated Romano cheese (optional)**

1. Cook orzo according to package directions; drain well.

2. Meanwhile, in a large skillet, heat margarine over medium-high heat; stir in the mushrooms, leek, pepper, salt, and garlic.

3. Cook, uncovered, for 5 minutes. Add the water, dried marjoram (if using), and bouillon granules. Reduce heat; cook until liquid is almost absorbed, about 6 minutes. Stir in fresh marjoram (if using).

4. Toss mushroom mixture with pasta. Sprinkle with Romano cheese, if desired.

Per serving: 167 cal., 4 g total fat (2 g sat. fat), 8 mg chol., 209 mg sodium, 29 g carbo., 2 g fiber, 5 g pro.

Pasta and Sweet Pepper Primavera

Pasta and Sweet Pepper Primavera ♥

Skip a step! Here, you add the vegetables to the pasta during the last three minutes of cooking; just heat up a little Alfredo sauce, add a touch of tarragon and crushed red pepper, and you've got an Italian classic at its fresh-and-simple best.

Start to Finish: 20 minutes **Makes:** 4 servings

- 14 ounces asparagus spears
- 8 ounces dried cavatappi (corkscrews) or rotini pasta (about 2½ cups)
- 1 large red or yellow sweet pepper, cut into 1-inch pieces
- 4 baby sunburst squash, halved (½ cup)
- ½ medium yellow summer squash or zucchini, sliced (½ cup)
- 1 10-ounce container refrigerated light Alfredo sauce
- 2 tablespoons snipped fresh tarragon or thyme
- ¼ teaspoon crushed red pepper

1. Snap off and discard woody bases from asparagus. Bias-slice asparagus into 1-inch pieces (you should end up with about 1½ cups).

2. Cook pasta according to package directions, adding asparagus, sweet pepper, and squash to pasta during the last 3 minutes of cooking; drain. Return pasta and vegetables to hot saucepan.

3. Meanwhile, in a small saucepan, combine Alfredo sauce, tarragon, and crushed red pepper. Cook and stir over medium heat about 5 minutes or until mixture is heated through. Pour over pasta and vegetables; toss gently to coat.

Per serving: 421 cal., 12 g total fat (6 g sat. fat), 31 mg chol., 622 mg sodium, 66 g carbo., 2 g fiber, 15 g pro.

Quick Tip Purchase sweet peppers that have richly colored, shiny skin, and are firm and heavy for their size. Avoid those that are limp, shriveled, or which have soft or bruised spots.

Tortellini Stir-Fry

Bottled stir-fry sauce provides a dozen seasoning ingredients in a single step. Keep one or two varieties on hand.

Start to Finish: 20 minutes **Makes:** 4 servings

- 1 9-ounce package refrigerated cheese-filled tortellini
- 1 tablespoon cooking oil
- 1 16-ounce package fresh cut or frozen stir-fry vegetables (such as broccoli, snow peas, carrots, and celery)
- ¾ cup peanut stir-fry sauce
- ¼ cup chopped dry-roasted cashews

1. Cook tortellini according to package directions. Drain and set aside.

2. In a wok or large skillet, heat oil over medium-high heat. Add fresh cut vegetables; cook and stir for 3 to 5 minutes (7 to 8 minutes for frozen vegetables) or until crisp-tender. Add tortellini and stir-fry sauce; toss gently to coat. Heat through. Sprinkle with cashews; serve immediately.

Per serving: 400 cal., 16 g total fat (3 g sat. fat), 30 mg chol., 1,256 mg sodium, 48 g carbo., 4 g fiber, 18 g pro.

Angel Hair Pasta with Asparagus, Tomatoes, And Basil ♥

Angel hair pasta is one of the quickest-cooking pastas around—and the refrigerated version is even speedier! That makes it the perfect pasta for the equally speedy sauce in this recipe.

Start to Finish: 20 minutes **Makes:** 3 servings

- 16 fresh asparagus spears
- 1 9-ounce package refrigerated angel hair pasta
- 1 tablespoon olive oil
- 4 cloves garlic, minced
- ¼ teaspoon ground black pepper
- 6 medium plum (Roma) tomatoes, seeded and chopped (2¼ cups)
- ¼ cup dry white wine
- ¼ teaspoon salt
- 1 tablespoon butter
- ¼ cup shredded fresh basil

1. Trim asparagus; rinse in cold water. Remove tips; set tips aside. Bias-slice remaining asparagus stalks into 1- to 1½-inch pieces; set aside.

2. Cook pasta according to package directions; drain. Return pasta to saucepan.

3. Meanwhile, in a large skillet, heat oil over medium heat. Add garlic and pepper; cook for 1 minute, stirring constantly. Add tomatoes and cook about 2 minutes, stirring often.

4. Add asparagus stalks, wine, and salt. Cook, uncovered, for 3 minutes. Add asparagus tips; cook uncovered, for 1 minute more. Add butter; stirring until melted. Add asparagus mixture and basil to pasta; toss gently to coat. Transfer to a warm serving dish.

Per serving: 484 cal., 11 g total fat (3 g sat. fat), 10 mg chol., 185 mg sodium, 81 g carbo., 15 g fiber, 15 g pro.

Farfalle with Spinach and Mushrooms

Farfalle with Spinach And Mushrooms 🖤

To make this quick recipe even quicker, look for sliced fresh mushrooms, prewashed spinach, and shredded Parmesan cheese. If your spinach hasn't been washed, be sure to rinse it well to wash away all the sand.

Start to Finish: 15 minutes **Makes:** 4 servings

- 6 ounces dried farfalle (bow tie) pasta
- 1 tablespoon butter
- 1 medium onion, chopped
- 1 cup sliced portobello mushrooms or other fresh mushrooms
- 2 cloves garlic, minced
- 4 cups thinly sliced fresh spinach or
     2 cups thinly sliced sorrel and 2 cups thinly sliced fresh spinach
- 1 teaspoon snipped fresh thyme
- ⅛ teaspoon ground black pepper
- 1 tablespoon licorice-flavored liqueur (optional)
- 2 tablespoons shredded Parmesan cheese

1. Cook pasta according to package directions; drain.

2. Meanwhile, in a large skillet, melt butter over medium heat. Add onion, mushrooms, and garlic; cook and stir for 2 to 3 minutes or until mushrooms are nearly tender. Stir in spinach, thyme, and pepper; cook 1 minute or until heated through and spinach is slightly wilted. Stir in cooked pasta and, if desired, liqueur. Toss gently to mix. Sprinkle with cheese.

Per serving: 214 cal., 6 g total fat (1 g sat. fat), 39 mg chol., 127 mg sodium, 33 g carbo., 2 g fiber, 9 g pro.

Tortilla Lasagna

This layered casserole goes together in a jiffy using off-the-shelf ingredients.

Prep: 10 minutes **Bake:** 35 minutes
Stand: 10 minutes **Oven:** 400°F **Makes:** 8 servings

- 1 7-ounce package Spanish rice mix
- 1 11-ounce can whole kernel corn with sweet peppers, undrained
- 2 15-ounce cans black beans, undrained
- 10 6-inch corn tortillas
- 2 cups shredded Monterey Jack cheese with jalapeño peppers (8 ounces)

1. Preheat oven to 400°F. Prepare the rice according to package directions, except substitute undrained corn for ½ cup of the liquid. Place undrained beans in a medium bowl; mash slightly.

2. Place five tortillas in the bottom of a greased 3-quart rectangular baking dish, overlapping and placing slightly up the sides of the dish (cut tortillas as necessary to fit). Spoon beans evenly over tortillas. Sprinkle with 1 cup of the cheese. Top with the remaining tortillas. Spoon cooked rice over tortillas.

3. Bake, covered, for 30 minutes. Uncover and sprinkle with remaining 1 cup cheese. Bake about 5 minutes more or until cheese is melted. Let stand 10 minutes before serving.

Per serving: 406 cal., 12 g total fat (7 g sat. fat), 34 mg chol., 1,101 mg sodium, 60 g carbo., 11 g fiber, 20 g pro.

Udon Noodles With Tofu ♥ one

Look for Japanese udon noodles near the Asian ingredients in your supermarket or use linguine.

Start to Finish: 25 minutes
Makes: 6 servings

- **8**   **ounces dried udon noodles or whole wheat linguine**
- **2**   **6- to 8-ounce packages smoked teriyaki-flavored or plain firm tofu (fresh bean curd), cut into ½-inch pieces**
- **1½**   **cups chopped cucumber**
- **1**   **large carrot, cut into thin bite-size pieces**
- **½**   **cup sliced green onion**
      Ginger-Soy Vinaigrette

1. Cook pasta according to package directions; drain. Cool pasta slightly.
2. Meanwhile, in a large bowl, combine tofu, cucumber, carrot, and green onion. Add drained pasta; toss gently to mix.
3. Drizzle Ginger-Soy Vinaigrette onto cooked pasta mixture. Toss salad gently to coat.

Ginger-Soy Vinaigrette: In a small bowl, whisk together 2 tablespoons rice vinegar or cider vinegar, 1 tablespoon toasted sesame oil, 2 teaspoons reduced-sodium soy sauce, 4 minced cloves garlic, 1 teaspoon grated fresh ginger, and ¼ teaspoon crushed red pepper. Makes ¼ cup.

Per serving: 231 cal., 4 g total fat (0 g sat. fat), 0 mg chol., 571 mg sodium, 39 g carbo., 3 g fiber, 7 g pro.

Make-Ahead Directions: Prepare as directed. Cover and chill for up to 6 hours.

Udon Noodles with Tofu

Linguine with Gorgonzola Sauce

Linguine and asparagus cook together in the same pan, then share a cheesy Gorgonzola sauce and a sprinkling of toasted nuts.

Start to Finish: 20 minutes **Makes:** 4 servings

- 1 **9-ounce package refrigerated linguine pasta**
- 1 **pound fresh asparagus, trimmed and cut into 1-inch pieces, or one 10-ounce package frozen cut asparagus**
- 1 **cup half-and-half or light cream**
- 1 **cup crumbled Gorgonzola or other blue cheese (4 ounces)**
- ¼ **teaspoon salt**
- 2 **tablespoons chopped walnuts, toasted**

1. Cook linguine and asparagus according to package directions for the linguine; drain. Return pasta mixture to pan.

2. Meanwhile, in a medium saucepan, combine half-and-half, ¾ cup of the Gorgonzola cheese, and the salt. Bring to boiling over medium heat; reduce heat. Simmer, uncovered, for 3 minutes, stirring frequently.

3. Pour sauce over linguine mixture; toss gently to coat. Transfer to a warm serving dish. Sprinkle with the remaining ¼ cup Gorgonzola cheese and the walnuts.

Per serving: 399 cal., 20 g total fat (11 g sat. fat), 111 mg chol., 590 mg sodium, 39 g carbo., 3 g fiber, 18 g pro.

Pasta with Broccoli and Asiago

Semisoft cheese makes a smooth sauce for broccoli and pasta of any shape. Italian Asiago has a nutty flavor and shreds or grates easily.

Start to Finish: 25 minutes **Makes:** 2 servings

- 4 **ounces dried spaghetti, linguine, fettuccine, or angel hair pasta**
- 1 **cup chopped broccoli**
- ½ **of a 5.2-ounce container semisoft cheese with garlic and herbs**
- ¼ **cup milk**
  Finely shredded Asiago or Parmesan cheese

1. Cook pasta according to package directions, adding the broccoli the last 4 minutes of cooking. Drain and return pasta mixture to pan.

2. In a small saucepan, combine semisoft cheese and milk. Cook and stir until smooth. Pour over pasta; toss to coat. Sprinkle with Asiago cheese.

Per serving: 411 cal., 20 g total fat (13 g sat. fat), 11 mg chol., 316 mg sodium, 47 g carbo., 3 g fiber, 14 g pro.

Trattoria-Style Spinach Fettuccine ♥

A trattoria is a family-run restaurant that serves up casual, simple fare. What makes this recipe particularly tasty is the spiced feta cheese, which brings a windfall of flavor in one easy measure.

Start to Finish: 18 minutes **Makes:** 4 servings

- 1 **9-ounce package refrigerated spinach fettuccine**
- 1 **medium carrot**
- 1 **tablespoon olive oil**
- 1 **medium shallot or 2 green onions, chopped (2 tablespoons)**
- 4 **red and/or yellow tomatoes, chopped (2 cups)**
- ¼ **cup oil-packed dried tomatoes, drained and snipped**
- ½ **cup crumbled garlic and herb or peppercorn feta cheese (2 ounces)**

1. Cut pasta strands in half with kitchen shears. Cook the pasta according to package directions; drain. Return pasta to hot pan.

2. Meanwhile, peel carrot. Using a sharp vegetable peeler, slice carrot lengthwise into wide, flat "ribbons." Set ribbons aside.

3. In a large skillet, heat oil over medium heat. Cook shallot for 30 seconds. Stir in fresh tomatoes, carrot ribbons, and dried tomatoes. Cook, covered, for 5 minutes, stirring once.

4. Spoon tomato mixture over cooked pasta; toss gently. Sprinkle with cheese.

Per serving: 311 cal., 11 g total fat (4 g sat. fat), 73 mg chol., 250 mg sodium, 44 g carbo., 2 g fiber, 13 g pro.

Quick Tip For the best flavor, look for fresh tomatoes that are marked "vine-ripened." Many of the tomatoes that supermarkets carry have been picked green and ripened with ethylene gas and never have the flavor of tomatoes that are allowed to ripen on the vine. If the tomatoes you purchase are not quite ripe yet, place them with an apple in a paper bag poked with a few holes. Let them stand at room temperature for 2 to 3 days.

Trattoria-Style Spinach Fettuccine

Couscous-Stuffed Peppers

Couscous-Stuffed Peppers

Vary this vegetable-and-rice main dish according to your family's preferences and what you have on hand. Use any color sweet pepper, any variety of pasta sauce, or another Italian-style cheese, such as provolone.

Prep: 15 minutes **Bake:** 25 minutes **Oven:** 350°F
Makes: 4 servings

- 1 **6-ounce package toasted pine nut couscous mix**
- 1 **medium carrot, shredded, or ½ cup purchased shredded carrot**
- 2 **large or 4 small red, yellow, green, or orange sweet peppers**
- ½ **cup shredded Italian cheese blend (2 ounces)**
- 1½ **cups mushroom and olive or tomato basil pasta sauce**

1. Preheat oven to 350°F. Prepare couscous mix according to package directions, omitting oil and adding the shredded carrot with the couscous.

2. Meanwhile, cut large peppers in half lengthwise (for small peppers, cut off tops and reserve). Remove seeds and membranes from peppers. Cook peppers (and tops, if using) in boiling water for 5 minutes. Drain on paper towels. Place peppers, cut sides up, in a 2-quart rectangular baking dish. Spoon cooked couscous mixture into peppers.

3. Bake, covered, for 20 to 25 minutes or until filling is heated through and peppers are tender. Sprinkle cheese over peppers. Bake, uncovered, about 5 minutes more or until cheese is melted.

4. Meanwhile, in a small saucepan, heat the pasta sauce. Serve peppers with sauce. (For small peppers, place pepper tops on top of couscous filling.)

Per serving: 259 cal., 6 g total fat (3 g sat. fat), 10 mg chol., 801 mg sodium, 42 g carbo., 7 g fiber, 11 g pro.

Cheesy Tortellini and Vegetables

Just about any frozen vegetable combination will work in this creamy pasta.

Start to Finish: 20 minutes **Makes:** 4 servings

- 1 **6-ounce package dried cheese-filled tortellini**
- 1 **16-ounce package loose-pack frozen broccoli, cauliflower, and carrots**
- 1¼ **cups milk**
- ½ **of a 1.8-ounce envelope white sauce mix (about 3 tablespoons)**
- 6 **ounces Havarti cheese with dill, cubed**

1. Cook tortellini according to package directions, adding the frozen vegetables for the last 5 minutes of cooking. Drain well. Return tortellini mixture to hot pan; cover to keep warm.

2. Meanwhile, for the sauce, in a small saucepan, whisk together milk and white sauce mix. Bring to boiling; reduce heat. Cook and stir for 1 minute. Remove from heat. Add cheese, stirring until melted. Pour sauce over tortellini mixture. Toss lightly.

Per serving: 453 cal., 24 g total fat (1 g sat. fat), 59 mg chol., 1,004 mg sodium, 38 g carbo., 4 g fiber, 22 g pro.

Fontina-Topped Angel Hair and Vegetables ♥

Angel hair is great in the summer, when you want to enjoy a quick veggie-pasta toss, like this recipe, but don't want to heat up the kitchen to boil longer-cooking noodles.

Start to Finish: 25 minutes
Makes: 4 servings

- 1 **tablespoon olive oil**
- 1 **pound fresh asparagus spears, trimmed and cut into 1-inch pieces (3 cups)**
- 1½ **cups assorted sliced fresh mushrooms, such as button, shiitake, or oyster**
- 1 **small red onion, thinly sliced**
- 2 **cloves garlic, minced**
- ¼ **cup dry white wine or chicken broth**
- 8 **ounces dried angel hair pasta, broken in half**
- 2 **medium tomatoes, coarsely chopped (2 cups)**
- 1 **tablespoon snipped fresh oregano**
- ½ **cup shredded fontina cheese (2 ounces)**
  Coarsely ground black pepper

1. In a large skillet, heat oil over medium heat. Add asparagus, mushrooms, onion, and garlic and cook for 3 to 4 minutes or until tender. Carefully stir in wine. Bring to boiling; reduce heat. Simmer, uncovered, 3 minutes or until liquid is almost evaporated.

2. Meanwhile, cook pasta according to package directions; drain. Add drained pasta to asparagus mixture in skillet. Stir in tomatoes and oregano, tossing to coat.

3. Transfer pasta and asparagus mixture to a serving platter. Top with fontina and sprinkle with black pepper. Serve immediately.

Per serving: 242 cal., 6 g total fat (2 g sat. fat), 11 mg chol., 83 mg sodium, 36 g carbo., 2 g fiber, 10 g pro.

Black Bean and Corn Quesadillas [one]

Flour tortillas come in an array of flavors, sizes, and colors. Store opened bags of tortillas in the refrigerator and watch their expiration date or freeze sealed bags for up to three months.

Start to Finish: 20 minutes **Oven:** 300°F
Makes: 4 servings

1	8-ounce package shredded 4-cheese Mexican blend cheese (2 cups)
8	8-inch whole wheat or flour tortillas
1½	cups bottled black bean and corn salsa
1	medium avocado, seeded, peeled, and chopped Dairy sour cream

1. Preheat oven to 300°F. Divide cheese evenly among tortillas, sprinkling cheese over half of each tortilla. Top each tortilla with 1 tablespoon of the salsa. Divide the avocado among tortillas. Fold tortillas in half, pressing gently.

2. Heat a large skillet over medium-high heat for 2 minutes; reduce heat to medium. Cook two of the quesadillas for 2 to 3 minutes or until lightly browned and cheese is melted, turning once. Remove quesadillas from skillet; place on a baking sheet. Keep warm in the preheated oven. Repeat with remaining quesadillas, cooking two at a time.

3. Cut quesadillas into wedges. Serve with sour cream and the remaining salsa.

Per serving: 647 cal., 35 g total fat (16 g sat. fat), 61 mg chol., 1,405 mg sodium, 48 g carbo., 23 g fiber, 31 g pro.

Tomatoes and Ravioli With Escarole ♥

If you're craving something fresh and green during the winter months, you're in luck. Escarole is in season, and it adds a unique, pungent flavor to this easy dish.

Start to Finish: 30 minutes **Makes:** 4 servings

1	tablespoon olive oil or cooking oil
1	medium onion, chopped (½ cup)
2	cloves garlic, minced
8	ounces fresh mushrooms, sliced (3 cups)
6	plum tomatoes, chopped (2 cups)
¾	cup chicken broth
4	cups coarsely chopped escarole
1	tablespoon snipped fresh basil
1	teaspoon snipped fresh rosemary
1	9-ounce package refrigerated cheese-filled ravioli
¼	cup pine nuts, toasted

1. For the sauce, in a large skillet, heat oil over medium heat. Cook onion and garlic for 2 minutes. Add mushrooms, tomatoes, and broth. Bring to boiling. Reduce heat; simmer, uncovered, about 7 minutes or until mushrooms are tender and sauce is slightly reduced (you should have about 3 cups). Add escarole, basil, and rosemary, stirring just until the escarole is wilted.

2. Meanwhile, cook pasta according to package directions; drain. Return pasta to saucepan. Pour sauce over pasta; toss to coat. Transfer to a warm serving dish. Sprinkle with pine nuts.

Per serving: 339 cal., 14 g total fat (3 g sat. fat), 34 mg chol., 454 mg sodium, 43 g carbo., 4 g fiber, 16 g pro.

Cauliflower and Chickpea Gratin

A truly unique gratin, this dish features chickpeas, a legume used extensively in Mediterranean cooking. Don't let the labels fool you; chickpeas and garbanzo beans are the same thing.

Prep: 30 minutes **Cook:** 15 minutes **Broil:** 1 minute
Makes: 6 servings.

3	tablespoons extra-virgin olive oil
2	cups chopped onion
2	14.5-ounce cans diced tomatoes, drained
1	15-ounce can garbanzo beans (chickpeas), rinsed and drained
6	cloves garlic, minced (1 tablespoon minced)
¼	cup chopped fresh flat-leaf parsley
2	tablespoons capers, rinsed and drained
1	tablespoon chopped fresh oregano
1	tablespoon lemon juice
1	teaspoon chopped fresh thyme
½	teaspoon salt
¼	teaspoon freshly ground black pepper
1¾	pounds cauliflower, cut into florets
4	ounces feta cheese, crumbled

1. In a large saucepan, heat olive oil over medium-high heat. Add onion; cook about 5 minutes or until tender, stirring occasionally. Add drained tomatoes, garbanzo beans, and garlic. Bring to boiling; reduce heat to low. Cover and simmer for 15 minutes. Stir in parsley, drained capers, oregano, lemon juice, thyme, salt, and pepper.

2. Meanwhile, in a covered Dutch oven, cook cauliflower in a small amount of boiling water about 5 minutes or just until tender. Drain and keep warm.

3. Transfer cauliflower to a 2- to 2½-quart broilerproof baking dish. Top with hot tomato mixture. Sprinkle with feta cheese. Broil 3 to 4 inches from the heat for 1 to 2 minutes or just until cheese begins to brown. Serve immediately.

Per serving: 271 cal., 12 g total fat (4 g sat. fat), 17 mg chol., 951 mg sodium, 35 g carbo., 9 g fiber, 10 g pro.

Macaroni and Cheese
with Caramelized Onions

Macaroni and Cheese With Caramelized Onions

For an Italian spin of this dressed-up American favorite, use 4 slices of pancetta—a rolled bacon cured with salt and spices, but not smoked—in place of the bacon strips.

Prep: 25 minutes **Bake:** 30 minutes
Stand: 10 minutes **Oven:** 350°F **Makes:** 4 servings

- **4** **strips bacon**
- **1** **large sweet onion, halved and thinly sliced**
- **1½** **cups regular or multigrain dried elbow macaroni pasta (6 ounces)**
- **2** **cups shredded mozzarella cheese (8 ounces)**
- **4** **ounces processed Gruyère cheese, shredded,**
- **1** **cup half-and-half or light cream**
- **⅛** **teaspoon ground black pepper**

1. Preheat oven to 350°F. In a large skillet, cook bacon over medium heat until crisp, turning once. Drain bacon on paper towels; crumble. Reserve bacon drippings in skillet.

2. Cook onion in reserved bacon drippings for 5 to 8 minutes or until onion is tender and golden brown. Set aside.

3. In a large saucepan, cook macaroni according to package directions. Drain and return to saucepan. Stir in the crumbled bacon, onion, 1½ cups of the mozzarella cheese, the Gruyère cheese, half-and half, and pepper. Toss gently to combine. Spoon into a 1½-quart casserole.

4. Bake, uncovered, for 20 minutes. Stir gently. Top with the remaining mozzarella cheese. Bake for 10 minutes more or until top of casserole is brown and bubbly. Let stand 10 minutes.

Per serving: 632 cal., 39 g total fat (21 g sat. fat), 110 mg chol., 617 mg sodium, 37 g carbo., 4 g fiber, 33 g pro.

Chunky Chipotle Pork Chili, **page 175**

Beef, Orzo, and Escarole Soup, **page 170**

White Bean Soup with Sausage and Kale, **page 177**

Mexican Vegetable Soup, **page 187**

Soups and Stews

Maybe soups and stews cannot always cure what ails you, but they are certainly cheering and comforting. With these quick-to-prepare recipes, you can enjoy homemade soup more often with less effort.

Quick Hamburger Soup ♥ one

Thanks to this easy—and fast— recipe, you can feed a crowd in practically no time.

Start to Finish: 30 minutes **Makes:** 12 servings

- 8 ounces extra-lean ground beef
- 8 ounces uncooked ground turkey breast
- 2 medium onions, finely chopped
- 2 carrots, coarsely shredded
- 2 stalks celery, sliced
- 2 cloves garlic, minced
- 6 cups reduced-sodium beef broth
- 2 14.5-ounce cans diced tomatoes, undrained
- 1 tablespoon snipped fresh sage or 1 teaspoon dried sage, crushed
- 2 teaspoons snipped fresh thyme or 1 teaspoon dried thyme, crushed
- 1 teaspoon snipped fresh rosemary or ½ teaspoon dried rosemary, crushed
- ¼ teaspoon salt
- ¼ teaspoon ground black pepper
- 2 medium potatoes, chopped (2 cups)
  Fresh sage (optional)

1. In a Dutch oven, combine beef, turkey, onions, carrots, celery, and garlic; cook until meat is brown and onion is tender. Drain off fat. Stir broth, undrained tomatoes, 1 tablespoon sage, thyme, rosemary, salt, and pepper into beef mixture in Dutch oven. Bring to boiling; stir in potatoes. Reduce heat. Cover and simmer for 10 to 15 minutes or until vegetables are tender. If desired, garnish with additional fresh sage.

Per serving: 103 cal., 2 g total fat (1 g sat. fat), 19 mg chol., 418 mg sodium, 10 g carbo., 1 g fiber, 10 g pro.

Zesty Meatball-Noodle Soup one

With meatballs and fill-you-up fettuccine, this soup is a meal in a bowl. It gets its kick from a can of tomatoes with green chiles.

Start to Finish: 30 minutes **Makes:** 4 servings

- 3 14-ounce cans reduced-sodium chicken broth
- 1 14.5-ounce can diced tomatoes with green chiles, undrained
- 1½ teaspoons bottled minced garlic
- 1 teaspoon ground cumin
- 8 ounces lean ground beef
- ⅛ teaspoon salt
- ⅛ teaspoon ground black pepper
- 3 ounces dried spaghetti pasta, broken
- 1 large zucchini, coarsely chopped
- ½ cup shredded Monterey Jack cheese (2 ounces)

1. In a large saucepan, combine broth, undrained tomatoes, 1 teaspoon of the garlic, and the 1 teaspoon cumin. Bring to boiling; reduce heat. Cover and simmer for 5 minutes.

2. Meanwhile, in a medium bowl, combine remaining garlic, beef, salt, and pepper. Shape beef mixture into ¾-inch meatballs.

3. Add meatballs to broth. Return to boiling; reduce heat. Cover and simmer 4 minutes. Add fettuccine; return to boiling. Reduce heat. Simmer, uncovered, 12 minutes more or until fettuccine is tender, adding zucchini the last 2 minutes of cooking. Sprinkle each serving with cheese.

Per serving: 267 cal., 10 g total fat (5 g sat. fat), 48 mg chol., 1,190 mg sodium, 23 g carbo., 3 g fiber, 22 g pro.

Beef, Orzo, and Escarole Soup one

Orzo, sometimes called "rosamarina," is a small, rice-shaped pasta. If orzo is not available, substitute spaghetti or linguine broken into ¼- to ½-inch-long pieces.

Prep: 5 minutes **Cook:** 25 minutes **Makes:** 4 servings

- 12 ounces lean ground beef
- 1 small fennel bulb, chopped (about ⅔ cup)
- 1 medium onion, chopped (about ½ cup)
- 2 cloves garlic, minced
- 4 cups beef broth
- 2 cups water
- 1 teaspoon dried oregano, crushed
- 2 bay leaves
- ¼ teaspoon cracked black pepper
- ½ cup orzo pasta
- 4 cups shredded escarole, curly endive, and/or spinach
- 3 ounces Parmesan cheese with rind, cut into 4 wedges (optional)

1. In a large saucepan, combine beef, fennel, onion, and garlic. Cook, uncovered, over medium-high heat for 5 minutes or until meat is browned and vegetables are nearly tender, stirring occasionally. Drain fat, if necessary.

2. Stir in broth, the water, oregano, bay leaves, and pepper. Bring to boiling; reduce heat. Simmer, covered, for 10 minutes. Remove bay leaves; discard.

3. Add orzo. Return to boiling; reduce heat to medium. Boil gently, uncovered, for 10 minutes or until pasta is just tender, stirring occasionally. Remove from heat; stir in escarole.

4. If desired, place a wedge of cheese in each of 4 soup bowls. Ladle hot soup into bowls.

Per serving: 262 cal., 10 g total fat (4 g sat. fat), 54 mg chol., 873 mg sodium, 22 g carbo., 7 g fiber, 21 g pro.

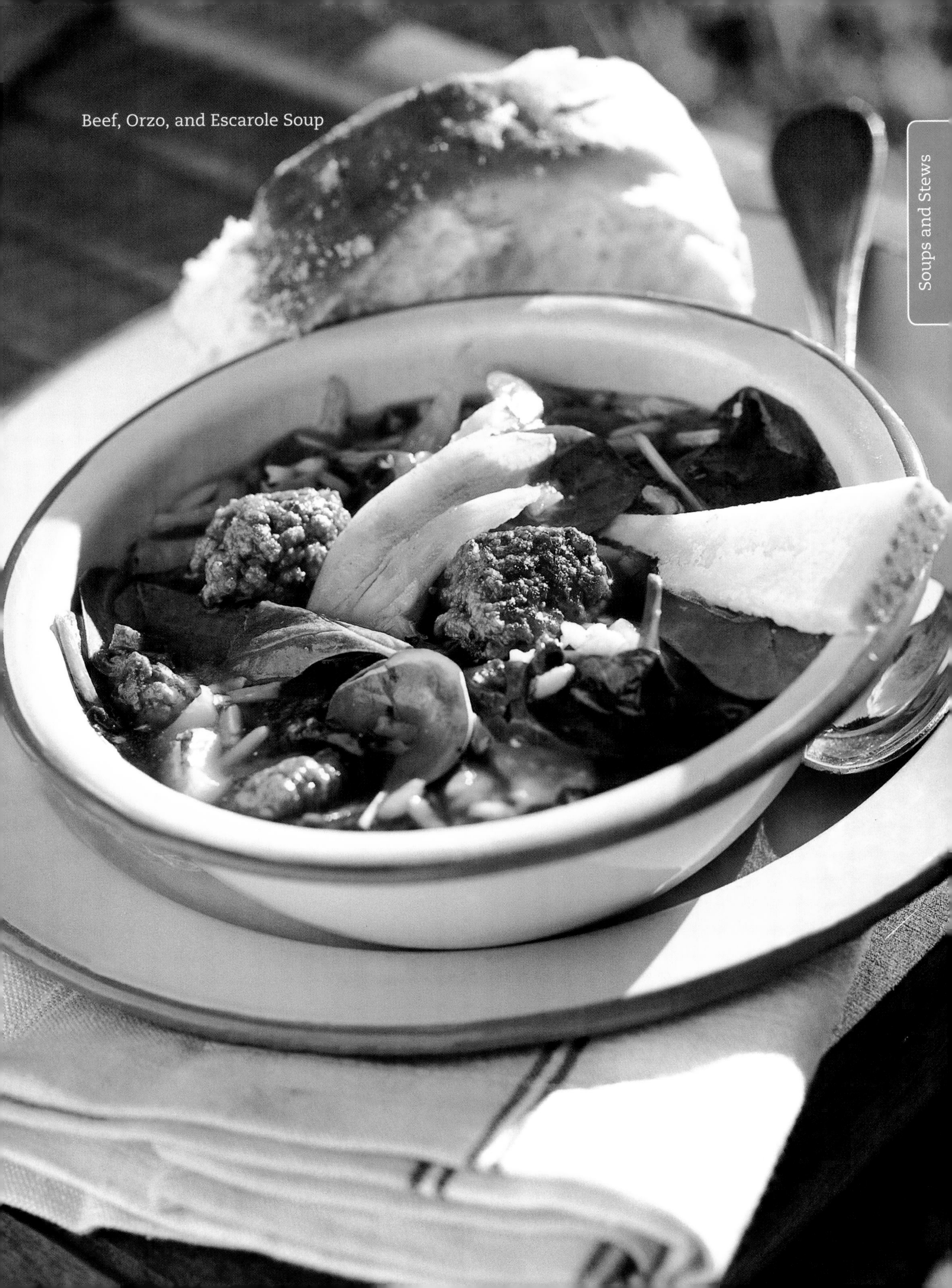

Beef, Orzo, and Escarole Soup

Italian Meatball Soup

Italian Meatball Soup [one]

With the ingredients on hand and this recipe flagged and waiting, you'll always have something filling and wonderful that's ready in a hurry. What to do with the leftover packaged meatballs? Another night, pair them with prepared pasta sauce for a quick and classic spaghetti-and-meatball dinner.

Prep: 15 minutes **Cook:** 10 minutes **Makes:** 4 servings

- 1   **14.5-ounce can diced tomatoes with onion and garlic, undrained**
- 1   **14-ounce can beef broth**
- 1½ **cups water**
- ½   **teaspoon Italian seasoning, crushed**
- ½   **of a 16-ounce package frozen Italian-style cooked meatballs**
- ½   **cup small dried pasta (such as orzo, tripolini, ditalini, or stellini)**
- 1   **cup loose-pack frozen mixed vegetables**
     Finely shredded Parmesan cheese

1. In a large saucepan, stir together undrained tomatoes, beef broth, the water, and Italian seasoning. Bring mixture to boiling.

2. Add frozen meatballs, pasta, and frozen vegetables. Return to boiling; reduce heat. Cover and simmer about 10 minutes or until pasta and vegetables are tender. Top each serving with cheese.

Per serving: 337 cal., 16 g total fat (7 g sat. fat), 42 mg chol., 1,419 mg sodium, 31 g carbo., 4 g fiber, 18 g pro.

Stuffed Green Pepper Soup [one]

Love stuffed peppers? Try this soup that combines the same ingredients in a brand-new way.

Prep: 25 minutes **Cook:** 20 minutes **Makes:** 6 servings

- 8   **ounces lean ground beef**
- 2   **14.5-ounce cans diced tomatoes with green peppers and onions, undrained**
- 3   **cups water**
- 1   **14-ounce can beef broth**
- 1   **5.7-ounce package tomato basil risotto mix**
- ¾ **cup chopped green sweet pepper (1 medium)**

1. In a large saucepan, cook beef until brown. Drain off fat.

2. Stir undrained tomatoes, the water, beef broth, risotto mix and seasoning packet, and sweet pepper into beef in saucepan. Bring to boiling; reduce heat. Cover and simmer about 20 minutes or until rice is tender.

Per serving: 245 cal., 6 g total fat (2 g sat. fat), 23 mg chol., 990 mg sodium, 33 g carbo., 2 g fiber, 11 g pro.

Vegetable-Beef Soup [one]

Although this soup simmers long and slow to blend flavors, using a blend of frozen vegetables eliminates time-consuming peeling and chopping.

Prep: 5 minutes **Cook:** 1 hour and 35 minutes **Makes:** 6 servings

- 1   **tablespoon cooking oil**
- 1   **pound beef stew meat or boneless beef chuck roast, cut into ¾-inch cubes**
- 3   **14-ounce cans beef broth**
- 1   **14.5-ounce can diced tomatoes with basil, oregano, and garlic, undrained**
- 1   **16-ounce package frozen broccoli, green beans, pearl onions, and red sweet pepper**

1. In a Dutch oven, heat oil over medium-high heat. Add half of the beef; cook until brown. Remove beef from Dutch oven. Add remaining beef to Dutch oven; cook until brown (add additional oil if necessary).

2. Return all beef to Dutch oven. Stir in broth and undrained tomatoes. Bring to boiling; reduce heat. Cover and simmer for 1½ to 1¾ hours or until beef is tender.

3. Stir in vegetables. Return to boiling; reduce heat. Cover and simmer about 5 minutes more or just until vegetables are tender.

Per serving: 179 cal., 6 g total fat (2 g sat. fat), 45 mg chol., 1095 mg sodium, 11 g carbo., 2 g fiber, 20 g pro.

Broccoli-Swiss Soup [one]

Broccoli and cheese always make a delicious pair. Add ham and roasted garlic and you have a sure winner.

Prep: 15 minutes **Cook:** 10 minutes **Makes:** 4 servings

- 2   **14-ounce cans chicken broth**
- 1   **16-ounce package fresh broccoli florets**
- 1   **medium onion, chopped**
- 2   **teaspoons bottled roasted garlic**
- 1   **cup shredded Swiss cheese (4 ounces)**
- 1   **cup half-and-half or light cream**
- ½ **cup cubed ham**
     Salt
     Ground black pepper

1. In a large saucepan, combine broth, broccoli, onion, and garlic. Bring to boiling; reduce heat. Cover and simmer about 10 minutes or until broccoli is very tender. In a blender or food processor blend or process the broccoli mixture, in 2 or 3 batches, until smooth.

2. Return to saucepan. Return to a simmer. Add cheese; cook, stirring constantly, until melted. Stir in half-and-half and ham. Season to taste with salt and pepper.

Per serving: 283 cal., 18 g total fat (10 g sat. fat), 58 mg chol., 1,213 mg sodium, 14 g carbo., 4 g fiber, 18 g pro.

Chunky Chipotle Pork Chili

Chunky Chipotle Pork Chili [one]

Lean pork tenderloin cooks to perfection in just minutes. As for the simmered-all-day flavor, give much of the credit to the smoky chipotle chile peppers.

Start to Finish: 30 minutes **Makes:** 4 servings

- 1 **tablespoon cooking oil**
- 1 **small onion, chopped**
- 2 **teaspoons bottled minced garlic (4 cloves)**
- 12 **ounces pork tenderloin, cut into ¾-inch cubes**
- 2 **teaspoons chili powder**
- 2 **teaspoons ground cumin**
- 1 **yellow or red sweet pepper, cut into ½-inch pieces**
- 1 **cup beer or beef broth**
- ½ **cup bottled picante sauce or salsa**
- 1 **to 2 tablespoons finely chopped canned chipotle chile peppers in adobo sauce***
- 1 **15-ounce can small red beans or pinto beans, rinsed and drained**
- ½ **cup dairy sour cream**
  Fresh cilantro or flat-leaf parsley sprigs (optional)

1. In a large saucepan, heat oil over medium-high heat. Add onion and garlic; cook about 3 minutes or until tender.

2. In a medium bowl, toss pork with chili powder and cumin; add to saucepan. Cook and stir until pork is browned. Add sweet pepper, beer, picante sauce, and chipotle chile peppers. Bring to boiling; reduce heat. Cover and simmer about 5 minutes or until pork is tender. Stir in beans; heat through. Top each serving with sour cream. If desired, garnish with cilantro.

Per serving: 328 cal., 11 g total fat (4 g sat. fat), 65 mg chol., 625 mg sodium, 29 g carbo., 7 g fiber, 26 g pro.

***Note:** Because chile peppers contain volatile oils that can burn your skin and eyes, avoid direct contact with them as much as possible. When working with chile peppers, wear plastic or rubber gloves. If your bare hands do touch the peppers, wash your hands and nails well with soap and warm water.

Quick Pork-Bean Soup [one]

Round out your meal with crusty rolls and creamy coleslaw.

Prep: 15 minutes **Cook:** 15 minutes **Makes:** 4 servings

- 12 **ounces lean boneless pork**
- 1 **large onion, chopped**
- 2 **tablespoons cooking oil**
- 2 **cups water**
- 1 **11.5-ounce can condensed bean with bacon soup**
- 3 **medium carrots, sliced**
- 1 **teaspoon Worcestershire sauce**
- ¼ **teaspoon dry mustard**

1. Cut pork into thin bite-size strips. In a large skillet, cook pork and onion in hot oil for 3 to 4 minutes or until pork is browned. Stir in the water, soup, carrots, Worcestershire sauce, and dry mustard.

2. Bring to boiling; reduce heat. Cover and simmer for 15 minutes.

Per serving: 312 cal., 13 g total fat (3 g sat. fat), 52 mg chol., 678 mg sodium, 23 g carbo., 6 g fiber, 24 g pro.

Speedy Beef Stew [one]

There's nothing more comforting on a frosty day than beef stew. This version of the old-fashioned classic is ready in less than half an hour.

Start to Finish: 25 minutes **Makes:** 4 servings

- 1 **17-ounce package refrigerated cooked beef roast au jus**
- 2 **10.75-ounce cans condensed beefy mushroom soup**
- 1 **16-ounce package frozen stew vegetables**
- 1½ **cups milk**
- 4 **teaspoons snipped fresh basil or 1½ teaspoons dried basil, crushed**

1. Cut beef into bite-size pieces if necessary. In a 4-quart Dutch oven, combine beef and au jus, soup, frozen vegetables, and dried basil, if using. Bring to boiling; reduce heat. Cover and simmer for 10 minutes. Stir in milk and fresh basil, if using. Heat through.

Per serving: 386 cal., 15 g total fat (7 g sat. fat), 80 mg chol., 1,688 mg sodium, 33 g carbo., 5 g fiber, 33 g pro.

Black Bean and Sausage Posole

Posole is a thick, hearty soup that's a tradition come Christmas in Mexico. Comprised of hominy, garlic, onion, and broth plus meat and seasonings, it's a one-pot meal that comes together in a jiffy. Feel free to experiment with the type of sausage you choose to use—let your own tastes guide you.

Prep: 15 minutes **Cook:** 30 minutes
Makes: 6 servings

- 1 **12-ounce package light bulk turkey-and-pork sausage**
- 2 **14-ounce cans reduced-sodium chicken broth**
- 1 **15-ounce can black beans, rinsed and drained**
- 1 **14.5-ounce can golden hominy, rinsed and drained**
- 1 **14.5-ounce can Mexican-style stewed tomatoes, undrained**
- 1 **cup loose-pack frozen diced hash brown potatoes**
- ½ **cup chopped green sweet pepper**
- ⅓ **cup chopped onion (1 small)**
- ½ **teaspoon bottled minced garlic (1 clove)**
- 1 **teaspoon dried oregano, crushed**
- ½ **teaspoon chili powder**

1. In a large saucepan, cook the sausage until brown; drain off fat.

2. Stir in broth, drained beans, drained hominy, undrained tomatoes, hash brown potatoes, sweet pepper, onion, garlic, oregano, and chili powder. Bring to boiling; reduce heat. Cover and simmer for 30 minutes.

Per serving: 292 cal., 14 g total fat (1 g sat. fat), 45 mg chol., 1,295 mg sodium, 26 g carbo., 4 g fiber, 17 g pro.

Black Bean and Sausage Posole

Cheese-Tortellini Soup

Served with a hunk of fresh bread, this hearty soup is the perfect meal on a cold winter's night. For variety, try vegetable- or meat-filled tortellini.

Start to Finish: 25 minutes **Makes:** 4 servings

- 3 **slices packaged ready-to-serve cooked bacon, chopped**
- 1 **small onion, chopped**
- 2 **cloves garlic, minced**
- 1 **32-ounce box reduced-sodium chicken broth (4 cups)**
- 3 **cups frozen cheese-filled tortellini (12 ounces)**
- 1 **10-ounce package frozen chopped spinach, thawed and drained**
  Ground black pepper
  Parmesan cheese shavings (optional)

1. In a large saucepan, cook bacon over medium-high heat until crisp, about 3 minutes. Add onion and cook 3 minutes more. Stir in garlic and cook 1 minute more.

2. Increase heat to high; add broth and bring to boiling. Stir in tortellini. Return to boiling. Reduce heat and simmer, uncovered, according to package directions, adding the spinach for the last 3 minutes of cooking time.

3. Season to taste with pepper and, if desired, garnish with Parmesan cheese.

Per serving: 229 cal., 5 g total fat (3 g sat. fat), 26 mg chol., 938 mg sodium, 31 g carbo., 3 g fiber, 14 g pro.

Sausage-Corn Chowder

This five-ingredient soup goes together quickly for hungry youngsters any day of the week.

Start to Finish: 20 minutes
Makes: 4 servings

- 12 **ounces cooked link smoked turkey sausage or frankfurters**
- 1 **10.75-ounce can condensed cream of potato soup**
- 1⅓ **cups milk**
- 1 **8.75-ounce can cream-style corn**
- 2 **or 3 slices American cheese, torn into pieces (2 or 3 ounces)**

1. Cut sausage links in half lengthwise; cut into ½-inch slices. Set aside.

2. In a 2-quart saucepan, combine soup, milk, and corn. Stir in sausage and cheese. Cook and stir over medium heat until heated through.

Per serving: 312 cal., 15 g total fat (6 g sat. fat), 80 mg chol., 1,774 mg sodium, 24 g carbo., 1 g fiber, 21 g pro.

White Bean Soup with Sausage and Kale

White Bean Soup with Sausage and Kale

Speedy, speedier, speediest. It takes a couple minutes to chop a fresh onion the old-fashioned way (with a knife), and a little less time if you use a mini food processor. If you're really pressed for time, look for frozen chopped onions, which can be added to soups and stews in seconds.

Start to Finish: 30 minutes   **Makes:** 5 servings

12	ounces fresh mild Italian sausage links, sliced ½ inch thick
¼	cup water
1	tablespoon cooking oil
1	medium onion, chopped (½ cup)
1	teaspoon bottled minced garlic
2	15-ounce cans white kidney (cannellini) beans, rinsed and drained
2	14 ounce cans reduced-sodium chicken broth
1	14.5-ounce can diced tomatoes with basil, oregano, and garlic, undrained
4	cups coarsely chopped kale or spinach
	Ground black pepper

1. In a large skillet, combine sausage and water. Bring to boiling; reduce heat. Simmer, covered, about 10 minutes or until sausage is no longer pink. Uncover and cook about 5 minutes more or until sausage is browned, stirring frequently. Remove sausage with a slotted spoon; set aside.

2. Meanwhile, in a large saucepan, heat oil. Cook onion and garlic in hot oil about 5 minutes or until onion is tender. Stir in drained beans, broth, and undrained tomatoes. Cover and bring to boiling; reduce heat. Simmer, covered, for 5 minutes.

3. Stir in cooked sausage and kale. Simmer, uncovered, about 3 minutes more or until kale is wilted. Season to taste with pepper.

Per serving: 394 cal., 19 g total fat (7 g sat. fat), 46 mg chol., 1,510 mg sodium, 38 g carbo., 10 g fiber, 25 g pro.

Quick Tip Look for kale with firm, deeply colored leaves and moist hardy stems. The leaves should appear fresh, unwilted, and have no signs of browning. Choose kale with smaller leaves because they will be more tender and have a milder flavor than those with large leaves.

Sausage Soup

Sausage Soup ⬚one

This hearty soup is packed with zesty Italian flavors. To add some spiciness, use hot Italian sausage.

Prep: 30 minutes **Cook:** 1 hour + 30 minutes
Makes: 8 servings

 1   **pound bulk Italian sausage**
 1   **large onion, chopped**
 1   **medium carrot, chopped**
 1   **stalk celery, chopped**
 8   **cups chicken broth**
 1   **14.5-ounce can diced tomatoes, undrained**
 1   **8-ounce can tomato sauce**
 1   **clove garlic, minced**
 2   **teaspoons dried Italian seasoning, crushed**
 1   **bay leaf**
 ½   **cup dried orzo pasta or finely broken capellini pasta**
     Finely shredded Parmesan cheese (optional)

1. In a 4-quart Dutch oven, cook sausage, onion, carrot, and celery over medium heat until sausage is brown. Drain well.

2. Add broth, undrained diced tomatoes, tomato sauce, garlic, Italian seasoning, and bay leaf to sausage mixture in Dutch oven. Bring to boiling; reduce heat. Cover and simmer for 1 hour. Add uncooked pasta. Return to boiling; reduce heat. Cook, uncovered, for 30 minutes more. Discard bay leaf. If desired, serve with shredded Parmesan cheese.

Per serving: 285 cal., 18 g total fat (6 g sat. fat), 46 mg chol., 1,600 mg sodium, 17 g carbo., 1 g fiber, 11 g pro.

Winter Vegetable Soup ⬚one

Bits of smoky kielbasa sausage accent the sweet flavors of tender squash and carrots in this seasonal soup.

Start to Finish: 30 minutes **Makes:** 6 servings

 6   **ounces kielbasa or smoked sausage, halved lengthwise and sliced**
 1   **small onion, chopped (⅓ cup)**
 2   **14-ounce cans chicken broth**
 2   **cups water**
 ½   **of a small (8 ounces) butternut squash, peeled, seeded, and cubed (about 1⅓ cups)**
 2   **medium carrots, sliced**
 ⅛   **to ¼ teaspoon ground black pepper**
 1   **cup dried ditalini or orzo pasta**
 1   **15- to 16-ounce can red kidney beans, rinsed and drained**
 2   **cups prewashed baby spinach leaves**

1. In a 4-quart Dutch oven, cook kielbasa and onion over medium-high heat for 5 minutes or until onion is tender, stirring occasionally. Add broth, the water, squash, carrots, and pepper. Cover; bring to boiling. Reduce heat. Simmer, covered, for 5 minutes.

2. Stir in pasta and drained beans. Return to boiling; reduce heat. Cover and boil gently for 6 minutes or until pasta and vegetables are tender, stirring occasionally. Stir in spinach. Serve immediately.

Per serving: 350 cal., 12 g total fat (4 g sat. fat), 28 mg chol., 1,598 mg sodium, 48 g carbo., 7 g fiber, 15 g pro.

Chicken-Lime Chili ⬚one

Top this zesty soup with salsa, tortilla chips, and cilantro for an exciting but easy-to-make weeknight dinner.

Start to Finish: 15 minutes
Makes: 4 servings

 1   **medium onion, chopped**
 1   **tablespoon cooking oil**
 1   **15- to 16-ounce can hominy, rinsed and drained**
 1   **15- to 16-ounce can Great Northern beans, rinsed and drained**
 1   **14-ounce can reduced-sodium chicken broth**
 1   **9-ounce package frozen cooked chicken breast strips**
 ¼   **cup lime juice**
 2   **tablespoons chopped fresh cilantro**
 ¼   **teaspoon ground cumin**
 ¼   **teaspoon ground black pepper**
 ½   **cup shredded Colby and Monterey Jack cheese, Monterey Jack, or cheddar cheese (2 ounces)**
     Bottled green salsa
     Corn tortilla chips
     Fresh cilantro leaves

1. In a large saucepan, cook onion in hot oil over medium heat for 3 minutes. Stir in drained hominy, drained beans, broth, frozen chicken, lime juice, the 2 tablespoons cilantro, cumin, and pepper. Cover and bring to boiling over high heat, stirring occasionally. Serve topped with cheese, salsa, tortilla chips, and fresh cilantro.

Per serving: 434 cal., 14 g total fat (5 g sat. fat), 58 mg chol., 1,001 mg sodium, 48 g carbo., 9 g fiber, 31 g pro.

Curried Chicken-Noodle Soup one

The aromatic Asian flavors in this soup provide a welcome change from traditional chicken-noodle soup.

Start to Finish: 30 minutes **Makes:** 6 servings

- **3   14-ounce cans reduced-sodium chicken broth**
- **1   to 2 tablespoons green or red Thai curry paste**
- **2   skinless, boneless chicken breast halves (about 10 ounces)**
- **1   5-ounce package dried Japanese curly wheat-flour noodles or angel hair pasta**
- **1   medium sweet potato, peeled and chopped (about 1½ cups)**
- **1   medium tomato, chopped**
- **1   cup unsweetened coconut milk**
- **½   cup lightly packed fresh cilantro leaves**

1. In a 4-quart Dutch oven, combine broth and curry paste. Cover and bring to boiling.

2. Meanwhile, slice chicken breasts crosswise into ¼-inch strips; sprinkle lightly with salt and set aside. Add noodles, sweet potato, and tomato to broth mixture. Return to boiling; reduce heat. Cover and simmer for 2 minutes, stirring once to break up noodles. Add chicken; simmer, covered, 2 to 3 minutes more or until chicken is tender and no longer pink. Stir in coconut milk. Remove soup from heat and sprinkle with cilantro.

Per serving: 273 cal., 9 g total fat (7 g sat. fat), 27 mg chol., 690 mg sodium, 30 g carbo., 2 g fiber, 18 g pro.

Italian Chicken Orzo Soup one

A spoonful of purchased basil pesto gives this quick-to-make soup a fresh and flavorful finish.

Start to Finish: 25 minutes **Makes:** 4 to 6 servings

- **2   14-ounce cans reduced-sodium chicken broth**
- **1   pound skinless, boneless chicken breast halves or thighs, cubed**
- **1   14.5-ounce can diced tomatoes with basil, garlic, and oregano, undrained**
- **½   cup dried orzo pasta**
- **1   cup chopped zucchini**
- **1   teaspoon finely shredded lemon peel**
- **1   tablespoon lemon juice**
- **Salt**
- **Ground black pepper**
- **4   to 6 tablespoons purchased basil pesto**

1. In a large saucepan, combine broth, chicken, undrained tomatoes, and orzo. Bring to boiling; reduce heat. Simmer, uncovered, for 6 minutes.

2. Add zucchini, lemon peel, and lemon juice. Return to boiling; reduce heat. Simmer, uncovered, for 3 to 4 minutes or until orzo and zucchini are tender and chicken is no longer pink. Season to taste with salt and pepper.

3. Ladle into bowls. Top with pesto.

Per serving: 371 cal., 12 g total fat (0 g sat. fat), 68 mg chol., 1,180 mg sodium, 30 g carbo., 1 g fiber, 35 g pro.

Chicken Soup with Spinach and Orzo one

Deli-roasted chicken and cooked deli ham are perfect in this cold-weather soup. However, if you have leftover cooked chicken or ham on hand, by all means use them.

Start to Finish: 20 minutes **Makes:** 6 servings

- **4   14-ounce cans reduced-sodium chicken broth**
- **1   cup dried orzo**
- **12   ounces fresh asparagus spears, trimmed and bias-sliced into 1½-inch pieces**
- **3   cups chopped fresh spinach, Swiss chard, or kale, or one 10-ounce package frozen chopped spinach, thawed**
- **1½   cups chopped fresh tomato (3 medium)**
- **1½   cups shredded cooked chicken (8 ounces)**
- **⅓   cup cubed cooked ham**
- **Salt**
- **Ground black pepper**
- **Snipped fresh chives and/or parsley (optional)**

1. In a covered 5- to 6-quart Dutch oven, bring chicken broth to boiling. Add orzo. Return to boiling; reduce heat. Simmer, uncovered, for 6 minutes. Add asparagus; simmer about 2 minutes more or until orzo is tender and asparagus is crisp-tender.

2. Stir in spinach, tomato, chicken, and ham; heat through. Season to taste with salt and pepper. If desired, sprinkle each serving with chives.

Per serving: 221 cal., 4 g total fat (1 g sat. fat), 35 mg chol., 837 mg sodium, 28 g carbo., 3 g fiber, 20 g pro.

Chicken Soup with Spinach and Orzo

Turkey and Rice Soup

Chicken-Vegetable Soup [one]

Keep several cans of seasoned tomatoes on hand. The spices and herbs they contain lend bonus flavor any time you use them.

Start to Finish: 25 minutes **Makes:** 4 servings

1   16-ounce package frozen Italian vegetables (zucchini, carrots, cauliflower, lima beans, and Italian beans)
1   14.5-ounce can Italian-style stewed tomatoes, undrained
1   12-ounce can vegetable juice
1   cup chicken broth
1½ cups chopped cooked chicken or turkey (about 8 ounces)

1. In a large saucepan, combine frozen vegetables, undrained tomatoes, vegetable juice, and broth.

2. Bring to boiling; reduce heat. Cover and simmer about 10 minutes or until vegetables are tender. Stir in chicken. Heat through.

Per serving: 186 cal., 4 g total fat (1 g sat. fat), 47 mg chol., 888 mg sodium, 17 g carbo., 5 g fiber, 18 g pro.

Turkey and Rice Soup ♥ [one]

Serve crispy breadsticks with this homey meal-in-a-bowl.

Start to Finish: 25 minutes **Makes:** 6 servings

2   14-ounce cans reduced-sodium chicken broth
1½ cups water
1   teaspoon snipped fresh rosemary or ¼ teaspoon dried rosemary, crushed
¼   teaspoon ground black pepper
1   medium carrot, thinly sliced
1   stalk celery, thinly sliced
1   small onion, thinly sliced
1   cup quick-cooking rice
½   cup loose-pack frozen cut green beans
2   cups chopped cooked turkey or chicken (about 10 ounces)
1   14.5-ounce can diced tomatoes, undrained
    Fresh rosemary sprigs (optional)

1. In a large saucepan or Dutch oven, combine broth, the water, snipped or dried rosemary, and pepper. Add carrot, celery, and onion. Bring to boiling.

2. Stir in uncooked rice and green beans. Return to boiling; reduce heat. Cover and simmer for 10 to 12 minutes or until vegetables are tender. Stir in turkey and undrained tomatoes; heat through. If desired, garnish with rosemary sprigs.

Per serving: 177 cal., 2 g total fat (1 g sat. fat), 35 mg chol., 500 mg sodium, 20 g carbo., 1 g fiber, 17 g pro.

Chicken Tortilla Soup 🔲

Serve the tortilla chips on the side or break up a few in the bottom of the bowls and ladle the soup over them.

Start to Finish: 25 minutes **Makes:** 4 servings

- 2 **14-ounce cans chicken broth with roasted garlic**
- 1 **14.5-ounce can Mexican-style stewed tomatoes, undrained**
- 2 **cups chopped cooked chicken**
- 2 **cups frozen sweet pepper and onion stir-fry vegetables**
  Tortilla chips
  Sliced fresh jalapeño chile peppers (optional)
  Lime wedges (optional)

1. In a large saucepan, combine chicken broth, undrained tomatoes, chicken, and frozen vegetables. Bring to boiling; reduce heat. Cover and simmer for 5 minutes.

2. To serve, ladle soup into warm soup bowls. Serve with tortilla chips. If desired, top with sliced jalapeño chile peppers and serve with lime wedges.

Per serving: 266 cal., 9 g total fat (2 g sat. fat), 65 mg chol., 1,260 mg sodium, 22 g carbo., 1 g fiber, 24 g pro.

Curry Lentil Soup 🔲

We added just enough curry to this vegetarian soup to give it zest without making it too spicy. The red sweet pepper adds a hint of sweetness to the soup.

Prep: 10 minutes **Cook:** 22 minutes **Makes:** 4 servings

- 2 **teaspoons vegetable oil**
- 1 **onion, chopped**
- 1 **teaspoon curry powder**
- ½ **teaspoon cumin**
- 1 **red sweet pepper, chopped**
- 1 **clove garlic, minced**
- 4 **cups water**
- 1 **cup red or yellow lentils**
- 1 **teaspoon salt**

1. In a large saucepan, heat oil over medium-high heat. Stir in onion, curry powder, and cumin, and cook 4 minutes. Stir in red pepper and garlic, and cook 3 minutes more.

2. Stir in water, lentils, and salt. Bring to a boil. Reduce heat; simmer until lentils are soft, about 15 minutes.

Per serving: 207 cal., 3 g total fat (1 g sat. fat), 0 mg chol., 886 mg sodium, 33 g carbo., 7 g fiber, 14 g pro.

Chicken Tortilla Soup

Tortellini Chicken Soup

Tortellini Chicken Soup [one]

Just a pinch of saffron goes a long way in adding flavor and more intense color to food. The aromatic spice is a tad expensive, so feel free to leave it out. This soup is terrific with or without it.

Start to Finish: 25 minutes **Makes:** 4 servings

	Nonstick cooking spray
12	ounces skinless, boneless chicken breast halves, cut into ½-inch cubes
6	cups reduced-sodium chicken broth
½	cup sliced leek or chopped onion
1	tablespoon grated fresh ginger
¼	teaspoon saffron threads, slightly crushed (optional)
1	9-ounce package refrigerated herb chicken tortellini or vegetable ravioli
½	cup fresh baby spinach leaves or shredded fresh spinach

1. Lightly coat an unheated large saucepan with cooking spray. Preheat over medium-high heat. Add chicken; cook and stir for 3 minutes. Carefully add broth, leek, ginger, and, if desired, saffron.

2. Bring to boiling. Add tortellini. Return to boiling; reduce heat. Simmer, uncovered, for 5 to 9 minutes or until tortellini is tender, stirring occasionally. Remove from heat. Top each serving with spinach.

Per serving: 222 cal., 3 g total fat (0 g sat. fat), 59 mg chol., 1,221 mg sodium, 21 g carbo., 3 g fiber, 29 g pro.

Turkey-Bean Soup [one]

All the goods for this hearty soup keep well in the fridge and pantry. Have them ready for a satisfying meal when the weather cools and a steaming bowl of soup sounds divine.

Start to Finish: 30 minutes
Makes: 4 servings

2	15-ounce cans Great Northern or white kidney (cannellini) beans, rinsed and drained
1	10.75-ounce can condensed cream of celery soup
8	ounces cooked smoked turkey sausage, halved lengthwise and sliced
1½	cups milk
1	teaspoon dried minced onion
½	teaspoon dried thyme, crushed
⅛	to ¼ teaspoon ground black pepper
1	teaspoon bottled minced garlic (2 cloves) or ¼ teaspoon garlic powder

1. In a large saucepan, combine beans, soup, and sausage. Stir in milk, dried minced onion, thyme, pepper, and garlic.

2. Bring to boiling over medium-high heat, stirring occasionally; reduce heat. Cover and simmer for 10 minutes, stirring occasionally.

Per serving: 434 cal., 11 g total fat (3 g sat. fat), 54 mg chol., 1,129 mg sodium, 57 g carbo., 11 g fiber, 29 g pro.

Asian Chicken Noodle Soup [one]

Udon or soba noodles and miso (MEE-soh) give this soup Asian character. Miso is fermented soybean paste and a common flavoring in Japanese cuisine. Look for both the noodles and miso in Asian markets.

Start to Finish: 20 minutes **Makes:** 4 servings

2	**14-ounce cans reduced-sodium chicken broth**
1	**cup water**
3	**ounces udon or soba noodles, broken in half (1 cup)**
1	**medium red sweet pepper, bias-sliced into bite-size strips (½ cup)**
⅓	**cup sliced green onion**
1	**tablespoon white miso**
1	**tablespoon grated fresh ginger**
⅛	**teaspoon crushed red pepper**
1½	**cups chopped cooked chicken or turkey**
1	**cup fresh snow pea pods, halved crosswise, or ½ of a 6-ounce package frozen snow pea pods, thawed and halved crosswise**
	Crushed red pepper (optional)

1. In a large saucepan, combine broth and water. Bring to boiling. Add noodles. Return to boiling; reduce heat. Simmer, covered, for 6 minutes.

2. Stir sweet pepper, green onion, miso, ginger, and the ⅛ teaspoon crushed red pepper into broth mixture. Add chicken. Return to boiling; reduce heat. Simmer, covered, for 3 minutes. Stir in pea pods. Simmer, uncovered, for 1 minute more or until pea pods are crisp-tender. Ladle soup into bowls. If desired, sprinkle with crushed red pepper.

Per serving: 225 cal., 6 g total fat (1 g sat. fat), 51 mg chol., 937 mg sodium, 22 g carbo., 2 g fiber, 23 g pro.

Quick Tip Snow peas are also called Chinese pea pods. Choose snow peas that are thin and crisp and have an almost translucent bright green pod. Avoid pods that are limp or broken. Store unwashed snow peas in a plastic bag in the refrigerator for up to 3 days. Before using, wash the pods, then snap off the ends, using them to pull on and remove the string, if present.

Asian Chicken Noodle Soup

Mexican Vegetable Soup

Mexican Vegetable Soup [one]

Shredded spinach adds freshness to this no-meat chili, plus chickpeas and jicama offer an unexpected twist to the traditional chili ingredients.

Start to Finish: 25 minutes **Makes:** 4 servings

- 1   teaspoon cumin seeds
- ¼   teaspoon chili powder
- 2   14-ounce cans vegetable broth or chicken broth
- 1   15-ounce can chickpeas (garbanzo beans), rinsed and drained
- 1   cup peeled jicama, cut into bite-size pieces
- ⅓   cup sliced green onion
- 3   cups torn fresh spinach
- ¼   cup crushed baked tortilla chips

1. In a medium saucepan, heat and stir cumin seeds and chili powder over medium heat for 1 to 2 minutes or until slightly fragrant. Remove from heat; carefully add broth and drained chickpeas.

2. Bring to boiling; stir in jicama and green onions. Return to boiling. Stir in spinach. Immediately divide among 4 soup bowls. Sprinkle each serving with some of the crushed tortilla chips.

Per serving: 201 cal., 3 g total fat (0 g sat. fat), 0 mg chol., 1,599 mg sodium, 33 g carbo., 9 g fiber, 11 g pro.

Speedy Southwestern-Style Tomato Soup [one]

Southwestern-style seasonings give canned soup character and punch. If you wish, sprinkle additional snipped cilantro on top.

Start to Finish: 10 minutes **Makes:** 5 or 6 servings

- 1   32-ounce jar ready-to-serve tomato soup
- 1   14.5-ounce can Mexican-style chopped tomatoes, undrained
- ⅛   teaspoon ground cumin
      Dash cayenne pepper or several dashes bottled hot pepper sauce
- 2   tablespoons snipped fresh cilantro
- ¼   cup dairy sour cream (optional)

1. In a large saucepan, combine tomato soup, undrained tomatoes, cumin, and cayenne pepper. Cook, covered, over medium heat until heated through, stirring occasionally. Stir in cilantro. If desired, top each serving with sour cream.

Per serving: 125 cal., 2 g total fat (1 g sat. fat), 7 mg chol., 787 mg sodium, 23 g carbo., 2 g fiber, 3 g pro.

Jalapeño Corn Chowder ♥ [one]

Frozen corn makes this soup easy to prepare. Fresh jalapeños give it a spicy kick.

Prep: 15 minutes **Cook:** 5 minutes **Makes:** 4 servings

- 3   cups frozen whole kernel corn
- 1   14-ounce can vegetable broth or chicken broth
- ⅔   cup dried small pasta (such as ditalini or tiny shell macaroni)
- 1   cup milk, half-and-half, or light cream
- ¼   cup bottled roasted red sweet peppers, drained and chopped
- 1   or 2 fresh jalapeño chile peppers, seeded and finely chopped*
- ½   cup shredded Cheddar cheese (optional)

1. In a blender or food processor, combine half of the corn and all of the broth. Cover and blend or process until nearly smooth.

2. In a large saucepan, combine the broth mixture and the remaining corn; bring to a boil. Add pasta. Reduce heat; simmer, uncovered, for 5 to 7 minutes or until pasta is tender. Stir in milk, roasted sweet peppers, and chile peppers; heat through. Ladle soup into bowls. If desired, sprinkle with cheese.

Per serving: 219 cal., 2 g total fat (1 g sat. fat), 5 mg chol., 419 mg sodium, 45 g carbo., 3 g fiber, 8 g pro.

*Note: Because chile peppers contain volatile oils that can burn your skin and eyes, avoid direct contact with them as much as possible. When working with chile peppers, wear plastic or rubber gloves. If your bare hands do touch the chile peppers, wash your hands and nails well with soap and warm water.

Jalapeño Corn Chowder

Thai-Style Shrimp Soup

Thai-Style Shrimp Soup ⊡one

The lemon grass for this simple soup can be found in Asian specialty markets or larger supermarkets.

Prep: 20 minutes **Cook:** 4 minutes
Makes: 3 or 4 servings

- 1   **14.5-ounce can chicken broth**
- 1   **small zucchini, cut into match-stick-size pieces (about 1½ cups)**
- 1   **green onion, bias-cut into 1¼-inch slices (2 tablespoons)**
- 2   **tablespoons minced fresh ginger**
- 2   **tablespoons minced fresh lemon grass or 1½ teaspoons finely shredded lemon peel**
- ¼   **teaspoon crushed red pepper**
- 12   **ounces small shrimp, peeled and deveined**
- 1   **14-ounce can unsweetened coconut milk**
- 2   **tablespoons shredded fresh basil**
- 2   **tablespoons toasted shaved coconut
  Fresh basil (optional)**

1. In a saucepan, bring broth to boiling. Add zucchini, green onion, ginger, lemon grass, and crushed red pepper. Return to boiling; reduce heat. Simmer, uncovered, 3 minutes, stirring occasionally.

2. Add shrimp. Simmer, uncovered, 1 to 3 minutes or until shrimp turn opaque. Add coconut milk. Heat through (do not boil).

3. To serve, ladle into bowls. Top with shredded basil, coconut, and, if desired, fresh basil.

Per serving: 445 cal., 37 g total fat (31 g sat. fat), 115 mg chol., 708 mg sodium, 12 g carbo., 4 g fiber, 21 g pro.

Vegetable Cheese Chowder ⊡one

If you've never tried a smoked cheese, you'll be surprised at the complex flavor it can add to a simple chowder.

Start to Finish: 20 minutes **Makes:** 4 servings

- 1   **16-ounce package frozen broccoli, cauliflower, and carrots**
- ½   **cup water**
- 2   **cups milk**
- ⅓   **cup all-purpose flour**
- 1   **14-ounce can chicken broth**
- 1   **cup shredded smoked or regular Gouda cheese (4 ounces)**

1. In a large saucepan, combine the frozen vegetables and water. Bring to boiling; reduce heat. Cover and simmer about 4 minutes or until vegetables are just tender. Do not drain.

2. Meanwhile, in a screw-top jar, combine ⅔ cup of the milk and the flour; cover and shake well. Add to vegetable mixture in saucepan; add remaining 1⅓ cups milk and the broth. Cook and stir until thickened and bubbly. Cook and stir for 1 minute more. Add the cheese; cook and stir over low heat until cheese nearly melts.

Per serving: 370 cal., 20 g total fat (13 g sat. fat), 81 mg chol., 942 mg sodium, 22 g carbo., 3 g fiber, 25 g pro.

Salmon Confetti Chowder ♥ ⊡one

If watercress isn't available, use snipped fresh parsley, spinach, or basil instead.

Start to Finish: 25 minutes **Makes:** 4 servings

- 2   **cups frozen (yellow, green, and red) pepper and onion stir-fry vegetables**
- 2   **tablespoons minced seeded fresh jalapeño chile pepper***
- 1   **tablespoon butter or margarine**
- 2   **tablespoons all-purpose flour**
- 2   **cups milk**
- 1   **cup half-and-half or light cream**
- 2   **cups refrigerated diced potatoes with onions**
- 1   **15-ounce can salmon, drained and flaked**
- ¼   **cup snipped fresh watercress**
- ½   **teaspoon finely shredded lemon peel**
- ½   **teaspoon salt**
- ½   **teaspoon ground black pepper**

1. In a large saucepan, cook stir-fry vegetables and chile pepper in hot butter for 3 to 5 minutes or until tender. Stir in flour. Stir in milk and half-and-half. Cook and stir until slightly thickened. Cook and stir for 2 minutes more.

2. Stir in diced potatoes, salmon, watercress, lemon peel, salt, and black pepper. Cook and stir until chowder is heated through.

Per serving: 410 cal., 17 g total fat (8 g sat. fat), 40 mg chol., 531 mg sodium, 30 g carbo., 3 g fiber, 34 g pro.

*Note: Because chile peppers contain volatile oils that can burn your skin and eyes, avoid direct contact with them as much as possible. When working with chile peppers, wear plastic or rubber gloves. If your bare hands do touch the peppers, wash your hands and nails well with soap and warm water.

Spiced Pumpkin and Shrimp Soup

Spiced Pumpkin and Shrimp Soup ♥ one

Fresh ginger and allspice add a pleasant hint of spice to this healthful seafood soup.

Start to Finish: 30 minutes   **Makes:** 4 servings

- 2 **tablespoons butter or margarine**
- 2 **medium onions, sliced**
- 2 **medium carrots, sliced (1 cup)**
- 1 **tablespoon snipped fresh cilantro**
- 2 **teaspoons grated fresh ginger**
- ½ **teaspoon ground allspice**
- 2 **cloves garlic, minced**
- 1 **14-ounce can chicken broth**
- 1 **15-ounce can pumpkin**
- 1 **cup milk**
- 1 **8-ounce package frozen, peeled and deveined cooked shrimp, thawed**
  Plain yogurt or dairy sour cream (optional)
  Snipped fresh chives (optional)

1. In a large saucepan, melt butter. Add onions, carrots, cilantro, ginger, allspice, and garlic to hot butter and cook, covered, for 10 to 12 minutes or until vegetables are tender, stirring once or twice.

2. Transfer vegetable mixture to a blender or food processor. Add ½ cup of the broth. Cover and blend or process until nearly smooth.

3. In the same saucepan, combine pumpkin, milk, and remaining 1¼ cups broth. Stir in blended vegetable mixture and shrimp; heat through. If desired, serve topped with yogurt and chives.

Per serving: 247 cal., 10 g total fat (5 g sat. fat), 134 mg chol., 537 mg sodium, 20 g carbo., 5 g fiber, 21 g pro.

Quick Tip Fresh ginger is available year-round in most supermarkets. Also referred to as mature ginger, it has a tan-colored skin that must be removed. Look for ginger with a smooth skin and spicy fragrance. If the skin is wrinkled or cracked, the root has become dry and is past its prime. Store unpeeled ginger in a plastic bag in the vegetable drawer of your refrigerator for up to 3 weeks.

Cajun Fish Soup `one`

Jazz up the mild fish in this soup with peppery Cajun seasoning.

Start to Finish: 20 minutes **Makes:** 4 servings

- **12 ounces fresh or frozen sea bass, cod, or orange roughy fillets**
- **4 cups assorted stir-fry vegetables from a salad bar or produce department or one 16-ounce package frozen stir-fry vegetables**
- **4 cups reduced-sodium chicken broth**
- **2 teaspoons Cajun seasoning**
- **1 14.5-ounce can diced tomatoes, undrained**

1. Thaw fish, if frozen. Rinse fish; cut into 1-inch pieces. Set fish aside.

2. In a large saucepan, combine vegetables, broth, and Cajun seasoning. Bring to boiling; reduce heat. Cover and simmer for 3 to 5 minutes or until vegetables are crisp-tender. Stir in fish and undrained tomatoes. Return to boiling; reduce heat. Simmer, covered, for 2 to 3 minutes or until fish flakes when tested with a fork.

Per serving: 157 cal., 2 g total fat (0 g sat. fat), 35 mg chol., 968 mg sodium, 12 g carbo., 3 g fiber, 21 g pro.

Manhattan-Style Clam Chowder `one`

On the East Coast, chowder fans still argue which is better—Manhattan-style chowder made with tomatoes or cream-based New England-style chowder. This easy-to-make version could have you favoring the red.

Start to Finish: 25 minutes **Makes:** 4 servings

- **2 6.5-ounce cans minced clams**
- **2 slices bacon, coarsely chopped**
- **1 cup chopped celery (2 stalks)**
- **1 cup chopped onion (1 large)**
- **1 14.5-ounce can diced tomatoes with basil, oregano, and garlic, undrained**
- **¼ teaspoon salt**
- **⅛ teaspoon ground black pepper**

1. Drain canned clams, reserving juice. If necessary, add enough water to reserved clam juice to equal 2 cups. Set clams and juice aside.

2. In a large saucepan, cook bacon until crisp. Remove bacon from pan, reserving drippings in pan. Drain bacon on paper towels.

3. Cook celery and onion in reserved drippings in the saucepan until tender. Stir in the reserved clam juice and the undrained tomatoes. Bring to boiling; reduce heat. Simmer, uncovered, for 5 minutes. Stir in clams, bacon, salt, and pepper; heat through.

Per serving: 133 cal., 5 g total fat (3 g sat. fat), 10 mg chol., 1,026 mg sodium, 14 g carbo., 2 g fiber, 4 g pro.

Fish Provençale `one`

The sweet essence of fresh fennel blends nicely with fish, tomatoes, garlic, and onion in this classic French soup.

Start to Finish: 30 minutes **Makes:** 4 servings

- **8 ounces fresh or frozen skinless haddock, grouper, or halibut fillets**
- **1 small fennel bulb**
- **3 cups vegetable or chicken broth**
- **1 cup finely chopped onion**
- **1 cup cubed yellow summer squash**
- **1 cup dry white wine**
- **1 teaspoon finely shredded orange peel or lemon peel**
- **3 cloves garlic, minced**
- **2 cups chopped tomatoes or one 14.5-ounce can diced tomatoes, undrained**
- **2 tablespoons snipped fresh thyme**

1. Thaw fish, if frozen. Cut fish into 1-inch pieces; set aside.

2. Cut off and discard upper stalks of fennel. Remove any wilted outer layers and cut a thin slice from the base. Wash fennel; cut in half lengthwise and thinly slice.

3. In a large saucepan, combine fennel, broth, onion, squash, wine, orange peel, and garlic. Bring to boiling; reduce heat. Simmer, covered, for 10 minutes. Stir in fish, tomatoes, and thyme. Cook about 3 minutes more or until fish flakes easily with a fork.

Per serving: 165 cal., 1 g total fat (0 g sat. fat), 32 mg chol., 798 mg sodium, 17 g carbo., 4 g fiber, 13 g pro.

Fish Provençale

Pork Tenderloin with
Tomato-Peach Chutney, **page 204**

Bull's-Eye Onion Burgers,
page 196

Grilled Chicken
and Kiwi Tacos, **page 213**

Grilled Asparagus with
Lemon, **page 225**

From the Grill

It is no wonder that many home cooks agree that grilling is their favorite way to cook. Hot coals bring out so much succulent flavor in food that few extra ingredients are needed. Look here for innovative recipes that are sure to wow cookout guests.

Country French Ribeyes

Country French Ribeyes

Elevate yourself to the rank of master griller with this juicy, lavender-infused ribeye. If you have time to plan ahead, you can boost the lavender flavor by applying the rub a few hours in advance and chilling the steaks in the refrigerator.

Prep: 10 minutes **Grill:** 16 minutes **Makes:** 4 servings

5	green onions
2	teaspoons dried lavender, crushed
2	teaspoons dried thyme, crushed
1	teaspoon coarsely ground black pepper
½	teaspoon coarse salt
4	6- to 8-ounce boneless beef ribeye steaks, cut 1 to 1¼ inches thick
1	tablespoon olive oil
4	to 8 plum tomatoes

1. Mince one of the green onions; set remaining green onions aside. In a small bowl, combine minced green onion, lavender, thyme, pepper, and salt. Sprinkle green onion mixture over steaks; rub in with your fingers. Brush steaks with half of the oil. Brush tomatoes and remaining green onions with the remaining olive oil.

2. Place steaks on the lightly oiled rack of an uncovered grill directly over medium-high heat. Grill for 8 minutes. Place tomatoes and green onions alongside steaks on the grill. Turn steaks; grill for 8 to 10 minutes more or until desired doneness (145°F for medium-rare doneness; 160°F for medium doneness). Grill tomatoes and onions for 8 to 10 minutes or until slightly charred, turning several times.

Per serving: 326 cal., 17 g total fat (6 g sat. fat), 99 mg chol., 340 mg sodium, 5 g carbo., 2 g fiber, 36 g pro.

All-American Burgers

If you love cheeseburgers, add a slice of cheddar, Swiss, or pepper cheese to this classic favorite.

Prep: 10 minutes **Grill:** 14 minutes **Makes:** 4 servings

2	tablespoons ketchup
1	tablespoon Worcestershire sauce
1	tablespoon bottled steak sauce
1	teaspoon sugar
1	teaspoon cooking oil
1	teaspoon vinegar
½	teaspoon bottled minced garlic (1 clove) or 2 tablespoons finely chopped onion
	Few dashes bottled hot pepper sauce
1	pound lean ground beef
¼	teaspoon salt
¼	teaspoon ground black pepper
4	whole wheat hamburger buns, split and toasted
	Purchased fresh salsa
	Lettuce, pickles, radish halves, and/or cucumber slices (optional)

1. For the sauce, in a small saucepan, combine ketchup, Worcestershire sauce, steak sauce, sugar, oil, vinegar, garlic, and hot pepper sauce. Bring to boiling; reduce heat. Simmer, uncovered, for 5 minutes. Set aside.

2. In a medium bowl, combine meat, salt, and black pepper; mix well. Shape meat mixture into four ¾-inch-thick patties.

3. Place patties on the rack of an uncovered grill directly over medium heat. Grill for 14 to 18 minutes or until done (160°F),* turning once and brushing often with sauce. Discard any remaining sauce.

4. Serve burgers on buns topped with purchased salsa. If desired, serve with lettuce, pickles, radish halves, and/or cucumber slices.

Per serving: 336 cal., 15 g total fat (5 g sat. fat), 71 mg chol., 572 mg sodium, 26 g carbo., 2 g fiber, 25 g pro.

*Note: The internal color of a burger is not a reliable doneness indicator. A beef patty cooked to 160°F is safe, regardless of color. To measure the doneness of a beef patty, insert an instant-read thermometer through the side of the beef patty to a depth of 2 to 3 inches.

All-American Burgers

Caesar-Beef-Vegetable Kabobs

Named after the Caesar salad dressing used here as a marinade, this meat and veggie combo is also tasty when marinated in Italian salad dressing.

Prep: 30 minutes **Grill:** 12 minutes
Marinate: 2 to 4 hours **Makes:** 4 servings

1	**pound boneless beef sirloin steak, cut 1 inch thick**
8	**cherry tomatoes**
8	**whole fresh button mushrooms**
1	**large yellow or green sweet pepper, cut into 1-inch pieces**
½	**cup bottled Caesar salad dressing**
½	**teaspoon ground black pepper**

1. Cut steak into 1-inch cubes. Place steak cubes, tomatoes, mushrooms, and sweet pepper pieces in a resealable plastic bag set in a shallow dish. For the marinade, combine salad dressing and black pepper. Pour marinade over steak and vegetables. Seal bag; turn to coat steak and vegetables. Marinate in the refrigerator for 2 to 4 hours, turning bag occasionally.

2. Remove steak and vegetables from marinade; discard marinade. On eight 6- to 8-inch metal skewers, alternately thread steak, tomatoes, mushrooms, and sweet pepper pieces, leaving a ¼-inch space between pieces.

3. Grill kabobs on the rack of an uncovered grill directly over medium heat for 12 to 14 minutes for medium doneness, turning once.

Per serving: 338 cal., 23 g total fat (4 g sat. fat), 69 mg chol., 385 mg sodium, 7 g carbo., 1 g fiber, 26 g pro.

Gorgonzola-and-Herb-Stuffed Burgers

These juicy burgers feature an Italian trifecta of Gorgonzola, basil, and garlic.

Prep: 20 minutes **Grill:** 14 minutes **Makes:** 4 servings

½	**cup crumbled Gorgonzola cheese or other blue cheese**
¼	**cup snipped fresh basil**
1	**clove garlic, minced**
1¼	**pounds lean ground beef**
	Salt and ground black pepper
4	**kaiser rolls, split and toasted**
1½	**cups arugula or fresh spinach leaves (optional)**
1	**large tomato, sliced (optional)**

1. In a small bowl, combine Gorgonzola cheese, basil, and garlic; shape into four slightly flattened mounds. Shape ground beef into eight ¼-inch-thick patties. Place a cheese mound in the center of four of the patties. Top with remaining patties; press gently to seal edges. Season with salt and pepper.

2. Grill patties on the rack of an uncovered grill directly over medium heat for 14 to 18 minutes or until beef is done (160°F), turning once halfway through grilling.

3. Serve burgers on kaiser rolls with, if desired, arugula and tomato.

Per serving: 448 cal., 20 g total fat (8 g sat. fat), 100 mg chol., 704 mg sodium, 31 g carbo., 1 g fiber, 34 g pro.

Bull's-Eye Onion Burgers

Not only are these scrumptious burgers shaped with a bull's-eye on top, but they're also tastefully targeted to hit the spot.

Prep: 20 minutes **Grill:** 10 minutes **Makes:** 4 servings

1	**large sweet onion**
1	**pound lean ground beef**
1½	**teaspoons garlic powder**
½	**teaspoon salt**
¼	**teaspoon ground black pepper**
4	**slices Swiss cheese (4 ounces)**
4	**¾-inch slices hearty bread or Texas toast, toasted**
	Lettuce (optional)
	Sliced tomatoes (optional)

1. Peel and cut onion into four ¼-inch slices; refrigerate remaining onion for another use. Shape beef loosely into four ½-inch-thick patties; sprinkle with garlic powder, salt, and pepper. Press one onion slice into the center of each patty and shape beef around onion until top of onion is flush with the surface of the beef patty.

2. Place patties, onion sides up, on the rack of an uncovered grill directly over medium heat. Grill for 10 to 13 minutes or until meat is done (160°F), turning once halfway through grilling. Top with cheese slices before the last minute of grilling.

3. Serve burgers on toast and, if desired, with lettuce and tomato slices.

Per serving: 475 cal., 24 g total fat (10 g sat. fat), 147 mg chol., 648 mg sodium, 31 g carbo., 2 g fiber, 36 g pro.

Bull's-Eye Onion Burgers

Top Loins with Gorgonzola Butter

The delectable flavor of Gorgonzola, the Italian blue-veined cheese, is out of this world on top of a juicy grilled steak.

Prep: 15 minutes **Grill:** 10 minutes **Makes:** 4 servings

- **2 tablespoons crumbled Gorgonzola or blue cheese**
- **2 tablespoons tub-style cream cheese spread with chive and onion**
- **1 to 2 tablespoons butter, softened**
- **1 tablespoon chopped pine nuts or walnuts, toasted**
- **4 boneless beef top loin steaks, cut 1 inch thick**
  Salt

1. For Gorgonzola butter, in a small bowl, combine Gorgonzola cheese, cream cheese spread, butter, and pine nuts. Shape cheese mixture into a 1-inch-diameter log. Wrap in plastic wrap. Refrigerate until firm.

2. Trim fat from steaks. Grill steaks on the rack of an uncovered grill directly over medium heat until steaks reach desired doneness, turning once halfway through grilling. Allow 10 to 12 minutes for medium-rare (145°F) or 12 to 15 minutes for medium (160°F).

3. To serve, halve each steak. Season with salt to taste. Cut Gorgonzola butter log into eight slices. Place one slice of butter on each steak piece.

Per serving: 268 cal., 19 g total fat (8 g sat. fat), 82 mg chol., 110 mg sodium, 0 g carbo., 0 g fiber, 23 g pro.

Top Loins with Gorgonzola Butter

Italian Kabobs with Orzo

Because of their petite size, cipollini onions are time-consuming to peel. Drop them into boiling water for 30 seconds, and the peel will be easier to remove.

Prep: 50 minutes **Grill:** 12 minutes
Marinate: 6 to 24 hours **Makes:** 4 servings

2	tablespoons olive oil
12	cipollini onions, peeled and ends trimmed
12	medium cremini mushrooms
1	large red sweet pepper, cut into 12 pieces
1½	pounds boneless beef sirloin steak, cut into 1½-inch cubes
1	8-ounce bottle purchased Italian vinaigrette salad dressing (about 1 cup)
	Herbed Orzo

1. In a large skillet, heat oil over medium heat. Arrange onions in an even layer in hot oil; cook for 2 to 3 minutes on each side or until browned and just tender, turning once (do not stir). Reduce heat; add mushrooms. Cook, covered, for 3 to 5 minutes or until mushrooms are almost tender. Transfer onions and mushrooms to a dish; set aside until cool.

2. Place onions, mushrooms, sweet pepper, and beef in a large resealable plastic bag set in a shallow dish. Pour salad dressing over beef mixture; seal bag. Marinate in the refrigerator for 6 to 24 hours, turning bag occasionally. On four 12- to 14-inch metal skewers, thread beef and vegetables. Transfer remaining marinade to a saucepan; bring to boiling. Set aside.

3. Grill kabobs on the rack of an uncovered grill directly over medium heat for 12 to 14 minutes for medium doneness (160°F), turning occasionally and brushing with some of the remaining marinade during the last 2 minutes of grilling.

Herbed Orzo: Prepare 1 cup orzo pasta according to package directions; drain. Stir in 2 tablespoons olive oil and 1 tablespoon snipped fresh herb, such as oregano, marjoram, and/or thyme. Season to taste with salt and black pepper. If desired, top with freshly grated Parmesan cheese.

Per serving: 803 cal., 48 g total fat (8 g sat. fat), 80 mg chol., 836 mg sodium, 49 g carbo., 4 g fiber, 45 g pro.

Teriyaki Beef Spirals ♥

Score the steak with a sharp knife and pound it with a meat mallet to make it more tender and easier to roll into a spiral.

Prep: 20 minutes **Grill:** 12 minutes **Makes:** 4 servings

1	cup loosely packed fresh spinach leaves
½	cup finely chopped water chestnuts
¼	cup chopped green onion (2)
¼	cup reduced-sodium teriyaki sauce
¾	to 1 pound beef flank steak
	Salt
	Ground black pepper
	Cooked rice noodles (optional)
	Sliced green onion (optional)

1. Remove stems from spinach leaves. Layer spinach leaves on top of each other; slice crosswise into thin strips. In a medium bowl, combine spinach, water chestnuts, the ¼ cup green onions, and 2 tablespoons of the teriyaki sauce.

2. Trim fat from steak. Score steak on both sides by making shallow cuts at 1-inch intervals in a diamond pattern. Place steak between 2 pieces of plastic wrap. Pound lightly with the flat side of a meat mallet into a 10×8-inch rectangle. Remove plastic wrap. Sprinkle steak with salt and pepper.

3. Spread spinach mixture over steak. Starting from a short side, roll steak up. Secure with wooden toothpicks at 1-inch intervals, starting ½ inch from one end. Slice between toothpicks into eight 1-inch slices. Thread two slices onto each of four long wooden* or metal skewers. Brush slices with some of the remaining teriyaki sauce.

4. Grill slices on the rack of an uncovered grill directly over medium heat for 12 to 14 minutes for medium doneness, turning once and brushing with remaining teriyaki sauce halfway through grilling. If desired, toss noodles with sliced green onion and serve with steak.

Per serving: 135 cal., 6 g total fat (2 g sat. fat), 42 mg chol., 135 mg sodium, 2 g carbo., 1 g fiber, 18 g pro.

*Note: If using wooden skewers, soak in water for 30 minutes; drain.

Spice-Rubbed Ribeyes 🖤

Chili-style seasonings—smoky with a hint of spice—bring out the best flavor of these delectable ribeyes.

Prep: 5 minutes **Grill:** 11 minutes **Makes:** 4 servings

- **4   teaspoons chili powder**
- **1   teaspoon ground coriander**
- **1   teaspoon cumin seeds**
- **½   teaspoon ground black pepper**
- **4   6-ounce boneless beef ribeye steaks, cut 1 inch thick**

1. For spice rub, in a small nonstick skillet, cook and stir chili powder, coriander, cumin seeds, and pepper over medium heat for 1 minute; cool. Rub spice mixture onto both sides of steaks.

2. Grill steaks on the rack of an uncovered grill directly over medium heat until desired doneness, turning once halfway through grilling. Allow 11 to 15 minutes for medium rare (145°F) and 14 to 18 minutes for medium (160°F).

Per serving: 267 cal., 11 g total fat (4 g sat. fat), 81 mg chol., 115 mg sodium, 2 g carbo., 1 g fiber, 38 g pro.

Sizzling Beef Salad

Pungent red chile paste and savory hoisin sauce add an Asian accent to beef.

Prep: 20 minutes **Grill:** 14 minutes **Stand:** 30 minutes **Makes:** 4 servings

- **12   ounces boneless beef top sirloin steak, cut 1 inch thick**
- **Salt**
- **1   to 2 tablespoons purchased red chile paste**
- **⅓   cup lime juice**
- **3   tablespoons cooking oil**
- **2   tablespoons bottled hoisin sauce**
- **6   cups shredded romaine lettuce**
- **1   medium fresh papaya, seeded, peeled, and sliced**
- **2   tablespoons chopped honey-roasted peanuts**

1. Sprinkle both sides of steak lightly with salt. Spread one or both sides of steak with chile paste. Place in a resealable plastic bag set in a shallow dish. Seal bag. Let stand at room temperature for 30 minutes. (Or refrigerate for at least 4 hours or up to 24 hours.)

2. Grill steak on the rack of an uncovered grill directly over medium heat until desired doneness, turning once halfway through grilling. Allow 14 to 18 minutes for medium-rare doneness (145°F) or 18 to 22 minutes for medium doneness (160°F).

3. Meanwhile, for the dressing, in a screw-top jar combine lime juice, oil, and hoisin sauce. Cover and shake well. Arrange lettuce on 4 chilled dinner plates. To serve, thinly slice steak. Arrange steak slices on lettuce; add papaya slices. Drizzle with dressing; sprinkle with peanuts.

Per serving: 369 cal., 20 g total fat (5 g sat. fat), 57 mg chol., 259 mg sodium, 25 g carbo., 4 g fiber, 22 g pro.

Zesty Grilled Sirloin

Thanks to marinating in a paste of dried chili and cumin, the finished steak will be juicy with just the right flavor.

Prep: 20 minutes **Grill:** 24 minutes
Stand: 30 minutes **Marinate:** 24 hours
Makes: 12 servings

- **1½   ounces dried red chile peppers, such as guajillo, ancho, or pasilla (7 or 8 chiles)**
- **1   tablespoon ground cumin**
- **½   cup olive oil**
- **1   2.75- to 3-pound beef sirloin steak, cut 2 inches thick**

1. Wearing plastic or rubber gloves, use scissors or a sharp knife to remove the stalk ends from the chile peppers. Split peppers; remove and discard seeds. In a heavy skillet, toast peppers (without oil) over medium heat for 3 to 4 minutes or until they give off a fragrance, turning once or twice with tongs.

2. Transfer chile peppers to a small bowl. Cover with hot water and soak for 30 minutes. Drain, reserving 1 cup soaking water. Place chile peppers in a blender or food processor.

3. In the same skillet, toast cumin over medium heat for 1 to 2 minutes or until it becomes fragrant, stirring often. Add cumin and oil to chile peppers in blender or food processor. Blend or process until nearly smooth, adding enough of the soaking water to make a medium-thick paste; set aside.

4. Trim fat from steak. Place steak in a resealable plastic bag set in a shallow dish. Spread chile pepper paste on both sides of steak. Seal bag. Marinate in the refrigerator for 24 hours, turning bag occasionally.

5. Drain the steak, reserving marinade. Grill steak on the rack of an uncovered grill directly over medium heat for 24 to 26 minutes for medium rare (145°F) or 26 to 30 minutes for medium (160°F), turning once halfway through grilling and brushing occasionally with reserved marinade during the first half of grilling. Discard remaining marinade. To serve, thinly slice steak across the grain.

Per serving: 233 cal., 14 g total fat (3 g sat. fat), 63 mg chol., 56 mg sodium, 3 g carbo., 1 g fiber, 23 g pro.

Grilled Steak Sandwiches

These tantalizing sandwiches are stuffed with a blend of marinated beef, grilled peppers, and a tangy mayonnaise.

Prep: 15 minutes **Grill:** 10 minutes
Marinate: 4 to 24 hours **Makes:** 4 servings

- **2 8-ounce boneless beef top loin steaks, cut 1 inch thick**
- **½ cup dried tomato vinaigrette or Italian salad dressing**
- **¼ cup light mayonnaise or salad dressing**
- **2 teaspoons finely chopped sweet pickle**
- **1 teaspoon drained capers, chopped (optional)**
- **½ teaspoon lemon juice**
- **⅛ teaspoon ground black pepper**
- **2 large yellow sweet peppers, each cut into 8 strips**
- **4 French-style rolls or kaiser rolls, split and toasted**
- **1 cup fresh spinach leaves**

1. Trim fat from steak. Place steak in resealable plastic bag set in shallow dish. Pour vinaigrette over steak; seal bag. Marinate in refrigerator for 4 to 24 hours, turning bag occasionally.

2. Meanwhile, for the sauce, in small bowl, combine mayonnaise, pickle relish, capers (if desired), lemon juice, and black pepper. Cover and chill for 4 to 24 hours.

3. Drain steaks, discarding salad dressing. Place steak and sweet pepper strips on rack of uncovered grill directly over medium heat. Grill until steak is desired doneness and pepper strips are crisp-tender, turning once halfway through grilling. For steak, allow 10 to 12 minutes for medium-rare (145°F) or 12 to 15 minutes for medium (160°F). Cut steak into ¼-inch slices.

4. To assemble, spread sauce on bottom and top halves of rolls. Fill with spinach, steak slices, and sweet pepper strips.

Per serving: 496 cal., 16 g total fat (4 g sat. fat), 72 mg chol., 872 mg sodium, 54 g carbo., 4 g fiber, 33 g pro.

Grilled Steak Sandwiches

Peanut-Crusted Chops

Keep the grill cover handy for this one. We recommend that you cover the grill after adding the peanut "crust" to the pork chops so they get slightly crispy.

Prep: 15 minutes **Grill:** 11 minutes **Makes:** 4 servings

- ⅓ **cup creamy peanut butter**
- ⅓ **cup pineapple juice**
- 2 **tablespoons finely chopped green onion (1)**
- 1 **tablespoon soy sauce**
- 1 **tablespoon honey**
- 1 **teaspoon grated fresh ginger or ¼ teaspoon ground ginger**
- ½ **teaspoon dry mustard**
  Several dashes bottled hot pepper sauce
- ⅓ **cup finely chopped honey-roasted peanuts**
- 2 **tablespoons fine dry bread crumbs**
- 1 **tablespoon toasted sesame seeds**
- 4 **boneless pork sirloin chops, cut ¾ inch thick**
- 4 **ounces Chinese egg noodles or dried angel hair pasta**

1. For peanut sauce, in a small saucepan, heat peanut butter until melted; gradually whisk in pineapple juice, green onion, soy sauce, honey, ginger, mustard, and hot pepper sauce. Set aside 2 tablespoons of the peanut butter sauce. Keep remaining peanut butter sauce warm. For crust, in a small bowl, combine peanuts, bread crumbs, and sesame seeds; set aside.

2. Grill chops on the rack of an uncovered grill directly over medium heat for 6 minutes. Turn chops and brush with the reserved 2 tablespoons peanut butter sauce. Sprinkle chops with crust mixture. With the back of a metal spatula, press crust onto chops. Cover and grill for 5 to

Peanut-Crusted Chops

7 minutes more or until chops are slightly pink in center and juices run clear (160°F).

3. Meanwhile, cook noodles according to package directions; drain. Toss noodles with the remaining peanut sauce. Serve with chops.

Per serving: 510 cal., 23 g total fat (5 g sat. fat), 89 mg chol., 518 mg sodium, 39 g carbo., 6 g fiber, 42 g pro.

Stout-Glazed Ribs

Stout beer glazes the ribs with gorgeous, dark color and deep, rich flavor. The darker the beer the better.

Prep: 15 minutes **Cook:** 10 minutes **Grill:** 1½ hours
Marinate: 6 to 24 hours **Makes:** 4 servings

- 4 **pounds pork loin back ribs or meaty pork spareribs**
- 1 **12-ounce bottle stout**
- ½ **cup chopped onion (1 medium)**
- ¼ **cup honey mustard**
- 3 **cloves garlic, minced, or 1½ teaspoons bottled minced garlic**
- 1 **teaspoon caraway seeds (optional)**
  Salt
  Ground black pepper

1. Trim fat from ribs. Place ribs in a resealable plastic bag set in a shallow dish. For marinade, in a medium bowl, combine stout, onion, honey mustard, garlic, and, if desired, caraway seeds. Pour marinade over ribs. Seal bag; turn to coat ribs. Marinate in the refrigerator for 6 to 24 hours, turning bag occasionally.

2. Drain ribs, reserving marinade. Sprinkle ribs with salt and pepper. Pour marinade into a small saucepan. Bring to boiling; reduce heat. Simmer, uncovered, for 10 minutes.

3. For a charcoal grill, arrange medium-hot coals around a drip pan. Test for medium heat above pan. Place ribs, bone sides down, on grill rack over drip pan. Cover and grill for 1½ to 1¾ hours or until ribs are tender, brushing frequently with marinade during the last 10 minutes of grilling. Discard any remaining marinade. (For a gas grill, preheat grill. Adjust for indirect cooking. Grill as above.)

Per serving: 482 cal., 20 g total fat (7 g sat. fat), 135 mg chol., 296 mg sodium, 5 g carbo., 0 g fiber, 63 g pro.

Quick Tip Stout is a strong beer made from dark-roasted barley. It has an intensely dark color, bitter flavor, and extremely dense body. Always store any type of beer standing upright. Laying the bottle on its side exposes more of the liquid to the air in the bottle, which will diminish the beer's flavor.

Stout-Glazed Ribs

Pork Tenderloin with
Tomato-Peach Chutney

Pork Tenderloin with ♥ Tomato-Peach Chutney

This guest-worthy tenderloin roast is grilled on a cedar plank for added flavor and also to keep the meat moist and succulent. Find cedar planks near other grilling products at large supermarkets or at specialty food stores.

Prep: 20 minutes **Grill:** 30 minutes **Stand:** 1 hour
Makes: 6 servings

- 1   **15×7×½-inch cedar plank**
- 2   **teaspoons ground allspice**
- 1½   **teaspoons freshly ground black pepper**
- 1   **teaspoon salt**
- 2   **12- to 16-ounce pork tenderloins**
- 1   **tablespoon olive oil**
- 6   **to 8 cups arugula, mesclun, or mixed baby greens**
       Tomato-Peach Chutney

1. At least 1 hour before grilling, soak plank in enough water to cover. Weight down plank to keep it submerged during soaking. Drain plank.

2. In a small bowl, stir together allspice, pepper, and salt; set aside. Trim fat from pork. Brush pork with oil. Sprinkle spice mixture evenly over pork, rubbing it in with your fingers.

3. Place plank on the grill rack directly over medium heat; heat about 5 minutes or until plank begins to crackle and smoke. Place pork on plank. Cover; grill for 30 to 35 minutes or until an instant-read thermometer inserted into the center of the pork registers 155°F. Remove pork from grill. Cover with foil and let stand for 5 minutes.

4. To serve, line a platter or each plate with greens. Cut pork diagonally into 1-inch slices. Arrange pork slices on greens and top with some of the Tomato-Peach Chutney. Pass remaining chutney.

Tomato-Peach Chutney: In a medium saucepan, heat 1 tablespoon olive oil over medium-high heat. Add ¼ cup chopped onion, ¼ cup chopped red sweet pepper, and 2 cloves garlic, minced. Cook and stir until onion is tender. Stir in 1 cup cored, seeded, and chopped tomato, 2 tablespoons sugar, 2 tablespoons cider vinegar, and ¼ cup golden raisins. Bring to boiling; reduce heat. Simmer, uncovered, for 10 minutes or until mixture is thickened, stirring occasionally. Stir in 1 cup chopped, peeled fresh or thawed frozen peaches and ¼ cup jalapeño jelly. Heat and stir until jelly melts. Serve chutney warm or cooled. Makes about 1¾ cups.

Per serving: 279 cal., 8 g total fat (2 g sat. fat), 73 mg chol., 386 mg sodium, 26 g carbo., 3 g fiber, 25 g pro.

Memphis-Style Pork Chops

What's considered "good" barbecue varies with the part of country you're in. This Southern-style recipe opts for chili sauce in place of ketchup and includes molasses and cider vinegar.

Prep: 15 minutes **Grill:** 12 minutes **Makes:** 4 servings

- ½ **cup bottled chili sauce**
- 2 **tablespoons molasses**
- 2 **tablespoons cider vinegar**
- 1 **teaspoon chili powder**
- 4 **boneless pork loin chops, cut ¾ to 1 inch thick (about 1¼ pounds total)**
- 1 **teaspoon dried basil, crushed**
- ½ **teaspoon paprika**
- ¼ **teaspoon salt**
- ¼ **teaspoon onion powder**
- ¼ **teaspoon cayenne pepper**

1. In a small saucepan, stir together chili sauce, molasses, vinegar, and chili powder. Bring to boiling; reduce heat. Simmer, uncovered, for 3 minutes. Remove from heat.

2. Trim fat from chops. In a small bowl, stir together basil, paprika, salt, onion powder, and cayenne pepper. Sprinkle evenly over both sides of each chop; rub in with your fingers.

3. Place chops on the rack of an uncovered grill directly over medium heat. Grill for 12 to 15 minutes or until juices run clear (160°F), turning once and brushing with chili sauce mixture during the last 5 minutes of grilling.

Per serving: 260 cal., 7 g total fat (3 g sat. fat), 83 mg chol., 623 mg sodium, 16 g carbo., 2 g fiber, 31 g pro.

Spicy Orange-Glazed Pork Chops ♥

The glaze is sweet, so wait until the last minutes of grilling before brushing it onto the chops. If added too soon it's likely to burn.

Prep: 10 minutes **Grill:** 12 minutes **Makes:** 4 servings

- ¼ **cup orange marmalade**
- 2 **teaspoons Dijon-style mustard**
- 1 **teaspoon lemon juice**
- ⅛ **to ¼ teaspoon cayenne pepper**
- 4 **boneless pork loin chops, cut ¾ inch thick**
  Salt and ground black pepper

1. For the glaze, in a small bowl, stir together orange marmalade, mustard, lemon juice, and cayenne pepper. Set glaze aside.

2. Trim fat from chops. Sprinkle chops with salt and black pepper. Grill chops on the greased rack of an uncovered grill directly over medium heat for 12 to 15 minutes or until done (160°F), turning once and brushing frequently with glaze during the last few minutes of grilling.

Per serving: 263 cal., 10 g total fat (3 g sat. fat), 92 mg chol., 126 mg sodium, 5 g carbo., 0 g fiber, 37 g pro.

Quick Tip When purchasing pork, look for meat that is pale pink with a small amount of marbling. Store fresh pork that will be used within 6 hours of purchasing in the refrigerator in the store packaging. Otherwise, remove it from the packaging, wrap it in waxed paper, and store it in the coldest part of the refrigerator for up to 2 days.

Memphis-Style Pork Chops

Apple-Smoked Pork Loin

Apple-Smoked Pork Loin ♥

Flavored wood chips are sold in a variety of flavors, from hickory and mesquite to cherry and pecan. In this oregano-rubbed pork recipe, apple wood chips impart a subtle sweetness and full-bodied smoky flavor.

Prep: 10 minutes **Soak:** 1 hour **Grill:** 1 hour
Stand: 15 minutes **Makes:** 8 servings

3	cups apple wood or orange wood chips or 6 to 8 apple wood or orange wood chunks
1	2- to 2½-pounds boneless pork top loin roast (single loin)
2	teaspoons dried oregano, crushed
4	cloves garlic, minced, or 2 teaspoons bottled minced garlic
½	teaspoon salt
½	teaspoon coarsely ground black pepper

1. At least 1 hour before cooking, soak wood chips or chunks in enough water to cover.

2. Meanwhile, trim fat from roast. Place roast in a shallow dish. In a small bowl, stir together oregano, garlic, salt, and pepper. Sprinkle evenly over all sides of roast; rub in with your fingers.

3. Drain wood chips. For a charcoal grill, arrange medium coals around a drip pan. Test for medium-low heat over drip pan. Sprinkle half of the drained wood chips over the coals. Place roast on grill rack directly over drip pan. Cover and grill for 1 to 1½ hours or until done (155°F). Add more coals and remaining wood chips as needed during grilling. (For a gas grill, preheat grill. Reduce heat to medium. Adjust for indirect cooking. Grill as above following manufacturer's directions for use of wood chips.)

4. Remove roast from grill. Cover with foil; let stand for 15 minutes before slicing. (The temperature of the roast will rise 5°F during standing.)

Per serving: 190 cal., 9 g total fat (3 g sat. fat), 74 mg chol., 214 mg sodium, 1 g carbo., 0 g fiber, 24 g pro.

Skewered Five-Spice Pork

Oyster sauce is a thick, concentrated mixture of oysters, brine, and soy sauce. Asian cooks enjoy the way it brings richness and depth to recipes, yet doesn't compete with other natural flavors in a dish.

Prep: 30 minutes **Grill:** 10 minutes
Marinate: 4 to 24 hours **Makes:** 4 servings

1	pound boneless pork loin, cut into bite-size strips
¼	cup bottled salsa
2	tablespoons soy sauce
2	tablespoons bottled oyster sauce
1	tablespoon sugar
1	teaspoon five-spice powder
⅛	to ¼ teaspoon ground red pepper
1	medium red sweet pepper, cut into 1-inch pieces
4	green onions, cut diagonally into 1½-inch pieces
8	large fresh mushrooms
1	tablespoon cooking oil

1. Place pork in a resealable plastic bag set in a medium bowl. In a small bowl, stir together salsa, soy sauce, oyster sauce, sugar, five-spice powder, and ground red pepper. Pour over pork in bag; close bag. Turn to coat pork. Marinate in the refrigerator for 4 to 24 hours, turning bag occasionally. Drain pork, reserving marinade.

2. Brush sweet pepper and onions lightly with cooking oil. Alternately thread pork, sweet pepper, green onions, and mushrooms onto four 12- to 14-inch metal skewers.

3. Grill kabobs on the rack of an uncovered grill directly over medium heat for 10 to 12 minutes or until meat is done (160°F) and vegetables are tender, turning and brushing with marinade halfway through grilling. Discard any remaining marinade.

Per serving: 318 cal., 19 g total fat (6 g sat. fat), 67 mg chol., 829 mg sodium, 11 g carbo., 2 g fiber, 26 g pro.

Curried Apricot Pork Pockets

Shaping these delightful pork-and-fruit patties into ovals rather than rounds makes them easier to tuck into pita bread halves.

Prep: 30 minutes **Grill:** 14 minutes **Makes:** 4 servings

- 1 egg
- ¼ cup finely snipped dried apricots
- ¼ cup mango chutney (finely chop any large pieces of fruit)
- ¼ cup finely crushed whole wheat crackers
- 1¼ teaspoons curry powder
- ¼ teaspoon salt
- 1 pound lean ground pork
- 2 tablespoons apricot preserves
- 1 teaspoon lemon juice
- 2 large pita bread rounds, halved crosswise
- 1 cup shredded spinach or romaine

1. In a large bowl, beat egg with a whisk; stir in snipped apricots, chutney, wheat crackers, 1 teaspoon of the curry powder, and the salt. Add ground pork; mix well. Shape into four ¾-inch-thick oval patties. In a small bowl, combine apricot preserves, lemon juice, and the remaining ¼ teaspoon curry powder; set aside.

2. Place patties on the grill rack directly over medium heat; grill for 14 to 18 minutes or until done (160°F), turning once halfway through grilling and brushing with the preserves mixture during the last 2 minutes of grilling.

3. Serve patties in pita bread halves with shredded spinach.

Per serving: 519 cal., 26 g total fat (10 g sat. fat), 134 mg chol., 584 mg sodium, 43 g carbo., 2 g fiber, 25 g pro.

Texas Rib Sandwiches With Coleslaw

Coleslaw is an indispensable ingredient for this down-home classic. Pick up a creamy- or vinaigrette-base slaw from your supermarket's deli.

Prep: 10 minutes **Grill:** 1½ hours **Makes:** 6 servings

- 2 pounds boneless pork country-style ribs
- ¾ cup bottled barbecue sauce
- 6 crusty dinner rolls or hamburger buns, split and toasted
  Bottled hot pepper sauce (optional)
- 1 cup purchased deli coleslaw

1. Trim fat from ribs. For a charcoal grill, arrange medium-hot coals around a drip pan. Test for medium heat above pan. Place ribs on grill rack over pan. Cover and grill for 1½ to 2 hours or until ribs are tender, brushing occasionally with barbecue sauce during the last 10 minutes of grilling. (For a gas grill, preheat grill. Reduce heat to medium. Adjust for indirect cooking. Grill as above.) Remove ribs from grill and brush with the remaining sauce.

2. Thinly slice ribs. To serve, top the roll bottoms with rib slices and, if desired, sprinkle with hot pepper sauce. Spoon coleslaw on top of sandwiches. Add roll tops.

Per serving: 464 cal., 22 g total fat (7 g sat. fat), 89 mg chol., 635 mg sodium, 37 g carbo., 1 g fiber, 28 g pro.

Balsamic-Glazed Lamb Chops 🖤

A captivating quartet of orange juice, balsamic vinegar, honey, and soy sauce brings out the best in succulent lamb rib chops.

Prep: 15 minutes **Cook:** 15 minutes
Grill: 12 minutes **Marinate:** 4 hours **Makes:** 4 servings

- 8 lamb rib chops, cut 1 inch thick (1½ pounds total)
- ¼ teaspoon salt
- ¼ teaspoon ground black pepper
- ½ cup orange juice
- ¼ cup balsamic vinegar
- 1 tablespoon honey
- 1 tablespoon reduced-sodium soy sauce

1. Trim fat from chops. Season chops with salt and pepper. Place chops in a resealable plastic bag set in a shallow dish. For marinade, in a small bowl, stir together orange juice, balsamic vinegar, honey, and soy sauce. Pour marinade over chops. Seal bag; turn to coat chops. Marinate in the refrigerator for 4 to 24 hours, turning bag occasionally.

2. Drain chops, reserving marinade. For glaze, pour marinade into a small heavy saucepan. Bring to boiling; reduce heat. Boil gently, uncovered, about 15 minutes or until reduced to about ⅓ cup; set aside.

3. Grill chops on the rack of an uncovered grill directly over medium heat until chops reach desired doneness, turning once and brushing with glaze halfway through grilling. Allow 12 to 14 minutes for medium-rare (145°F) or 15 to 17 minutes for medium (160°F). Discard any remaining glaze.

Per serving: 161 cal., 6 g total fat (2 g sat. fat), 48 mg chol., 334 mg sodium, 10 g carbo., 0 g fiber, 15 g pro.

Balsamic-Glazed Lamb Chops

Thai-Spiced Chicken Kabobs

Thai-Spiced Chicken Kabobs ♥

Dress up skewered chicken with this spicy Thai-inspired glaze. As you assemble the kabobs, leave at least a ¼-inch space between the pieces to allow the chicken to cook evenly.

Prep: 30 minutes **Grill:** 12 minutes **Makes:** 4 servings

1   **small fresh pineapple (3 to 3½ pounds)**
    Nonstick cooking spray or cooking oil
1   **pound skinless, boneless chicken breast halves,**
      cut into 1-inch pieces
    Thai Brushing Sauce
1   **tablespoon butter, melted**
1   **tablespoon packed brown sugar (optional)**
    Hot cooked rice (optional)
    Fresh basil leaves (optional)
    Whole fresh red chile peppers (optional)

1. Cut off pineapple ends. Halve pineapple lengthwise; cut each half crosswise into 4 slices. Lightly coat pineapple slices with nonstick cooking spray or brush with oil. Set aside.

2. Thread chicken pieces onto 4 long skewers, leaving a ¼-inch space between pieces.

3. Place skewers on the grill rack directly over medium heat; grill for 7 minutes. Turn skewers; brush with ¼ cup of the Thai Brushing Sauce. Discard any remaining brushing sauce. Arrange pineapple slices on grill rack directly over medium heat. Grill chicken and pineapple for 6 to 8 minutes or until chicken is no longer pink (170°F) and pineapple is heated through, turning once.

4. In a small bowl, combine remaining Thai Brushing Sauce, melted butter, and, if desired, brown sugar; serve with chicken and pineapple. If desired, serve with rice and garnish with basil and chile peppers.

Thai Brushing Sauce: In a small bowl, combine ⅔ cup sweet-and-sour sauce, 2 tablespoons snipped fresh basil, 1 teaspoon Thai seasoning or five-spice powder, and 1 minced clove garlic. Makes about ¾ cup.

Per serving: 285 cal., 4 g total fat (2 g sat. fat), 73 mg chol., 292 mg sodium, 35 g carbo., 3 g fiber, 36 g pro.

Make-Ahead Directions: Up to 24 hours ahead, prepare Thai Brushing Sauce, cut pineapple into slices, and thread chicken onto skewers. Cover and store separately in refrigerator.

Cheesy Tuscan Chicken Pockets

Some skinless, boneless chicken breast halves are thicker than others. Shop for thick ones for this dish so it's easier to cut the pockets.

Prep: 15 minutes **Grill:** 12 minutes **Makes:** 4 servings

- **4** **skinless, boneless chicken breast halves (about 1¼ pounds)**
- **¼** **cup semisoft cheese with garlic and herb**
- **3** **to 4 ounces thinly sliced prosciutto**
- **⅓** **cup bottled Parmesan Italian salad dressing with basil**

1. Using a sharp knife, cut a pocket in the side of each chicken breast half. Spread 1 tablespoon of the cheese in each pocket; top with a folded slice of prosciutto. Secure pockets with wooden toothpicks. Brush chicken with some of the salad dressing.

2. Grill chicken on the rack of an uncovered grill directly over medium heat for 12 to 15 minutes or until chicken is no longer pink (170°F), turning once and brushing with remaining salad dressing halfway through grilling.

Per serving: 312 cal., 15 g total fat (5 g sat. fat), 113 mg chol., 888 mg sodium, 2 g carbo., 0 g fiber, 40 g pro.

Ginger-Apple-Glazed Chicken

Triple the apple action with apple jelly in the glaze, plus cider and apples with the chicken.

Prep: 20 minutes **Grill:** 12 minutes **Makes:** 4 servings

- **Ginger-Apple-Glaze**
- **4** **skinless, boneless chicken breast halves (about 1¼ pounds)**
- **Nonstick cooking spray**
- **2** **medium apples, cored and sliced**
- **1** **medium leek, sliced, or ⅓ cup chopped onion**
- **2** **cloves garlic, minced**
- **2** **tablespoons apple juice, apple cider, or chicken broth**
- **1** **10-ounce bag prewashed spinach, stems removed (about 10 cups)**
- **Salt**
- **Ground black pepper**

1. Measure ¼ cup of the Ginger-Apple Glaze. Place chicken on the grill rack directly over medium heat; grill for 12 to 15 minutes or until no longer pink (170°F), turning once halfway through grilling and brushing often with the ¼ cup Ginger-Apple Glaze during the last 5 minutes of grilling.

2. Meanwhile, lightly coat an unheated large saucepan or Dutch oven with nonstick cooking spray. Preheat over medium heat. Add apples, leek, and garlic; cook for 3 minutes. Add ¼ cup of the Ginger-Apple Glaze and the apple juice; bring to boiling. Add spinach; toss just until wilted. Season to taste with salt and pepper.

3. To serve, slice each chicken breast crosswise into 6 to 8 pieces. On 4 dinner plates, arrange spinach mixture; top with sliced chicken.

Ginger-Apple Glaze: In a small saucepan, combine ½ cup apple jelly, 2 tablespoons soy sauce, 1 tablespoon snipped fresh thyme or 1 teaspoon dried thyme (crushed), 1 teaspoon finely shredded lemon peel, and 1 teaspoon grated fresh ginger. Heat and stir just until jelly is melted. Makes ⅔ cup.

Per serving: 345 cal., 2 g total fat (.5 g sat. fat), 82 mg chol., 728 mg sodium, 47 g carbo., 4 g fiber, 36 g pro.

Quick Tip Purchase firm, well-colored apples with a fresh, not musty, fragrance. The skin should be tight, smooth, and free of bruises or punctures. Store apples in a cool, dark place, or in a plastic bag in the refrigerator. If possible, do not let the apples touch during storage—they will keep longer.

Ginger-Apple-Glazed Chicken

Barbecued Chicken Thighs ♥

Serve this lip-smacking-good chicken with coleslaw and baked beans from the deli section of your supermarket.

Prep: 10 minutes **Grill:** 12 minutes **Makes:** 4 servings

- ¼ **cup packed brown sugar**
- 2 **tablespoons finely chopped onion**
- 2 **tablespoons vinegar**
- 1 **tablespoon yellow mustard**
- ¼ **teaspoon celery seeds**
- ⅛ **teaspoon garlic powder**
- 1 **teaspoon paprika**
- ¼ **teaspoon salt**
- ¼ **teaspoon ground black pepper**
- 8 **skinless, boneless chicken thighs**

1. For the sauce, in a small saucepan, combine brown sugar, onion, vinegar, mustard, celery seeds, and garlic powder. Bring to boiling, stirring until sugar dissolves. Set aside.

2. In a small bowl, combine paprika, salt, and pepper. Sprinkle paprika mixture evenly over chicken thighs; rub in with your fingers.

3. Place chicken thighs on the rack of an uncovered grill over medium heat. Grill for 12 to 15 minutes or until no longer pink (180°F), turning once halfway through grilling and brushing with sauce during the last 5 minutes of grilling.

Per serving: 305 cal., 8 g total fat (2 g sat. fat), 158 mg chol., 329 mg sodium, 16 g carbo., 0 g fiber, 40 g pro.

Broiling Directions: Preheat broiler. Place chicken on the unheated rack of a broiler pan. Broil 4 to 5 inches from heat for 12 to 15 minutes or until no longer pink (180°F), turning once halfway through broiling and brushing with sauce during the last 5 minutes of broiling.

Grilled Tomato and Chicken Kabobs ♥

Grill the tomatoes separately to keep them from overcooking and perhaps dropping off the skewer into the heat.

Prep: 20 minutes **Grill:** 10 minutes
Marinate: 4 to 6 hours **Makes:** 6 servings

- 1 **pound skinless, boneless chicken breast halves, cut into 1-inch pieces**
- 12 **fresh small white mushrooms or button mushrooms, stems removed**
- ¼ **cup reduced-sodium soy sauce**
- 1 **tablespoon sesame oil**
- 12 **cherry tomatoes**
- 1 **tablespoon sesame seeds, toasted (optional)**

1. Place chicken pieces and mushrooms in a resealable plastic bag set in a shallow dish. For the marinade, in a small bowl, combine soy sauce and sesame oil. Pour over chicken and mushrooms. Seal bag; turn bag to coat chicken and mushrooms. Marinate in the refrigerator for 4 to 6 hours, turning bag occasionally.

2. Drain chicken and mushrooms, reserving marinade. On five 10-inch metal skewers, alternately thread chicken and mushrooms, leaving ¼-inch space between pieces. Thread tomatoes on another 10-inch metal skewer.

3. Grill chicken and mushroom kabobs on the rack of an uncovered grill directly over medium heat for 10 to 12 minutes or until chicken is no longer pink (170°F), turning once and brushing occasionally with reserved marinade the last 5 minutes of grilling. Add tomato kabob to the grill during the last 3 to 4 minutes, grilling until softened and heated through. Discard any remaining marinade. If desired, sprinkle kabobs with sesame seeds.

Per serving: 124 cal., 3 g total fat (1 g sat. fat), 44 mg chol., 436 mg sodium, 3 g carbo., 1 g fiber, 20 g pro.

Hot Barbecued Chicken

Fans of buffalo wings will go for that heated-up flavor in these chicken pieces.

Prep: 10 minutes **Grill:** 50 minutes
Marinate: 2 to 3 hours **Makes:** 6 servings

- 2½ **to 3 pounds meaty chicken pieces (breast halves, thighs, and drumsticks)**
- 1 **2-ounce bottle hot pepper sauce (¼ cup)**
- 3 **tablespoons ketchup**
- 3 **tablespoons Worcestershire sauce**

1. Place chicken pieces in a resealable plastic bag set in a shallow bowl. For the marinade, in a small bowl, combine hot pepper sauce, ketchup, and Worcestershire sauce. Pour marinade over chicken pieces in bag. Seal bag; turn to coat chicken. Marinate in the refrigerator for 2 to 3 hours.

2. Drain chicken, discarding marinade. For a charcoal grill, arrange medium-hot coals around a drip pan. Test for medium heat above the pan. Place chicken pieces, bone sides down, on a grill rack over drip pan. Cover and grill for 50 to 60 minutes or until chicken is no longer pink (170°F for breasts; 180°F for thighs and drumsticks). (For a gas grill, preheat grill. Reduce heat to medium. Adjust for indirect cooking. Grill as above.)

Per serving: 285 cal., 17 g total fat (5 g sat. fat), 110 mg chol., 201 mg sodium, 2 g carbo., 0 g fiber, 29 g pro.

Grilled Chicken and Kiwi Tacos

Grilled Chicken and Kiwi Tacos 💙

Fried flour tortillas give these terrific tacos a homemade flair. Another time, save a few minutes—and some mess—by using purchased taco shells.

Start to Finish: 30 minutes **Makes:** 6 tacos

- ½ **teaspoon ground cumin**
- ¼ **teaspoon salt**
- ⅛ **to ¼ teaspoon crushed red pepper**
- 8 **ounces skinless, boneless chicken breast halves**
- 1 **teaspoon cooking oil**
     Fried Taco Shells (below) or 6 purchased taco shells
- 1 **cup shredded romaine lettuce**
- ½ **cup shredded Monterey Jack cheese or Monterey Jack cheese with jalapeño chile peppers (2 ounces)**
- 3 **kiwifruit, peeled and chopped**
- 1 **small tomato, chopped**
- 1 **tablespoon lime juice or lemon juice**

1. In a small bowl, combine cumin, salt, and crushed red pepper. Brush chicken breasts with oil. Sprinkle brushed chicken breasts evenly with cumin mixture. Place each breast half between 2 pieces of plastic wrap; gently pound with the flat side of a meat mallet to ½-inch thickness.

2. Place chicken on the lightly oiled rack of an uncovered grill directly over medium-high heat. Grill for 6 to 8 minutes or until done (170°F) and juices run clear, turning once. Remove chicken; set aside until cool enough to handle. Meanwhile, prepare Fried Taco Shells or heat purchased taco shells according to the package directions.

3. Cut chicken into thin strips and arrange in taco shells. Top with lettuce and cheese. In a small bowl, toss together chopped kiwifruit, tomato, and lime juice. Sprinkle onto tacos.

Fried Taco Shells: In a large heavy skillet, heat ½ inch cooking oil over medium heat. Using six 5-inch flour tortillas, add tortillas, one at a time, to hot oil; cook just until golden. Using tongs, remove from hot oil. Fold fried tortillas over a paper-towel-wrapped rolling pin or a wire tortilla rack placed over a paper-towel-lined pan. Let cool until firm.

Per taco: 170 cal., 7 g total fat (3 g sat. fat), 30 mg chol., 219 mg sodium, 13 g carbo., 2 g fiber, 13 g pro.

Indian-Style Chicken

Indian-Style Chicken ♥

If you prefer flavorful dark meat, this recipe is for you. The robust four-ingredient sauce is just right with drumsticks and thighs.

Prep: 5 minutes   **Grill:** 35 minutes   **Makes:** 6 servings

- ½   **cup bottled barbecue sauce**
- ¼   **cup peanut butter**
- ½   **teaspoon finely shredded orange peel**
- 1   **to 2 tablespoons orange juice**
- 1½ **pounds chicken drumsticks and/or thighs**

1. For the sauce, in a small bowl, stir together barbecue sauce, peanut butter, orange peel, and enough orange juice to make desired consistency. Set sauce aside.

2. Grill chicken on the rack of an uncovered grill directly over medium heat for 35 to 45 minutes or until chicken is no longer pink (180°F), turning once and brushing with sauce during the last 5 minutes of grilling.

3. If desired, place any remaining sauce in a 1-cup glass measure. Microwave on 100-percent power (high) for 30 to 60 seconds or until boiling. Serve remaining sauce with chicken.

Per serving: 171 cal., 8 g total fat (2 g sat. fat), 49 mg chol., 338 mg sodium, 10 g carbo., 1 g fiber, 16 g pro.

Grilled Chicken Sandwiches with Lime Dressing ♥

Sliced grilled zucchini gives these dressed-up chicken sandwiches a unique Mediterranean twist that will have your grill-out guests swooning. Add a lively bit of heat to the lime-scented dressing by stirring in ⅛ teaspoon cayenne pepper before chilling.

Prep: 15 minutes **Grill:** 12 minutes **Makes:** 4 servings

- ¼ **cup fat-free mayonnaise dressing or salad dressing**
- ½ **teaspoon finely shredded lime peel or lemon peel**
- 1 **medium zucchini or yellow summer squash, cut lengthwise into ¼-inch slices**
- 3 **tablespoons Worcestershire sauce for chicken**
- 4 **skinless, boneless chicken breast halves (about 1¼ pounds)**
- 4 **whole wheat or white hamburger buns, split and toasted**

1. For the lime dressing, in a small bowl, combine mayonnaise dressing and lime peel. Cover and chill until serving time.

2. Brush zucchini slices with 1 tablespoon of the Worcestershire sauce; set aside. Brush all sides of chicken with the remaining 2 tablespoons Worcestershire sauce.

3. Place chicken on the rack of an uncovered grill directly over medium heat. Grill for 12 to 15 minutes or until no longer pink (170°F), turning once halfway through grilling. Add zucchini slices to grill for the last 6 minutes of grilling time for chicken, turning once and grilling until zucchini slices are softened and lightly browned.

4. To serve, spread lime dressing onto cut sides of toasted buns. If desired, halve zucchini slices crosswise. Place chicken and zucchini slices on bun bottoms; add bun tops.

Per serving: 259 cal., 2 g total fat (0 g sat. fat), 66 mg chol., 488 mg sodium, 27 g carbo., 3 g fiber, 31 g pro.

Quick Tip For added color, use half of a medium zucchini and half of a medium yellow summer squash.

Grilled Chicken Sandwiches with Lime Dressing

Lemon Grass Chicken and Rice Noodles

Lemon Grass Chicken And Rice Noodles ♥

Fresh ginger adds a slightly hot, spicy flavor and fragrant aroma that are hard to resist. Peel fresh ginger with a vegetable peeler and use a grater with fine openings.

Prep: 25 minutes **Cook:** 12 minutes **Makes:** 4 servings

- ¼ **cup finely chopped green onions**
- ¼ **cup finely chopped lemon grass**
- 1 **tablespoon grated fresh ginger**
- 6 **cloves garlic, minced**
- 4 **skinless, boneless chicken breast halves (about 1¼ pound total)**
- 8 **ounces dried rice noodles**
- ¼ **cup fish sauce**
- 3 **to 4 tablespoons fresh lime juice**
- 2 **tablespoons packed brown sugar**
- 1 **or 2 cloves garlic, minced**
- 1 **cup shredded carrot**
- ¼ **cup coarsely snipped fresh cilantro**
- ¼ **cup coarsely chopped peanuts**

1. For the rub, in a food processor or blender, combine green onions, lemon grass, ginger, and the 6 cloves garlic. Cover and process or blend with a few on-off turns until mixture forms a paste. Use your fingers to rub lemon grass-ginger paste evenly onto both sides of chicken breast halves.

2. Grill chicken on the rack of an uncovered grill directly over medium heat for 12 to 15 minutes or until chicken is tender and no longer pink, turning once halfway through grilling. Cut chicken into thin, diagonal slices. Set chicken aside.

3. Meanwhile, cook noodles in a large amount of boiling water for 3 to 4 minutes or until just tender; drain. In a medium bowl, combine fish sauce, lime juice, brown sugar, and the 1 or 2 cloves garlic; stir until brown sugar dissolves. Add hot cooked noodles, carrot, cilantro, and peanuts; toss lightly to coat.

4. Arrange sliced chicken over hot noodle mixture. Serve immediately.

Per serving: 431 cal., 6 g total fat (1 g sat. fat), 66 mg chol., 471 mg sodium, 63 g carbo., 2 g fiber, 30 g pro.

Grilled Chicken and Wild Rice Salad

Be sure you're using a plain rice mix instead of one with salty seasonings.

Prep: 30 minutes **Grill:** 12 minutes **Chill:** 2 hours
Makes: 6 servings

- 1 **6-ounce package long grain and wild rice mix**
- ⅔ **cup bottled fat-free Italian salad dressing**
- 6 **skinless, boneless chicken breast halves (about 1½ to 1¾ pounds)**
- 1 **cup loose-pack frozen French-cut green beans**
- 1 **14-ounce can artichoke hearts, drained and quartered**
- 2½ **cups packaged shredded cabbage with carrot (coleslaw mix)**
   Lettuce leaves (optional)

1. Prepare long grain and wild rice mix according to package directions. Transfer to a medium bowl. Cover and refrigerate about 2 hours or until chilled.

2. Place 3 tablespoons of the salad dressing in a small bowl. Set aside remaining salad dressing.

3. Place chicken on the rack of an uncovered grill directly over medium heat. Grill for 12 to 15 minutes or until chicken is tender and no longer pink (170°F), turning once and brushing chicken with the 3 tablespoons salad dressing during the last 2 minutes.

4. Meanwhile, rinse green beans with cool water for 30 seconds; drain well. In a large bowl, toss together green beans, chilled cooked rice, drained artichoke hearts, and coleslaw mix. Pour the reserved salad dressing over rice mixture; toss to gently coat.

5. Remove chicken from grill. Slice chicken; serve with wild rice mixture. If desired, garnish salad with lettuce leaves.

Per serving: 262 cal., 2 g total fat (0 g sat. fat), 66 mg chol., 982 mg sodium, 29 g carbo., 3 g fiber, 31 g pro.

Grilled Chicken and Wild Rice Salad

Margarita Fajitas with Lime Salsa

Margarita Fajitas with Lime Salsa

Say the word margarita and you immediately think of a kicked-back, celebrate-the-evening kind of mood. So when you stir the lime juice and tequila into this grilled chicken marinade, you know a fiesta meal will be happening soon.

Prep: 20 minutes **Grill:** 12 minutes
Marinate: 1 hour **Makes:** 4 servings

- 1 **15-ounce can black beans, rinsed and drained**
- 1 **8-ounce can pineapple tidbits (juice pack), drained**
- ¼ **cup finely chopped red onion**
- 2 **fresh jalapeño chile peppers, seeded and finely chopped***
- 2 **tablespoons snipped fresh cilantro**
- 1 **canned chipotle pepper in adobo sauce, drained and finely chopped***
- 4 **teaspoons lime juice**
- ¼ **teaspoon salt**
- 4 **skinless, boneless chicken breast halves (about 1¼ pounds)**
- ¼ **cup tequila**
- ¼ **cup lime juice**
- 1 **tablespoon cooking oil**
- ¼ **teaspoon salt**
- ¼ **teaspoon black pepper**
- 8 **6- to 7-inch flour tortillas**

1. For the salsa, in a medium bowl, stir together drained beans, pineapple, onion, chile peppers, cilantro, chipotle pepper, the 4 teaspoons lime juice, and ¼ teaspoon salt. Cover and refrigerate while chicken marinates.

2. Place the chicken in a large resealable plastic bag set in a large bowl. In a small bowl, stir together tequila, the ¼ cup lime juice, the oil, ¼ teaspoon salt, and black pepper. Pour over chicken in bag; seal bag. Marinate in the refrigerator for 1 hour, turning bag occasionally. Meanwhile, wrap tortillas in heavy foil; set aside.

3. Drain chicken, discarding marinade. Place chicken on the rack of an uncovered grill directly over medium heat. Grill for 12 to 15 minutes or until chicken is tender and no longer pink (170°F), turning once halfway through grilling. During the last 5 minutes of grilling, place foil-wrapped tortillas next to chicken on the grill rack until heated through, turning once. Remove chicken to a cutting board.

4. Cut chicken into ½-inch slices. Divide chicken among tortillas and top with salsa. Roll up.

Per serving: 489 cal., 7 g total fat (2 g sat. fat), 82 mg chol., 835 mg sodium, 61 g carbo., 8 g fiber, 46 g pro.

***Note:** Because chile peppers contain oils that can burn your skin and eyes, avoid direct contact with them as much as possible. When working with chile peppers, wear plastic or rubber gloves. If your bare hands do touch chile peppers, wash them well with soap and water.

Turkey with Onion-Cilantro Relish 🖤

You can store cilantro and other fresh herbs for a few days in the refrigerator. Immerse the fresh-cut stems in about 2 inches of water and cover loosely with plastic wrap.

Prep: 5 minutes **Grill:** 15 minutes **Makes:** 4 servings

- ½ cup chopped onion (1 medium)
- ¼ cup cilantro sprigs
- ⅛ teaspoon salt
- ⅛ teaspoon ground black pepper
- 2 turkey breast tenderloins, halved horizontally (about 1 pound total)
- 3 tablespoons lime or lemon juice

1. In a blender or food processor, combine onion, cilantro, salt, and pepper; cover and blend or process until mixture is very finely chopped.

2. Dip turkey tenderloins in lime juice. Grill turkey on the rack of an uncovered grill directly over medium heat for 7 minutes. Turn and brush with lime juice. Spread the onion mixture over turkey. Grill for 8 to 11 minutes more or until turkey is no longer pink (170°F).

Per serving: 141 cal., 2 g total fat (1 g sat. fat), 68 mg chol., 130 mg sodium, 3 g carbo., 1 g fiber, 27 g pro.

Quick Tip When purchasing onions, choose ones that are heavy for their size with dry, papery skins. Avoid onions with soft areas, spotted skins, or ones that have begun to sprout.

Grilled Chicken with 🖤 Cucumber Yogurt Sauce

If you prefer, peel the cucumber for the sauce before you chop it.

Prep: 20 minutes **Grill:** 12 minutes **Makes:** 4 servings

- 1 6-ounce carton plain low-fat yogurt
- ¼ cup thinly sliced green onion
- 2 teaspoons snipped fresh mint
- ½ teaspoon ground cumin
- ¼ teaspoon salt
- ⅛ teaspoon ground black pepper
- 1 cup chopped, seeded cucumber
- 4 skinless, boneless chicken breast halves (1 to 1¼ pounds total)
- ⅛ teaspoon ground black pepper

1. In a medium bowl, combine yogurt, green onion, mint, cumin, salt, and ⅛ teaspoon pepper. Transfer half of the yogurt mixture to a small bowl; set aside. For cucumber yogurt sauce, stir cucumber into remaining yogurt mixture.

2. Sprinkle chicken breasts with ⅛ teaspoon pepper.

3. Place chicken on the rack of an uncovered grill directly over medium heat. Grill for 12 to 15 minutes or until chicken is no longer pink (170°F), turning once halfway through grilling and brushing with reserved yogurt mixture for the last half of grilling. Discard any remaining yogurt mixture.

4. Serve chicken with the cucumber-yogurt sauce.

Per serving: 159 cal., 2 g total fat (1 g sat. fat), 68 mg chol., 251 mg sodium, 5 g carbo., 0 g fiber, 29 g pro.

Grilled Chicken with Cucumber Yogurt Sauce

Grilled Lemon Chicken

Grilled Lemon Chicken 🖤

Instead of using oil to keep the chicken moist while cooking, spritz it occasionally with broth.

Prep: 20 minutes **Grill:** 12 minutes
Marinate: 1 to 2 hours **Makes:** 4 servings

- **3** **lemons**
- **4** **skinless, boneless chicken breast halves (about 1¼ pounds)**
- **½** **cup reduced-sodium chicken broth**
- **1** **tablespoon snipped fresh lemon thyme or thyme**
- **¼** **teaspoon ground black pepper**
   Fresh lemon thyme or thyme sprigs (optional)

1. Finely shred enough lemon peel from one lemon to make 1 tablespoon peel. Cut the lemon in half and squeeze both halves to make ¼ cup juice. Set lemon peel and lemon juice aside.

2. Place the chicken in a resealable plastic bag in a shallow bowl. For the marinade, in a small bowl, stir together chicken broth, the lemon peel, the lemon juice, the 1 tablespoon snipped thyme, and pepper. Pour over chicken. Seal bag; turn to coat chicken. Marinate in the refrigerator for 1 to 2 hours, turning bag occasionally.

3. Drain chicken, reserving marinade. Cut remaining 2 lemons in half. Grill chicken on the rack of an uncovered grill directly over medium heat for 12 to 15 minutes or until no longer pink (170°F), turning once and brushing with marinade halfway through grilling. Add lemon halves to grill for the last 3 minutes of grilling. Discard any remaining marinade.

4. Serve chicken with grilled lemons and, if desired, garnish with additional fresh thyme.

Per serving: 161 cal., 2 g total fat (0 g sat. fat), 82 mg chol., 140 mg sodium, 1 g carbo., 0 g fiber, 33 g pro.

Spiced Cider Salmon

This salty-sweet brine features allspice for exotic flavor and delectable moistness.

Prep: 10 minutes **Grill:** 10 minutes **Chill:** 2 hours
Makes: 6 servings

- **1** **1½-pound fresh or frozen skinless salmon fillet, ¾ inch thick**
- **4** **cups apple cider or apple juice**
- **3** **tablespoons coarse salt**
- **2** **tablespoons packed brown sugar**
- **1** **teaspoon ground allspice**
   Nonstick cooking spray
- **2** **tablespoons apple jelly (optional)**

1. Thaw fish, if frozen. For the brine, in a large bowl, combine apple cider, salt, brown sugar, and allspice. Stir until salt and brown sugar dissolve. Add salmon. Cover and chill for 2 to 3 hours, turning salmon occasionally.

2. Drain salmon, discarding brine. Rinse salmon; pat dry with paper towels. Cut salmon into six serving-size pieces. Tear off a 28×12-inch piece of heavy foil; fold in half to make a 14×12-inch rectangle. Cut several slits in the foil rectangle. Lightly coat one side of the foil with cooking spray. Place salmon on the coated side of the foil.

3. For a charcoal grill, arrange medium-hot coals around a drip pan. Test for medium heat above pan. Place salmon on foil over drip pan. Cover and grill about 10 minutes or until salmon flakes easily when tested with a fork. (For a gas grill, preheat grill. Reduce heat to medium. Adjust for indirect cooking. Cover and grill as above.) If desired, spread apple jelly over salmon just before serving.

Per serving: 223 cal., 12 g total fat (2 g sat. fat), 66 mg chol., 550 mg sodium, 4 g carbo., 0 g fiber, 23 g pro.

Cilantro-Lime Orange Roughy 🖤

The distinctive flavors of fresh lime and cilantro lend themselves deliciously to light, slightly sweet orange roughy.

Start to Finish: 30 minutes **Makes:** 4 servings

- **1¼** **pounds fresh or frozen orange roughy, ocean perch, cod, or haddock fillets, ¾ to 1 inch thick**
   Salt
   Ground black pepper
- **¼** **cup snipped fresh cilantro**
- **1** **tablespoon butter, melted**
- **1** **teaspoon finely shredded lime peel**
- **1** **tablespoon lime juice**
   Lime and/or radish wedges (optional)

1. Thaw fish, if frozen. Rinse fish; pat dry with paper towels. If necessary, cut fish into four serving-size pieces. Sprinkle fish with salt and pepper.

2. Place fish in a well-greased grill basket, tucking under any thin edges. Grill fish on the rack of an uncovered grill directly over medium heat for 4 to 6 minutes per ½-inch thickness of fish or until fish flakes easily when tested with a fork, turning basket once halfway through grilling.

3. Meanwhile, in a small bowl, stir together cilantro, melted butter, lime peel, and lime juice. Spoon cilantro mixture over fish. If desired, serve with lime wedges.

Per serving: 127 cal., 4 g total fat (2 g sat. fat), 36 mg chol., 259 mg sodium, 1 g carbo., 0 g fiber, 21 g pro.

Mustard-Glazed Halibut Steaks ♥

Because of its dense, firm texture, halibut is one of the best seafood choices for grilling.

Start to Finish: 20 minutes **Makes:** 4 servings

- **4 6-ounce fresh or frozen halibut steaks, 1 inch thick**
- **2 tablespoons butter or margarine**
- **2 tablespoons lemon juice**
- **1 tablespoon Dijon-style mustard**
- **2 teaspoons snipped fresh basil or ½ teaspoon dried basil, crushed**

1. Thaw fish, if frozen. Rinse fish and pat dry with paper towels. In a small saucepan, heat butter, lemon juice, mustard, and basil over low heat until butter is melted. Brush both sides of fish with mustard mixture.

2. Grill fish on the greased rack of an uncovered grill directly over medium heat for 8 to 12 minutes or until fish flakes easily when tested with a fork, carefully turning once halfway through grilling and brushing occasionally with mustard mixture.

Per serving: 243 cal., 10 g total fat (4 g sat. fat), 70 mg chol., 254 mg sodium, 1 g carbo., 0 g fiber, 36 g pro.

Spicy Grilled Shrimp ♥

Orange marmalade, honey, and Cajun seasoning create a delectable sweet-spicy sauce for succulent grilled shrimp.

Prep: 15 minutes **Grill:** 7 minutes
Marinate: 1 hour **Makes:** 4 servings

- **1½ pounds fresh or frozen peeled and deveined extra-large shrimp**
- **¼ cup orange marmalade**
- **¼ cup honey**
- **2 to 3 teaspoons Cajun seasoning**
- **1 tablespoon olive oil**
- **2 cups hot cooked rice (optional)**

Spicy Grilled Shrimp

1. Thaw shrimp, if frozen. If using wooden skewers, soak in water for 1 hour. Rinse shrimp; pat dry with paper towels. For sauce, in a small saucepan, stir together marmalade, honey, and ½ teaspoon of the Cajun seasoning; set aside.

2. Place shrimp in a resealable plastic bag set in a shallow bowl. For the marinade, in a small bowl, combine oil and remaining Cajun seasoning. Pour marinade over shrimp; seal bag. Marinate in refrigerator for 1 hour, turning bag occasionally.

3. Drain shrimp, discarding marinade. Thread shrimp onto skewers, leaving ¼-inch space between shrimp. Grill skewers on the greased rack of an uncovered grill directly over medium heat for 7 to 9 minutes or until shrimp turn opaque, turning once halfway through grilling.

4. Stir marmalade sauce over low heat for 2 to 3 minutes or until melted. Place skewers on plates. Drizzle sauce over shrimp on skewers. If desired, serve with hot cooked rice.

Per serving: 327 cal., 6 g total fat (1 g sat. fat), 259 mg chol., 356 mg sodium, 33 g carbo., 0 g fiber, 35 g pro.

Prosciutto-Stuffed Trout ♥

If you don't catch your own trout, shop for fish with bright, clear eyes; red or pink gills; shiny, elastic skin; and a mild (not strong) aroma.

Prep: 10 minutes **Grill:** 6 minutes **Makes:** 8 servings

- **4 fresh or frozen pan-dressed, boned trout (about 8 ounces each)**
- **⅛ teaspoon ground black pepper**
- **4 slices prosciutto or thinly sliced cooked ham, chopped (3 ounces)**
  Nonstick cooking spray
  Sliced red onion
  Fresh herb sprigs (optional)

1. Thaw fish, if frozen. Rinse; pat dry with paper towels. Sprinkle insides of trout with pepper and prosciutto.

2. Place trout in a well-greased grill basket or directly on greased grill rack over medium heat. Grill for 6 to 9 minutes or until trout flakes easily when tested with a fork, turning basket or trout over once halfway through grilling.

3. Meanwhile, if desired, coat an unheated nonstick skillet with cooking spray. Preheat over medium heat. Add onion slices to hot skillet; cook until almost tender. Garnish fish with onion slices and, if desired, fresh herb sprigs. To serve, cut each trout into 2 portions.

Per serving: 151 cal., 7 g total fat (1 g sat. fat), 50 mg chol., 218 mg sodium, 0 g carbo., 0 g fiber, 20 g pro.

Prosciutto-Stuffed Trout

Grilled Herb Corn on the Cob

Grilled Asparagus
with Lemon

Grilled Herb Corn On the Cob ♥

The corn steams in its own husks on the grill. How easy is that?

Prep: 20 minutes **Grill:** 25 minutes **Makes:** 12 servings

- **6** fresh ears of corn
- **2** tablespoons snipped fresh oregano or
      2 teaspoons dried oregano, crushed
- **2** tablespoons snipped fresh thyme or
      2 teaspoons dried basil, crushed
- **1** tablespoon snipped fresh tarragon or
      1 teaspoon dried basil, crushed
- **2** tablespoons olive oil
- **½** teaspoon salt
- **¼** teaspoon ground black pepper

1. Peel back corn husks, but do not remove. Discard silks. Soak in cold water for 15 minutes; pat dry.

2. In a small bowl, combine oregano, thyme, and tarragon; set aside. In another small bowl, combine oil, salt, and black pepper.

3. Brush corn with oil mixture. Sprinkle with herb mixture. Fold husks back around cobs. Tie with 100-percent-cotton kitchen string.

4. Place corn in a grill basket or directly on grill rack over medium heat. Grill for 25 to 30 minutes or until tender, turning and rearranging a few times during grilling.

Per serving: 87 cal., 3 g total fat (0 g sat. fat), 0 mg chol., 109 mg sodium, 15 g carbo., 2 g fiber, 3 g pro.

Quick Tip Choose ears of corn with bright green, tight-fitting husks, and fresh-looking, golden silk. The silk should be dry, not soggy. The kernels should be plump and milky and extend all the way to the ear's tip; the rows should be tightly spaced. Store fresh corn in a plastic bag in the refrigerator for no more than a day after purchase.

Grilled Asparagus with Lemon ♥

Partially precooking the asparagus ensures it is tender after grilling without burning, and allows the asparagus to absorb more flavors from the marinade.

Prep: 15 minutes **Grill:** 3 minutes
Marinate: 30 minutes **Makes:** 4 to 6 servings

- **1** to 1½ pounds fresh asparagus spears
- **2** tablespoons olive oil
- **2** tablespoons lemon juice
- **½** teaspoon salt
- **¼** teaspoon ground black pepper
      Lemon wedges

1. Snap off and discard woody bases from asparagus. If desired, scrape off scales. In a large skillet, cook the asparagus in a small amount of boiling water for 3 minutes; drain well.

2. Meanwhile, for marinade, in a 2-quart rectangular baking dish, stir together olive oil, lemon juice, salt, and pepper. Add asparagus, turning to coat. Cover and marinate at room temperature for 30 minutes.

3. Drain asparagus, discarding marinade. Place asparagus on a grill tray or in a grill basket. Grill asparagus on the rack of an uncovered grill directly over medium heat for 3 to 5 minutes or until asparagus is tender and beginning to brown, turning once halfway through grilling.

4. To serve, arrange asparagus on a serving platter. Serve with lemon wedges.

Per serving: 87 cal., 7 g total fat (1 g sat. fat), 0 mg chol., 294 mg sodium, 7 g carbo., 3 g fiber, 3 g pro.

Turkey with Creamy
Alfredo Sauce, **page 248**

German-Style
Beef Roast, **page 230**

Sweet Pork
Sandwiches, **page 244**

Three-Bean Vegetarian
Chili, **page 253**

Slow and Simple

For families busy with a multitude of tasks, errands, and activities, this is the way to cook. Put all the recipe ingredients in a slow cooker, cover, and turn on. Plan to get a dozen things done while dinner cooks the no-tend way.

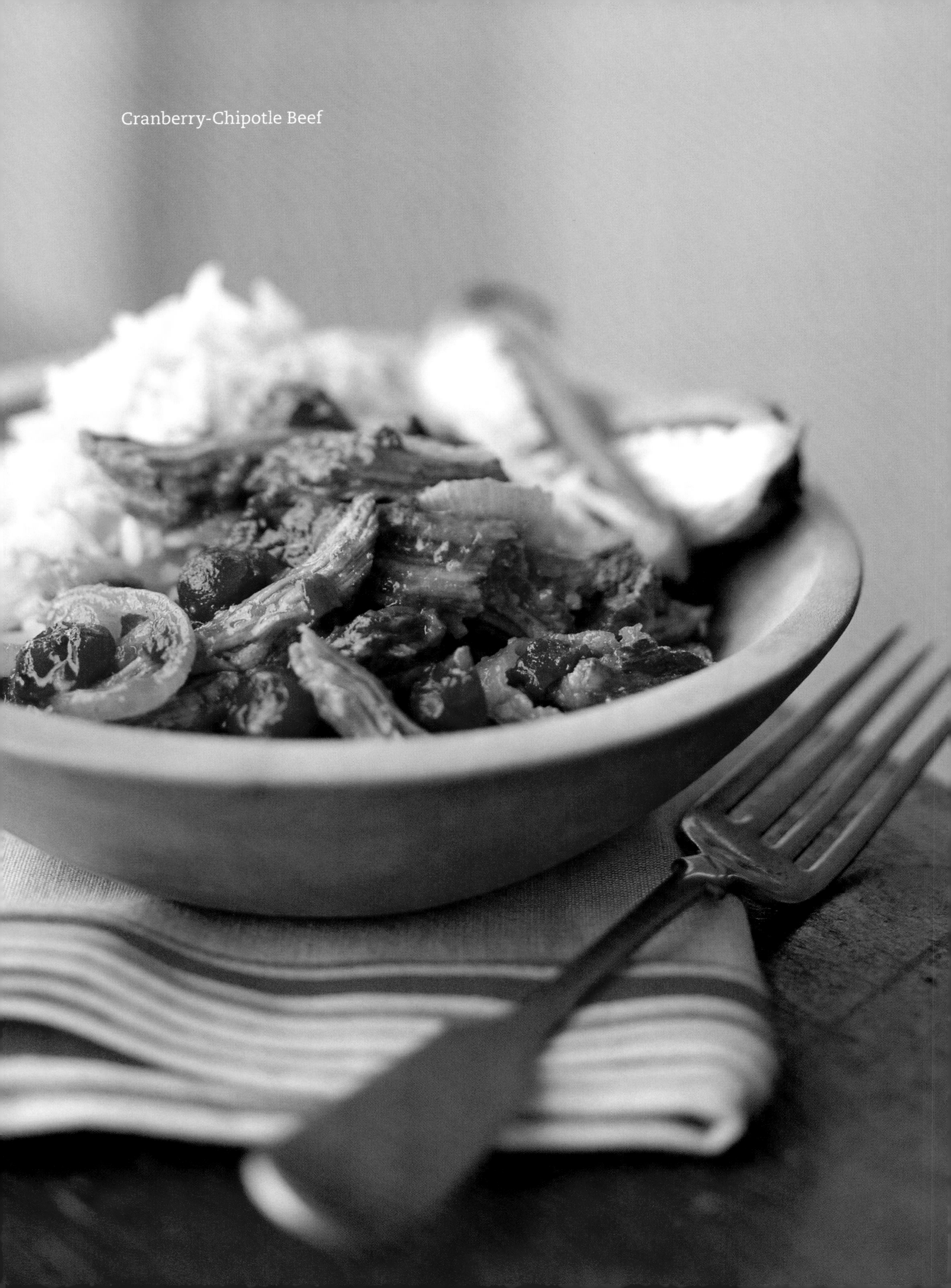
Cranberry-Chipotle Beef

Cranberry-Chipotle Beef

Looking for a roast to serve for a special dinner at home? This fiery chipotle-seasoned chuck roast is a delicious possibility.

Prep: 10 minutes
Cook: 6 to 8 hours (low) or 3 to 4 hours (high)
Makes: 4 servings

1	medium onion, cut into thin wedges
1½	pounds beef chuck roast
¼	teaspoon salt
¼	teaspoon ground black pepper
2	cloves garlic, minced
1	16-ounce can whole cranberry sauce
1	to 2 teaspoons finely chopped canned chipotle chile peppers in adobo sauce*
2	cups instant brown rice
	Fresh jalapeño chile peppers, halved (optional)*

1. Place onion in a 4-quart slow cooker. If necessary, cut beef to fit into cooker; add to cooker. Sprinkle with salt, black pepper, and garlic. Combine cranberry sauce and chipotle peppers. Pour over all.

2. Cover and cook on low-heat setting for 6 to 8 hours or on high-heat setting for 3 to 4 hours. If no heat setting is available, cook for 4½ to 5½ hours.

3. To serve, cook rice according to package directions, except omit salt and butter. Serve beef mixture with rice. If desired, garnish with jalapeño peppers.

Per serving: 506 cal., 7 g total fat (2 g sat. fat), 101 mg chol., 296 mg sodium, 71 g carbo., 4 g fiber, 40 g pro.

*Note: Because chile peppers contain volatile oils that can burn your skin and eyes, avoid direct contact with them as much as possible. When working with chile peppers, wear plastic or rubber gloves. If your bare hands do touch the chile peppers, wash your hands and nails well with soap and warm water.

Bloody Mary Steak ♥

Sassy and lively—just like the classic cocktail—this easy-fixing steak is sensational.

Prep: 20 minutes
Cook: 8 to 9 hours (low) or 4 to 4½ hours (high)
Makes: 6 servings

1	2-pound beef round steak, cut ¾ inch thick
	Nonstick cooking spray
¾	cup hot-style tomato juice
2	cloves garlic, minced
¼	cup water
4	teaspoons cornstarch
2	tablespoons cold water
2	teaspoons prepared horseradish
	Salt and ground black pepper

1. Trim fat from steak. Cut steak into six serving-size pieces. Lightly coat a large skillet with cooking spray; heat skillet over medium-high heat. Add steak pieces; cook until brown, turning once. Place steak in a 2½- to 3½-quart slow cooker. Add tomato juice, garlic, and the ¼ cup water. Cover and cook on low-heat setting for 8 to 9 hours or on high-heat setting for 4 to 4½ hours.

2. Transfer steak to a serving platter, reserving cooking juices. If desired, slice steak; cover and keep warm.

3. For the gravy, pour cooking juices into a glass measuring cup; skim off fat. Measure juices; if necessary, add water to reach 1½ cups liquid. In a small saucepan, combine cornstarch and the 2 tablespoons cold water; stir in cooking juices. Cook and stir over medium heat until thickened and bubbly. Cook and stir for 2 minutes more. Stir in horseradish. Season to taste with salt and pepper. Serve steak with gravy.

Per serving: 196 cal., 4 g total fat (1 g sat. fat), 85 mg chol., 272 mg sodium, 3 g carbo., 0 g fiber, 35 g pro.

Bloody Mary Steak

Beer Brisket ♥

Beer and chili sauce do great things to beef brisket and sliced onions. Fork slices of meat onto rolls for a hearty sandwich.

Prep: 15 minutes
Cook: 10 to 12 hours (low) or 5 to 6 hours (high)
Makes: 9 to 12 servings

1	3- to 4-pound fresh beef brisket
2	large onions, sliced
1	12-ounce bottle or can beer
½	cup bottled chili sauce
2	teaspoons dried steak seasoning
9	to 12 kaiser rolls, split and toasted (optional)

1. Trim fat from brisket. If necessary, cut brisket to fit into a 3½- or 4-quart slow cooker. Place onions in the cooker. Top with brisket. In a medium bowl, stir together beer, chili sauce, and steak seasoning. Pour over onions and brisket in cooker.

2. Cover and cook on low-heat setting for 10 to 12 hours or on high-heat setting for 5 to 6 hours.

3. To serve, remove brisket from cooking liquid. Thinly slice brisket across the grain. Using a slotted spoon, remove the onions from the cooking liquid and place on top of the brisket. Drizzle with some of the cooking liquid. If desired, serve sliced brisket and onions on kaiser rolls.

Per serving: 265 cal., 10 g total fat (4 g sat. fat), 94 mg chol., 378 mg sodium, 8 g carbo., 2 g fiber, 31 g pro.

Greek Beef and Orzo

Cinnamon, orzo, and artichoke hearts give this hearty stew its Greek flair.

Prep: 15 minutes
Cook: 8 to 10 hours (low) or 4 to 5 hours (high) + 30 minutes (high) **Makes:** 4 servings

	Nonstick cooking spray
2	large onions, cut into thin wedges (1 cup)
1	pound beef stew meat cut into 1-inch pieces
¼	teaspoon salt
¼	teaspoon ground black pepper
1	14-ounce can beef broth
½	of a 6-ounce can tomato paste (⅓ cup)
¼	teaspoon ground cinnamon
¾	cup dried orzo
1	9-ounce package frozen artichoke hearts, thawed

1. Lightly coat a 3½- to 4-quart slow cooker with cooking spray. Place onions in cooker; top with beef. Sprinkle with salt and pepper. In a medium bowl, whisk together beef broth, tomato paste, and cinnamon; pour on top of beef.

2. Cover and cook on low-heat setting for 8 to 10 hours or on high-heat setting for 4 to 5 hours. If using low-heat setting, turn to high. Stir in orzo and artichoke hearts. Cover and cook 30 minutes more.

Per serving: 348 cal., 5 g total fat (1 g sat. fat), 67 mg chol., 648 mg sodium, 41 g carbo., 7 g fiber, 33 g pro.

German-Style Beef Roast ♥

Red wine, chopped dill pickles, and hearty mustard set this succulent beef pot roast apart from the rest.

Prep: 25 minutes
Cook: 8 to 10 hours (low) or 4 to 5 hours (high)
Makes: 8 servings

1	2½- to 3-pound boneless beef chuck pot roast
1	tablespoon cooking oil
2	cups sliced carrot
2	cups chopped onion
1	cup sliced celery
¾	cup chopped kosher-style dill pickles
½	cup dry red wine or beef broth
⅓	cup German-style mustard
½	teaspoon coarsely ground black pepper
¼	teaspoon ground cloves
2	bay leaves
2	tablespoons all-purpose flour
2	tablespoons dry red wine or beef broth
	Hot cooked spaetzle or cooked noodles
	Snipped fresh parsley (optional)

1. Trim fat from roast. If necessary, cut roast to fit in a 3½- or 4-quart slow cooker. In a large skillet, brown the roast slowly on all sides in hot oil.

2. Meanwhile, in the cooker, combine carrot, onion, celery, and pickles. Place the roast on the vegetables. In a small bowl, combine the ½ cup red wine, the mustard, pepper, cloves, and bay leaves. Pour over roast.

3. Cover and cook on low-heat setting for 8 to 10 hours or on high-heat setting for 4 to 5 hours.

4. Transfer roast to serving platter; cover to keep warm. For the gravy, transfer vegetables and cooking liquid to a 2-quart saucepan. Skim off fat. Discard bay leaves. In a small bowl, stir together flour and the 2 tablespoons red wine. Stir into vegetable mixture in saucepan. Cook and stir over medium heat until thickened and bubbly. Cook and stir for 1 minute more. Slice roast. Serve roast and vegetables with gravy and hot cooked spaetzle. If desired, sprinkle with parsley.

Per serving: 372 cal., 25 g total fat (9 g sat. fat), 82 mg chol., 414 mg sodium, 10 g carbo., 2 g fiber, 24 g pro.

German-Style Beef Roast

Orange-Spiced Corned Beef
with Dried Fruit

Orange-Spiced Corned Beef with Dried Fruit

Perfect for a special dinner, the mixed dried fruit, orange juice, molasses, and spices dress up ordinary corned beef with lively new flavor.

Prep: 15 minutes
Cook: 8 to 10 hours (low) or 4 to 5 hours (high)
Makes: 6 servings

1	2½- to 3-pound corned beef brisket
1	7-ounce package mixed dried fruit
½	cup dried cranberries
2	tablespoons quick-cooking tapioca
½	cup orange juice
½	cup water
1	tablespoon mild-flavored molasses
¼	teaspoon ground cinnamon
⅛	teaspoon ground nutmeg

1. Trim fat from brisket. If necessary, cut brisket to fit into a 3½- or 4-quart slow cooker. If a seasoning packet is present, discard it. Place brisket in the cooker.

2. Cut any large pieces of mixed dried fruit into quarters. Sprinkle mixed dried fruit, dried cranberries, and tapioca over brisket in cooker. In a small bowl, combine orange juice, the water, molasses, cinnamon, and nutmeg. Pour over brisket mixture in cooker.

3. Cover and cook on low-heat setting for 8 to 10 hours or on high-heat setting for 4 to 5 hours.

4. Remove brisket from cooker. Thinly slice brisket across the grain. Arrange meat slices on a serving platter. Spoon fruit mixture over meat.

Per serving: 617 cal., 36 g total fat (12 g sat. fat), 185 mg chol., 2,151 mg sodium, 38 g carbo., 2 g fiber, 35 g pro.

Quick Tip Store dried fruit in an airtight container in the refrigerator. If your dried fruit has hardened, soften it by covering it with boiling water and letting it steep for 15 minutes. Drain and blot with paper towels before use. Use kitchen shears to cut dried fruit, such as apples, apricots, and dates. To keep the fruit from sticking, dip the shears in hot water or granulated sugar as needed.

Gingered Beef and Vegetables ♥

Grated fresh ginger and soy sauce team up to make a snappy sauce for meat and vegetables.

Prep: 20 minutes
Cook: 9 to 10 hours (low) or 4½ to 5 hours (high), + 20 minutes (high) **Makes:** 6 servings

1½	pounds boneless beef round steak, cut into 1-inch cubes
4	medium carrots, bias-cut into ½-inch slices
½	cup bias-sliced green onion
2	cloves garlic, minced
1½	cups water
2	tablespoons soy sauce
2	teaspoons grated fresh ginger
1½	teaspoons instant beef bouillon granules
¼	teaspoon crushed red pepper
3	tablespoons cornstarch
3	tablespoons cold water
½	cup chopped red sweet pepper
2	cups loose-pack frozen sugar snap peas, thawed Hot cooked rice

1. In a 3½- or 4-quart slow cooker, combine beef, carrots, green onion, and garlic. In a medium bowl, combine the 1½ cups water, the soy sauce, ginger, bouillon granules, and crushed red pepper; pour over mixture in cooker.

2. Cover and cook on low-heat setting for 9 to 10 hours or on high-heat setting for 4½ to 5 hours.

3. If using low-heat setting, turn to high-heat setting. In a small bowl, stir together cornstarch and the 3 tablespoons cold water; stir into beef mixture along with sweet pepper. Cover and cook for 20 to 30 minutes or until thickened, stirring once. Stir in sugar snap peas. Serve with hot cooked rice.

Per serving: 350 cal., 10 g total fat (4 g sat. fat), 68 mg chol., 400 mg sodium, 35 g carbo., 3 g fiber, 29 g pro.

Gingered Beef and Vegetables

Family-Style Chili and
Dumplings

Family-Style Chili and Dumplings

Because the dumplings start with a corn muffin mix, they stir together easily. If you have a round rather than an oval slow cooker, bake the extra dumpling batter in the oven.

Prep: 25 minutes   **Cook:** 8 to 10 hours (low) or 4 to 5 hours (high) + 20 to 25 minutes (high)
Makes: 6 to 8 servings

- 1 **pound boneless beef round steak or boneless pork shoulder, trimmed and cut into ½-inch cubes***
- 1 **large onion, chopped**
- 1 **large green, red, or yellow sweet pepper, seeded and chopped**
- 1 **15-ounce can chili beans with chili gravy**
- 1 **15-ounce can kidney or pinto beans, rinsed and drained**
- 1 **14.5-ounce can Mexican-style stewed tomatoes, undrained, cut up**
- 1 **cup beef broth**
- 1 **to 2 teaspoons chopped canned chipotle chile peppers in adobo sauce** or ¼ to ½ teaspoon crushed red pepper**
- 1 **teaspoon ground cumin**
- ¾ **teaspoon garlic salt**
- ½ **teaspoon dried oregano, crushed**
  Corn Bread Dumplings
  Shredded cheddar cheese
  Green onions, cut into strips (optional)

1. In a 3½- to 4-quart slow cooker, stir together beef, onion, sweet pepper, undrained chili beans with chili gravy, drained kidney beans, undrained tomatoes, beef broth, chipotle chile peppers, cumin, garlic salt, and oregano.

2. Cover; cook on low-heat setting for 8 to 10 hours or on high-heat setting for 4 to 5 hours.

3. If using low-heat setting, turn to high-heat setting. If you have an oval slow cooker, drop all of the Corn Bread Dumplings batter onto the bubbling mixture in the slow cooker. (If you have a round cooker, preheat oven to 400°F. Drop half of the Corn Bread Dumplings batter onto the bubbling mixture. Spoon remaining batter into two or three greased muffin cups. Bake for 15 to 18 minutes or until a toothpick inserted in the center comes out clean.)

4. Cover cooker; cook for 20 to 25 minutes more or until a toothpick inserted into dumplings comes out clean. Top each serving with cheese. If desired, garnish with green onion strips.

Corn Bread Dumplings: In a large bowl, combine one 8.5-ounce package corn muffin mix; ½ cup shredded cheddar cheese, Monterey Jack cheese, or Mexican cheese blend (2 ounces); and ¼ cup sliced green onion. In a small bowl, beat 1 egg with a fork; stir in ¼ cup dairy sour cream. Stir egg mixture into cheese mixture.

Per serving: 529 cal., 17 g total fat (6 g sat. fat), 101 mg chol., 1,256 mg sodium, 61 g carbo., 9 g fiber, 35 g pro.

***Note:** If desired, substitute 1 pound ground beef or pork for the beef round steak or pork shoulder. In a large skillet, brown ground beef or pork; drain off fat before using.

****Note:** Because chile peppers contain volatile oils that can burn your skin and eyes, avoid direct contact with them as much as possible. When working with chile peppers, wear plastic or rubber gloves. If your bare hands do touch the chile peppers, wash your hands and nails well with soap and warm water.

French Dips with Mushrooms

Meaty portobello mushrooms add a new dimension to classic French dip sandwiches. Serve the seasoned broth in bowls just large enough to dunk a corner of the sandwich.

Prep: 25 minutes
Cook: 8 to 9 hours (low) or 4 to 4½ hours (high)
Stand: 10 minutes **Makes:** 8 servings

1   **3- to 3½-pound beef bottom round or rump roast**
    Nonstick cooking spray
4   **portobello mushrooms (3 to 4 inches in diameter)**
1   **14-ounce can onion-flavor beef broth**
1   **large red onion, sliced (optional)**
8   **hoagie buns, split and toasted**

1. Trim fat from roast. If necessary, cut roast to fit into a 3½- to 4-quart slow cooker. Lightly coat a large skillet with cooking spray; heat over medium heat. Brown roast on all sides in hot skillet. Place roast in the slow cooker.

2. Clean mushrooms; remove and discard stems. Cut mushrooms into ¼-inch slices. Add to cooker. Pour broth over roast and mushrooms.

3. Cover and cook on low-heat setting for 8 to 9 hours or on high-heat setting for 4 to 4½ hours. Remove roast from cooker; cover and let stand for 10 minutes.

4. Meanwhile, using a slotted spoon, remove mushrooms and set aside. Thinly slice roast. Arrange roast, mushroom slices, and, if desired, onion slices on toasted buns. Pour cooking juices into a measuring cup; skim off fat. Drizzle some of the juices onto each sandwich and pour the remaining juices into bowls to serve with sandwiches.

Per serving: 646 cal., 17 g total fat (4 g sat. fat), 98 mg chol., 970 mg sodium, 74 g carbo., 4 g fiber, 50 g pro.

Quick Tip When purchasing a beef roast, look for brightly colored red to deep red cuts. If the meat will be cooked within 6 to 8 hours of purchase, leave it in the store packaging. Otherwise, remove the beef roast and wrap it in waxed paper. Store beef roasts in the coldest part of the refrigerator for up to 3 days or freeze (tightly wrapped) for up to 3 months.

French Dips with Mushrooms

Italian Steak Rolls

Stuffed with veggies and Parmesan cheese, these beef bundles cook up moist and tender in bottled meatless spaghetti sauce. Add a dash of crushed red pepper for added spice.

Prep: 20 minutes
Cook: 8 to 10 hours (low) or 4 to 5 hours (high)
Makes: 6 servings

½	**cup shredded carrot**
⅓	**cup chopped zucchini**
⅓	**cup chopped red or green sweet pepper**
¼	**cup sliced green onion**
2	**tablespoons grated Parmesan cheese**
1	**tablespoon snipped fresh parsley**
1	**clove garlic, minced**
¼	**teaspoon ground black pepper**
6	**tenderized beef round steaks (about 2 pounds total)**
2	**cups purchased meatless spaghetti sauce**

1. For the vegetable filling, in a small bowl, combine carrot, zucchini, sweet pepper, green onion, Parmesan cheese, parsley, garlic, and black pepper. Spoon ¼ cup of the vegetable filling onto each piece of steak. Roll up steak around the filling; secure each roll with 100-percent-cotton string or wooden toothpicks.

2. Place steak rolls in a 3½- or 4-quart slow cooker. Pour spaghetti sauce over the steak rolls.

3. Cover; cook on low-heat setting for 8 to 10 hours or on high-heat setting for 4 to 5 hours.

4. Discard string or toothpicks. Serve sauce with steak rolls.

Per serving: 261 cal., 9 g total fat (3 g sat. fat), 73 mg chol., 523 mg sodium, 7 g carbo., 2 g fiber, 36 g pro.

*Note: If you can't find tenderized round steak, ask a butcher to tenderize 2 pounds boneless beef round steak and cut it into 6 pieces. Or cut 2 pounds boneless beef round steak into 6 serving-size pieces; place each steak piece between 2 pieces of plastic wrap. Using a meat mallet, pound the steak pieces ¼ to ½ inch thick.

Italian Steak Rolls

Pot Roast with Root Vegetables

Pot Roast with Root ♥ Vegetables

Carrots, red potatoes, parsnips, and rutabaga are tasty additions to pot roast. Another time, try substituting other root vegetables, such as sweet potatoes or celery root.

Prep: 30 minutes
Cook: 10 to 12 hours (low) or 5 to 6 hours (high)
Makes: 10 servings

1	**3-pound boneless beef chuck pot roast**
2½	**teaspoons Homemade Garam Masala or purchased garam masala**
½	**teaspoon salt**
30	**small carrots with tops trimmed to 2 inches (about 12 ounces) or 2 cups packaged peeled baby carrots**
1	**pound round red potatoes, quartered**
2	**medium parsnips, peeled and cut into ½-inch slices**
1	**medium rutabaga, peeled and cut into 1-inch pieces**
1	**medium red onion, cut into wedges**
1	**cup beef broth**
¼	**cup dry red wine or beef broth**
2	**tablespoons cornstarch**
2	**tablespoons cold water**
1	**teaspoon garam masala**
1	**8-ounce carton plain low-fat yogurt Salt and ground black pepper**

1. Trim fat from beef. For the rub, in small bowl, combine 2½ teaspoons garam masala and salt. Sprinkle rub evenly over beef; rub in with your fingers. Place beef in 5- to 6-quart slow cooker. Add carrots, potatoes, parsnips, rutabaga, onion, broth, and wine.

2. Cover and cook on low-heat setting for 10 to 12 hours or on high-heat setting for 5 to 6 hours. Transfer beef and vegetables to serving platter. Cover to keep warm.

3. For the gravy, skim and discard fat from cooking liquid. Strain cooking liquid. Measure 1½ cups of the cooking liquid; pour into small saucepan. Discard remaining cooking liquid. In small bowl, combine cornstarch, the cold water, and 1 teaspoon garam masala. Add to liquid in saucepan. Cook and stir over medium heat until thickened and bubbly. Cook and stir for 2 minutes more. Stir in yogurt; heat through but do not boil. Season to taste with salt and pepper. Serve gravy with beef and vegetables.

Homemade Garam Masala: In a medium skillet, combine 1 tablespoon cardamom seeds, 1 tablespoon cumin seeds, 1 tablespoon black peppercorns, 12 whole cloves, and a 3-inch-long piece of stick cinnamon; cook and stir over medium-low heat about 3 minutes or until aromatic. Remove from heat and cool. Place the cinnamon stick in a resealable plastic bag; seal. Using a rolling pin or mallet, crush the cinnamon. In a spice grinder or blender, combine the spices. Cover and grind or blend to a fine powder. Store in a covered container for up to 6 months. Makes about ¼ cup.

Per serving: 274 cal., 7 g total fat (2 g sat. fat), 82 mg chol., 381 mg sodium, 18 g carbo., 3 g fiber, 32 g pro.

Steak Sandwiches with Ratatouille ♥

Serve open-face steak sandwiches with a culinary twist, just like those served in bistros.

Prep: 25 minutes **Cook:** 7 to 9 hours (low) or 3½ to 4½ hours (high), + 30 minutes (high)

Makes: 6 to 8 servings

1½ pounds beef flank steak
1 teaspoon dried Italian seasoning, crushed
   Salt and ground black pepper
1½ cups sliced fresh mushrooms
1 medium onion, finely chopped
2 cloves garlic, minced
1 14.5-ounce can tomatoes, cut up
2 tablespoons red wine vinegar
1 medium yellow summer squash and/or zucchini, halved lengthwise and cut into ¼-inch-thick slices
1 cup red and/or yellow sweet pepper strips
1 6-ounce jar marinated artichoke hearts, drained and halved
   Focaccia (about a 9-inch round), split
⅓ cup finely shredded Asiago or Parmesan cheese

1. Trim fat from steak. Sprinkle both sides of steak with Italian seasoning, salt, and black pepper. If necessary, cut steak to fit into a 3½- or 4-quart slow cooker. Place mushrooms, onion, and garlic in cooker. Add steak. Pour undrained tomatoes and vinegar over all.

2. Cover; cook on low-heat setting for 7 to 9 hours or on high-heat setting for 3½ to 4½ hours. If using low-heat setting, turn to high-heat setting. Add squash and/or zucchini and sweet pepper to cooker. Cover; cook on high-heat setting for 30 minutes more.

3. Remove steak from cooker. Stir in drained artichoke hearts. Thinly slice steak across grain. Arrange steak on the focaccia. Using a slotted spoon, place vegetable mixture over steak. Drizzle with enough of the cooking liquid to moisten. Sprinkle with cheese. Replace top of focaccia. To serve, cut into wedges.

Per serving: 440 cal., 15 g total fat (5 g sat. fat), 58 mg chol., 369 mg sodium, 46 g carbo., 4 g fiber, 34 g pro.

Pesto Meatball Stew

When you're ready for spring but the temperatures won't oblige, let this meatball stew warm you from the inside. Made with fresh-tasting basil pesto, it's sure to conjure images of spring.

Prep: 10 minutes
Cook: 5 to 6 hours (low) or 2½ to 3 hours (high)
Makes: 6 servings

1 16-ounce package frozen cooked Italian-style meatballs (32), thawed
2 14.5-ounce cans Italian-style stewed tomatoes, undrained
1 15- to 19-ounce can cannellini beans (white kidney beans), rinsed and drained
½ cup water
¼ cup purchased basil pesto
½ cup finely shredded Parmesan cheese (2 ounces)

1. In a 3½- or 4-quart slow cooker, combine the meatballs, undrained tomatoes, beans, the water, and pesto.

2. Cover and cook on low-heat setting for 5 to 6 hours or on high-heat setting for 2½ to 3 hours. Ladle soup into bowls. Sprinkle with Parmesan cheese.

Per serving: 408 cal., 27 g total fat (10 g sat. fat), 34 mg chol., 1,201 mg sodium, 24 g carbo., 6 g fiber, 17 g pro.

Steak Sandwiches with Ratatouille

Pesto Meatball Stew

No-Hassle Honey-Mustard
Barbecue Pork Ribs

No-Hassle Honey-Mustard Barbecue Pork Ribs

Boneless country-style ribs offer more meat with less mess than regular ribs.

Prep: 15 minutes
Cook: 8 to 10 hours (low) or 4 to 5 hours (high)
Makes: 6 to 8 servings

3½ **pounds boneless pork country-style ribs**
1 **cup bottled barbecue sauce**
1 **8-ounce jar honey mustard**
2 **teaspoons zesty herb grill seasoning blend**

1. Place ribs in a 3½- or 4-quart slow cooker. In a small bowl, stir together barbecue sauce, honey mustard, and seasoning blend. Pour over ribs in cooker. Stir to coat.

2. Cover and cook on low-heat setting for 8 to 10 hours or on high-heat setting for 4 to 5 hours.

3. Transfer ribs to a serving platter. Strain sauce; skim fat from sauce. Drizzle some of the sauce over the ribs and pass remaining sauce.

Per serving: 322 cal., 12 g total fat (4 g sat. fat), 94 mg chol., 497 mg sodium, 18 g carbo., 1 g fiber, 29 g pro.

Ham and Potatoes au Gratin

Kids will like the yummy rich cheese flavor of this golden casserole. Roasted red peppers add flavor and color.

Prep: 15 minutes
Cook: 7 to 8 hours (low) or 3½ to 4 hours (high)
Makes: 6 servings

Nonstick cooking spray
2 **5.5-ounce packages dry au gratin potato mix**
2 **cups diced cooked ham**
¼ **cup bottled roasted red sweet pepper, drained and chopped**
3 **cups water**
1 **10.75-ounce can condensed Cheddar cheese soup**

1. Lightly coat a 3½- or 4-quart slow cooker with cooking spray. Place au gratin potato mixes with contents of seasoning packets, the ham, and roasted sweet pepper in the prepared cooker. In a large bowl, stir together the water and soup. Pour over potato mixture in cooker.

2. Cover and cook on low-heat setting for 7 to 8 hours or on high-heat setting for 3½ to 4 hours.

Per serving: 255 cal., 7 g total fat (3 g sat. fat), 29 mg chol., 2,087 mg sodium, 45 g carbo., 3 g fiber, 15 g pro.

Taco Chili

It looks like chili but tastes like a taco. The hominy contributes its subtle sweet flavor. Scoop some sour cream or grated cheese on top or sprinkle with corn chips or sliced green onions.

Prep: 20 minutes
Cook: 4 to 6 hours (low) or 2 to 3 hours (high)
Makes: 4 to 6 servings

1 **pound lean ground beef**
2 **15-ounce cans seasoned tomato sauce with diced tomatoes**
1 **15-ounce can chili beans with chili gravy**
1 **15-ounce can hominy or whole-kernel corn, undrained**
1 **1.25-ounce package taco seasoning mix**
   Dairy sour cream (optional)
   Shredded Cheddar cheese (optional)

1. In a large skillet, cook beef over medium heat until brown; drain off fat.

2. In a 3½- or 4-quart slow cooker, combine the beef, tomato sauce, beans with chili gravy, undrained hominy, and taco seasoning mix.

3. Cover and cook on low-heat setting for 4 to 6 hours or on high-heat setting for 2 to 3 hours. If desired, top each serving with sour cream and cheese.

Per serving: 477 cal., 18 g total fat (6 g sat. fat), 71 mg chol., 1,998 mg sodium, 49 g carbo., 12 g fiber, 35 g pro.

Beefy Shepherd's Pie

This dish is for the kid in all of those who crave homey foods. A sprinkling with a bit of shredded cheddar cheese before serving is optional. If you must be a grown-up, serve it with a salad on the side.

Prep: 20 minutes   **Cook:** 6 to 8 hours (low) or 3 to 4 hours (high)   **Makes:** 8 servings

2 **pounds lean ground beef**
1 **cup chopped onion (1 large)**
1 **16-ounce package frozen mixed vegetables**
2 **10.75-ounce cans condensed tomato soup**
8 **servings refrigerated or frozen mashed potatoes**

1. In a large skillet, cook beef and onion until beef is brown and onion is tender; drain off fat.

2. In a 3½- or 4-quart slow cooker, combine beef mixture, frozen vegetables, and soup.

3. Cover and cook on low-heat setting for 6 to 8 hours or on high-heat setting for 3 to 4 hours.

4. Meanwhile, prepare mashed potatoes according to package directions. Serve beef mixture with potatoes.

Per serving: 575 cal., 27 g total fat (13 g sat. fat), 106 mg chol., 836 mg sodium, 51 g carbo., 7 g fiber, 32 g pro.

Orange Sesame Ribs

Try ribs done the Asian-flavor way with an aromatic, sweet, dark sauce that glazes the meat.

Prep: 15 minutes
Cook: 8 to 10 hours (low) or 4 to 5 hours (high)
Makes: 4 servings

2½   to 3 pounds boneless country-style pork ribs
      Nonstick cooking spray
1   10-ounce jar orange marmalade
1   7.25-ounce jar hoisin sauce
3   cloves garlic, minced, or 1½ teaspoons bottled minced garlic
1   teaspoon toasted sesame oil
      Hot cooked rice (optional)

1. Trim fat from ribs. Lightly coat a large skillet with cooking spray; heat over medium heat. Brown ribs on all sides in hot skillet; drain fat. Place in a 3½- or 4-quart slow cooker.

2. In a medium bowl, stir together marmalade, hoisin sauce, garlic, and sesame oil. Pour over ribs in cooker; stir to coat ribs with sauce.

3. Cover and cook on low-heat setting for 8 to 10 hours or on high-heat setting for 4 to 5 hours. Transfer ribs to a serving platter. Skim fat from sauce. Spoon some of the sauce over the ribs. Pass remaining sauce. If desired, serve with hot cooked rice.

Per serving: 532 cal., 16 g total fat (5 g sat. fat), 101 mg chol., 696 mg sodium, 66 g carbo., 0 g fiber, 33 g pro.

Southwest Pork Chops

Corn and fresh cilantro contribute a lively dose of flavor to this slow-simmered Tex-Mex dish. Complete the menu with a fresh spinach salad and you have a meal that's fit for company.

Prep: 15 minutes
Cook: 5½ hours (low) or 2½ hours (high) + 30 minutes (high)   **Makes:** 6 servings

6   pork rib chops, cut ¾ inch thick (about 2½ pounds)
1   15-ounce can Mexican-style or Tex-Mex-style chili beans
1¼   cups bottled salsa
1   cup fresh* or frozen whole kernel corn
2   cups hot cooked rice
      Snipped fresh cilantro (optional)

1. Trim excess fat from chops. Place chops in the bottom of a 3½- or 4-quart crockery cooker. Add chili beans and salsa. Cover; cook on low-heat setting for 5 hours or high-heat setting for 2½ hours.

2. Turn to high-heat setting, if necessary. Stir in corn. Cover and cook 30 minutes longer on high-heat setting. Serve over rice. If desired, sprinkle with cilantro.

Per serving: 334 cal., 7 g total fat (2 g sat. fat), 77 mg chol., 716 mg sodium, 34 g carbo., 4 g fiber, 33 g pro.

*Note: 2 medium ears of fresh corn equal about 1 cup of whole kernel corn.

Orange Sesame Ribs

Pork Pot Roast with Apples

Pork Pot Roast with Apples

Teamed with apples, parsnips, sweet potatoes, and an onion, this ready-when-you-are pork shoulder is a sure winner.

Prep: 30 minutes
Cook: 7 to 9 hours (low) or 3½ to 4½ hours (high)
Makes: 6 servings

1	**2½- to 3-pound boneless pork shoulder roast**
1	**tablespoon cooking oil**
6	**small parsnips, peeled and quartered**
2	**small sweet potatoes, peeled and quartered**
1	**small onion, sliced**
1	**cup beef broth**
½	**cup apple cider or apple juice**
1	**teaspoon dried basil, crushed**
1	**teaspoon dried marjoram, crushed**
½	**teaspoon salt**
¼	**teaspoon ground black pepper**
2	**small cooking apples, cored and cut into wedges**
½	**cup cold water**
¼	**cup all-purpose flour**
	Salt
	Ground black pepper
	Fresh flat-leaf parsley (optional)

1. Trim fat from roast. In a large skillet, heat oil over medium-high heat. Brown roast in hot oil, turning to brown on all sides. In a 4½- to 6-quart slow cooker, combine parsnips, sweet potatoes, and onion. Place roast on vegetables. In a medium bowl, combine broth, apple cider, basil, marjoram, the ½ teaspoon salt, and the ¼ teaspoon pepper. Pour over roast.

2. Cover; cook on low-heat setting for 7 to 9 hours or on high-heat setting for 3½ to 4½ hours, adding apple wedges the last 30 minutes of cooking. Remove roast, vegetables, and apples to a serving platter; keep warm.

3. For gravy, skim fat from cooking liquid; strain liquid through a fine mesh sieve. Measure 1¾ cups of the cooking liquid; pour into a medium saucepan. In a small bowl, stir the cold water into the flour; stir into cooking liquid in saucepan. Cook and stir until thickened and bubbly. Cook and stir for 1 minute more. Season to taste with additional salt and additional pepper. Pass gravy with roast. If desired, garnish with parsley.

Per serving: 485 cal., 16 g total fat (5 g sat. fat), 126 mg chol., 492 mg sodium, 45 g carbo., 8 g fiber, 40 g pro.

Quick Tip Purchase firm, small to medium, well-shaped parsnips. Avoid those that are limp, shriveled, or spotted. Store parsnips in a plastic bag in the refrigerator for up to 2 weeks.

Sweet Pork Sandwiches

Root beer concentrate adds rich flavor and pleasant sweetness. You'll find it in the spice section of your supermarket.

Prep: 15 minutes
Cook: 8 to 10 hours (low) or 4 to
5 hours (high) **Makes:** 8 to 10 servings

1	2½- to 3-pound boneless pork shoulder roast
½	teaspoon salt
½	teaspoon ground black pepper
2	medium onions, cut into thin wedges
3	12-ounce bottles or cans root beer*
1	cup bottled chili sauce
¼	teaspoon root beer concentrate (optional)
	Several dashes bottled hot pepper sauce (optional)
8	to 10 hamburger buns, split (and toasted, if desired)
	Lettuce leaves (optional)
	Tomato slices (optional)

1. Trim fat from meat. If necessary, cut pork roast to fit into a 3½- to 4-quart slow cooker. Sprinkle pork roast with salt and pepper. Place pork roast in cooker. Add onions and one bottle root beer.

2. Cover and cook on low-heat setting for 8 to 10 hours or on high-heat setting for 4 to 5 hours.

3. Meanwhile, for sauce, in a medium saucepan, combine 2 bottles or cans root beer and chili sauce. Bring to boiling; reduce heat. Boil gently, uncovered, for 30 to 35 minutes or until desired consistency, stirring occasionally. If desired, stir in root beer concentrate and hot pepper sauce.

4. Transfer pork roast to a bowl. Using a slotted spoon, remove onions from cooking liquid and place in bowl with pork roast. Discard cooking liquid. Using two forks, gently shred the pork roast.

5. If desired, line buns with lettuce leaves and tomato slices. Add shredded meat and onions; spoon on sauce.

Per serving: 399 cal., 10 g total fat (3 g sat. fat), 92 mg chol., 884 mg sodium, 42 g carbo., 3 g fiber, 33 g pro.

*Note: Do not use diet root beer.

Pork Chops and Corn Bread Stuffing

Try this when you get a craving for Thanksgiving-type fare. Browned chops slow-cook over vegetables and stuffing.

Prep: 20 minutes
Cook: 5 to 6 hours (low) or 2½ to 3 hours (high)
Makes: 4 servings

    Nonstick cooking spray
4   **pork rib chops, cut ¾ inch thick**
1   **10.75-ounce can condensed golden mushroom or cream of mushroom soup**
¼   **cup butter, melted**
1   **16-ounce package frozen broccoli, cauliflower, and carrots**
½   **of a 16-ounce package corn bread stuffing mix (about 3 cups)**

1. Lightly coat a 5½- or 6-quart slow cooker with cooking spray; set aside. Lightly coat a 10-inch skillet with cooking spray; heat over medium heat. Brown the chops, half at a time, in the hot skillet. Remove chops from skillet; set aside.

2. In an extra large bowl, stir together soup and melted butter. Add frozen vegetables and stuffing mix; stir to combine. Transfer stuffing mixture to prepared cooker. Arrange chops on top of stuffing mixture.

3. Cover and cook on low-heat setting for 5 to 6 hours or on high-heat setting for 2½ to 3 hours.

Per serving: 558 cal., 22 g total fat (10 g sat. fat), 89 mg chol., 1,533 mg sodium, 56 g carbo., 7 g fiber, 30 g pro.

Smoky Turkey and Cheesy Potato Casserole

Frozen hash brown potatoes and canned cream of chicken soup make this creamy casserole a snap to prepare.

Prep: 20 minutes **Cook:** 5 to 6 hours (low)
Makes: 6 servings

    Nonstick cooking spray
1   **10.75-ounce can condensed cream of chicken with herbs soup**
1   **8-ounce carton dairy sour cream**
1½   **cups shredded smoked Cheddar cheese (6 ounces)**
1   **28-ounce package frozen loose-pack diced hash brown potatoes with onion and peppers, thawed**
3   **cups chopped smoked or roasted turkey or chicken**
    Crushed croutons (optional)

1. Lightly coat the inside of a 3½- or 4-quart slow cooker with cooking spray. In the cooker, stir together the soup, sour cream, cheese, potatoes, and turkey.

2. Cover and cook on low-heat setting for 5 to 6 hours. If desired, top each serving with crushed croutons.

Per serving: 402 cal., 21 g total fat (12 g sat. fat), 84 mg chol., 1,384 mg sodium, 29 g carbo., 3 g fiber, 26 g pro.

Spicy Chicken with Peppers and Olives ♥

Spicy red pepper sauce is the choice for this recipe. If you can't find it, use a favorite variety of pasta sauce.

Prep: 20 minutes
Cook: 6 to 7 hours (low) or 3 to 3½ hours (high)
Makes: 6 servings

2½   **to 3 pounds meaty chicken pieces (breasts, thighs, and drumsticks), skinned**
    Salt
    Ground black pepper
½   **cup coarsely chopped yellow sweet pepper (1 small)**
½   **cup sliced, pitted ripe olives and/or pimiento-stuffed green olives**
1   **26-ounce jar spicy red pepper pasta sauce**
    Hot cooked pasta (optional)

1. Place the chicken pieces in a 3½- or 4-quart slow cooker. Sprinkle lightly with salt and black pepper. Add sweet pepper and olives to cooker. Pour pasta sauce over chicken mixture in cooker.

2. Cover and cook on low-heat setting for 6 to 7 hours or on high-heat setting for 3 to 3½ hours. If desired, serve chicken and sauce over hot cooked pasta.

Per serving: 239 cal., 10 g total fat (2 g sat. fat), 77 mg chol., 592 mg sodium, 10 g carbo., 3 g fiber, 27 g pro.

Ginger Chicken

Ginger Chicken

This sweet-and-sour chicken relies on mango chutney and chili sauce for intense flavor. Serve rice alongside to absorb every last drop of the tasty sauce.

Prep: 20 minutes
Cook: 5 to 6 hours (low) or 2½ to 3 hours (high)
Makes: 6 servings

½   **cup mango chutney or orange marmalade**
¼   **cup bottled chili sauce**
2   **tablespoons quick-cooking tapioca**
1½   **teaspoons grated fresh ginger**
12   **chicken thighs, skinned (about 4 pounds)**
     Hot cooked brown rice (optional)
     Sliced green onions (optional)

1. Cut up any large pieces of fruit in the chutney. In a 4- to 5-quart slow cooker, combine chutney, chili sauce, tapioca, and ginger. Add chicken, turning pieces in chutney mixture to coat.

2. Cover and cook on low-heat setting for 5 to 6 hours or on high-heat setting for 2½ to 3 hours. If desired, serve chicken over rice and sprinkle with green onions.

Per serving: 264 cal., 7 g total fat (2 g sat. fat), 143 mg chol., 494 mg sodium, 16 g carbo., 1 g fiber, 34 g pro.

Quick Tip Skinning chicken dramatically reduces the fat content the chicken contributes to a dish. If you can't find packaged skinned chicken thighs in your supermarket's meat section, ask a butcher to skin the thighs for you.

Herbed Chicken and Mushrooms

For a company-special meal, pair this beguiling chicken-and-pasta dish with a tossed salad, crispy breadsticks, and your favorite wine.

Prep: 30 minutes
Cook: 7 to 8 hours (low) or 3½ to 4 hours (high)
Makes: 6 servings

- 5 cups sliced assorted fresh mushrooms (such as shiitake, button, cremini, and oyster)
- 1 medium onion, chopped (½ cup)
- 1 medium carrot, chopped (½ cup)
- ¼ cup dried tomato pieces (not oil-packed)
- ¾ cup chicken broth
- ¼ cup dry white wine or chicken broth
- 3 tablespoons quick-cooking tapioca, crushed
- 1 teaspoon dried thyme, crushed
- ½ teaspoon dried basil, crushed
- ½ teaspoon garlic salt
- ¼ to ½ teaspoon ground black pepper
- 3 pounds chicken thighs and/or drumsticks, skinned
- 4½ cups hot cooked plain and/or spinach linguine or fettuccine, or hot cooked rice

1. In a 4- to 5-quart slow cooker, combine mushrooms, onion, carrot, and dried tomato. Pour the ¾ cup broth and the wine over mixture in cooker. Sprinkle with tapioca, thyme, basil, garlic salt, and pepper. Place chicken pieces on mixture in cooker.

2. Cover and cook on low-heat setting for 7 to 8 hours or on high-heat setting for 3½ to 4 hours.

3. To serve, arrange chicken and vegetables over pasta; drizzle with cooking juices.

Per serving: 360 cal., 7 g total fat (2 g sat. fat), 107 mg chol., 350 mg sodium, 39 g carbo., 3 g fiber, 34 g pro.

Herbed Chicken and Mushrooms

Turkey with Creamy 🖤 Alfredo Sauce

The velvety sauce for this tender chicken is a tantalizing blend of golden mushroom soup, white wine, and cream cheese with chives and onion.

Prep: 20 minutes   **Cook:** 5½ hours to 6½ hours
Makes: 6 to 8 servings

- 1 2½- to 3½-pound boneless turkey breast portion, rolled and tied
- 1 10.5-ounce can reduced-fat and reduced-sodium condensed cream of chicken soup
- 1 1.25-ounce envelope Alfredo sauce mix
- ½ of an 8-ounce tub cream cheese with chives and onion, softened
- 1 5-ounce can evaporated milk
- ½ cup water
- 4 cups hot cooked red pepper fettuccine, plain fettuccine, or angel hair pasta
     Shredded Parmesan cheese (optional)
     Steamed sugar snap peas (optional)

1. Place turkey in a 3½- or 4-quart slow cooker. In a medium bowl, stir together soup, sauce mix, and cream cheese; whisk in milk and water. Pour over the chicken. Cover and cook on low-heat setting for 5½ to 6½ hours.

2. Remove turkey from slow cooker; remove string. Slice turkey. Whisk sauce in cooker until nearly smooth. Serve turkey and sauce over hot cooked pasta. If desired, sprinkle with Parmesan cheese and serve with sugar snap peas.

Per serving: 489 cal., 13 g total fat (7 g sat. fat), 150 mg chol., 600 mg sodium, 34 g carbo., 2 g fiber, 55 g pro.

Zesty Ginger-Tomato 🖤 Chicken

Chicken drumsticks or thighs are great for the slow cooker. They stay moist and tender during the long cooking time.

Prep: 15 minutes
Cook: 6 to 7 hours (low) or 3 to 3½ hours (high)
Makes: 6 servings

- 12 chicken drumsticks and/or thighs, skinned (2½ to 3 pounds total)
- 2   14.5-ounce cans tomatoes, undrained
- 2   tablespoons quick-cooking tapioca
- 1   tablespoon grated fresh ginger
- 1   tablespoon snipped fresh cilantro or parsley
- 4   cloves garlic, minced
- 2   teaspoons packed brown sugar (optional)
- ½   teaspoon crushed red pepper
- ½   teaspoon salt

1. Place chicken pieces in a 3½- or 4-quart slow cooker.

2. Drain one can of the tomatoes; chop tomatoes from both cans. For the sauce, in a medium bowl, combine chopped tomatoes and the juice from one can of tomatoes, the tapioca, ginger, cilantro, garlic, brown sugar (if desired), crushed red pepper, and salt. Pour sauce over chicken.

3. Cover; cook on low-heat setting for 6 to 7 hours or on high-heat setting for 3 to 3½ hours.

4. Skim fat from sauce. Serve sauce with chicken.

Per serving: 168 cal., 4 g total fat (1 g sat. fat), 81 mg chol., 472 mg sodium, 10 g carbo., 1 g fiber, 23 g pro.

Turkey with Creamy Alfredo Sauce

Zesty Ginger-Tomato Chicken

Smoked Sausage-Lentil Soup

Smoked Sausage-Lentil Soup ♥

Cooked fennel provides a subtle, sweet flavor to smoked sausage in this warming soup.

Prep: 25 minutes
Cook: 6 to 7 hours (low) or 3 to 3½ hours (high)
Makes: 6 servings

1	**small fennel bulb**
6	**cups water**
6	**ounces smoked sausage, cut into ½-inch pieces**
1¼	**cups dry brown lentils, rinsed and drained**
2	**carrots, chopped**
1	**medium onion, chopped**
4	**cloves garlic, minced**
¾	**teaspoon salt**
¼	**teaspoon ground black pepper**
2	**tablespoons red wine vinegar**
	Kosher salt, sea salt, or regular salt
	Freshly ground black pepper

1. Remove fennel tops and reserve for garnish. Chop enough of the fennel bulb to equal 1 cup.

2. In a 3½- to 5-quart slow cooker, combine fennel, the water, sausage, lentils, carrots, onion, garlic, the salt, and the ¼ teaspoon pepper.

3. Cover and cook on low-heat setting for 6 to 7 hours or on high-heat setting for 3 to 3½ hours.

4. Before serving, stir in vinegar. Season to taste with additional salt and pepper. Garnish with reserved fennel tops.

Per serving: 273 cal., 10 g total fat (3 g sat. fat), 19 mg chol., 776 mg sodium, 30 g carbo., 13 g fiber, 17 g pro.

Italian Sausage Stew

Visit your favorite Italian grocer to pick up some sausage for this hearty and satisfying stew.

Prep: 15 minutes
Cook: 5 to 6 hours + 30 minutes (low) or 2½ to 3 hours + 15 minutes (high)
Makes: 6 servings

1	**pound Italian sausage**
2	**14-ounce cans seasoned chicken broth with Italian herbs**
1	**15- to 19-ounce can white kidney (cannellini) beans, rinsed and drained**
1	**14.5-ounce can diced tomatoes with basil, oregano, and garlic, undrained**
1	**9-ounce package refrigerated cheese-filled tortellini pasta**
	Finely shredded Parmesan cheese (optional)

1. In a large skillet, cook sausage over medium heat until brown; drain off fat.

2. In a 3½- to 4½-quart slow cooker, combine cooked sausage, broth, beans, and undrained tomatoes.

3. Cover and cook on low-heat setting for 5 to 6 hours or on high-heat setting for 2½ to 3 hours. Stir in tortellini. Cover and cook on low-heat setting for 30 minutes more or on high-heat setting for 15 minutes more. Ladle soup into bowls. If desired, sprinkle each serving with Parmesan cheese.

Per serving: 441 cal., 20 g total fat (8 g sat. fat), 72 mg chol., 1,597 mg sodium, 40 g carbo., 5 g fiber, 24 g pro.

Quick Tip Uncooked, fresh sausage, such as bulk Italian sausage, is very perishable and should be refrigerated, tightly wrapped, for only up to 2 days after purchase.

Mexican Meatball Stew

The meatballs hail from Italy, but the spicy sauce is definitely Mexican. Eat this culturally blended stew with warm corn bread.

Prep: 10 minutes
Cook: 6 to 7 hours (low) or 3 to 3½ hours (high)
Makes: 8 to 10 servings

2	**14.5-ounce cans Mexican-style stewed tomatoes**
2	**12-ounce packages frozen cooked turkey meatballs (24), thawed**
1	**15-ounce can black beans, rinsed and drained**
1	**14-ounce can chicken broth with roasted garlic**
1	**10-ounce package frozen corn, thawed**

1. In a 4- to 5-quart slow cooker, combine tomatoes, meatballs, drained beans, broth, and corn.

2. Cover and cook on low-heat setting for 6 to 7 hours or on high-heat setting for 3 to 3½ hours.

Per serving: 268 cal., 10 g total fat (3 g sat. fat), 66 mg chol., 1,328 mg sodium, 30 g carbo., 8 g fiber, 20 g pro.

Cheese Enchilada Chowder

Need a new party stew? This one's festive and great for a group. Set the chowder on a buffet table next to bowls, spoons, and toppings. Guests will eat it up in no time!

Prep: 25 minutes
Cook: 6 to 8 hours (low) or 3 to 4 hours (high)
Makes: 6 servings

- 1   15-ounce can black beans, rinsed and drained
- 1   14.5-ounce can diced tomatoes, drained
- 1   10-ounce package frozen whole kernel corn
- ½   cup chopped onion
- ½   cup chopped yellow, green, or red sweet pepper
- 1   small jalapeño chile pepper, seeded, if desired, and finely chopped*
- 1   10-ounce can enchilada sauce
- 1   10.75-ounce can condensed cream of chicken soup
- 2   cups milk
- 1   cup shredded Monterey Jack cheese (4 ounces)
- 1   cup shredded Cheddar cheese (4 ounces)
    Dairy sour cream (optional)
    Guacamole (optional)
    Tortilla chips, coarsely broken (optional)

1. In a 3½- to 5-quart slow cooker, combine drained beans, drained tomatoes, corn, onion, sweet pepper, and jalapeño pepper. In a large bowl, whisk together enchilada sauce and soup. Gradually whisk in milk until smooth. Pour sauce mixture over ingredients in cooker.

2. Cover; cook on low-heat setting for 6 to 8 hours or on high-heat setting for 3 to 4 hours. Stir in shredded Monterey Jack cheese and Cheddar cheese until melted. Ladle into bowls. If desired, top each serving with sour cream, guacamole, and tortilla chips.

Per serving: 374 cal., 18 g total fat (10 g sat. fat), 47 mg chol., 1,536 mg sodium, 37 g carbo., 6 g fiber, 21 g pro.

*Note: Because chile peppers contain volatile oils that can burn your skin and eyes, avoid direct contact with them as much as possible. When working with chile peppers, wear plastic or rubber gloves. If your bare hands do touch the chile peppers, wash your hands and nails well with soap and warm water.

Southwestern Bean Soup ♥

To make sure the fluffy mounds cook through, don't lift the slow-cooker lid until you're ready to test the dumplings for doneness.

Prep: 25 minutes **Cook:** 10 to 12 hours + 30 minutes (low), or 5 to 6 hours + 20 minutes (high)
Makes: 6 servings

- 3   cups water
- 1   15-ounce can red kidney beans, rinsed and drained
- 1   15-ounce can black beans, pinto beans, or Great Northern beans, rinsed and drained
- 1   14.5-ounce can Mexican-style stewed tomatoes, undrained
- 1   10-ounce package frozen whole kernel corn
- 1   cup sliced carrot
- 1   large onion, chopped
- 1   4-ounce can diced green chile peppers, undrained
- 2   tablespoons instant beef or chicken bouillon granules
- 1   to 2 teaspoons chili powder
- 2   cloves garlic, minced
- ⅓   cup all-purpose flour
- ¼   cup yellow cornmeal
- 1   teaspoon baking powder
    Dash ground black pepper
- 1   egg white
- 2   tablespoons milk
- 1   tablespoon cooking oil

1. In a 3½- or 4-quart slow cooker, combine the water, drained beans, undrained tomatoes, corn, carrot, onion, chile peppers, bouillon granules, chili powder, and garlic.

2. Cover and cook on low-heat setting for 10 to 12 hours or on high-heat setting for 5 to 6 hours.

3. For dumplings, in a medium bowl, stir together flour, cornmeal, baking powder, and black pepper. In a small bowl, whisk together egg white, milk, and oil. Add to flour mixture; stir with a fork just until combined.

4. Drop dumpling dough into six mounds on top of the bubbling soup. Cover and cook on low-heat setting about 30 minutes more or on high-heat setting about 20 minutes more or until a toothpick inserted in center of a dumpling comes out clean. (Do not lift lid while dumplings are cooking.)

Per serving: 263 cal., 4 g total fat (1 g sat. fat), 1 mg chol., 1,434 mg sodium, 51 g carbo., 11 g fiber, 15 g pro.

Three-Bean Vegetarian Chili 🤍

Chocolate-flavored syrup adds an intriguing undertone to this Cajun-accented chili.

Prep: 20 minutes
Cook: 6 to 8 hours (low) or 3 to 4 hours (high)
Makes: 4 servings

- 1 **15-ounce can no-salt-added red kidney beans, rinsed and drained**
- 1 **15-ounce can small white beans, rinsed and drained**
- 1 **15-ounce can low-sodium black beans, rinsed and drained**
- 1 **14.5-ounce can diced tomatoes and green chile peppers, undrained**
- 1 **cup beer or chicken broth**
- 3 **tablespoons chocolate-flavored syrup**
- 1 **tablespoon chili powder**
- 2 **teaspoons Cajun seasoning**
  Dairy sour cream (optional)
  Shredded Cheddar cheese (optional)

1. In a 3½- or 4-quart slow cooker, combine drained kidney beans, drained white beans, drained black beans, undrained tomatoes and green chile peppers, beer, chocolate syrup, chili powder, and Cajun seasoning.

2. Cover and cook on low-heat setting for 6 to 8 hours or on high-heat setting for 3 to 4 hours.

3. If desired, top each serving with sour cream and cheese.

Per serving: 308 cal., 1 g total fat (0 g sat. fat), 0 mg chol., 569 mg sodium, 60 g carbo., 21 g fiber, 21 g pro.

Grilled Formaggio Sandwiches, **page 270**

Brats with Onion-Pepper Relish, **page 260**

Open-Face Crab Ciabatta, **page 269**

Veggie Salad in a Pocket, **page 279**

Sandwiches and Pizzas

For meals with big appeal, turn to hearty sandwiches and pizzas. The possible combinations for these family favorites are almost endless. Just pile on a new ingredient or try a different bread or spread to bring new appeal to these stacked-up dinners.

Barbecue Beef Wrap

Roast Beef and Red Pepper Sandwiches

Roast Beef and Red ♥ Pepper Sandwiches

Italian sandwich breads—such as focaccia or ciabatta—taste delicious in this Mediterranean-style sandwich. Flag this recipe for nights when everyone eats at a different time. Portions keep well up to 24 hours when wrapped and chilled in the refrigerator.

Start to Finish: 25 minutes
Makes: 12 servings (one-half sandwich each)

- ⅓ **cup light mayonnaise dressing or mayonnaise**
- ⅓ **cup Dijon-style mustard**
- 2 **to 4 tablespoons prepared horseradish**
- 6 **6- to 7-inch rustic Italian sandwich breads**
- 12 **ounces thinly sliced cooked roast beef**
- 1 **12-ounce jar roasted red sweet peppers, drained and cut into ¼-inch-wide strips**
- 6 **ounces thinly sliced Monterey Jack cheese**
- 2 **cups fresh watercress, tough stems removed**
- 2 **cups fresh spinach**

1. In a small bowl, combine mayonnaise dressing, mustard, and horseradish. Using a serrated knife, slice bread in half horizontally.

2. For each sandwich, spread one bread half with mayonnaise mixture. Top each with roast beef, peppers, cheese, watercress, spinach, and remaining half of bread. To serve, cut each sandwich in half.

Per serving: 303 cal., 14 g total fat (4 g sat. fat), 41 mg chol., 656 mg sodium, 27 g carbo., 2 g fiber, 20 g pro.

Barbecue Beef Wrap ♥

With this delicious wrap, no more noses turned up at leftovers.

Start to Finish: 10 minutes **Makes:** 4 servings

- 8 **ounces leftover roast beef, shredded (⅓ cup)**
- 4 **7- to 8-inch flour tortillas**
- ¼ **cup bottled barbecue sauce**
- ½ **cup shredded Monterey Jack cheese**
- ½ **cup packaged shredded broccoli (broccoli slaw mix)**

1. Arrange beef on the tortillas. Drizzle with barbecue sauce and top with cheese and broccoli; roll up. Serve immediately or wrap tightly in plastic wrap and chill for up to 24 hours.

Per serving: 280 cal., 13 g total fat (6 g sat. fat), 57 mg chol., 367 mg sodium, 17 g carbo., 1 g fiber, 21 g pro.

Deli Roast Beef Sandwiches

Deli Roast Beef ♥ Sandwiches

Try coleslaw on a sandwich for a delicious lunch option. Pair it with chips or raw veggies for a quick meal for two.

Start to Finish: 10 minutes **Makes:** 2 sandwiches

8	ounces thinly sliced deli roast beef
4	slices pumpernickel, rye, or whole wheat bread
½	cup purchased coleslaw
	Herb pepper seasoning

1. Arrange roast beef on 2 of the bread slices. Spread coleslaw over roast beef; sprinkle with herb pepper seasoning. Top with the remaining 2 bread slices.

Nutrition Facts Per sandwich: 369 cal., 8 g total fat (2 g sat. fat), 80 mg chol., 507 mg sodium, 34 g carbo., 5 g fiber, 39 g pro.

Calzones ♥

Pizza sauce and refrigerated pizza dough make quick work of folded half-moon pizzas.

Start to Finish: 30 minutes **Bake:** 8 minutes
Oven: 425°F **Makes:** 6 servings

8	ounces lean ground beef
½	cup sliced fresh mushrooms
¼	cup chopped green sweet pepper
½	cup shredded mozzarella cheese (2 ounces)
⅓	cup pizza sauce
1	10-ounce package refrigerated pizza dough
1	tablespoon milk
	Grated Parmesan cheese (optional)
	Warmed pizza sauce (optional)

1. Preheat oven to 425°F.

2. In a medium skillet, cook beef, mushrooms, and sweet pepper until beef is no longer pink; drain. Stir in the mozzarella cheese and the ⅓ cup pizza sauce.

3. Unroll pizza dough. Roll or stretch dough into a 10×15-inch rectangle. Cut dough into six 5-inch squares. Divide the beef mixture evenly over one-half of each square. Brush dough edges with water. Lift a corner and stretch dough over beef mixture to opposite corner. Seal the edges by pressing with the tines of a fork.

4. Place calzones on a greased baking sheet. Prick tops with a fork to allow steam to escape. Brush with milk. If desired, sprinkle with Parmesan cheese. Bake for 8 to 10 minutes or until golden brown. Let stand for 5 minutes before serving. If desired, serve with warmed pizza sauce.

Per serving: 235 cal., 8 g total fat (3 g sat. fat), 31 mg chol., 358 mg sodium, 26 g carbo., 1 g fiber, 13 g pro.

Canadian Bacon Pizza `one`

This fast-grilling entrée puts all of the sizzle and smoke you love into one of the world's most popular treats. Purchased Italian bread shells make the recipe a real snap to prepare.

Prep: 20 minutes **Grill:** 5 minutes **Makes:** 4 servings

1	6-ounce jar marinated artichoke hearts, quartered
2	6-inch Italian bread shells
1	cup shredded fontina or mozzarella cheese (4 ounces)
6	slices Canadian-style bacon, cut into strips (about 5 ounces)
3	plum tomatoes, sliced
¼	cup crumbled feta cheese (1 ounce)
2	green onions, thinly sliced
1	tablespoon snipped fresh oregano or basil

1. Drain artichoke hearts, reserving marinade. Brush the bread shells with some of the reserved marinade (discard any remaining marinade). Sprinkle half of the fontina cheese over bread shells. In a large bowl, toss together artichoke hearts, Canadian-style bacon, tomatoes, feta cheese, green onions, and oregano; divide among bread shells. Sprinkle with the remaining fontina cheese.

2. Transfer the bread shells to a pizza grill pan or a large piece of double-thickness heavy foil. On a grill that has a cover, place the pan or foil on the rack of the grill directly over medium coals. Cover and grill for 5 to 8 minutes or until cheese is melted and pizza is heated through. Or, preheat oven to 450°F. Bake for 10 to 12 minutes or until heated through.

Per serving: 384 cal., 19 g total fat (7 g sat. fat), 58 mg chol., 1,246 mg sodium, 33 g carbo., 1 g fiber, 23 g pro.

Canadian Bacon Pizza

Brats with Onion-Pepper Relish

Brats with Onion-Pepper Relish

These slimmed-down brats give you all the flavor you expect with a lot fewer calories than the concession stand variety.

Start to Finish: 30 minutes **Makes:** 4 servings

- **4**   **uncooked turkey bratwurst**
- **½**   **cup water**
- **1**   **small onion, thinly sliced**
- **1**   **small red or green sweet pepper, cut into thin strips**
- **¼**   **teaspoon ground black pepper**
- **⅛**   **teaspoon salt**
- **2**   **teaspoons butter or margarine**
- **4**   **bratwurst buns, split and toasted**
- **3**   **tablespoons spicy brown mustard**

1. In a large nonstick skillet, cook bratwurst over medium heat about 5 minutes or until brown, turning frequently. Carefully add the water. Bring to boiling; reduce heat. Cover and simmer for 15 to 20 minutes or until an instant-read meat thermometer inserted from the end of a bratwurst into the center registers 165°F. Drain on paper towels.

2. Meanwhile, in a covered medium saucepan, cook onion, sweet pepper, black pepper, and salt in hot butter for 3 minutes. Stir onion mixture. Cook, covered, for 3 to 4 minutes more or until onion is golden brown.

3. Spread cut sides of toasted buns with mustard. Serve bratwurst in buns topped with onion mixture.

Per serving: 284 cal., 12 g total fat (4 g sat. fat), 43 mg chol., 1,100 mg sodium, 27 g carbo., 2 g fiber, 17 g pro.

Hot Sub Sandwich

With options for every ingredient, the possibilities for this sandwich are almost limitless. Check your refrigerator and create your own combination.

Start to Finish: 30 minutes   **Makes:** 6 to 8 servings

- 1 **16-ounce loaf brown-and-serve French or Italian bread**
- 6 **ounces sliced American, Cheddar, and/or Swiss cheese**
- 12 **ounces thinly sliced deli turkey, ham, roast beef, or chicken**
   Ranch salad dressing or other creamy salad dressing

1. Bake the bread according to package directions. Cool slightly.

2. Using a long serrated knife, cut the baked loaf of bread in half horizontally. Arrange the cheese on bottom half of bread. Arrange the deli meat over the cheese.

3. Place the top half of the bread on the sandwich. Return to oven; bake about 5 minutes more or until the cheese melts. Remove sandwich from the oven and cool slightly.

4. Slice sandwich. Serve warm. Pass the salad dressing to use as a dipping sauce or to drizzle over deli meat.

Per serving: 433 cal., 16 g total fat (7 g sat. fat), 52 mg chol., 1,648 mg sodium, 46 g carbo., 2 g fiber, 29 g pro.

Chipotle Brisket Sandwich [one]

Sassy coleslaw slides over a serving of beef brisket as an alternative to lettuce and tomato for a tangy filling.

Start to Finish: 15 minutes   **Makes:** 6 servings

- 1 **17-ounce package refrigerated cooked, seasoned, and sliced beef brisket with barbecue sauce**
- 1 **to 2 canned chipotle chile peppers in adobo sauce, chopped***
- ½ **of a 16-ounce package shredded cabbage with carrot (coleslaw mix) (about 4 cups)**
- ⅓ **cup bottled coleslaw dressing**
- 6 **kaiser rolls, split and toasted**

1. In a large saucepan, combine the beef brisket with barbecue sauce and the chipotle peppers. Cook and stir about 5 minutes or until heated through.

2. Meanwhile, in a large bowl, combine shredded cabbage mixture and coleslaw dressing; toss to coat.

3. To serve, spoon beef mixture onto roll bottoms. Top with coleslaw mixture. Add roll tops.

Per serving: 414 cal., 18 g total fat (5 g sat. fat), 39 mg chol., 1,085 mg sodium, 47 g carbo., 2 g fiber, 16 g pro.

***Note:** Because chile peppers contain volatile oils that can burn your skin and eyes, avoid direct contact with them as much as possible. When working with chile peppers, wear plastic or rubber gloves. If your bare hands do touch the chile peppers, wash your hands and nails well with soap and warm water.

Roast Beef Sandwich With Horseradish Slaw

Horseradish and beef, common sandwich partners, pair up once again. Here the horseradish seasons crunchy broccoli slaw.

Start to Finish: 15 minutes   **Makes:** 4 servings

- ⅓ **cup light dairy sour cream**
- 2 **tablespoons snipped fresh chives**
- 2 **tablespoons spicy brown mustard**
- 1 **teaspoon prepared horseradish**
- ½ **teaspoon sugar**
- ¼ **teaspoon salt**
- 1 **cup packaged shredded broccoli with carrots (broccoli slaw mix)**
- 8 **ounces thinly sliced cooked roast beef**
- 8 **½-inch slices sourdough bread, toasted**

1. In a medium bowl, combine sour cream, chives, brown mustard, horseradish, sugar, and salt. Add shredded broccoli; toss to coat.

2. To assemble, divide roast beef among 4 of the bread slices. Top with broccoli mixture. Top with remaining bread slices. If desired, secure sandwiches with wooden toothpicks.

Per serving: 315 cal., 11 g total fat (4 g sat. fat), 53 mg chol., 630 mg sodium, 30 g carbo., 2 g fiber, 23 g pro.

Roast Beef Sandwich with Horseradish Slaw

Ham Calzones

Ham Calzones [one]

Leftover ham works deliciously in these individual pizza pockets. Purchase sliced ham from the supermarket deli if you do not have leftover ham on hand.

Prep: 20 minutes **Bake:** 20 minutes
Oven: 375°F **Makes:** 4 calzones

- **4 cups torn fresh spinach with stems removed**
- **1 16-ounce loaf frozen white bread dough, thawed**
- **3 cloves garlic, minced**
- **1 teaspoon dried Italian seasoning, crushed**
- **1 cup ricotta cheese or cottage cheese, drained**
- **4 ounces thinly sliced ham, chopped (1 cup)**
- **4 ounces thinly sliced Swiss cheese**
- **1 cup tomato and herb pasta sauce, heated**

1. Preheat oven to 375°F. In a large bowl, pour enough boiling water over spinach to cover. Let stand for 5 minutes. Drain well, squeezing out liquid; set aside.

2. Divide bread dough into four equal portions. On lightly floured surface, roll each portion of dough into 7-inch circle. Brush circles with garlic and Italian seasoning. Divide ricotta cheese evenly among circles, spreading only on half of each circle and to within ½ inch of edges. Layer spinach, ham, and Swiss cheese over ricotta cheese.

3. Moisten edges of dough with water. Fold dough in half over filling. Seal edges with tines of fork. Prick tops three or four times with fork. Place calzones on lightly greased baking sheet.

4. Bake about 20 minutes or until golden. Serve with warm pasta sauce.

Per serving: 484 cal., 6 g total fat (2 g sat. fat), 32 mg chol., 802 mg sodium, 64 g carbo., 2 g fiber, 32 g pro.

Make-Ahead Directions: Prepare calzones as above. Cool. Cover and chill the calzones overnight. To reheat, place calzones on a baking sheet. Bake calzones, uncovered, in a 375°F oven for 12 to 15 minutes or until heated through.

Ham and Pear Melt 🔲one

Serve these tortilla-wrapped sandwiches with soup for a satisfying lunch. At party time, roll the filled tortillas into spirals and cut into 1-inch pieces.

Start to Finish: 10 minutes **Makes:** 2 servings

- **2 7- to 8-inch whole wheat flour tortillas**
- **6 ounces very thinly sliced ham**
- **2 small ripe pears, cored and thinly sliced**
- **1 cup finely shredded Swiss, Colby-Monterey Jack, or mozzarella cheese (4 ounces)**

1. Place tortillas on a baking sheet or broiler pan. Broil tortillas 4 to 5 inches from the heat just until warm. Layer half the ham, half the sliced pears, and half the shredded cheese on each warm tortilla.

2. Broil layered tortillas about 2 minutes or until cheese is melted and bubbly. Fold tortillas in half or roll up into a spiral. Cut each in half.

Per serving: 474 cal., 25 g total fat (13 g sat. fat), 100 mg chol., 1,446 mg sodium, 29 g carbo., 11 g fiber, 33 g pro.

Mock Monte Cristo Sandwiches 🔲one

Traditionally dipped in beaten egg and grilled, this sandwich is a true classic. You'll like our simple baked version.

Prep: 10 minutes **Bake:** 15 minutes **Oven:** 400°F **Makes:** 3 servings

- **6 slices frozen French toast**
- **2 tablespoons honey mustard**
- **3 ounces thinly sliced cooked turkey breast**
- **3 ounces thinly sliced cooked ham**
- **3 ounces thinly sliced Swiss cheese**

1. Preheat oven to 400°F. Lightly grease a baking sheet; set aside.

2. To assemble sandwiches, spread one side of each of the frozen French toast slices with honey mustard. Layer three of the toast slices, mustard sides up, with the turkey, ham, and cheese. Cover with remaining toast slices, mustard sides down. Place sandwiches on prepared baking sheet.

3. Bake for 15 to 20 minutes or until sandwiches are heated through, turning sandwiches over once. Cut each sandwich in half diagonally.

Per serving: 445 cal., 18 g total fat (8 g sat. fat), 150 mg chol., 1,370 mg sodium, 43 g carbo., 1 g fiber, 27 g pro.

Provolone and Ham Melt 🔲one

You can mix and match the ingredients in this sandwich to satisfy both children and adults. For kids, try combining Cheddar cheese, ham, and fruit. Offer grown-ups a mix of provolone cheese, roasted pepper, and prosciutto.

Prep: 15 minutes **Cook:** 8 minutes **Makes:** 4 servings

- **8 slices multigrain, whole wheat, poppy seed, white, or pumpernickel bread**
  Butter or margarine, softened
- **4 teaspoons mayonnaise or salad dressing**
- **4 ounces provolone and/or Cheddar cheese, thinly sliced**
- **⅓ cup roasted red sweet peppers, well drained and cut into strips**
- **1 pear or apple, cored and thinly sliced, or 4 canned pineapple rings, well drained and patted dry**
- **4 ounces thinly sliced cooked ham and/or prosciutto**
- **2 tablespoons mango chutney**
  Fresh fruit such as sliced pears and apples, pineapple wedges, or grapes (optional)

1. Spread one side of each bread slice with butter. Place four of the bread slices, buttered sides down, on griddle. Spread mayonnaise on the four bread slices on the griddle. Top with cheese, red sweet peppers, and pear slices. Top with ham and/or prosciutto.

2. Cut up any large pieces of chutney; spread the unbuttered sides of the four remaining bread slices with chutney. Place over bread slices on griddle, buttered sides up.

3. Cook sandwiches over medium heat about 8 minutes or until bread is toasted and cheese is melted, turning once halfway through cooking. If desired, serve with additional fresh fruit.

Per serving: 466 cal., 22 g total fat (11 g sat. fat), 53 mg chol., 1,085 mg sodium, 48 g carbo., 7 g fiber, 20 g pro.

BBQ Chicken Sandwiches ♥

Next time you fix chicken breast halves, cook a couple extra ones and freeze them to have ready for these supper sandwiches.

Start to Finish: 15 minutes **Makes:** 4 servings

- **2 cups cooked chicken or turkey breast, cut into strips**
- **½ cup shredded carrot (1 medium)**
- **½ cup bottled barbecue sauce**
- **1 16-ounce loaf French bread, split and toasted, or 4 hamburger buns, split and toasted**
- **½ cup shredded Monterey Jack cheese (2 ounces) (optional)**
- **Pickle slices (optional)**

1. In a medium saucepan, heat the chicken, carrot, and barbecue sauce over medium heat until bubbly.

2. Spoon chicken mixture onto bottom half of bread loaf. If desired, top chicken mixture with cheese. Place on a baking sheet. Broil 3 to 4 inches from heat for 1 to 2 minutes or until cheese melts. If desired, top with pickle slices. Cover with bread top. If using bread, cut into serving-size pieces.

Per serving: 269 cal., 6 g total fat (2 g sat. fat), 53 mg chol., 520 mg sodium, 27 g carbo., 2 g fiber, 25 g pro.

Barbecue Beef Calzones 🔲one

A smart combination of refrigerated pizza dough, packaged shredded beef in barbecue sauce, packaged veggies, and shredded cheese produces a savory hot baked meal in no time.

Prep: 20 minutes **Bake:** 30 minutes **Oven:** 400°F
Makes: 4 calzones

- **1 13.8-ounce package refrigerated pizza dough**
- **½ of an 18- to 20-ounce package refrigerated cooked shredded beef with barbecue sauce**
- **½ of a 16-ounce package (2 cups) frozen stir-fry vegetables (yellow, green, and red peppers and onion), thawed**
- **1 cup shredded Monterey Jack cheese with jalapeño peppers (4 ounces)**
- **2 tablespoons cornmeal**
- **1 tablespoon milk**
- **¼ teaspoon garlic salt**

1. Preheat oven to 400°F. Grease a 15×10×1-inch baking pan; set aside. On a lightly floured surface, unroll pizza dough. Roll to a 12-inch square. Cut into four 6-inch squares.

2. Divide shredded beef, thawed vegetables, and cheese among dough squares, placing ingredients on half of each square. Fold remaining half of each dough square over filling to form a rectangle. Press edges with the tines of a fork to seal.

3. Sprinkle 1 tablespoon of the cornmeal on prepared baking pan. Place calzones on pan; brush tops lightly with milk. In a small bowl combine remaining 1 tablespoon cornmeal and the garlic salt; sprinkle over calzones.

4. Bake about 30 minutes or until golden. Serve warm.

Per calzone: 434 cal., 17 g total fat (8 g sat. fat), 69 mg chol., 832 mg sodium, 42 g carbo., 2 g fiber, 28 g pro.

Roasted Vegetable and Pastrami Panini ♥ 🔲one

A panini grill presses a sandwich as it cooks from both sides. You can get the same effect in an open griddle or skillet by using a foil-wrapped brick or a heavy pan as a weight.

Start to Finish: 30 minutes **Makes:** 4 servings

- **4 thin slices provolone cheese (2 ounces)**
- **8 ½-inch slices sourdough or Vienna bread**
- **1 cup roasted or grilled vegetables from the deli or deli-marinated vegetables, coarsely chopped**
- **4 thin slices pastrami (3 ounces)**
- **1 tablespoon olive oil or basil-flavored olive oil**

1. Place a cheese slice on each of four of the bread slices. Spread vegetables evenly over cheese. Top with pastrami and remaining 4 bread slices. Brush the outsides of the sandwiches with oil.

2. If desired, wrap a brick completely in foil. Heat a nonstick griddle or large skillet over medium heat. Place a sandwich on heated pan; place brick on top to flatten slightly.* Cook for 4 to 6 minutes or until sandwich is golden and cheese is melted, turning once. Repeat for remaining sandwiches.

Per serving: 314 cal., 16 g total fat (6 g sat. fat), 29 mg chol., 689 mg sodium, 30 g carbo., 2 g fiber, 12 g pro.

***Note:** Or place sandwich on a covered indoor grill or panini grill. Close lid; grill for 4 to 5 minutes or until golden and cheese is melted.

Chicken-Artichoke
Sandwiches

Chicken-Artichoke Sandwiches

A whole cooked deli chicken or frozen cooked chicken breast (thawed) provide quick sources of cooked chicken for these open-face sandwiches. You can also try leftover turkey from a special dinner.

Start to Finish: 20 minutes **Bake:** 12 minutes
Oven: 450°F **Makes:** 6 servings

- **6** **½-inch bias slices of Italian bread**
- **⅓** **cup refrigerated basil pesto**
- **3** **ounces thinly sliced prosciutto**
- **1** **14-ounce can artichoke hearts, drained and thinly sliced**
- **1** **7-ounce jar roasted red peppers, drained and cut into strips**
- **12** **ounces cooked chicken or turkey, cut into bite-size strips (about 2¼ cups)**
- **4** **to 6 ounces shredded provolone cheese (1 to 1½ cups)**

1. Preheat oven to 450°F.

2. Lightly spread pesto on one side of each bread slice. Top slices with prosciutto, artichoke slices, red pepper strips, and chicken strips.

3. Place sandwiches on a large foil-lined baking sheet. Cover loosely with foil. Bake about 8 minutes or until nearly heated through. Uncover sandwiches and sprinkle with cheese. Bake 4 to 5 minutes more or until cheese melts.

Per serving: 387 cal., 20 g total fat (6 g sat. fat), 67 mg chol., 855 mg sodium, 20 g carbo., 1 g fiber, 31 g pro.

Quick Tip To make your own pesto for this sandwich, combine in a food processor or blender, ¼ cup olive oil, ½ cup pine nuts, 2 cups packed basil leaves, ½ cup grated Parmesan cheese, 4 cloves of garlic, and ¼ teaspoon salt. Cover and process or blend until smooth. Makes ¾ cup. Place unused portion in a small airtight container and refrigerate for 1 to 2 days or freeze for up to 3 months.

Turkey Caesar Sandwiches

Hail, Caesar! That's what diners will be saying when they bite into these scrumptious grilled turkey sandwiches made with fluffy pita bread. No pita? That's okay—use toasted kaiser or other rolls instead.

Prep: 10 minutes **Grill:** 12 minutes **Makes:** 4 servings

2	**8-ounce turkey tenderloins or 4 skinless, boneless chicken breast halves**
½	**cup bottled Caesar salad dressing**
4	**teaspoons olive oil**
½	**teaspoon bottled minced garlic (1 clove)**
4	**thick pita bread rounds, split horizontally**
	Lettuce leaves
2	**medium tomatoes, sliced**
1	**medium avocado, peeled and sliced (optional)**
	Shaved Parmesan cheese

1. Split each turkey tenderloin in half horizontally. Place turkey on the rack of an uncovered grill directly over medium coals. Grill for 12 to 15 minutes or until turkey is tender and no longer pink, turning once. Set aside half of the salad dressing; brush remaining salad dressing on the turkey during the last 5 minutes of grilling.

2. Meanwhile, in a small bowl, stir together oil and garlic. Using a pastry brush, brush oil mixture over one side of each pita bread. Place pita bread, brushed sides down, on grill rack directly over medium heat. Grill for 2 to 3 minutes or until toasted.

3. To assemble, cut turkey tenderloins crosswise into ½-inch slices. Place lettuce leaves on broiled side of four of the pita bread halves. Top with tomato, turkey, and, if desired, avocado; drizzle with reserved salad dressing. Top with shaved Parmesan cheese. Top with remaining pita bread halves.

Per serving: 535 cal., 26 g total fat (5 g sat. fat), 74 mg chol., 823 mg sodium, 37 g carbo., 2 g fiber, 36 g pro.

Honey Chicken Sandwiches one

These are definitely no ordinary chicken sandwiches! Honey mellows and sweetens the red onion, while earthy, fragrant thyme adds an intriguing new dimension of flavor to these croissant chicken sandwiches.

Start to Finish: 20 minutes **Makes:** 4 sandwiches

- 3 **tablespoons honey**
- 2 **teaspoons snipped fresh thyme or ½ teaspoon dried thyme, crushed**
- 1 **small red onion, halved and thinly sliced**
- 12 **ounces thinly sliced cooked chicken, halved crosswise**
- 4 **purchased croissants, halved horizontally and toasted**

1. In a medium skillet, combine honey, thyme, and red onion. Cook and stir over medium-low heat just until hot (do not boil). Stir in chicken; heat through. Arrange chicken mixture in halved croissants.

Per sandwich: 445 cal., 18 g total fat (8 g sat. fat), 118 mg chol., 498 mg sodium, 40 g carbo., 2 g fiber, 29 g pro.

Easy Meatball Panini

Check the frozen food aisle for cooked Italian-style meatballs, which make this sandwich-shop classic easy as can be.

Start to Finish: 25 minutes **Makes:** 4 servings

- 16 **frozen Italian-style cooked meatballs (about 1 pound)**
- 1 **15-ounce can pizza sauce**
- 4 **Italian rolls or hoagie buns**
- 4 **slices provolone cheese**
- 1 **cup loosely packed large basil or spinach leaves**

1. Preheat the broiler. In a large saucepan, combine meatballs and pizza sauce. Cover and cook over medium-low heat for 10 minutes or until heated through, stirring occasionally.

2. Meanwhile, cut a thin slice from the top of rolls; hollow out roll leaving a ¼- to ½-inch-thick shell. (Discard or save bread from rolls for another use). Place hollowed-out rolls and roll tops, cut sides up, on a baking sheet. Broil 3 to 4 inches from the heat for 1 to 2 minutes or until lightly toasted. Remove roll tops from baking sheet.

3. Spoon meatballs and sauce into toasted rolls. Top with cheese. Broil about 1 minute more or until cheese is melted. To serve, place basil or spinach leaves on top of cheese and replace roll tops.

Per serving: 740 cal., 38 g total fat (18 g sat. fat), 98 mg chol., 1,570 mg sodium, 63 g carbo., 8 g fiber, 36 g pro.

Tall Turkey Sandwiches

Tall Turkey Sandwiches

The typical turkey sandwich is more than ready for a modern-day update. Here a yogurt and horseradish spread provides tang, while snow peas impart snap. For even more kick, use an extra teaspoon of horseradish.

Start to Finish: 15 minutes
Makes: 4 sandwiches.

- ¼ **cup fat-free plain yogurt**
- 3 **tablespoons horseradish mustard**
- 8 **slices multigrain bread, toasted**
- 12 **lettuce leaves**
- 8 **to 12 ounces deli-sliced cooked turkey breast**
- 1 **tomato, sliced**
- 1 **yellow sweet pepper, sliced**
- 1 **cup fresh pea pods**

1. In a small bowl, stir together yogurt and horseradish mustard. Spread yogurt mixture on 4 of the toasted bread slices.

2. Top the remaining bread slices with lettuce, turkey, tomato, sweet pepper, and pea pods. Top with remaining bread slices, spread sides down.

Nutrition Facts per sandwich: 235 cal., 3 g total fat (0 g sat. fat), 23 mg chol., 1163 mg sodium, 34 g carbo., 6 g fiber, 22 g pro.

Individual Turkey Pizzas

Individual Turkey Pizzas 🖼️one

A fun way to enjoy leftover turkey, this recipe uses some terrific convenience products—salad mix, ranch dressing, bottled minced garlic, bottled roasted red sweet peppers, and Italian bread shells.

Prep: 20 minutes **Broil:** 5 minutes **Makes:** 4 servings

4	**cups mixed baby greens**
¼	**cup bottled peppercorn ranch salad dressing**
1	**tablespoon olive oil**
½	**teaspoon bottled minced garlic or bottled roasted minced garlic**
4	**8-inch Italian bread shells**
3	**cups chopped cooked turkey**
¾	**cup bottled roasted red sweet peppers, drained and chopped**
1½	**cups shredded mozzarella cheese (6 ounces)**

1. In a large bowl, combine greens and salad dressing; toss to coat. Set aside.

2. In a small bowl, combine olive oil and minced garlic. Lightly brush one side of each bread shell with oil mixture. Place bread shells, oiled sides up, on a very large baking sheet or two large baking sheets. Broil 4 to 5 inches from the heat for 2 to 3 minutes or until bread shells are light brown (if using two sheets, broil one sheet at a time).

3. Top bread shells with turkey and sweet peppers. Sprinkle with cheese. Broil about 2 minutes more or until cheese melts. Top with greens.

Per serving: 827 cal., 36 g total fat (13 g sat. fat), 116 mg chol., 1,287 mg sodium, 70 g carbo., 3 g fiber, 55 g pro.

Quick Tip If you like, use chopped cooked ham or chicken in place of the turkey in this recipe.

Tuna and Roasted Sweet Pepper Pizza [one]

Alfredo sauce, refrigerated or canned, is a very useful kitchen staple. Add pizza topping to the list of terrific dishes the creamy sauce helps create.

Prep: 20 minutes **Bake:** 17 minutes
Oven: 425°F **Makes:** 4 servings

- 1 **13.8-ounce package refrigerated pizza dough**
- 1 **10-ounce container refrigerated Alfredo pasta sauce**
- 1 **6- or 6.5-ounce can chunk white tuna (water pack), drained and broken into chunks**
- 1 **cup bottled roasted red sweet peppers, drained and cut into bite-size strips**
- 1 **tablespoon capers, drained (optional)**
- 1 **cup shredded mozzarella cheese (4 ounces)**

1. Preheat oven to 425°F. Lightly grease a large baking sheet. Unroll pizza dough and transfer to prepared baking sheet. Press dough with your hands into a 15×11-inch rectangle; build up edges slightly. Prick generously with a fork. Bake for 7 to 10 minutes or until lightly browned.

2. Spread Alfredo sauce over the hot crust. Top with tuna, sweet peppers, and, if desired, drained capers. Sprinkle with mozzarella cheese.

3. Bake for 10 to 12 minutes more or until cheese melts and pizza is heated through.

Per serving: 496 cal., 23 g total fat (12 g sat. fat), 78 mg chol., 1,185 mg sodium, 45 g carbo., 3 g fiber, 26 g pro.

Open-Face Crab Ciabatta ♥

Top crusty bread with dressed-up deli crab salad for this sophisticated sandwich.

Start to Finish: 15 minutes **Makes:** 6 servings

- 1 **½-pint container purchased deli crab salad**
- ½ **cup smoked almonds, chopped, or dried fruit-and-nut trail mix, chopped**
- 1 **teaspoon snipped fresh rosemary**
- 6 **½-inch slices ciabatta or French bread, toasted**

1. In a small bowl, combine crab salad, smoked almonds, and rosemary. To serve, spread on toasted bread.

Per serving: 192 cal., 11 g total fat (1 g sat. fat), 24 mg chol., 373 mg sodium, 15 g carbo., 2 g fiber, 9 g pro.

Quick Tip When purchasing fresh herbs, such as rosemary, look for a clean, fresh fragrance and bright color; avoid ones that show signs of wilting or browning around the edges. Store fresh herbs in the refrigerator, wrapped loosely in a damp paper towel and sealed in a plastic bag for up to 5 days.

Open-Face Crab Ciabatta

Eggplant Panini [one]

Why say sandwich when you can say panini? The Italian word sounds so much more enticing, with a promise of unexpected delights for the taste buds.

Start to Finish: 25 minutes **Makes:** 6 servings

- **1 cup torn arugula**
- **2 teaspoons red wine vinegar**
- **1 teaspoon olive oil**
- **⅓ cup seasoned fine dry bread crumbs**
- **2 tablespoons grated pecorino Romano cheese or Parmesan cheese**
- **1 egg**
- **1 tablespoon milk**
- **2 tablespoons all-purpose flour**
- **½ teaspoon salt**
- **1 medium eggplant, cut crosswise into ½-inch slices**
- **1 tablespoon olive oil**
- **3 ounces fresh mozzarella cheese, thinly sliced**
- **6 individual focaccia rolls or one 12-inch plain or seasoned Italian flatbread (focaccia),* halved horizontally**
- **1 large tomato, thinly sliced**

1. In a small bowl, toss together arugula, vinegar, and the 1 teaspoon oil; set aside. In a shallow dish, stir together the bread crumbs and Romano cheese. In another shallow dish, beat together the egg and milk. In a third shallow dish, stir together the flour and salt. Dip the eggplant slices into flour mixture to coat. Dip the eggplant slices into egg mixture; coat both sides with bread crumb mixture.

2. In a 12-inch nonstick skillet, heat the 1 tablespoon oil over medium heat. Add eggplant slices; cook for 6 to 8 minutes or until lightly browned, turning once. (Add more oil as necessary during cooking.) Top the eggplant with mozzarella cheese; reduce heat to low. Cook, covered, just until cheese begins to melt.

3. To serve, place the tomato slices on bottom halves of rolls. Top with eggplant slices, cheese sides up, and the arugula mixture. Add top halves of rolls. (Or place tomato slices on bottom half of bread. Top with eggplant slices, arugula mixture, tomato slices, and top half of bread. Cut into wedges.)

Per serving: 271 cal., 10 g total fat (3 g sat. fat), 53 mg chol., 687 mg sodium, 37 g carbo., 3 g fiber, 12 g pro.

*Note: For easier slicing, purchase focaccia that is at least 2½ inches thick.

Grilled Formaggio [one] Sandwiches

As easy as a grilled-cheese sandwich, this sophisticated sandwich melds sparkling green fresh spinach and nutty Scamorza cheese. Serve the sandwiches with your family's favorite canned tomato soup for a satisfying lunch or dinner.

Start to Finish: 30 minutes **Makes:** 4 servings

- **4 teaspoons butter or olive oil**
- **4 wedges Italian flatbread (focaccia) (about 1 inch thick), split in half horizontally***
- **8 slices Scamorza or provolone cheese (about 8 ounces)**
- **12 to 16 fresh spinach leaves, washed and patted dry**
- **¼ cup finely crumbled cooked bacon or turkey bacon**

1. Spread 1 teaspoon of the butter on one side of each slice of bread. Place two slices cheese, three to four spinach leaves, and 1 tablespoon cooked bacon between the unbuttered sides of the bread.

2. Place one sandwich in a large skillet or on a griddle. Cook over medium-high heat for 3 to 4 minutes on each side or until the cheese is melted and the bread is golden brown. If necessary to prevent overbrowning, reduce heat to medium or brush on extra butter.

3. Repeat with remaining sandwiches.

Per serving: 442 cal., 25 g total fat (14 g sat. fat), 55 mg chol., 657 mg sodium, 33 g carbo., 3 g fiber, 24 g pro.

*Note: If using thin focaccia bread, use two unsplit wedges to make each sandwich.

Quick Tip Purchase spinach with crisp, dark green leaves that have a fresh fragrance. Avoid leaves that are limp, damaged, or have yellow spots. To wash spinach, remove the stems and place the leaves in a large container full of cold water. Swish the leaves around using your hands, then let stand for a few minutes to allow any dirt and sand to sink to the bottom. Lift the leaves out of the water. If the spinach is very gritty, wash it a second time.

Grilled Formaggio Sandwiches

Thai-Style Veggie Pizza

Thai-Style Veggie Pizza ♥

An Italian bread shell, bottled peanut sauce, and purchased shredded carrot from the supermarket can help you put this pizza together in almost no time.

Start to Finish: 20 minutes **Makes:** 4 servings

- **2 8-inch Italian bread shells**
  Nonstick cooking spray
- **1 cup sliced fresh shiitake or button mushrooms**
- **2/3 cup fresh pea pods, cut into thin strips**
- **4 tablespoons coarsely shredded carrot**
- **4 tablespoons sliced green onion**
- **4 to 6 tablespoons bottled peanut sauce**
- **2 tablespoons chopped peanuts**
  Fresh cilantro leaves

1. Preheat oven to 450°F. Place bread shells on an ungreased baking sheet. Bake for 5 to 7 minutes or until lightly browned and crisp. Meanwhile, lightly coat a large nonstick skillet with cooking spray. Preheat skillet over medium heat. Add mushrooms, pea pods, and carrot; cook about 2 minutes or just until tender. Stir in green onion. Remove from heat.

2. Carefully divide peanut sauce between hot bread shells. Top with hot vegetable mixture; sprinkle with peanuts and cilantro leaves. Cut each pizza in half to serve.

Per serving: 283 cal., 10 g total fat (3 g sat. fat), 0 mg chol., 634 mg sodium, 40 g carbo., 3 g fiber, 11 g pro.

Egg and Asparagus Pizza ♥

When you're looking for something terrific to serve for breakfast or brunch, try this egg-and-veggie pizza with bacon or sausage and fresh fruit on the side.

Start to Finish: 20 minutes **Makes:** 6 servings

- **1 14-ounce Italian bread shell**
- **6 eggs**
- **1/3 cup milk**
- **2 teaspoons snipped fresh tarragon or oregano**
- **1/8 teaspoon salt**
- **1/8 teaspoon ground black pepper**
- **2 tablespoons butter or margarine**
- **1 cup asparagus bias-sliced into 1-inch pieces**
- **1 clove garlic, minced**
- **1 large tomato, halved and sliced**

1. Preheat oven to 450°F.

2. Place bread shell on an ungreased 12-inch pizza pan. Bake for 8 to 10 minutes or until heated through.

3. Meanwhile, in a medium bowl, beat together eggs, milk, tarragon, salt, and pepper; set aside. In a large skillet, melt butter over medium heat. Add asparagus and garlic; cook for 3 minutes. Pour egg mixture over asparagus mixture in skillet. Cook over medium heat, without stirring, until mixture begins to set on the bottom and around the edge.

4. Using a spatula, lift and fold the partially cooked egg mixture so the uncooked portion flows underneath. Continue cooking over medium heat for 2 to 3 minutes or until egg mixture is cooked through, but still glossy and moist. Remove from heat.

5. Arrange tomato slices evenly around the edge of the baked bread shell. Spoon scrambled egg mixture into the center. Serve immediately.

Per serving: 327 cal., 14 g total fat (4 g sat. fat), 227 mg chol., 575 mg sodium, 36 g carbo., 2 g fiber, 16 g pro.

Mediterranean Pita Pockets

Poppy seed dressing and Swiss cheese are enticing additions to this fruit and garbanzo bean sandwich.

Start to Finish: 20 minutes **Makes:** 4 sandwiches

- **1 15-ounce can garbanzo beans, rinsed and drained**
- **1 cup shredded spinach or lettuce**
- **2/3 cup seedless grapes, halved**
- **1/2 cup finely chopped red sweet pepper**
- **1/3 cup thinly sliced celery**
- **1/4 cup finely chopped onion**
- **1/4 cup mayonnaise or salad dressing**
- **2 tablespoons bottled poppy seed salad dressing or desired creamy salad dressing**
- **4 pita bread rounds, halved crosswise**
- **1/2 cup finely shredded Swiss cheese (2 ounces)**

1. In a large bowl, combine beans, spinach, grapes, sweet pepper, celery, and onion.

2. In a small bowl, stir together mayonnaise and salad dressing. Add to bean mixture; toss gently to coat.

3. To serve, spoon the bean mixture into pita bread halves. Top with cheese.

Per sandwich: 476 cal., 21 g total fat (5 g sat. fat), 21 mg chol., 857 mg sodium, 58 g carbo., 6 g fiber, 15 g pro.

Pizza Margherita

Pizza Margherita

Though this pizza was originally created in 1889 as a tribute to Queen Margherita of Savoy, you'll need no royal baking staff to make it. Up-to-date shortcuts include a focaccia crust and preshredded pizza cheese.

Start to Finish: 25 minutes **Bake:** 15 minutes
Oven: 425°F **Makes:** 4 servings

- 4 6- to 7-inch individual-size packaged Italian flatbreads (focaccia) or prebaked pizza crusts
- 1½ cups shredded pizza cheese
- ½ cup finely shredded fresh basil
- 4 fresh roma tomatoes or 2 medium tomatoes, cut into thin wedges or slices
- 2 to 3 teaspoons olive oil
- ¼ cup pine nuts (optional)

1. Preheat oven to 425°F.

2. Place pizza crusts on a very large baking sheet. Bake for 5 minutes. Remove from oven; sprinkle with cheese. Top with fresh basil. Arrange the tomato wedges in a circular pattern on top. Drizzle tomatoes with oil and, if desired, sprinkle with pine nuts.

3. Bake for 10 minutes more. Serve immediately.

Per serving: 369 cal., 15 g total fat (9 g sat. fat), 30 mg chol., 631 mg sodium, 41 g carbo., 5 g fiber, 19 g pro.

Mediterranean Alfredo Pizza

This gourmet pizza is topped with a creamy Alfredo sauce, fresh spinach, mushrooms, tomatoes, and artichoke hearts.

Prep: 30 minutes **Bake:** 15 minutes
Oven: 400°F **Makes:** 6 to 8 servings

- 1 16-ounce Italian bread shell crust
- ⅓ cup refrigerated Alfredo sauce
- 8 to 10 fresh spinach leaves
- 1 cup fresh mushrooms, sliced (about 3 ounces)
- 1 small tomato, thinly sliced
- 4 canned marinated artichoke hearts, quartered or sliced
- 1½ teaspoons snipped fresh oregano or ½ teaspoon dried oregano, crushed
- 1½ cups shredded mozzarella cheese

1. Preheat oven to 400°F. Spread bread shell with Alfredo sauce. Arrange spinach leaves over sauce; sprinkle with mushrooms. Arrange tomato slices and artichoke hearts over mushrooms. Sprinkle with oregano and mozzarella cheese.

2. Bake for 12 to 15 minutes or until cheese is bubbly around edges.

Per serving: 270 cal., 12 g total fat (4 g sat. fat), 28 mg chol., 384 mg sodium, 29 g carbo., 2 g fiber, 11 g pro.

Open-Face Portobello Sandwiches

Love bread-stuffed mushroom caps? Turn the same great flavors into an open-face sandwich that's ready in minutes.

Start to Finish: 25 minutes **Makes:** 4 servings

- 1 medium tomato, chopped (⅔ cup)
- 2 teaspoons snipped fresh basil, thyme, and/or oregano
- ⅛ teaspoon salt
- 2 medium fresh portobello mushrooms (about 4 inches in diameter)
- 1 teaspoon balsamic vinegar or red wine vinegar
- ½ teaspoon olive oil
- ½ of a 12-inch Italian flatbread (focaccia), quartered, or one-half of a 12-inch thin-crust Italian bread shell
- Finely shredded Parmesan cheese (optional)

1. Preheat broiler. In a small mixing bowl, combine tomato, basil, and salt; set aside.

2. Clean mushrooms; cut off stems even with caps. Discard stems. Combine vinegar and oil; gently brush mixture over the mushrooms. Place mushrooms on the unheated rack of the broiler pan.

3. Broil mushrooms 4 to 5 inches from the heat for 6 to 8 minutes or just until tender, turning once. Drain mushrooms on paper towels. Thinly slice mushrooms.

4. Place bread on a baking sheet. Place under broiler for 2 to 3 minutes or until heated through.

5. To serve, top toasted bread with mushroom slices and tomato mixture. If desired, top with Parmesan cheese.

Per serving: 161 cal., 3 g total fat (1 g sat. fat), 2 mg chol., 71 mg sodium, 29 g carbo., 3 g fiber, 7 g pro.

Mediterranean Alfredo Pizza

Fresh Tomato Pizza with Pesto `one`

Meatless pizzas get revved-up flavor from pesto and olives.

Prep: 20 minutes **Bake:** 10 minutes **Oven:** 425°F
Makes: 6 to 8 servings

- ½   **cup purchased pesto**
- 1   **16-ounce Italian bread shell or one 12-inch purchased prebaked pizza crust**
- 3   **ripe medium tomatoes, thinly sliced**
     Freshly ground black pepper
- 2   **cups shredded Monterey Jack or mozzarella cheese (8 ounces)**
- 1   **2.25-ounce can sliced pitted ripe olives, drained (about ⅔ cup)**

1. Preheat oven to 425°F. Spread pesto evenly over bread shell. Place on a large pizza pan or baking sheet. Arrange tomato slices on top. Sprinkle with pepper. Top with cheese and olives.

2. Bake for 10 to 15 minutes or until cheese melts and tomatoes are warm. Cut into wedges.

Per serving: 468 cal., 27 g total fat (10 g sat. fat), 42 mg chol., 831 mg sodium, 38 g carbo., 2 g fiber, 22 g pro.

Peasant Pizza with Goat Cheese ♥ `one`

Tired of heavy, abundantly cheesy pizzas that weigh you down? Just a little goat cheese (sometimes labeled chèvre) goes a long way to add a creamy, almost decadent richness to pizza without loading on extra fat and calories.

Start to Finish: 25 minutes **Bake:** 12 minutes
Oven: 400°F **Makes:** 6 servings

- 1   **16-ounce Italian bread shell**
- 2   **ounces cream cheese**
- 2   **ounces semisoft goat cheese or feta cheese, crumbled (about ¼ cup)**
- 1   **clove garlic, minced**
- ⅛   **teaspoon ground black pepper**
- 3   **plum tomatoes, thinly sliced**
- 1   **small yellow, orange, or green sweet pepper, cut into thin bite-size strips**
- 2   **tablespoons snipped fresh basil**

1. Preheat oven to 400°F. Place the Italian bread shell on a baking sheet.

2. In a small mixing bowl, stir together the cream cheese, goat cheese or feta, garlic, and black pepper. Spread cheese mixture over the bread shell. Place the tomato slices and sweet pepper strips over the cheese mixture.

3. Bake about 12 minutes or until heated through. Sprinkle with fresh basil. To serve, cut into wedges.

Per serving: 281 cal., 11 g total fat (4 g sat. fat), 21 mg chol., 494 mg sodium, 36 g carbo., 2 g fiber, 25 g pro.

Peppery Artichoke Pitas ♥

Black-eyed peas add texture and substance to these vegetarian pita pockets. To prepare the sandwiches to take on the go, wrap them tightly in waxed paper. Add some baby carrots or some pretzels for a healthy—and convenient—lunch.

Start to Finish: 20 minutes **Makes:** 6 sandwiches

- 1   **15-ounce can black-eyed peas, rinsed and drained**
- 1   **13.75- to 14-ounce can artichoke hearts, drained and cut up**
- ½   **cup packaged torn mixed salad greens**
- ¼   **cup bottled creamy Italian salad dressing or creamy garlic salad dressing**
- ¼   **teaspoon ground black pepper**
- 1   **small tomato, sliced**
- 3   **pita bread rounds, halved crosswise***

1. In a medium bowl, combine drained black-eyed peas, drained artichoke hearts, mixed greens, salad dressing, and pepper. Place tomato slices inside pita bread halves. Spoon artichoke mixture into pita bread halves.

Per sandwich: 211 cal., 5 g total fat (1 g sat. fat), 0 mg chol., 746 mg sodium, 34 g carbo., 6 g fiber, 8 g pro.

***Note:** For softer pita breads, wrap the pita bread rounds in foil and warm in a 350°F oven for 10 minutes. Soft pita bread rounds are easier to split.

Quick Tip To renew salad greens that have begun to wilt, place them in ice water and 2 tablespoons lemon juice. Cover and refrigerate the greens for 1 hour; drain. If you have time, wrap the moist greens in dry paper towels and refrigerate for about 4 hours.

Peppery Artichoke Pitas

Roasted Pepper and Artichoke Pizza

Nutty Cucumber Sandwich ♥ [one]

Purchase chèvre cheese that has been rolled in cracked black pepper to add another flavor dimension to this sandwich.

Start to Finish: 15 minutes **Makes:** 4 sandwiches

- ½ **cup fresh snow pea pods, trimmed**
- ½ **of a medium cucumber**
- 8 **thin slices rye bread**
- 3 **to 4 ounces soft goat cheese (chèvre)**
- ⅓ **cup seasoned roasted soy nuts (such as ranch- or garlic-seasoned)**
- 1 **medium tomato, thinly sliced**
  Salt

1. In a covered small saucepan, cook the pea pods in a small amount of boiling lightly salted water for 2 minutes. Drain; rinse with cold water. Drain again. Place pea pods in a small bowl; chill until needed.

2. Use a vegetable peeler to remove a few lengthwise strips of peel from the cucumber. Thinly slice cucumber.

3. Spread one side of each bread slice with cheese. Sprinkle four of the bread slices with soy nuts, gently pressing nuts into the cheese. Top soy nuts with cucumber slices, tomato slices, and pea pods. Sprinkle with salt. Top with remaining bread slices, cheese sides down.

Per serving: 276 cal., 9 g total fat (4 g sat. fat), 10 mg chol., 540 mg sodium, 36 g carbo., 6 g fiber, 14 g pro.

Roasted Pepper and Artichoke Pizza ♥ [one]

No leftover cooked chicken? Look for frozen chopped cooked chicken in your supermarket's freezer case.

Prep: 20 minutes **Bake:** 7 minutes + 13 minutes
Oven: 425°F **Makes:** 8 servings

- 1 **6- to 6.5-ounce package pizza crust mix**
- 1 **teaspoon dried oregano or basil, crushed**
- ½ **cup pizza sauce**
- 1 **cup coarsely chopped or shredded cooked chicken (about 5 ounces)**
- 1 **6-ounce jar marinated artichoke hearts, drained and coarsely chopped**
- 1 **cup roasted red and/or yellow sweet peppers, cut into strips**
- ¼ **cup sliced green onion or chopped red onion**
- ½ **cup shredded part-skim mozzarella cheese (2 ounces)**
- 4 **ounces semisoft goat cheese (chèvre), crumbled**

1. Preheat oven to 425°F. Grease a large baking sheet; set aside. Prepare pizza crust according to package directions, except stir oregano into pizza crust mix. With floured hands, pat dough into a 15×10-inch rectangle on prepared baking sheet, building up edges slightly (crust will be thin). Bake for 7 minutes.

2. Spread pizza sauce evenly over crust. Top with chicken, drained artichoke hearts, sweet peppers, and green onion. Top with mozzarella cheese and goat cheese.

3. Bake for 13 to 15 minutes more or until edges of crust are golden brown.

Per serving: 203 cal., 9 g total fat (3 g sat. fat), 27 mg chol., 410 mg sodium, 20 g carbo., 1 g fiber, 12 g pro.

Veggie Salad in A Pocket ♥

The squash, broccoli, and tomatoes soften and sweeten as they marinate in the salad dressing.

Prep: 20 minutes **Chill:** 2 to 24 hours
Makes: 4 servings

- 1 **cup chopped yellow summer squash and/or zucchini**
- ¾ **cup chopped broccoli**
- 2 **plum tomatoes, seeded and chopped (about ⅔ cup)**
- 8 **pitted kalamata or ripe olives, chopped**
- 2 **tablespoons snipped fresh flat-leaf parsley**
- 2 **tablespoons bottled fat-free Italian salad dressing**
- 2 **6- to 7-inch whole wheat pita bread rounds or four 6- to 7-inch whole wheat flour tortillas**
- ½ **cup Spicy Navy Bean Hummus**

1. In a medium bowl, combine squash, broccoli, tomatoes, olives, and parsley; toss with salad dressing. Cover and chill for 2 to 24 hours.

2. If using pita bread, cut rounds in half crosswise; open pita halves to make pockets. Spread the inside of each pita bread pocket or one side of each tortilla with 2 tablespoons of the Spicy Navy Bean Hummus.

3. Spoon chilled vegetable mixture into pita pockets or onto tortillas. If using tortillas, fold or roll them.

Spicy Navy Bean Hummus: In a food processor, combine one 15- to 19-ounce can navy or cannellini beans (white kidney beans), rinsed and drained; ¼ cup bottled fat-free Italian salad dressing; and 1 tablespoon spicy brown mustard. Cover and process until smooth and spreadable. (Or mash beans with a potato masher or fork. Stir in salad dressing and mustard.) Transfer to an airtight storage container. Cover and chill for up to 1 week. Makes 1⅓ cups.

Per serving: 166 cal., 2 g total fat (0 g sat. fat), 0 mg chol., 599 mg sodium, 31 g carbo., 6 g fiber, 7 g pro.

Veggie Salad in a Pocket

Green Onion Parker House Biscuits, **page 303**

Layered Southwest
Bean Salad, **page 284**

Basil and Tomato
Pasta Salad, **page 295**

Crumb-Topped
Vegetables, **page 297**

Tasty Side Dishes

The salads, vegetables,
and breads that round
out a meal usually
command less thought
and attention than the
main dish, but they are
still important. Here
are easy and creative
recipes for side dishes
that are both nutritious
and satisfying.

Fennel, Carrot, and Spinach Toss

Grapefruit-Avocado Salad

Fennel, Carrot, and Spinach Toss one

The heat of the cooked carrots and fennel wilts the raw spinach just enough to make it easy to serve and eat.

Prep: 20 minutes **Cook:** 15 minutes
Makes: 4 to 6 servings

- 1½ **cups packaged peeled baby carrots**
- 1 **medium fennel bulb, trimmed and cut into thin wedges (about 1 pound)**
- 1 **tablespoon olive oil**
- ½ **teaspoon salt**
- ¼ **teaspoon cracked black pepper**
- 2 **tablespoons olive oil**
- 1 **10-ounce package prewashed spinach**
- ¼ **cup finely shredded Parmesan cheese (1 ounce)**

1. In a large bowl, combine carrots and fennel. Add the 1 tablespoon oil, the salt, and pepper; toss to coat.

2. In a large skillet, heat the 2 tablespoons oil over medium heat. Add vegetable mixture and cook for 15 to 20 minutes or until vegetables are tender, stirring occasionally. Remove pan from heat. Gradually add spinach to skillet, tossing until spinach wilts.

3. Transfer vegetable mixture to a serving plate. Sprinkle with Parmesan cheese.

Per serving: 134 cal., 11 g total fat (1 g sat. fat), 0 mg chol., 408 mg sodium, 9 g carbo., 3 g fiber, 3 g pro.

Grapefruit-Avocado Salad ♥

The versatile Orange Vinaigrette works with just about any combination of tossed salad ingredients.

Start to Finish: 15 minutes
Makes: 6 servings

- 4 **cups packaged fresh baby spinach**
- 1 **grapefruit, peeled and sectioned**
- 1 **small avocado, halved, seeded, peeled, and sliced**
- 1 **cup canned sliced beets**
- 1 **tablespoon sliced almonds, toasted**
  Orange Vinaigrette

1. Divide spinach among 4 salad plates. Arrange grapefruit, avocado, and beets on spinach. Top with almonds. Drizzle with Orange Vinaigrette.

Orange Vinaigrette: In a screw-top jar, combine 1 teaspoon finely shredded orange peel, ⅓ cup orange juice, 2 teaspoons red wine vinegar, 2 teaspoons salad oil, ⅛ teaspoon salt, and a dash of ground black pepper. Cover and shake well.

Per serving: 106 cal., 7 g total fat (1 g sat. fat), 0 mg chol., 122 mg sodium, 11 g carbo., 4 g fiber, 2 g pro.

Spinach Salad with Strawberries

Watercress adds peppery notes to the popular fruit-and-spinach salad. Serve this recipe to add sparkle to just about any meal.

Start to Finish: 20 minutes **Makes:** 4 servings

- **4** **cups torn fresh spinach**
- **1** **cup watercress leaves**
- **1** **cup sliced fresh strawberries**
- **½** **of a small red onion, thinly sliced**
- **½** **cup bottled oil and vinegar salad dressing**

1. In a large salad bowl, combine spinach, watercress, strawberries, and onion. Drizzle dressing over salad; toss to coat.

Per serving: 168 cal., 16 g total fat (2 g sat. fat), 0 mg chol., 468 mg sodium, 8 g carbo., 2 g fiber, 2 g pro.

Gingery Sugar Snap Peas

A light coating of sweet peach preserves, soy sauce, and ginger will tempt even the most finicky eater to enjoy the pleasures of crisp-tender sugar snap peas.

Start to Finish: 15 minutes **Makes:** 6 servings

- **3** **cups fresh sugar snap peas or loose-pack frozen sugar snap peas**
- **1** **tablespoon butter or margarine**
- **1** **tablespoon peach preserves**
- **1** **teaspoon soy sauce**
-    **Dash ground ginger**
-    **Dash black pepper**

1. Remove strings and tips from fresh sugar snap peas. In a covered medium saucepan, cook fresh peas in a small amount of boiling salted water for 2 to 4 minutes or until crisp-tender. (Or cook frozen sugar snap peas according to package directions.) Drain well; set aside.

2. In the same saucepan melt butter over low heat; stir in preserves, soy sauce, ginger, and pepper. Return sugar snap peas to saucepan, stirring to coat.

Per serving: 78 cal., 2 g total fat (1 g sat. fat), 5 mg chol., 85 mg sodium, 11 g carbo., 3 g fiber, 3 g pro.

Creamy Lemon-Pepper Coleslaw

Cabbage holds its crispness overnight when chilled so you can fix the salad while you're preparing dinner tonight and have it ready for a fast meal tomorrow night.

Prep: 10 minutes **Chill:** 2 hours **Makes:** 6 servings

- **½** **cup mayonnaise or salad dressing**
- **1** **teaspoon lemon-pepper seasoning**
- **½** **teaspoon dried thyme, crushed**
- **5** **cups packaged shredded cabbage with carrot (coleslaw mix)**
- **¼** **cup shelled sunflower seeds**

1. In a large salad bowl, combine mayonnaise, lemon-pepper seasoning, and thyme. Stir in shredded cabbage and sunflower seeds. Toss lightly to coat. Cover and chill for 2 to 24 hours.

Per serving: 188 cal., 18 g total fat (2 g sat. fat), 7 mg chol., 328 mg sodium, 5 g carbo., 2 g fiber, 2 g pro.

Layered Southwest Bean Salad

A twist of lime and the kick of peppers turns the familiar layered salad into a bronco-busting Tex-Mex favorite.

Prep: 30 minutes **Chill:** 2 to 24 hours
Makes: 8 to 12 servings

- **4** **cups shredded iceberg lettuce**
- **2** **15-ounce cans black beans, rinsed and drained**
- **1** **cup chopped red onion**
- **1** **4-ounce can diced green chile peppers, drained**
- **2** **cups chopped red and/or green sweet pepper**
- **2** **tablespoons snipped fresh cilantro**
- **1½** **cups dairy sour cream**
- **2** **tablespoons lime juice**
- **1** **teaspoon chili powder**
- **½** **teaspoon salt**
- **¼** **teaspoon garlic powder**
- **¾** **cup chopped seeded tomato**

1. Place the lettuce in a deep 3-quart serving bowl. Layer drained beans, red onion, drained chile peppers, sweet pepper, and cilantro on top of lettuce.

2. For the dressing, in a small bowl, stir together sour cream, lime juice, chili powder, salt, and garlic powder.

3. Cover salad and dressing; chill separately for at least 2 hours or up to 24 hours.

4. Drizzle dressing over salad; gently toss salad to coat vegetables with dressing. Sprinkle with chopped tomato.

Per serving: 173 cal., 8 g total fat (5 g sat. fat), 16 mg chol., 492 mg sodium, 22 g carbo., 7 g fiber, 9 g pro.

Layered Southwest Bean Salad

Orange-Asparagus Salad

Orange-Asparagus Salad ♥ 🔲

A citrus-and-mustard dressing brings out the best in this medley of garden-fresh asparagus and juicy orange sections.

Start to Finish: 20 minutes **Makes:** 2 servings

- **8 ounces fresh asparagus**
- **1 medium orange, peeled and sliced crosswise**
- **2 tablespoons orange juice**
- **2 teaspoons olive oil**
- **½ teaspoon Dijon-style mustard**
- **⅛ teaspoon salt**
- **Dash ground black pepper**

1. Snap off and discard woody bases from asparagus. If desired, scrape off scales. Cut stems into 2-inch-long pieces. In a covered small saucepan, cook asparagus in a small amount of boiling water for 1 minute; drain. Cool immediately in a bowl of ice water. Drain on paper towels.

2. Cut orange slices into two-section pieces; set aside.

3. For the dressing, in a medium bowl, whisk together orange juice, oil, mustard, salt, and pepper. Add asparagus and orange sections; stir gently to coat. Serve immediately. (Or cover and chill for up to 6 hours.)

Per serving: 94 cal., 5 g total fat (1 g sat. fat), 0 mg chol., 177 mg sodium, 12 g carbo., 3 g fiber, 2 g pro.

Romaine with Creamy Garlic Dressing

Cover and chill any leftover salad dressing for up to 3 days. It makes a good topper for any greens or vegetables.

Start to Finish: 5 minutes **Makes:** 4 servings

- **½ cup plain yogurt**
- **⅓ cup bottled Italian salad dressing**
- **1 garlic clove, minced, or ½ teaspoon bottled minced garlic**
- **4 cups torn romaine lettuce**
- **¼ cup finely shredded Parmesan cheese**

1. For the dressing, in a small bowl, stir together yogurt, salad dressing, and garlic.

2. Arrange lettuce on 4 salad plates. Drizzle each salad with 1 tablespoon of the dressing. Sprinkle with Parmesan cheese.

Per serving: 257 cal., 19 g total fat (7 g sat. fat), 26 mg chol., 744 mg sodium, 7 g carbo., 1 g fiber, 15 g pro.

Quick Tip When purchasing garlic, look for firm, plump bulbs with dry, papery skins. Avoid heads with soft, shriveled, or sprouting cloves. Store fresh garlic in an open container in a cool, dry place for 1 to 2 months.

Insalata Mista

Insalata Mista

This Italian mixed greens salad is generously topped with fresh mozzarella, a specialty cheese worth seeking for its hallmark sweet, mild flavor and soft texture. Look for it at larger supermarkets or specialty food stores.

Start to Finish: 15 minutes
Makes: 4 servings

- **4 cups torn mixed greens (such as radicchio, spinach, arugula, and/or chicory)**
- **1 cup yellow and/or red cherry tomatoes, halved**
- **¼ cup snipped fresh basil**
- **½ cup Greek olives**
- **Italian Vinaigrette**
- **3 ounces thinly sliced fresh mozzarella cheese**

1. In a large mixing bowl, toss together the mixed greens, tomatoes, basil, and olives. Drizzle Italian Vinaigrette over salad; toss to coat. Top with mozzarella cheese.

Italian Vinaigrette: In a screw-top jar, combine 2 tablespoons olive oil or salad oil, 2 tablespoons balsamic vinegar, 2 teaspoons snipped fresh oregano or basil, ⅛ teaspoon salt, and ⅛ teaspoon ground black pepper. Cover the jar; shake well. Serve immediately or cover and store in the refrigerator up to 2 weeks. Shake before serving. Makes about ¼ cup.

Per serving: 169 cal., 14 g total fat (4 g sat. fat), 16 mg chol., 255 mg sodium, 7 g carbo., 2 g fiber, 6 g pro.

Quick Bread Salad

Mexican Rice [one]

This rice side dish is packed with veggies and not too spicy. Another time try it with green beans, sweet peppers, or broccoli in place of the carrots and peas.

Prep: 10 minutes **Cook:** 15 minutes
Stand: 5 minutes **Makes:** 8 servings

1½ **cups uncooked long grain white rice**
1 **14.5-ounce can Mexican-style stewed tomatoes, undrained and cut up finely**
1 **14-ounce can chicken broth**
½ **cup water**
½ **cup chopped carrot (1 medium)**
½ **cup frozen peas or chopped fresh zucchini**
 Lime wedges (optional)

1. In a large saucepan, stir together rice, undrained tomatoes, broth, the water, and carrot. Bring to boiling; reduce heat. Cover and simmer for 15 to 20 minutes or until rice is tender and most of the liquid is absorbed.

2. Stir peas into rice. Let stand, covered, for 5 minutes. Fluff with a fork before serving. If desired, garnish with lime wedges.

Per serving: 155 cal., 0 g total fat (0 g sat. fat), 1 mg chol., 391 mg sodium, 33 g carbo., 1 g fiber, 4 g pro.

Quick Bread Salad

Bread salad—called panzanella in Italy—is a great use for day-old bread. Serve the salad alongside platters of fresh cheeses and pickled vegetables for an easy-going supper.

Start to Finish: 20 minutes **Makes:** 6 servings

¼ **cup olive oil**
3 **tablespoons red wine vinegar**
3 **tablespoons snipped fresh oregano**
½ **teaspoon sugar**
¼ **teaspoon salt**
¼ **teaspoon ground black pepper**
4 **ounces whole wheat sourdough or other country-style bread, cut into 1½-inch cubes**
½ **of a 10-ounce package Italian-style torn mixed salad greens (about 5 cups)**
1 **medium tomato, cut into thin wedges**
¼ **cup halved yellow cherry tomatoes or yellow sweet pepper cut into ½-inch pieces**
½ **cup Greek black olives or other olives**

1. For the dressing, in a screw-top jar, combine olive oil, wine vinegar, oregano, sugar, salt, and black pepper. Cover and shake well.

2. In a large salad bowl, combine bread cubes, mixed greens, tomato wedges, cherry tomatoes, and olives. Add dressing; toss gently to coat. Serve immediately.

Per serving: 151 cal., 11 g total fat (1 g sat. fat), 0 mg chol., 238 mg sodium, 13 g carbo., 1 g fiber, 2 g pro.

Tabbouleh With Edamame and Feta

Tabbouleh with Edamame and Feta [one]

Bulgur, the main ingredient in tabbouleh, is made from cracked whole wheat that has been soaked then baked. It is high in fiber and has a pleasant nutty flavor.

Start to Finish: 25 minutes
Makes: 6 servings

2½	**cups water**
1¼	**cups bulgur**
¼	**cup lemon juice**
3	**tablespoons purchased basil pesto**
2	**cups fresh or thawed frozen shelled sweet soybeans (edamame)**
2	**cups cherry tomatoes, cut up**
⅓	**cup crumbled feta cheese**
⅓	**cup thinly sliced green onion**
2	**tablespoons snipped fresh parsley**
¼	**teaspoon ground black pepper**
	Fresh parsley sprigs (optional)

1. In a medium saucepan, bring the water to boiling; add uncooked bulgur. Return to boiling; reduce heat. Cover and simmer about 15 minutes or until most of the liquid is absorbed. Remove from heat. Transfer to a large bowl.

2. In a small bowl, whisk together lemon juice and pesto. Add to bulgur along with soybeans, cherry tomatoes, feta cheese, green onions, the snipped parsley, and pepper. Toss gently to combine. If desired, garnish with parsley sprigs.

Per serving: 320 cal., 13 g total fat (2 g sat. fat), 8 mg chol., 175 mg sodium, 37 g carbo., 10 g fiber, 18 g pro.

Make-Ahead Directions: Prepare as directed. Cover and chill for up to 4 hours.

Quick Tip When purchasing green onions (also called scallions), look for crisp, bright green tops and a firm, white base. Generally, green onions that are no larger than ½ inch in diameter taste the best. Store green onions, unwashed, in a plastic bag in the refrigerator for up to 5 days.

Confetti Summer Salad

Confetti Summer Salad ♥ [one]

Fresh, crisp, and colorful—just what you're looking for in a summer salad. The fresh veggies in this dish are most abundant during summer months, but are available all year long so the salad never goes out of season.

Prep: 30 minutes **Chill:** 4 to 24 hours
Makes: 8 servings.

- **4 medium ears fresh corn or 2 cups frozen whole kernel corn, thawed**
- **4 baby zucchini, thinly sliced, or ½ of a small zucchini, halved lengthwise and thinly sliced (½ cup)**
- **2 medium tomatoes, seeded and chopped**
- **2 green onions, sliced**
- **1 medium yellow bell pepper, seeded and chopped**
- **1 medium red bell pepper, seeded and chopped**
- **½ cup bottled clear Italian salad dressing**
- **¼ teaspoon cayenne pepper (optional)**
  Fresh thyme (optional)

1. If using fresh corn, in a large covered saucepan, cook ears of corn in a small amount of boiling water for 4 minutes. Drain; rinse with cold water to cool. When cool enough to handle, cut corn from cobs (you should have about 2 cups of corn kernels).

2. In a large bowl, combine corn, zucchini, tomatoes, green onions, sweet pepper, salad dressing, and, if desired, cayenne pepper. Cover and chill for 4 to 24 hours, stirring occasionally. If desired, garnish with fresh thyme.

Per serving: 99 cal., 5 g total fat (1 g sat. fat), 0 mg chol., 253 mg sodium, 14 g carbo., 2 g fiber, 2 g pro.

Quick Tip To remove kernels from the cob, begin by cutting a small portion off the tip to make it flat. Holding the stem end, hold the cob upright on its flat end. Set it on a plate or cutting board and use a firm-bladed knife to cut downward, about 3 to 4 rows at a time.

Mushroom and Herb Rice ▣

The pairing of mushrooms with rice and Italian seasoning makes a savory side dish that takes almost no time to go from skillet to plate.

Start to Finish: 15 minutes **Makes:** 4 servings

- 1   **tablespoon olive oil or butter**
- 3   **cups packaged sliced fresh mushrooms (8 ounces)**
- 1   **8.8-ounce pouch cooked whole grain brown rice or long grain rice**
- ⅓   **cup shredded carrot**
- 2   **green onions, chopped**
- 2   **tablespoons water**
- 1   **teaspoon dried Italian seasoning, crushed**
- ¼   **teaspoon salt**
- ¼   **cup finely shredded Parmesan cheese (1 ounce)**

1. In a large skillet, heat oil over medium heat. Add mushrooms; cook until almost tender.

2. Add cooked rice, carrot, green onions, the water, Italian seasoning, and salt. Cook until heated through and vegetables are tender, stirring occasionally. Top with Parmesan cheese.

Per serving: 299 cal., 8 g total fat (3 g sat. fat), 4 mg chol., 241 mg sodium, 50 g carbo., 3 g fiber, 11 g pro.

Savory Couscous ♥ ▣

Add a garden-fresh note to any meal by jazzing up couscous with mushrooms, carrots, green onions, and dried basil. Bouillon granules give the couscous a good punch of flavor.

Start to Finish: 20 minutes **Makes:** 8 servings

- 2   **cups water**
- 1½ **cups sliced fresh mushrooms**
- ½   **cup shredded carrot**
- ⅓   **cup thinly sliced green onion**
- 1   **tablespoon butter or margarine**
- 2   **teaspoons instant chicken bouillon granules**
- ½   **teaspoon dried basil or thyme, crushed**
- 1   **10-ounce package quick-cooking couscous**

1. In a medium saucepan, combine the water, mushrooms, carrot, green onions, butter, bouillon granules, and basil; bring to boiling. Stir in couscous. Remove from heat.

2. Cover; let stand about 5 minutes or until liquid is absorbed. Fluff with a fork before serving.

Per serving: 158 cal., 2 g total fat (1 g sat. fat), 4 mg chol., 241 mg sodium, 29 g carbo., 2 g fiber, 5 g pro.

Quick Tip Store dried herbs in a cool, dark place for up to 6 months. To keep dried herbs tasting their best, be sure they are not exposed to air, light, or heat. The more airtight the storage container (screw-top glass jars work best), the longer the herbs will retain their flavor.

Savory Couscous

Beans, Barley, and Tomatoes

Beans, Barley, and Tomatoes

Find frozen green soybeans, also called edamame, in the frozen section of large supermarkets or at natural food stores.

Start to Finish: 30 minutes **Makes:** 4 servings

- 1 **14-ounce can vegetable broth or chicken broth**
- 1 **teaspoon Greek seasoning or garam masala**
- 1 **cup frozen green soybeans (shelled edamame)**
- ¾ **cup quick-cooking barley**
- ½ **cup packaged shredded carrot (1 medium)**
- 4 **cups packaged prewashed fresh spinach leaves**
- 4 **small to medium tomatoes, sliced**

1. In a medium saucepan, bring broth and seasoning to boiling. Add soybeans and barley. Return to boiling; reduce heat. Simmer, covered, for 12 minutes. Stir carrot into barley mixture.

2. Meanwhile, arrange spinach on 4 salad plates; top with tomato slices. Using a slotted spoon, spoon barley mixture over tomatoes (or drain barley mixture; spoon over tomato slices).

Per serving: 171 cal., 3 g total fat (0 g sat. fat), 0 mg chol., 484 mg sodium, 33 g carbo., 10 g fiber, 9 g pro.

Penne with Snap Peas And Tomatoes ♥

Sweet sugar snap peas, dried tomatoes, and garlic enliven this tasty pasta side dish. Cook the peas with the pasta to save washing another saucepan.

Start to Finish: 30 minutes **Makes:** 4 servings

- 8 **ounces dried penne (4 cups)**
- 8 **ounces fresh sugar snap peas, trimmed and halved lengthwise (about 2 cups)**
- 3 **oil-packed dried tomatoes, drained and snipped, reserving 1 tablespoon drained oil**
- 2 **cloves garlic, minced, or 1 teaspoon bottled minced garlic**
  Salt and ground black pepper

1. In a large saucepan, cook pasta according to package directions, adding peas for the last 3 minutes of the cooking time; drain.

2. Return pasta and peas to pan. Add drained tomatoes, reserved oil, and garlic; toss to coat. Season to taste with salt and pepper.

Per serving: 270 cal., 5 g total fat (1 g sat. fat), 0 mg chol., 157 mg sodium, 47 g carbo., 3 g fiber, 9 g pro.

Corn and Bean Quinoa Pilaf

Corn and Bean Quinoa Pilaf ♥ one

Quinoa is a grain-like seed that has been cultivated continuously in the Andes for more than 5,000 years. Not only does quinoa add a crunchy texture and nutty flavor to dishes, it's also high in protein and rich in calcium.

Start to Finish: 30 minutes **Makes:** 4 servings

- 1   teaspoon olive oil
- ½   cup chopped onion
- 2   cloves garlic, minced
- ½   cup quinoa
- 1   cup reduced-sodium chicken broth or vegetable broth
- ⅔   cup water
- ¾   cup Black Bean, Corn, and Jicama Salsa
  Fresh jalapeño chile pepper slices* (optional)

1. In a large saucepan, heat oil over medium heat. Add onion and garlic; cook about 5 minutes or until onion is tender, stirring occasionally. Add quinoa; cook and stir about 3 minutes or until quinoa is lightly browned.

2. Add broth and the water. Bring to boiling; reduce heat. Cover and simmer for 15 to 20 minutes or until all of the liquid is absorbed and the quinoa is tender. Add Black Bean, Corn, and Jicama Salsa to quinoa mixture; heat through. If desired, garnish with jalapeño slices.

Black Bean, Corn, and Jicama Salsa: In a medium bowl, toss together 1 15-ounce can black beans (rinsed and drained), 1 cup thawed frozen corn, 1 chopped large tomato, ½ cup chopped jicama, 2 thinly sliced green onions, 1 finely chopped jalapeño, 2 tablespoons snipped fresh cilantro, 2 tablespoons lime juice, ¼ teaspoon salt, and ¼ teaspoon ground cumin.

Nutrition Facts Per side-dish serving: 128 cal., 3 g total fat (0 g sat. fat), 0 mg chol., 227 mg sodium, 23 g carbo., 3 g fiber, 6 g pro.

Quick Tip Look for quinoa at a health food store or in the grains section of a large supermarket.

***Note:** Because chile peppers contain volatile oils that can burn your skin and eyes, avoid direct contact with them as much as possible. When working with chile peppers, wear plastic or rubber gloves. If your bare hands do touch the chile peppers, wash your hands and nails well with soap and warm water.

Basil and Tomato Pasta Salad

Barbecued Limas

A spunky barbecue sauce that starts with canned soup makes this old-fashioned bean-and-bacon combination a tasty reason to get out the can opener.

Start to Finish: 25 minutes   **Makes:** 6 servings

1	**16-ounce package frozen baby lima beans**
4	**slices bacon, cut into ½-inch pieces**
½	**cup chopped onion**
1	**teaspoon bottled minced garlic (2 cloves)**
1	**10.75-ounce can condensed tomato soup**
2	**tablespoons packed brown sugar**
1	**tablespoon white vinegar**
1	**tablespoon Worcestershire sauce**
2	**teaspoons yellow mustard**
1	**teaspoon chili powder**

1. In a large saucepan, cook lima beans according to package directions; drain and set aside.

2. Meanwhile, in another large saucepan, cook bacon, onion, and garlic over medium heat until bacon is brown and onion is tender. Stir in soup, brown sugar, vinegar, Worcestershire sauce, mustard, and chili powder. Bring to boiling; reduce heat. Cover and simmer for 5 minutes.

3. Stir cooked lima beans into soup mixture; heat through.

Per serving: 195 cal., 3 g total fat (1 g sat. fat), 5 mg chol., 487 mg sodium, 34 g carbo., 6 g fiber, 9 g pro.

Kale Sauté ♥

If you enjoy kale in salads, you'll love this wilted version that's sprinkled with toasted bread crumbs, Worcestershire sauce, and a squeeze of lemon.

Start to Finish: 15 minutes   **Makes:** 4 servings

12	**ounces kale, cut or torn into 1- to 2-inch pieces (about 12 cups)**
6	**teaspoons olive oil**
¼	**cup soft sourdough or French loaf bread crumbs**
⅛	**teaspoon ground black pepper**
1	**teaspoon Worcestershire sauce for chicken**
	Lemon wedges (optional)

1. Rinse kale leaves thoroughly under cold running water. Drain well; set aside.

2. In a small skillet, heat 2 teaspoons of the oil over medium heat. Add bread crumbs; cook and stir for 1 to 2 minutes or until browned. Season with pepper; set aside.

3. In a large nonstick skillet, heat the remaining 4 teaspoons oil. Add kale; cover and cook for 1 minute. Uncover. Cook and stir about 1 minute more or just until wilted.

4. Transfer kale to a serving dish. Drizzle with Worcestershire sauce. Sprinkle with the bread crumbs. If desired, squeeze lemon wedges over all.

Per serving: 89 cal., 5 g total fat (1 g sat. fat), 0 mg chol., 53 mg sodium, 9 g carbo., 4 g fiber, 3 g pro.

Basil and Tomato Pasta Salad ♥ [one]

To get the best flavor if you use dried herbs, chill the salad for at least two hours so they rehydrate.

Prep: 30 minutes   **Chill:** 2 to 4 hours
Makes: 16 servings

1	**pound dried gemelli pasta**
1	**pound red and/or yellow tomatoes, chopped**
1	**cup shredded reduced-fat mozzarella cheese (4 ounces)**
½	**cup thinly sliced red onion**
½	**cup quartered pitted kalamata or ripe olives**
¼	**cup thinly sliced fresh basil or 4 teaspoons dried basil, crushed**
2	**tablespoons snipped fresh oregano or 2 teaspoons dried oregano, crushed**
2	**tablespoons capers, rinsed and drained**
2	**cloves garlic, minced**
¼	**teaspoon salt**
⅛	**teaspoon ground black pepper**
2	**tablespoons olive oil**

1. Cook pasta according to package directions. Drain; rinse under cold water until cool. Drain again.

2. In a large bowl, combine cooked pasta, tomatoes, cheese, onion, olives, basil, oregano, drained capers, garlic, salt, and pepper. Add olive oil; toss gently to mix. Cover and chill for 2 to 4 hours.

Per serving: 152 cal., 4 g total fat (1 g sat. fat), 4 mg chol., 161 mg sodium, 23 g carbo., 1 g fiber, 6 g pro.

Quick Tip Capers, which are the dried flower buds of a native Mediterranean bush, range in size from the tiny nonpareil variety to giant buds which can be as large as the tip of your finger. For use in most recipes, look for the tiny variety. Store brine-packed capers, tightly sealed, in the refrigerator for up to 9 months. Before using them, be sure to thoroughly rinse off excess salt or brine.

Lemon-Pepper Baby Broccoli

Lemon-Pepper Baby Broccoli one

Baby broccoli, called broccolini, is a cross between broccoli and Chinese kale. Because of its tender stem, it cooks quickly.

Start to Finish: 20 minutes   **Makes:** 8 servings

1 cup reduced-sodium chicken broth
1 tablespoon snipped fresh dill
2 teaspoons finely shredded lemon peel
1 teaspoon olive oil
½ teaspoon coarse salt
⅛ teaspoon crushed red pepper
⅛ teaspoon ground black pepper
1 pound baby broccoli or broccoli rabe
2 tablespoons butter
  Lemon halves or slices (optional)

1. In a large skillet, combine broth, dill, lemon peel, oil, coarse salt, crushed red pepper, and black pepper. Bring to boiling; reduce heat. Cover and simmer for 5 minutes.

2. Add broccoli and butter to skillet. Cover and cook over medium heat for 6 to 8 minutes or until broccoli is tender. If desired, drain. Transfer broccoli mixture to a serving bowl. If desired, garnish with lemon halves.

Per serving: 47 cal., 3 g total fat (2 g sat. fat), 8 mg chol., 489 mg sodium, 4 g carbo., 2 g fiber, 2 g pro.

Pear-Pecan Stuffing

Pears, pecans, and nutmeg create a sweet and savory addition to old-fashioned stuffing. It is equally delicious baked in a casserole and served as a side dish.

Prep: 25 minutes   **Bake:** 20 minutes + 40 minutes
Oven: 350°F   **Makes:** 12 to 14 servings

1 pound firm-textured white bread
2 tablespoons butter
1 large onion, chopped (1 cup)
2 large firm ripe Bartlett pears, cored, peeled, and chopped
½ to ¾ cup water
¼ cup butter
1 cup pecan halves, toasted and coarsely chopped
2 tablespoons snipped fresh Italian parsley
¼ teaspoon ground nutmeg
⅛ teaspoon salt
  Dash ground black pepper

1. Preheat oven to 350°F. Spread bread slices on baking sheets. Place baking sheets in the preheated oven for 20 minutes or until bread is dry.

2. In a large skillet, place the 2 tablespoons butter, the onion, and pears; cook over medium heat about 4 minutes or until tender. Set aside.

3. Break the dried bread into small pieces. Place in an extra large bowl. Bring ½ cup water and the ¼ cup butter to boiling in a small saucepan. Add to bread crumbs and toss just until moistened.

4. Stir in pear mixture, pecans, parsley, nutmeg, salt, and pepper. Add remaining water as needed until stuffing mixture reaches desired moistness. Transfer stuffing to a 2-quart casserole and bake, covered, about 40 minutes or until heated through.

Per serving: 244 cal., 15 g total fat (4 g sat. fat), 16 mg chol., 291 mg sodium, 26 g carbo., 2 g fiber, 4 g pro.

Make-Ahead Directions: Let bread stand overnight at room temperature to dry on baking sheets. Store dried bread in a covered container at room temperature for up to 1 week. Omit Step 1.

Quick Tip Purchase pears that are fragrant, firm but not hard, and free of blemishes and soft spots. Store ripe pears in a plastic bag in the refrigerator for up to 5 days. Ripen unripe pears at room temperature by placing them in a paper bag with an apple. Pierce the bag in several places. If using them for cooking, they are ready to use when still fairly firm.

Crumb-Topped Vegetables

Crumb-Topped Vegetables

Crushed cheese-flavored crackers are the secret ingredient in the crust on this green bean side dish. Feel free to experiment with other varieties of frozen vegetables in this recipe.

Start to Finish: 10 minutes **Makes:** 4 to 6 servings

1	**12-ounce package frozen cut green beans in microwaveable steaming bag**
1	**cup cheese-flavored crackers, crushed**
½	**teaspoon dried thyme, crushed**
2	**tablespoons butter, melted**
¼	**cup finely shredded Parmesan cheese**

1. Steam beans in microwave according to package directions.

2. Meanwhile, in a small resealable plastic bag, place the crackers and thyme. Release the air from the bag and seal the bag. With your hands, crush the crackers until they resemble fine crumbs. Add melted butter to the bag. Seal bag and toss to combine.

3. Place beans in a serving dish. Top with cracker mixture. Sprinkle Parmesan cheese over top.

Per serving: 168 cal., 10 g total fat (6 g sat. fat), 20 mg chol., 249 mg sodium, 13 g carbo., 2 g fiber, 4 g pro.

Quick Tip If you like, you may use other frozen vegetables, such as corn or peas, in place of the green beans.

Beet Greens with Walnuts and Blue Cheese ♥ [one]

This sophisticated side dish showcases beet greens that are lightly cooked with walnuts and sprinkled with blue cheese.

Start to Finish: 15 minutes **Makes:** 4 servings

- **8 ounces fresh beet greens**
- **2 teaspoons cooking oil**
- **2 tablespoons chopped walnuts**
- **1 tablespoon crumbled blue cheese**
- **¼ teaspoon ground black pepper**

1. Thoroughly clean beet greens. Drain well. Cut beet greens into 1-inch strips. In a large skillet, heat oil over medium-high heat. Add walnuts. Cook and stir for 2 minutes.

2. Add beet greens to skillet. Cook and stir, uncovered, about 1 minute or just until wilted. Top with crumbled cheese and pepper.

Per serving: 55 cal., 5 g total fat (1 g sat. fat), 0 mg chol., 109 mg sodium, 3 g carbo., 2 g fiber, 2 g pro.

Quick Tip This recipe can also be prepared with fresh spinach or Swiss chard. Whichever greens you choose to use, be sure to clean them well under cold running water to remove any dirt or sand. Drain well.

Green Beans and Tomatoes ♥ [one]

Pair whole green beans and tiny tomatoes for a vegetable medley that's pleasing served at room temperature or chilled. Remember this recipe next time you need a great side dish for grilled or roasted meat.

Start to Finish: 20 minutes **Makes:** 6 to 8 servings

- **1½ pounds fresh green beans, trimmed**
- **1 pint small tomatoes (such as yellow pear, red grape, red and/or orange cherry), halved**
- **¼ cup bottled basil vinaigrette salad dressing Salt and freshly ground black pepper**

1. Cook beans, covered, in a small amount of boiling salted water for 10 to 15 minutes or until crisp-tender. Drain and rinse under cool water. Drain and pat dry with paper towels.

2. In a large bowl, combine green beans and tomatoes. Drizzle with vinaigrette salad dressing; toss to coat. If necessary, add more salad dressing. Season to taste with salt and pepper. Serve immediately or chill in the refrigerator up to 8 hours.

Per serving: 86 cal., 5 g total fat (1 g sat. fat), 0 mg chol., 106 mg sodium, 10 g carbo., 4 g fiber, 4 g pro.

Beet Greens with Walnuts and Blue Cheese

Glazed Brussels Sprouts

Glazed Brussels Sprouts ♥ one

Brussels sprouts are thought to have been first grown in Belgium several hundred years ago.

Start to Finish: 25 minutes   **Makes:** 8 servings

3	**tablespoons butter**
2	**10-ounce package frozen Brussels sprouts**
1	**10-ounce package frozen whole small onions**
⅓	**cup pure maple syrup**
1	**tablespoon butter or margarine**
	Salt and ground black pepper
¼	**cup chopped walnuts, toasted**

1. In a large skillet, melt butter over medium heat. Add Brussels sprouts and onions. Cook, covered, about 10 minutes, stirring occasionally.

2. Drizzle vegetables with maple syrup. Cook, uncovered, 1 to 2 minutes more, stirring occasionally. Season to taste with salt and pepper. Transfer vegetables to a serving bowl. Sprinkle with walnuts.

Per serving: 139 cal., 7 g total fat (3 g sat. fat), 12 mg chol., 83 mg sodium, 18 g carbo., 4 g fiber, 4 g pro.

Sweet Saucy Carrots and Pecans one

Orange marmalade, butter, and salt meld on the stove to glaze a quickly cooked bag of baby carrots that you'll top with chopped pecans. Elegant, luscious, and delicious.

Start to Finish: 20 minutes   **Makes:** 4 servings

1	**1-pound package peeled baby carrots**
2	**tablespoons orange marmalade**
1	**tablespoon butter or margarine**
½	**teaspoon salt**
2	**tablespoons pecan pieces, toasted**

1. In a large covered saucepan, cook the carrots in a small amount of boiling water for 8 to 10 minutes or until crisp-tender. Drain.

2. Return carrots to pan. Add orange marmalade, butter, and salt. Stir until carrots are coated. Top with the pecans.

Per serving: 124 cal., 6 g total fat (2 g sat. fat), 8 mg chol., 365 mg sodium, 19 g carbo., 4 g fiber, 2 g pro.

Cauliflower with Lemon Dressing

Cauliflower with Lemon Dressing

Cauliflower goes from ordinary to spectacular when it's drizzled with a lemon dressing and served with Serrano ham (a seasoned ham from Spain), Manchego cheese (a Spanish sheep's-milk cheese), capers, and toasted pine nuts.

Start to Finish: 20 minutes **Makes:** 4 servings

- 2 **small heads cauliflower**
- ½ **cup water**
- 2 **to 3 ounces thinly sliced Serrano ham, prosciutto, or cooked ham**
- 1 **ounce Manchego cheese or Monterey Jack cheese, thinly shaved**
- ¼ **cup olive oil or cooking oil**
- 2 **tablespoons lemon juice**
- ½ **teaspoon salt**
- ½ **teaspoon bottled minced garlic (1 clove)**
- ¼ **teaspoon sugar**
- ¼ **teaspoon dry mustard**
- ¼ **teaspoon freshly ground black pepper**
- 2 **tablespoons pine nuts, toasted**
- 2 **tablespoons capers, rinsed and drained**

1. Remove heavy leaves and tough stems from cauliflower; cut cauliflower into wedges. Place cauliflower in a microwave-safe 3-quart casserole. Add the water. Microwave, covered, on 100% power (high) for 7 to 9 minutes or just until tender. Remove with a slotted spoon to serving plates. Top with ham and cheese.

2. Meanwhile, in a screw-top jar, combine oil, lemon juice, salt, garlic, sugar, mustard, and pepper. Cover and shake well to combine; drizzle over cauliflower. Sprinkle with pine nuts and drained capers.

Per serving: 207 cal., 18 g total fat (3 g sat. fat), 10 mg chol., 848 mg sodium, 7 g carbo., 4 g fiber, 9 g pro.

Zucchini alla Romana ♥ 🔲one

Simple is very often best. Here's a quintessentially Italian recipe that combines quintessential Italian ingredients: basil, garlic, a little olive oil, and a sprinkling of Parmesan cheese.

Start to Finish: 15 minutes **Makes:** 6 servings

- 2 **cloves garlic**
- 2 **teaspoons olive oil**
- 4 **small zucchini, sliced (4 cups)**
- 1 **teaspoon dried basil, crushed**
- ¼ **teaspoon salt**
   Dash ground black pepper
- 2 **tablespoons finely shredded Romano or Parmesan cheese**

1. In a large skillet, cook whole garlic cloves in oil until lightly brown; discard garlic.

2. Add zucchini, basil, salt, and pepper to oil in skillet. Cook, uncovered, over medium heat about 5 minutes or until zucchini is crisp-tender, stirring occasionally.

3. To serve, sprinkle with Romano cheese.

Per serving: 35 cal., 2 g total fat (1 g sat. fat), 2 mg chol., 130 mg sodium, 3 g carbo., 1 g fiber, 2 g pro.

Hash Brown Potato Cakes

Hash Brown Potato Cakes ♥

For smooth cakes that hold together, be sure to slice the onion very thinly. Don't turn the cakes until the first side is golden brown.

Prep: 20 minutes **Cook:** 8 minutes per batch
Oven: 300°F **Makes:** 8 servings

- 1 **pound russet or round red potatoes**
- ½ **of a medium onion, very thinly sliced**
- 1 **tablespoon olive oil**
- 2 **teaspoons snipped fresh thyme or ¼ teaspoon dried thyme, crushed**
- ¼ **teaspoon salt**
- ⅛ **teaspoon ground black pepper**
  Nonstick cooking spray

1. Preheat oven to 300°F. Peel and coarsely shred potatoes; immediately rinse with cold water in a colander. Drain well, pressing lightly, then pat dry with paper towels; place in a large bowl. Quarter the onion slices. Stir onion, oil, thyme, salt, and pepper into potatoes.

2. Lightly coat an unheated very large nonstick skillet or griddle with cooking spray. Heat skillet over medium heat.

3. For each cake, scoop a slightly rounded measuring tablespoon of potato mixture onto skillet. Using a spatula, press potato mixture to flatten evenly to 2½- to 3-inch diameter. Cook for 5 minutes. Using a wide spatula, carefully turn potato cakes (be sure not to turn cakes too soon or they will not hold together). Cook for 3 to 5 minutes more or until golden brown. Remove cooked potato cakes from skillet; keep warm, uncovered, in oven while cooking remaining potato cakes. Repeat with remaining potato mixture, stirring mixture frequently.

Per serving: 59 cal., 2 g total fat (0 g sat. fat), 0 mg chol., 75 mg sodium, 9 g carbo., 1 g fiber, 1 g pro.

Southern Succotash

Southern Succotash

Fresh green beans give a summertime spin to this old-fashioned lima-bean-and-corn classic.

Start to Finish: 25 minutes **Makes:** 12 servings

- 1 **10-ounce package frozen lima beans**
- 1 **quart boiling water**
- 2½ **cups fresh French green beans (haricot verts) or green beans, trimmed**
- 2 **cups fresh or frozen yellow corn kernels**
- 1 **tablespoon butter**
- ½ **to 1 teaspoon cracked black pepper**

1. In a Dutch oven, cook lima beans in the boiling water for 10 minutes. Add green beans; cook for 5 minutes. Add corn and cook for 5 minutes more; drain. Stir in butter and pepper; toss to mix.

Per serving: 71 cal., 1 g total fat (1 g sat. fat), 3 mg chol., 24 mg sodium, 13 g carbo., 3 g fiber, 3 g pro.

Easy Parmesan Breadsticks

These versatile crispy, cheesy sticks can be served a couple of ways. Serve them restaurant-style as a meal starter. Or use them as a serve-along for soup or salad.

Prep: 15 minutes **Bake:** 10 minutes **Oven:** 375°F
Makes: 6 servings

- ½ **of a 12-ounce loaf baguette-style French bread (halve bread loaf crosswise)**
  Nonstick cooking spray
- ¼ **cup olive oil**
- 6 **tablespoons grated or finely shredded Parmesan cheese**
  Purchased marinara sauce, warmed, and/or flavored oils (such as lemon-, basil-, or garlic-flavored)

1. Preheat oven to 375°F. Cut bread lengthwise into quarters; cut into ¼- to ½-inch-wide strips. (Cut bread so there is crust on each strip.)

2. Line a 15×10×1-inch baking pan with foil; lightly coat foil with cooking spray. Arrange bread strips in a single layer; drizzle with oil. Using a spatula or tongs, carefully turn breadsticks to coat with oil. Sprinkle with Parmesan cheese.

3. Bake for 10 to 12 minutes or until browned and crisp. Serve with marinara sauce and/or flavored oils.

Per serving: 219 cal., 13 g total fat (3 g sat. fat), 4 mg chol., 539 mg sodium, 20 g carbo., 2 g fiber, 5 g pro.

Green Onion Parker House Biscuits

Refrigerated biscuit dough and softened herb-blended cheese make these biscuits so quick to prepare, you can serve them even when your schedule is the most hectic.

Prep: 10 minutes **Bake:** 8 minutes **Oven:** 400°F
Makes: 10 biscuits

- 1 **5.2-ounce container boursin cheese with garlic and herbs**
- ¼ **cup sliced green onion**
- 1 **12-ounce package (10) refrigerated biscuits**
- 1 **egg yolk**
- 1 **tablespoon water**
- 2 **tablespoons grated Parmesan cheese**
  Sliced green onion

1. Preheat oven to 400°F. In a small bowl, stir together boursin cheese and the ¼ cup green onions; set aside.

2. Unwrap biscuits. Using your fingers, gently split the biscuits horizontally. Place the biscuit bottoms on a greased baking sheet. Spread about 1 tablespoon of the cheese mixture over each biscuit bottom. Replace biscuit tops.

3. In a small bowl, use a fork to beat together egg yolk and the water. Brush biscuit tops with yolk mixture. Sprinkle with Parmesan cheese and additional sliced green onion. Bake for 8 to 10 minutes or until golden brown. Serve warm.

Per biscuit: 149 cal., 8 g total fat (5 g sat. fat), 23 mg chol., 394 mg sodium, 16 g carbo., 0 g fiber, 4 g pro.

Green Onion Parker House Biscuits

Broccoli Corn Bread

Broccoli Corn Bread ♥

Fold chopped broccoli, onion, and shredded Cheddar cheese into corn muffin mix and eggs for a filled bread that makes a fine complement to roast beef or chicken.

Prep: 10 minutes **Bake:** 30 minutes **Oven:** 350°F
Makes: 16 servings

- 1   **8.5-ounce package corn muffin mix**
- 3   **eggs**
- 1   **8-ounce package shredded Cheddar cheese (2 cups)**
- 1   **10-ounce package frozen chopped broccoli, thawed and well drained**
- ½   **cup chopped onion (1 medium)**

1. Preheat oven to 350°F. Grease a 9×9×2-inch baking pan; set aside.

2. In a large bowl, combine the corn muffin mix and eggs. Stir in cheese, broccoli, and onion. Spoon batter into the prepared pan, spreading evenly.

3. Bake about 30 minutes or until a wooden toothpick inserted near the center comes out clean. Serve warm.

Per serving: 138 cal., 7 g total fat (3 g sat. fat), 55 mg chol., 209 mg sodium, 12 g carbo., 1 g fiber, 6 g pro.

Honey and Poppy Seed Biscuits

Kids can help make these biscuits by brushing the tops with milk and sprinkling on the poppy seeds.

Prep: 15 minutes **Bake:** 10 minutes **Oven:** 450°F
Makes: 10 to 12 servings

- ½   **cup cream-style cottage cheese**
- ¼   **cup milk**
- 2   **tablespoons honey**
- 2¼   **cups packaged biscuit mix**
       Water
       Poppy seeds

1. Preheat oven to 450°F. In a food processor or blender, combine cottage cheese, milk, and honey. Cover and process or blend until nearly smooth.

2. Prepare biscuit mix according to package directions for rolled biscuits, except substitute the pureed cottage cheese mixture for the liquid called for on the package. Lightly brush with water and sprinkle with poppy seeds.

3. Bake for 10 to 12 minutes or until golden and bottoms are lightly browned.

Per serving: 143 cal., 5 g total fat (1 g sat. fat), 3 mg chol., 393 mg sodium, 21 g carbo., 1 g fiber, 4 g pro.

Parmesan Rosettes

Parmesan Rosettes

Rolled out and tied into individual rosettes, this dough gets brushed with an Italian-inspired blend of cheese and seasonings. The shapely baked rosettes are pretty in a bread basket or on a bread plate.

Prep: 15 minutes **Bake:** 15 minutes **Oven:** 375°F
Makes: 12 rosettes

- 1   **11-ounce package (12) refrigerated breadsticks**
- 3   **tablespoons grated Parmesan or Romano cheese**
- 1   **teaspoon sesame seeds**
- ½   **teaspoon dried Italian seasoning, crushed**
- ¼   **teaspoon garlic powder**
- 2   **tablespoons butter, melted**

1. Preheat oven to 375°F. Separate breadsticks and uncoil into 12 pieces. On a lightly floured surface, roll each piece into a 12-inch-long rope.

2. Tie each rope in a loose knot, leaving 2 long ends. Tuck the top end of the rope under roll. Bring bottom end up and tuck into center of roll.

3. In a shallow dish, combine Parmesan cheese, sesame seeds, Italian seasoning, and garlic powder. Brush top and sides of each rosette with melted butter. Carefully dip the top and sides of each rosette into the cheese mixture. Place rosettes 2 to 3 inches apart on an ungreased baking sheet.

4. Bake for about 15 minutes or until golden. Serve warm.

Per rosette: 135 cal., 5 g total fat (2 g sat. fat), 6 mg chol., 334 mg sodium, 18 g carbo., 1 g fiber, 4 g pro.

Cranberry-Pumpkin Bread Pudding
with Brandy-Butter Sauce, **page 317**

Praline Crunch Bars, **page 319**

Little Lemon Snowbites, **page 310**

Shortcut Malted Chocolate Cake, **page 321**

Sweet-Tooth Desserts

Not every menu requires a dessert, but something sweet at the end of a meal provides a delicious finale. Packaged mixes, purchased doughs, and flavor-packed ingredients are the keys to these pleasing treats.

Baked Fruit Ambrosia

Baked Fruit Ambrosia ♥

When you're having friends or family in for breakfast or brunch, begin with this easy cinnamon-spiced fruit duet.

Prep: 10 minutes **Bake:** 15 minutes **Oven:** 350°F
Makes: 4 servings

- 2 **medium oranges**
- 1 **8-ounce can pineapple tidbits (juice pack), drained**
- ¼ **teaspoon ground cinnamon**
- 2 **tablespoons shredded coconut**
   Fresh raspberries (optional)

1. Preheat oven to 350°F. Finely shred enough peel from one of the oranges to make ½ teaspoon peel; set aside. Peel and section the two oranges. Cut orange sections into bite-size pieces.

2. Divide orange pieces and pineapple among four 6-ounce custard cups. Sprinkle with orange peel and cinnamon. Top with coconut.

3. Bake about 15 minutes or until fruit is heated through and coconut is golden. If desired, garnish each serving with fresh raspberries. Serve warm.

Per serving: 66 cal., 1 g total fat (1 g sat. fat), 0 mg chol., 12 mg sodium, 14 g carbo., 2 g fiber, 1 g pro.

Quick Tip Purchase oranges that are firm and heavy for their size. Avoid any with spongy or moldy spots. A rough, brownish area called russeting occurs on the skin of some oranges and does not affect flavor or quality. Because oranges are sometimes dyed with food coloring, a bright color doesn't necessarily indicate quality.

Fluffy Cranberry Mousse

During the winter, serve this festive dessert as the luscious ending to a special meal. In summer, beat the heat with the same mixture frozen in small dessert dishes.

Start to Finish: 20 minutes **Makes:** 12 servings

- ½ **of an 8-ounce package cream cheese, softened**
- 2 **tablespoons sugar**
- ½ **teaspoon vanilla**
- ½ **cup frozen cranberry juice concentrate, thawed**
- 1 **16-ounce can whole cranberry sauce**
- 1½ **cups whipping cream**
   Sweetened Cranberries (optional)

1. In a large bowl, beat cream cheese with an electric mixer on medium speed for 30 seconds. Beat in sugar and vanilla until smooth. Slowly add cranberry concentrate, beating until very smooth. In a small bowl, stir the cranberry sauce to remove any large lumps; set aside.

2. In a chilled large bowl, beat cream with an electric mixer on low to medium speed until soft peaks form (tips curl over). Fold half of the cranberry sauce and half of the whipped cream into the cream cheese mixture. Fold in the remaining cranberry sauce and whipped cream.

3. Spoon cranberry mixture into 12 chilled small dessert dishes or a large serving bowl. If desired, spoon Sweetened Cranberries on top.

Sweetened Cranberries: In a medium skillet, combine 1 cup fresh cranberries, ⅓ cup sugar, and 2 tablespoons water. Cook and stir over medium heat until sugar dissolves and cranberries just begin to pop. Remove from heat. Cover and chill until serving time.

Per serving: 223 cal., 14 g total fat (9 g sat. fat), 51 mg chol., 45 mg sodium, 23 g carbo., 1 g fiber, 1 g pro.

Fluffy Cranberry Mousse

Little Lemon Snowbites ♥

Sugar cookies topped with lemon curd are delicious and unique. Lemon curd is a thick spread of sugar, butter, fresh lemon juice, and egg yolks.

Prep: 25 minutes **Bake:** 7 minutes per batch
Oven: 375°F **Makes:** about 24 sandwich cookies

- 1 **17.5-ounce package sugar cookie mix**
- ¼ **cup crushed hard lemon candies**
- ⅔ **cup purchased lemon curd**
- ⅔ **cup frozen whipped dessert topping, thawed**
- 2 **tablespoons powdered sugar**

1. Preheat the oven to 375°F. Line a cookie sheet with foil or parchment paper; set aside. Prepare cookie mix according to package directions. Stir in the crushed candies. If necessary, cover and chill dough about 1 hour or until easy to handle. Roll dough into 1-inch balls. Place balls 2 inches apart on prepared cookie sheet.

2. Bake for 7 to 9 minutes or until edges are firm and cookies are light brown on bottoms. Cool on cookie sheet for 1 minute. Transfer to a wire rack and let cool.

3. For filling, in a small bowl, stir together lemon curd and whipped topping; set aside. To assemble cookies, place a rounded teaspoon of filling on the bottom side of a cookie; top with another cookie, top-side-up. Repeat with remaining cookies and filling. Sprinkle tops of cookies with powdered sugar. Store filled cookies in the refrigerator for up to 3 days or freeze for up to 1 month.

Per sandwich cookie: 169 cal., 7 g total fat (3 g sat. fat), 26 mg chol., 87 mg sodium, 25 g carbo., 1 g fiber, 1 g pro.

Quick Tip For a different citrus flavor, you may use lime curd in place of the lemon curd in this recipe.

Easy Butter Bars ♥

Oh-so-rich cream-cheesy bars boast a big butter flavor. Sugared cranberries and fresh mint add a fruity garnish complement.

Prep: 20 minutes **Bake:** 25 minutes **Oven:** 350°F
Makes: 36 bars

- **Nonstick cooking spray**
- 1 **package 2-layer-size yellow or white cake mix**
- ½ **cup butter, softened**
- 1 **egg**
- 1 **8-ounce package cream cheese, softened**
- 2 **eggs**
- 1 **teaspoon butter flavoring**
- 3½ **cups powdered sugar**

1. Preheat oven to 350°F. Lightly coat a 15×10×1-inch baking pan with cooking spray.

2. For the crust, in a large mixing bowl, combine cake mix, butter, and 1 egg. Beat with an electric mixer on low speed until mixture is crumbly. Pat mixture evenly into the bottom of the prepared pan; set aside.

3. In another large mixing bowl, beat cream cheese with the electric mixer on medium speed until smooth. Add 2 eggs and butter flavoring; beat until smooth. Add the powdered sugar; beat on low speed until well combined. Spread on top of crust in pan.

4. Bake for 25 to 30 minutes or until the filling is set and golden brown. Cool in pan on a wire rack. (The filling may fall as it cools.) Using a sharp knife, cut into bars.

Per bar: 153 cal., 6 g total fat (4 g sat. fat), 31 mg chol., 136 mg sodium, 23 g carbo., 0 g fiber, 1 g pro.

Quick Tip Dip the knife in hot water and lightly pat dry between cuts to make cleaner cuts.

Little Lemon Snowbites

Sour Cream-Blueberry Pie

Sour Cream-Blueberry Pie

A scrumptious pecan topping adds the perfect finishing touch to this creamy fruit pie.

Prep: 15 minutes **Bake:** 40 minutes **Chill:** 4 hours
Oven: 400°F **Makes:** 8 servings

1	egg, beaten
1	8-ounce carton dairy sour cream
¾	cup sugar
2	tablespoons all-purpose flour
1	teaspoon vanilla
¼	teaspoon salt
2½	cups fresh blueberries
½	of a 15-ounce package rolled refrigerated unbaked piecrust (1 crust)
¼	cup all-purpose flour
¼	cup butter, softened
¼	cup chopped pecans or walnuts

1. Preheat oven to 400°F. Bring piecrust to room temperature according to package directions. In a large mixing bowl, combine egg, sour cream, sugar, the 2 tablespoons flour, the vanilla, and salt, stirring until smooth. Fold in blueberries. Unroll piecrust and ease into a 9-inch pie plate. Pour filling into piecrust.

2. Bake pie in preheated oven for 25 minutes. Meanwhile, in a small bowl, thoroughly combine the ¼ cup flour, the butter, and nuts. Pinch off small bits of flour mixture and sprinkle on top of pie. Bake pie for 15 minutes more. Cool on a wire rack. Chill for at least 4 hours before serving.

Per serving: 397 cal., 24 g total fat (10 g sat. fat), 54 mg chol., 211 mg sodium, 42 g carbo., 3 g fiber, 5 g pro.

Quick Tip Look for blueberries that are plump, firm, uniform in size, and a silver-frosted indigo blue color. To store blueberries, refrigerate them, tightly covered, for up to 10 days. Before use, discard any shriveled or moldy blueberries and remove any stems.

Raspberry-Pecan Bars

Keep just six ingredients on hand for those spur-of-the-moment potlucks. To change the recipe up a bit, try using a different type of preserves, such as cherry or apricot.

Prep: 15 minutes **Bake:** 45 minutes **Oven:** 350°F
Makes: 16 bars

1	**cup butter, softened**
1	**cup sugar**
1	**egg**
2¼	**cups all-purpose flour**
1	**cup chopped pecans**
1	**10-ounce jar raspberry preserves**

1. Preheat oven to 350°F. In a large mixing bowl, beat butter with an electric mixer on medium to high speed for 30 seconds. Add sugar; beat until combined. Add the egg; beat until combined. Beat in flour until crumbly. Stir in pecans. Measure 1½ cups of the mixture. Set aside.

2. Press the remaining flour mixture into the bottom of an ungreased 8×8×2-inch baking pan. Spread preserves evenly over crust, leaving a ½-inch border around sides. Crumble reserved mixture over the top.

3. Bake cookies for 45 to 50 minutes until top is browned. Cool in pan on a wire rack. Cut into bars.

Per bar: 308 cal., 17 g total fat (8 g sat. fat), 44 mg chol., 92 mg sodium, 38 g carbo., 1 g fiber, 3 g pro.

Ultimate Chocolate Sundaes

If you prefer less-sweet, darker chocolate, use bittersweet chocolate in this recipe.

Start to Finish: 30 minutes **Makes:** 8 servings

8	ounces semisweet or bittersweet chocolate, coarsely chopped
⅓	cup water
¼	cup sugar
¼	cup pear liqueur or pear nectar
4	small Forelle or Bosc pears (1 pound total)
3	tablespoons butter
2	tablespoons sugar
1	quart vanilla ice cream

1. For the chocolate sauce, in a small saucepan, combine chocolate, water, and the ¼ cup sugar. Melt chocolate over low heat, stirring slowly and constantly. Stir in pear liqueur. Set aside to cool slightly.

2. If desired, peel pears cut into halves and remove cores.* If desired, leave stem on one portion. In a large skillet, melt butter. Add pear halves; cook over medium heat about 12 minutes or until brown and tender, turning once. Add the 2 tablespoons sugar. Cook and stir gently until sugar is dissolved and pears are glazed.

3. To assemble, place scoops of ice cream in 8 dessert bowls. Spoon a pear half and some butter mixture around the ice cream in each bowl. Top with the chocolate sauce.

Per serving: 538 cal., 33 g total fat (20 g sat. fat), 132 mg chol., 119 mg sodium, 56 g carbo., 3 g fiber, 7 g pro.

*Note: If pears are larger, cut into sixths or eighths (should have about 16 pieces).

Ultimate Chocolate Sundaes

Caramel Apple Pastry

Refrigerated piecrust is a dessert lover's best friend. It's versatile, convenient, and—best of all—it tastes wonderful, especially when paired with sliced apples and brown sugar.

Prep: 10 minutes **Bake:** 15 minutes **Cool:** 5 minutes
Oven: 450°F **Makes:** 6 servings

½	of a 15-ounce package rolled refrigerated unbaked piecrust (1 crust)
1	tablespoon butter
2	20-ounce cans sliced apples, well drained
½	cup packed brown sugar
1	tablespoon lemon juice
1	teaspoon apple pie spice or ground cinnamon
1	tablespoon purchased cinnamon-sugar
	Cinnamon or vanilla ice cream (optional)
	Caramel ice cream topping (optional)

1. Preheat oven to 450°F. Bring piecrust to room temperature according to package directions; set aside. In a large ovenproof skillet, melt butter over high heat; stir in drained apple slices, brown sugar, lemon juice, and apple pie spice. Spread evenly in skillet. Cook until bubbly.

2. Meanwhile, on a lightly floured surface, unroll piecrust. Sprinkle piecrust with cinnamon-sugar; rub into piecrust with your fingers. Carefully place the piecrust over bubbly apple mixture in skillet, cinnamon-sugar side up. Tuck in piecrust around edge of skillet, using a spatula to press edge down slightly.

3. Bake about 15 minutes or until piecrust is golden brown. Cool for 5 minutes. Carefully invert skillet onto a serving platter; remove skillet. Serve warm. If desired, serve with ice cream and caramel topping.

Per serving: 381 cal., 12 g total fat (5 g sat. fat), 12 mg chol., 159 mg sodium, 69 g carbo., 3 g fiber, 1 g pro.

Quick Tip To make your own cinnamon-sugar, in a small bowl, stir together 1 tablespoon sugar and ¼ teaspoon ground cinnamon.

Gooey Chocolate-Caramel Fantasy

Gooey Chocolate-Caramel Fantasy

This luscious dessert is a chocolate lover's dream come true. The treat includes a chocolate crumb crust and caramel-pecan filling crowned with melted chocolate.

Prep: 20 minutes **Bake:** 11 minutes **Chill:** 2 hours
Oven: 350°F **Makes:** 12 servings

2	cups chocolate wafer crumbs (about 38 wafers)
⅓	cup butter, melted
30	vanilla caramels
½	cup caramel ice cream topping
½	cup whipping cream
2	cups chopped pecans, toasted
¾	cup semisweet chocolate pieces
	Pecan halves, optional

1. Preheat oven to 350°F. In a medium mixing bowl, stir together chocolate wafer crumbs and melted butter. Press onto the bottom of a 9-inch springform pan. Bake for 10 minutes. Cool slightly on a wire rack.

2. Meanwhile, in a medium heavy saucepan, melt caramels in caramel ice cream topping over low heat, stirring often. Stir in ¼ cup of the whipping cream. Remove from heat; stir in the chopped pecans. Spread over crust. Chill for 1 hour.

3. For the topping, in a small heavy saucepan, melt chocolate over low heat. Remove from heat; stir in remaining ¼ cup whipping cream. Drizzle or spread over caramel-pecan mixture. Cover and chill for at least 1 hour. If desired, garnish with additional pecan halves.

Per serving: 459 cal., 28 g total fat (9 g sat. fat), 29 mg chol., 253 mg sodium, 52 g carbo., 4 g fiber, 6 g pro.

Rocky Road Parfaits

Layer chocolate pudding into these dreamy two-tone desserts topped with a rocky road trio of chocolate, peanuts, and marshmallows.

Start to Finish: 20 minutes **Makes:** 4 servings

1	4-serving-size package chocolate or chocolate fudge instant pudding mix
2	cups milk
½	cup frozen whipped dessert topping, thawed
¼	cup unsalted peanuts, coarsely chopped
¼	cup tiny marshmallows
	Chocolate curls (optional)

1. Prepare pudding mix according to package directions using the milk. Remove ¾ cup of the pudding and place in a small bowl; fold in whipped topping until combined.

2. Divide remaining plain chocolate pudding among four 6-ounce glasses or dessert dishes. Top with dessert topping mixture. Let stand for 5 to 10 minutes or until set.

3. Sprinkle with peanuts and marshmallows just before serving. If desired, garnish with chocolate curls.

Per serving: 246 cal., 9 g total fat (4 g sat. fat), 10 mg chol., 412 mg sodium, 34 g carbo., 1 g fiber, 7 g pro.

Make-Ahead Directions: Prepare as directed through Step 2. Cover and chill parfaits for up to 24 hours. Serve as directed in Step 3.

Banana-Chocolate Bites ♥

When the weather's cool and the kids are romping outdoors, invite them indoors for a batch of these crescent-roll wrapped treats, still warm from the oven.

Prep: 20 minutes **Bake:** 11 minutes **Cool:** 10 minutes
Oven: 375°F **Makes:** 16 bites

1	8-ounce package refrigerated crescent rolls (8)
3	tablespoons chocolate-hazelnut spread
2	medium bananas, cut into sixteen ¾-inch slices
4	teaspoons lemon juice
1	egg yolk
1	tablespoon water

1. Preheat oven to 375°F. Grease a baking sheet; set aside.

2. Unroll crescent roll dough and separate into 8 triangles. Cut each triangle in half lengthwise, forming 16 long, narrow triangles. Place about ½ teaspoon of chocolate-hazelnut spread on wide end of each triangle. Brush each banana slice with some of the lemon juice. Place a banana slice on top of spread. Roll dough around bananas. Place bites on prepared baking sheet. In a small bowl, beat together egg yolk and water. Brush egg yolk mixture onto dough of each bite.

3. Bake in the preheated oven for 11 to 15 minutes or until golden brown. Remove bites from baking sheet and cool on a wire rack for 10 minutes. Serve warm or within 4 hours.

Per bite: 80 cal., 4 g total fat (1 g sat. fat), 13 mg chol., 118 mg sodium, 11 g carbo., 1 g fiber, 1 g pro.

Cranberry-Pumpkin Bread Pudding
with Brandy-Butter Sauce

Cranberry-Pumpkin Bread Pudding with Brandy-Butter Sauce

Rich, sweet, and full of seasonal flavors, this dessert makes a perfect special dinner alternative to standard pie. The luscious Brandy-Butter Sauce is a delicious high note.

Prep: 20 minutes **Bake:** 55 minutes
Stand: 15 minutes **Oven:** 350°F **Makes:** 15 servings

- **4 eggs, lightly beaten**
- **2 egg yolks, lightly beaten**
- **4 cups milk**
- **1 cup sugar**
- **1 15-ounce can pumpkin**
- **¼ cup brandy**
- **1½ teaspoons pumpkin pie spice**
- **9 slices whole wheat bread, cut into ½-inch cubes (about 8 cups)**
- **1 cup dried cranberries**
  Brandy-Butter Sauce

1. Preheat oven to 350°F. In an extra large bowl, combine eggs, egg yolks, milk, sugar, pumpkin, brandy, and pumpkin pie spice. Add bread cubes and cranberries; mix well. Let stand for 15 minutes. Transfer to a lightly greased 3-quart rectangular baking dish.

2. Bake, uncovered, for about 55 minutes or until a knife inserted in center comes out clean. Cool slightly. Serve warm with Brandy-Butter Sauce.

Brandy-Butter Sauce: In a small saucepan, melt ½ cup butter over medium heat. Stir in 1½ cups powdered sugar until mixture is smooth. Stir in 2 egg yolks; cook and stir just until bubbly. Remove from heat. Stir in 1 to 2 tablespoons brandy. Serve warm.

Per serving: 338 cal., 12 g total fat (6 g sat. fat), 136 mg chol., 216 mg sodium, 49 g carbo., 3 g fiber, 7 g pro.

Chocolate-Butter Mint Fondue

If you like the combination of salty and sweet, try chunky pretzels for dipping.

Start to Finish: 20 minutes **Makes:** 6 to 8 servings

- **1 14-ounce can sweetened condensed milk**
- **1 7-ounce jar marshmallow creme**
- **1 6-ounce package semisweet chocolate pieces**
- **⅓ cup crushed butter mints**
- **¼ cup milk**
- **2 tablespoons crème de cacao (optional)**
  Strawberries, pineapple chunks, cubed pound cake, and/or cubed angel food cake

1. In a medium saucepan, combine sweetened condensed milk, marshmallow creme, chocolate pieces, and butter mints. Cook and stir over low heat until chocolate melts. Stir in milk and, if desired, crème de cacao.

2. Transfer to a fondue pot; place over fondue burner. Spear strawberries, pineapple, pound cake, and/or angel food cake with fondue fork; dip into fondue mixture, swirling to coat.

Per serving: 665 cal., 22 g total fat (13 g sat. fat), 106 mg chol., 271 mg sodium, 114 g carbo., 3 g fiber, 10 g pro.

Raspberry Cheesecake Shake

Craving the richness of cheesecake, but don't have the time? Experience a glass of cheesecake heaven.

Start to Finish: 10 minutes **Makes:** 6 servings

- **1 12-ounce package frozen unsweetened red raspberries, thawed**
- **1 3-ounce package cream cheese, softened**
- **¼ teaspoon almond extract**
- **1 quart vanilla ice cream, softened**
- **2 12-ounce cans or bottles cream soda**
  Fresh raspberries

1. In a blender, combine raspberries, cream cheese, and almond extract; add half of the ice cream and ½ cup of the cream soda. Cover and blend until smooth.

2. Pour into six 16-ounce glasses. Add a scoop of the remaining ice cream to each glass. Top with remaining cream soda.

3. If desired, garnish with fresh raspberries. Serve immediately.

Per serving: 305 cal., 15 g total fat (9 g sat. fat), 54 mg chol., 130 mg sodium, 36 g carbo., 2 g fiber, 4 g pro.

Raspberry Cheesecake Shake

Chocolate-Peppermint Malts

Chocolate-Peppermint Malts

Chocolate malts are always in season, but with a delicious peppermint flavor, these malts are perfect for the holidays.

Start to Finish: 15 minutes **Makes:** 6 servings

- **3   cups chocolate milk**
- **1   quart vanilla or chocolate ice cream**
- **⅓   cup malted milk powder**
- **½   teaspoon peppermint extract**
- **Coarsely crushed hard peppermint candies**

1. In a blender, combine chocolate milk, half of the ice cream, the malted milk powder, and peppermint extract. Cover and blend until smooth.

2. Pour into 6 chilled tall glasses.

3. Top each malt with a scoop of remaining ice cream. Sprinkle with crushed candy pieces.

Per serving: 541 cal., 29 g total fat (18 g sat. fat), 150 mg chol., 237 mg sodium, 58 g carbo., 1 g fiber, 12 g pro.

Quick Tip To soften a quart of rock-hard ice cream, microwave it on medium-low power (30-percent) for about 30 seconds. Test the softness by inserting a knife or skewer into the ice cream. High-fat ice cream will soften more quickly than lower-fat ones.

Caramel Clementines ♥

Clementines, tangerines, satsuma oranges, and dancy oranges are all types of mandarin oranges and can be used interchangeably in this recipe. Typically, tangerines and dancy oranges have more seeds.

Prep: 15 minutes **Cook:** 15 minutes **Makes:** 6 servings

- **6   clementines or other orange variety**
- **1   14.5-ounce can apricot nectar (1¾ cups)**
- **½   cup sugar**
- **Dash cayenne pepper (optional)**
- **2   tablespoons Southern Comfort, orange liqueur, or orange juice**
- **Pomegranate seeds (optional)**

1. Peel clementines and remove any of the fibrous strands on the fruit. Place whole clementines in a medium saucepan; add apricot nectar, sugar, and, if desired, cayenne pepper. Bring to boiling; reduce heat. Cover and simmer for 5 minutes. Using a slotted spoon, transfer clementines to a serving dish. Continue to gently boil apricot nectar mixture about 15 minutes or until thick and syrupy. Remove from heat.

2. Stir Southern Comfort into apricot nectar mixture. Spoon over clementines. If desired, sprinkle with pomegranate seeds. Serve warm.

Per serving: 151 cal., 0 g total fat (0 g sat. fat), 0 mg chol., 3 mg sodium, 36 g carbo., 2 g fiber, 1 g pro.

Praline Crunch Bars

Toffee bits and pecans give basic cookie dough a tasty twist. Let the chocolate pieces melt from the heat of the bars then spread them for an easy topping.

Prep: 10 minutes **Bake:** 12 minutes
Stand: 5 minutes **Chill:** 10 minutes
Oven: 350°F **Makes:** 28 bars

- 1 **18-ounce roll refrigerated sugar cookie dough**
- ½ **cup toffee pieces**
- ½ **cup finely chopped pecans**
- 1 **12-ounce package miniature semisweet chocolate pieces**
- ⅓ **cup toffee pieces**

1. Preheat oven to 350°F. In a large resealable plastic bag, place cookie dough, the ½ cup toffee pieces, and the pecans; knead to combine. Press dough evenly over the bottom of an ungreased 13×9×2-inch baking pan.

2. Bake for 12 to 15 minutes or until golden brown. Sprinkle with chocolate pieces immediately after baking. Let stand for 5 to 10 minutes or until softened, then spread evenly over the bars. Sprinkle with the ⅓ cup toffee pieces.

3. Chill for 10 to 15 minutes to set chocolate. Cut into bars.

Per bar: 191 cal., 11 g total fat (4 g sat. fat), 8 mg chol., 105 mg sodium, 19 g carbo., 2 g fiber, 1 g pro.

To Store: Cover and chill for up to 3 days or freeze for up to 1 month.

Praline Crunch Bars

Lemon Cream Tart

Each bite of this luscious dessert showcases a soft nutty crust beneath creamy, rich, citrusy goodness.

Prep: 30 minutes **Chill:** 2 to 24 hours
Bake: 35 minutes **Cool:** 1 hour **Oven:** 350°F
Makes: 12 to 16 servings

- 1 **16.5-ounce package lemon bar mix**
- ½ **cup finely chopped macadamia nuts**
- 1 **8-ounce package cream cheese, softened**
- ½ **teaspoon vanilla**
- 1 **teaspoon finely shredded lemon peel**
- 1 **8-ounce carton dairy sour cream**
- 1 **tablespoon sugar**
- ½ **teaspoon vanilla**
- 1½ **to 2 cups fresh berries (blueberries, raspberries, and/or blackberries)**
  Fresh mint leaves, cut into long, thin strips (optional)

1. Preheat oven to 350°F. Prepare lemon filling mixture according to package directions for lemon bar mix; set aside. Press packaged lemon bar crust mixture into the bottom of a 10-inch springform pan or a 9×9×2-inch baking pan. Sprinkle macadamia nuts evenly over crust; press gently into crust. Bake in the preheated oven about 10 minutes or until light brown. Cool on a wire rack.

2. Meanwhile, in a medium mixing bowl, combine cream cheese and ½ teaspoon vanilla; beat with an electric mixer on medium to high speed until smooth. Add lemon filling mixture; beat until combined. Stir in lemon peel. Pour cream cheese mixture evenly over the crust in the pan.

3. Bake for about 25 minutes more or until set. Cool on wire rack for 1 hour. Cover and refrigerate for at least 2 hours or up to 24 hours.

4. Just before serving, in a small bowl, stir together sour cream, sugar, and ½ teaspoon vanilla. Spread sour cream mixture over tart. Sprinkle fresh berries and, if desired, mint leaf strips evenly over tart.

Per serving: 190 cal., 16 g total fat (8 g sat. fat), 82 mg chol., 109 mg sodium, 7 g carbo., 5 g fiber, 4 g pro.

Quick Tip When purchasing shelled nuts, such as macadamia nuts, look for nuts that are plump, crisp-looking, and uniform in color and size. Avoid those that are shriveled or discolored. Store nuts in an airtight container in a cool place. Refrigerate shelled nuts for up to 4 months or freeze them for up to 8 months.

Mississippi Mud Cake

Mississippi Mud Cake

A tasty topping of crunchy peanuts and mini marshmallows makes this dreamy cake a winner for kids and adults alike.

Prep: 15 minutes **Bake:** 30 minutes **Oven:** 350°F
Makes: 12 to 16 servings

- 1 **package 2-layer-size chocolate cake mix**
- 1¼ **cups water**
- ⅓ **cup cooking oil**
- ⅓ **cup creamy peanut butter**
- 3 **eggs**
- 1 **cup semisweet chocolate pieces (6 ounces)**
- 1 **16-ounce can chocolate fudge frosting**
- 1 **cup tiny marshmallows**
- 1 **cup chopped peanuts**

1. Preheat the oven to 350°F. Grease and lightly flour a 13×9×2-inch baking pan; set aside.

2. In a large bowl, combine cake mix, water, oil, peanut butter, and eggs. Beat with an electric mixer on low speed until moistened. Beat on medium speed for 2 minutes. Stir in chocolate pieces. Pour into prepared pan. Bake for 30 to 35 minutes or until a wooden toothpick inserted in center comes out clean. Cool in pan on wire rack.

3. Drop spoonfuls of frosting over cake; spread evenly. Sprinkle with marshmallows and peanuts.

Per serving: 591 cal., 30 g total fat (8 g sat. fat), 53 mg chol., 456 mg sodium, 76 g carbo., 3 g fiber, 9 g pro.

Coconut-Orange Cake

Orange juice concentrate and coconut join cake mix and fluffy frosting mix to produce a cake that tastes like sunshine.

Prep: 30 minutes **Bake:** 30 minutes **Cool:** 1 hour
Oven: 350°F **Makes:** 12 servings

- 1 **package 2-layer-size white cake mix**
- 1 **cup milk**
- 2 **egg whites**
- ½ **of a 6-ounce can (⅓ cup) frozen orange juice concentrate, thawed**
- ½ **cup flaked coconut**
- 1 **package fluffy white frosting mix (for 2-layer cake)**
- ⅓ **cup flaked coconut or large coconut flakes, toasted**

1. Preheat oven to 350°F. Grease and flour two 9×1½-inch round cake pans; set aside. In a large mixing bowl, combine cake mix, milk, egg whites, and orange juice concentrate. Beat with an electric mixer on medium speed for 2 minutes. Using a rubber scraper, gently fold in the ½ cup coconut. Divide batter evenly between prepared pans, spreading evenly.

2. Bake for 30 to 35 minutes or until a wooden toothpick inserted near centers comes out clean. Cool in pans on wire racks for 10 minutes. Remove cakes from pans. Cool thoroughly on wire racks.

3. Prepare frosting according to package directions. Fill and frost cake. Sprinkle toasted coconut on top of cake. Store frosted cake, covered, in the refrigerator.

Per serving: 291 cal., 6 g total fat (3 g sat. fat), 2 mg chol., 361 mg sodium, 57 g carbo., 0 g fiber, 3 g pro.

Snow Angel Cake

Try this on a snowy day when you want to celebrate the beauty of white fluff. Angel food cake dressed with whipped topping, shredded coconut, then drizzled with white chocolate. Serve it on a silver tray for a sparkling presentation.

Start to Finish: 15 minutes **Makes:** 12 servings

- **1** **purchased angel food cake**
- **2** **ounces white chocolate baking squares or ⅓ cup white baking pieces**
- **1** **8-ounce container frozen whipped dessert topping, thawed**
- **¼** **cup coconut**

1. Place cake on a serving plate; set aside.

2. In a small saucepan, melt white chocolate over low heat, stirring occasionally. Remove from heat.

3. Frost cake with whipped topping. Sprinkle with coconut. Drizzle with melted white chocolate.

Per serving: 152 cal., 6 g total fat (5 g sat. fat), 1 mg chol., 190 mg sodium, 22 g carbo., 1 g fiber, 2 g pro.

Chocolate Chip Ice Cream Cake

Hollow out an angel food cake, then stuff it with an ice cream-cream cheese blend for a unique fudge- or strawberry-topped dessert that both kids and adults will love.

Prep: 20 minutes **Freeze:** 6 to 24 hours
Makes: 10 to 12 servings

- **1** **3-ounce package cream cheese, softened**
- **1** **tablespoon sugar**
- **1½** **cups chocolate chip, strawberry, or vanilla ice cream**
- **1** **8- or 9-inch purchased angel food cake (15 or 16 ounces)**
- **⅓** **cup sliced fresh strawberries**
- **⅓** **cup chocolate fudge or strawberry ice cream topping**

1. For filling, in a small bowl, stir together cream cheese and sugar. In a medium bowl, use a wooden spoon to stir ice cream just until it begins to soften; fold cream cheese mixture into ice cream. Place in freezer while preparing the cake.

2. Use a serrated knife to cut off the top ½ inch of the cake; set aside. Hold the knife parallel to the center hole of the cake and cut around the hole, leaving about ¾-inch thickness of cake around the hole. Cut around the outer edge of the cake, leaving an outer cake wall about ¾ inch thick. Use a spoon to remove center of cake, leaving about a ¾-inch-thick base. (Reserve scooped-out cake for another use.)

3. Spoon filling into hollowed cake. Arrange sliced strawberries on the filling. Replace the top of the cake. Cover and freeze for at least 6 hours or up to 24 hours.

4. To serve, in a small saucepan, heat ice cream topping until drizzling consistency; drizzle over cake. Slice cake with a serrated knife.

Per serving: 219 cal., 7 g total fat (4 g sat. fat), 18 mg chol., 265 mg sodium, 37 g carbo., 0 g fiber, 5 g pro.

Shortcut Malted Chocolate Cake ♥

Malted milk powder adds a unique flair to packaged cake mix and store-bought frosting.

Prep: 10 minutes **Bake:** 30 minutes **Oven:** 350°F
Makes: 20 servings

- **1** **2-layer-size package dark chocolate fudge or devil's food cake mix**
- **⅓** **cup vanilla malted milk powder**
- **1** **12-ounce can whipped chocolate frosting**
- **¼** **cup vanilla malted milk powder**
- **1½** **cups coarsely chopped malted milk balls**

1. Preheat oven to 350°F. Prepare cake mix according to package directions, adding the ⅓ cup malted milk powder to batter. Pour batter into a greased 13×9×2-inch baking pan. Bake for 30 to 35 minutes or until a toothpick inserted near the center comes out clean. Place pan on a wire rack and cool completely.

2. In a medium bowl, stir together frosting and the ¼ cup malted milk powder. Spread evenly over cake. Top with chopped malted milk balls.

Per serving: 231 cal., 7 g total fat (2 g sat. fat), 2 mg chol., 281 mg sodium, 41 g carbo., 1 g fiber, 3 g pro.

Shortcut Malted Chocolate Cake

Index

Note: **Boldfaced** page numbers indicate photographs.